Barney Dreyfuss

ALSO BY BRIAN MARTIN
AND FROM McFARLAND

The Man Who Made Babe Ruth:
Brother Matthias of St. Mary's School (2020)

The Detroit Wolverines: The Rise and Wreck
of a National League Champion, 1881–1888 (2018)

Pud Galvin: Baseball's First 300-Game Winner (2016)

The Tecumsehs of the International Association:
Canada's First Major League Baseball Champions (2015)

Baseball's Creation Myth: Adam Ford,
Abner Graves and the Cooperstown Story (2013)

Barney Dreyfuss
Pittsburgh's Baseball Titan

Brian Martin

McFarland & Company, Inc., Publishers
Jefferson, North Carolina

This book has undergone peer review.

ISBN (print) 978-1-4766-7961-7
ISBN (ebook) 978-1-4766-4418-9

LIBRARY OF CONGRESS AND BRITISH LIBRARY
CATALOGUING DATA ARE AVAILABLE

Library of Congress Control Number 2021035948

© 2021 Brian Martin. All rights reserved

No part of this book may be reproduced or transmitted in any form or by any means, electronic or mechanical, including photocopying or recording, or by any information storage and retrieval system, without permission in writing from the publisher.

Front cover: Barney Dreyfuss (Library of Congress); Forbes Field, 1909 (Library of Congress)

Printed in the United States of America

*McFarland & Company, Inc., Publishers
Box 611, Jefferson, North Carolina 28640
www.mcfarlandpub.com*

To Pittsburgh and its loyal baseball fans

Table of Contents

Acknowledgments   viii
Preface   1

1. An Unshakeable Belief in Baseball   3
2. The Little Clerk, Big Dreams   15
3. A Fine Diversion   24
4. Louisville   33
5. Buying In   44
6. "I am tired of losing so much money…."   53
7. 1899: One Door Closes…   65
8. …Another Door Opens: The Colonels and a Captain   76
9. Success at Last   86
10. 1903: Making History   96
11. Riding High in the First Division: 1904 to 1908   106
12. Politics, Dirty Business and Tragedy   120
13. Champions   133
14. Departures and Decline   144
15. Retooling   154
16. Back on Top   165
17. Last Hurrah   176
18. After the Little Colonel   187

Epilogue   199
Chapter Notes   205
Bibliography   221
Index   225

Acknowledgments

The author owes a debt of gratitude to the following people who helped make possible this first comprehensive telling of the life and times of Barney Dreyfuss. A project of this scale is impossible without the assistance of others. Thank you all. And sincere apologies to anyone who may have been omitted inadvertently from this list.

Craig Britcher, project coordinator and assistant curator of the Western Pennsylvania Sports Museum, Senator John Heinz History Center, Pittsburgh, for his outstanding assistance to the author. His knowledge is vast and his willingness to help is deeply appreciated.

Len Martin, Pittsburgh, a baseball historian who has found many interesting ways to keep alive memories of Forbes Field. A technical illustrator, he published a book about Forbes Field that allows the reader to build it into a scale model of the famous ballpark. It is still available from his company, Point Four Ltd. and online. Len freely provided advice, terrific images and encouragement as this book was nearing completion. He is not related to the author.

Cassidy Lent, research librarian, National Baseball Hall of Fame and Museum in Cooperstown, New York, cheerfully and promptly responded to many requests for information.

Claudette Scrafford, manuscript archivist, National Baseball Hall of Fame.

John Horne, photo archivist, National Baseball Hall of Fame and Museum, was helpful and gracious, as is his habit.

Matt Rothenberg, of Ossining, New York, former manager of the Giamatti Research Center at the National Baseball Hall of Fame and avid researcher, provided some good information and leads.

Gabriel Schechter, of Salem, Oregon, former researcher at the National Baseball Hall of Fame, baseball historian and author, who helped shed light on a number of things when the author most needed help.

John Thorn, of Catskill, New York, Major League Baseball historian who has forgotten more about baseball than this author will ever know. He kindly provided advice at an early stage of this project. Despite his busy schedule he always finds time to assist others.

Bob Bailey, Gainesville, Florida, a well-known baseball historian and former resident of Louisville. He shared a wonderful unpublished manuscript he wrote about Louisville joining the American Association. He is particularly knowledgeable about baseball in the Kentucky city and has written several articles on the subject.

Harry Rothgerber, a baseball historian in Louisville, Kentucky, who kindly shared with the author insights into baseball and his city.

Nathan Lynn, of McCracken County Library, Paducah, Kentucky, provided information about early baseball in that area, and shared his "Short History of Paducah, Kentucky."

Randall Morgan, of Paducah, Kentucky, author of *Paducah's Native Baseball Team,* was kind and generous in sharing his knowledge with the author.

Jeff Youngblood, an historian and native Paducahan, now living in Oklahoma City, alerted the author to his 2009 paper: "Paducah and the World Series: The Life and Times of Barney Dreyfuss." This academic study can be found online and at the National Baseball Hall of Fame.

Diana Copsey Adams, of Denver, Colorado, a genealogical research wizard who provided significant help unraveling the complex Dreyfuss and Bernheim families. Her outstanding sleuthing has earned her the nickname "Sherlocka" and my enduring respect and admiration.

Sam Bernstein, of West Orange, New Jersey, who has written extensively about Barney Dreyfuss, shared some excellent information and provided encouragement.

Andrew North, of St. Marys, Ontario, a highly respected baseball researcher, founding director of the Centre for Canadian Baseball Research and volunteer at the Canadian Baseball Hall of Fame, provided solid advice and invaluable fact-checking and proofreading assistance. This book is better as a result of his efforts.

Don Murray, of London, Ontario, my good friend whose editing talents I utilized yet again. His advice, eye for detail and encouragement are always appreciated.

Kaitlyn Larsen, of Pittsburgh, normally a wedding photographer, expanded her horizons to capture some images needed to complete this book during a time of travel restrictions and pandemic. Her talent speaks for itself.

Dan Bonk and Mark Miner, Pittsburgh baseball historians who have written extensively about Forbes Field and Barney Dreyfuss. They shared images, information and documents that proved extremely helpful.

George Skornickel of Tarentum, Pennsylvania, a baseball historian and president of the Forbes Field Chapter of the Society for American Baseball Research, was always there to help and suggest contacts.

Herb Soltman of Pittsburgh, who keeps alive an important highlight of Pirates history from October 13, 1960, and shares it enthusiastically with everyone.

Preface

During a visit to Pittsburgh for the 48th Annual Convention of the Society for American Baseball Research in 2018, several of my fellow historians and I were chatting at lunch one day about the city's rich baseball history and how Barney Dreyfuss was such a major figure in it. We couldn't understand why a book had never been written about him. A seed was planted. It didn't take me long to get to work, knowing such a project would get me back to a city I have grown to admire.

Aside from being a great baseball city with a fine ballpark that provides one of the nicest views in the game, Pittsburgh has scrubbed up nicely since its steel-making days. Its riverside parks and trails are a treat, and the setting is sublime. The city has reinvented itself as a leader in education, health care, technology and financial services. And the air in the picturesque valley in which it sits no longer makes for dirty shirts by noon hour.

During my many visits, I've been struck by how much Pittsburghers enjoy all their sports teams, the Pirates, the football Steelers and hockey's Penguins. But mostly the Pirates. I wanted to know more about the origin of the love affair with the Pirates and all roads led to Barney Dreyfuss. He took an also-ran baseball operation and built it into a successful ball club that became among the top contenders in all of baseball from 1900 to his death in 1932. He erected Forbes Field in 1909 and helped establish the World Series, winning two of the four in which his Pirates appeared. Not bad for a little fellow from Germany who came to America in 1882 with little more than dreams and a work ethic and whose long-lasting affair with baseball was born in the Ohio Valley of Kentucky.

Barney Dreyfuss made significant contributions to the game that were recognized in 2008 with his induction into the National Baseball Hall of Fame. Other powerful figures in baseball have been similarly honored and many have had biographies penned about them. The time for Barney Dreyfuss has come.

Herewith the first effort to tell the full story of baseball's little titan.

A Note on Spellings

Baseball was often spelled "base ball" until about 1900.

Whiskey was usually spelled "whisky" until about the same time.

Pittsburgh. From 1891 to 1911, the "h" was dropped when the United States Board on Geographic Names sought to standardize spellings, thinking it was of Germanic origin. This was wrong. It is Scottish, as in Edinburgh, and appears with an "h" in the original city charter. Some businesses and a few newspapers dropped the "h," but others retained it during those 20 years. Because it was dropped in error, the author has opted to remain consistent throughout this book and include the "h," even if it appeared without the "h" in quotations.

Allegheny City. This is the city located on the north side of the Allegheny River, opposite downtown Pittsburgh. It was smaller than Pittsburgh but was home to most early teams that called Pittsburgh home. The first professional ball club was known as the Alleghenys just as other teams of the day were known as the Bostons, Detroits and Chicagos. The Pirates name was adopted in 1891 and in 1907, Allegheny City was annexed by Pittsburgh. Union Park (renamed Recreation Park), Exposition Park, Three Rivers Stadium and today's PNC Park were all located there. Today the area is known as Pittsburgh's North Side.

1

An Unshakeable Belief in Baseball

"'Dreyfuss's Folly,' mein arsch," the slight, nattily attired gentleman could have been forgiven for muttering, good-naturedly, under his breath. It was a remarkable early summer day of 1909 in Pittsburgh, and Barney Dreyfuss was busily accepting congratulations and handshakes at the main entrance to his sparkling new baseball palace, a tangible testament to his faith in his adopted country and its favorite game. Beaming broadly beneath his familiar derby, he thanked the many well-wishers in the massive crowd that milled about, his German accent coming as a surprise to those who had never before conversed with him.

Dreyfuss had been in the city barely nine years; in America more than twenty-five. Things were going well for the former bank clerk from a German duchy who migrated to Kentucky at the age of 17. Dreyfuss, now 44, was a wealthy man, a baseball magnate. This was opening day for Forbes Field, a $1 million state-of-the-art ballpark he built as a new home for his Pittsburgh Pirates.

Erected in less than six months, the three-tiered structure was built of concrete and steel and intended to be permanent and fireproof. Forbes Field was already the talk of baseball. This splendid day, its façade and gates were decorated with red, white and blue bunting while the Stars and Stripes fluttered on poles 50 feet apart along both the inner and outer edges of the roof above the grandstand. Clad in a buff-white terra cotta stone, with arched windows at street level, the handsome structure was topped by a copper-sheathed roof and all its structural steel was painted green. Access for fans included ramps between decks, a revolutionary design that eliminated stairs and eased ingress and egress. It was said the grandstand could be emptied in as little as eight minutes.[1] Meanwhile, elevators whisked patrons from the main lobby to exclusive boxes on the second and third tiers. Boxes with seven or eight seats sold for $8.75 and $10; reserved seats elsewhere were $1, while tickets cost 75 cents for general admission, 50 cents for the bleachers and 25 cents for temporary bleachers. Some of the latter were placed on the field of play this day. In all, 300 boxes could be found on all three tiers and by two weeks before opening day, all had been sold for the remainder of the season.[2] Boxes were new to Pittsburgh fans, but had been introduced elsewhere to improve the fan experience— and the bottom line for team owners. The new feature was explained by the local press as "boxes for the true lovers of the game who are willing to spend a little extra money to not only obtain a fine view of the field, but to be able to secure a quiet and comfortable time."[3]

Public telephones were available on every level of the grandstand and the spacious clubhouses included laundries. The main promenade at ground level was so large that everyone in the grandstand could seek cover there in the event of a sudden downpour, a first for a National League ballpark.[4] A special drainage system was installed in the field and patented canvas tarps protected the infield during inclement weather. Under the grandstand was a parking garage to accommodate more affluent patrons who could afford automobiles. About that feature, the *Pittsburgh Post* enthused "[it] will be the finest automobile garage in Pittsburgh."[5] Soon, even fans of more modest means could park there because, just months earlier, the first Model T had rolled off Henry Ford's assembly line.

The gleaming new park, with its focus on opulence and modern conveniences, was a template for many that followed. Of Forbes Field, it has been said in retrospect: "[its] cultural and commercial success in 1909 paved the way for not only the House that Ruth built, but numerous other majestic ballparks that would be unveiled throughout the twentieth century and beyond."[6]

Barney Dreyfuss knew precisely what he was doing. During his short time in Pittsburgh, he had converted the Pirates into a real contender in the National League, taking the pennant in 1903. Now the team had an impressive new home, with seating for 25,000, the biggest park in baseball, instantly rendering obsolete all existing frame-and-timber parks. It was located across Forbes Street from the Hotel Schenley where Dreyfuss lived for his first few years in Pittsburgh and had grown to know and like the area, removed as its was from the city's steel mills.

Despite his five-foot-six-inch frame that tipped the scales at barely 130 pounds, Dreyfuss liked to think big.[7] He was becoming a prominent figure in Pittsburgh—and in all of professional baseball. He had a keen eye for baseball talent and kept detailed notes on players in his "dope book" filled with information he gleaned from a variety of sources, friends, contacts and newspapers, including *Sporting Life* to which he subscribed. Dreyfuss was guided by doing what he felt was best for the game he loved and the city he adopted. His confidence was boundless. He has been described as "a fan first" who really understood the game and was guided by a sense of fairness and equity for players and for teams.[8] In 1908, *Baseball Magazine* said he was already widely known as one of the best judges of a baseball player in the business and more of a fan than a typical owner. "Usually the men who back the major league teams are too much interested in the financial end of the game, in the monetary returns from their invested funds to exhibit much feeling over the artistic part of the sport."[9] Upon his passing in 1932 *Sporting News* described Dreyfuss as the greatest fan among major league club owners "past or present." It noted he never missed a Pirates home game, occupying his regular seat in the second tier of the Forbes Field grandstand "where he passed critical judgment upon everything that his own and the opposing team did, as well as upon the work of the umpires."[10]

Decades later, in recognition of his significant and pioneering contribution as an executive, Dreyfuss was inducted into the National Baseball Hall of Fame in Cooperstown, hailed as an "innovative and highly respected team owner."[11]

This June 30 day was cloudless and warm, in the low 80s. Perfect for baseball. The opposition was the Chicago Cubs, the reigning National League champions. The Cubs appeared the previous day in the final game played in Exposition Park, the Pirates' old home. The Pirates, who were leading the National League, clobbered the visitors 8–1 in that contest to go 7–5 games ahead of the Cubs. It was a fine way to bid adieu to the ball club's home for the past 19 years.

This Wednesday afternoon marked the dawn of a new era in the professional game and for Pittsburgh. Forbes Field was located in the fashionable and leafy Oakland section of the gritty Steel City. Dreyfuss had been assisted in his search for a ballpark site by

The decorated main entrance to Forbes Field just days after it opened in 1909 during "Dedication Week." The state-of-the-art ballpark was located in the Oakland area of Pittsburgh, the growing educational and cultural sector of the city. Some critics panned the location as impractical and derided it as "Dreyfuss's Folly." In this image, the windows are incomplete and the canopy roof has not yet been installed above the main entrance (Library of Congress).

local industrialist and philanthropist Andrew Carnegie, who was anxious to see Oakland become a cultural hub for the city. But critics complained it was too far from downtown, three miles east of the Pirates' old home at Exposition Park. Even his business associates warned Dreyfuss that fans would never take the long trolley car ride out to Oakland, the growing cultural center of the city. But floods had frequently rendered the old park unusable and Dreyfuss felt it was located in the wrong neighborhood, a gritty industrial and working-class area with poor air quality. He complained that the "better class of citizens, especially when accompanied by their womenfolk, were loath to go there."[12] He viewed the game as entertainment for all and he wanted to extend its appeal beyond the working class. In particular, Dreyfuss sought to lure more affluent patrons, to further grow the game and increase his profits by offering exclusive boxes that would appeal to fans with money.

"When I first told people about the new ballpark and its location, they laughed," Dreyfuss recalled later. "It was on property belonging to Schenley Farms, complete with livery stable while a few cows roamed over the countryside."[13] But the ball club owner could see its potential. "The more I looked over the property, the better I liked it," he said. "I had a strong hunch, which amounted to a conviction, that Pittsburgh would grow eastward."[14] And as was so often the case with Dreyfuss, time would prove his hunches right.

When they first got wind of his preferred venue, some local skeptics wondered about his sanity. "They told Mr. Dreyfuss he was crazy," Bill Benswanger, Dreyfuss's son-in-law, told a newspaper writer during celebrations marking the 60th anniversary of the park that critics predicted would fail. "His business friends said people would never come all the way to Oakland to see a baseball game."[15]

Downtown interests were especially critical, dubbing the new park "Oakland's Orchard" and "Dreyfuss's Folly."[16] And even some of his supporters took issue with the name he chose for it. Forbes Field was named to honor British General John Forbes, who captured Fort Duquesne from the French in 1758, renamed it Fort Pitt, and began settling the area. Some Pittsburghers urged Dreyfuss to instead name the grand new baseball shrine after himself, the way Ben Shibe immodestly christened the new home for his Philadelphia Athletics of the American League, 300 miles to the east. Shibe spent $500,000 on a 23,000-seat concrete-and-steel structure with double-decked grandstand which he officially opened in April. Shibe Park featured an octagonal Beaux Arts tower and ornate brick-and-arch façade. It included terra cotta sculptures of Shibe and his co-owner and team manager, Connie Mack, which gazed down on visitors from perches high above the main entrance.[17] Dreyfuss was no Shibe, however. He disdained such recognition.

Previously, baseball parks were constructed primarily of wood and were prone to fires, posing a risk to fans and a liability for owners trying to build and develop the professional game. By its nature, wood also limited the size of grandstands and therefore profits. Dreyfuss himself had seen what fires could do to teams. In 1892, he was a director and part owner of the National League's Louisville Colonels when most of the club's ballpark burned to the ground. Only the right field bleachers were saved. The team was already a money-losing operation and the conflagration, believed set by an arsonist, was a significant setback.[18] Late in the 1899 season, a lightning strike triggered a fire in the rebuilt park that destroyed the grandstand. Few baseball team owners were prepared to invest in steel-reinforced concrete baseball palaces when the ongoing viability of professional baseball as a business was far from ensured at the outset of the twentieth century. Shibe and Dreyfuss had the confidence other baseball magnates lacked and were willing to invest heavily in the future.

"The concrete-and-steel stadiums not only represented a safety measure, but a leap of faith on how popular baseball would become," Major League Baseball historian John Thorn has said. "In effect, it was like *Field of Dreams*. They built in the hopes it would come. They built ballparks of great seating capacity and seeming posterity."[19]

When plans for Forbes Field were announced, however, Barney Dreyfuss was seen more as a fool than a visionary.

Even baseball executive Ned Hanlon, a former Pittsburgh player and manager, thought Dreyfuss had bitten off far too much, telling him he overspent and the park was far too large for a city whose population was approaching 530,000.[20] It was indeed a large edifice, twice the size of the Pirates' old home at Exposition Park on the North Side (formerly known as Allegheny City), directly across the Allegheny River from downtown.

The critics were wrong. As it turned out, Pittsburgh was ready for Barney Dreyfuss and his big dream. The city embraced the new park, already a tourist attraction as it rose rapidly along Bouquet Street at the edge of verdant Schenley Park. After a week of celebrations, the opening day crowd was immense, far more than the park was built to accommodate. The railroads provided extra cars to bring fans from neighboring cities and many businesses closed early to let their employees enjoy the game. The turnstiles counted 30,338 patrons, making it the largest crowd ever to witness a baseball game,

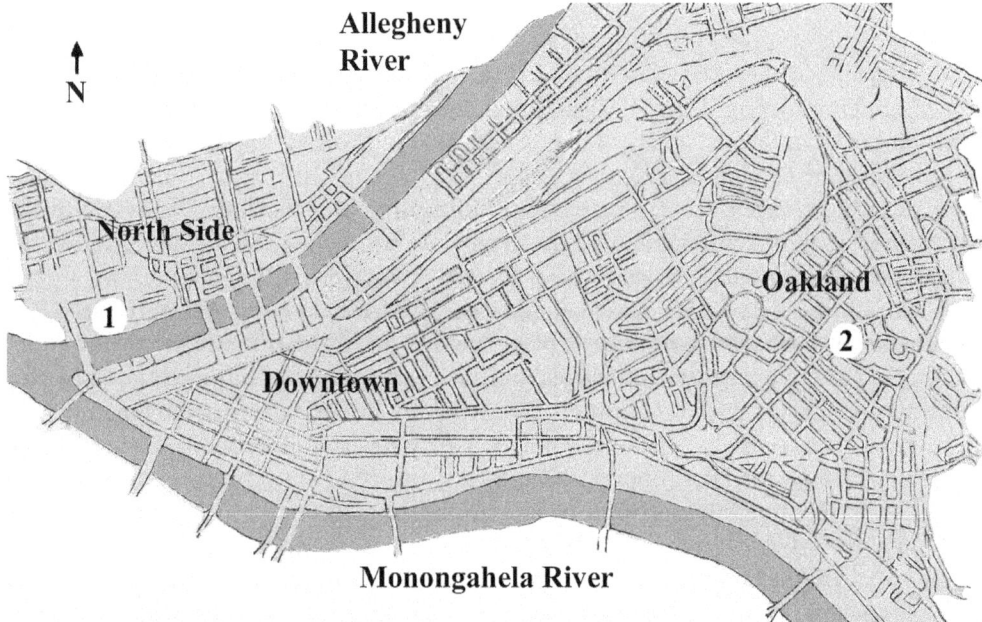

Sketch map of Pittsburgh in about 1915 showing the relative locations of (1) Exposition Park on the North Side, and (2) Forbes Field in the Oakland area, about three miles to the east (author's creation).

surpassing the previous high of 30,247 set the previous October in Chicago when Pittsburgh played there.[21] Everyone, it seemed, was wearing their Sunday best: men in suits, bow ties and straw boaters and Panama hats, while women wore fine dresses and bonnets. Boys and men unable to find seats, "were perched on girders or clung to pillars" while others sat atop walls. The outfield accommodated the overflow, with temporary seating and standing-room-only ticket holders held back by ropes.

It wasn't just the public that was impressed with the handiwork of Barney Dreyfuss. The *Pittsburgh Post* called Forbes Field "the World's Finest Baseball Grounds," while the *Pittsburgh Press* crowed that the opening day crowd was the "Largest Assemblage Ever Gathered in Any Ball Park Anywhere."[22] Positive comments appeared in sporting publications, like the *Reach Official American League Baseball Guide,* which described the opening day this way, resorting to decidedly purple prose: "Never, perhaps, in the history of the Old World or New—not excluding the assemblages in the Roman and Grecian amphitheaters and stadiums—was a scene more spectacular presented...."[23] Even after fine new stadiums began rising in other cities, *Baseball Magazine* said of Forbes Field: "it still stands pre-eminent as the most magnificent structure in baseball today.... All in all, Forbes Field, in the beauty of its surroundings and the fitness of its facilities, stands today without a peer."[24] Pittsburgh had a new landmark and Barney Dreyfuss had notched a major achievement in a long and storied baseball career.

"This is indeed the happiest day of my life," the normally reserved Dreyfuss told a reporter. "I used to dream of such things as I see here today, but it was not until a comparatively short time ago that I ever thought to see them as realities. I thank the people of Pittsburgh and Western Pennsylvania from the bottom of my heart for the appreciation shown here this afternoon."[25]

* * *

Baseball had been played in Pittsburgh for decades, with games often drawing good crowds. But it wasn't until Barney Dreyfuss arrived on the scene at the outset of the twentieth century that the city finally had a team whose success on the diamond gave Pittsburgh a real source of civic pride.

The professional game had its origins in Pittsburgh in 1876, when Denny McKnight established a semi-professional nine in Allegheny City, a city of 50,000 lying across the Allegheny River from downtown Pittsburgh, which was twice its population.

Amateur participation in baseball, however, predated the Civil War in the area. The earliest game is believed to have been played in 1857 in Allegheny City. By 1860, gentlemen from various occupations were playing each other in public parks in the same city, known as the East and West Common. By early June, two nines formed by members of the Duquesne Base Ball Club were reportedly playing each other while on June 15 the Duquesne club downed the Aliquippa nine by a score of 34 to 15.[26] Like other teams of the day, they played nine innings but used an antiquated method of scoring based on runs and "outs" recorded by each player. The *Pittsburgh Press* carried an account of an August 2 game on the West Common when the bank clerks in the Union Base Ball Club narrowly lost a close game against "nine other gentlemen belonging to the same club," the contest continuing "until it was almost too dark to see the ball."[27] The Fort Pitt and the Keystone clubs had scores of their games reported by the same newspaper. The Civil War itself helped spread the game and soldiers established new clubs upon their return home. Hostilities ended on May 9, 1865, just in time for warm weather and baseball. Within weeks, games were being played on the East and West Common. Teams such as the Olympics, the Xanthas and the Enterprise Club began to attract players and followers. Junior teams like the Allegheny, Resolute and Atlantic were formed. Many drew newspaper coverage as well as followers to their contests, some apparently unfamiliar with some aspects of the game. That situation prompted the *Pittsburgh Gazette*, while promoting an upcoming game between the Lincoln and Enterprise clubs, to issue this warning in August: "To prevent any interference, or inconvenience to those actively engaged in playing, it is respectfully requested of the spectators to remain outside of the lines, and under no circumstance to pick up the ball."[28]

The Philadelphia Athletics came to Allegheny City in mid–September for games against the Enterprise, the Lincolns, the Alleghenys, and a picked nine of the best Pittsburgh-area players. In anticipation of good crowds, an "amphitheater" capable of seating 2,500 was erected in the West Common.[29] The *Gazette* noted the growing popularity of baseball with "several fine clubs" in the area, each with from 20 to 40 active members, many of them based on occupation, such as bankers, clerks, merchants and salesmen. "Surely our young men will be benefitted by frequent visits to the ball ground … to learn the use of lungs and muscles," the paper said. "We would urge upon our readers, who can make it convenient, to attend one or more of these games and judge for themselves in reference to this fine American game."[30] Large crowds attended the four games, taking advantage of the first structure built specifically to accommodate spectators (then known as "cranks") for baseball and they willingly paid the 25-cent admission charge. The visiting Athletics swamped the local lads by lopsided scores, the worst an 88 to 13 drubbing of the Lincolns. The combined score for the four games was 247–42.[31]

Among the promising amateurs in the Pittsburgh area was returning Union Army soldier Al Pratt, born in Allegheny City late in 1848. He joined the army at age 15 and became an infantryman. The war introduced Pratt to the game and upon his return to civilian life, he and other veterans became active in the game locally. He may have been the "Pratt" who appeared with the Atlantic junior club as a catcher on the East Common in August of 1865.[32] By 1866, he was pitching for the Enterprise Club in Allegheny City, which became one of the best teams in the area. He soon moved on to the Allegheny Club, likely for money. In 1867, The Alleghenys entered what was billed as "The World's Base Ball Tournament" in Detroit, featuring $2,000 in prizes. The team placed second in the first division of the event, which attracted 23 teams, mainly from Michigan and Ontario, Canada. Pratt was named best pitcher in the tournament and was awarded a gold-mounted opera glass, a small binocular popular with theater patrons. His catcher, Ambrose Lynch, was named best catcher.[33] The following year, Pratt played in Portsmouth, Ohio, where he was paid $60 a month and provided college tuition.[34] He joined the Cleveland Forest Citys in 1869, as one of four professionals on that club.[35] Two years later, Cleveland became a charter member of the first professional baseball league, the National Association, with Pratt as their star pitcher. He played two seasons for Cleveland, in 1871 and 1872, earning 12 wins and 26 losses before leaving the team and returning to Pittsburgh, where he became a bartender. He was widely known as "Uncle" Al Pratt in the baseball community and is considered to be the first professional player from Pittsburgh.[36]

In 1869, the same year Pratt was hired by Cleveland, the Olympic club, which had become the Pittsburgh area's best nine, travelled down the Ohio River to challenge the Cincinnati Reds, baseball's first openly professional team. The Pennsylvania amateurs were no match for the Reds. They were humbled 54–2, giving the Reds yet another victory in their amazing string of 79 consecutive wins that was not broken until the following year in Brooklyn.[37]

Another Allegheny City man was instrumental in taking the game to a higher level in Pittsburgh. Harmar Denny McKnight, a member of a prominent family, played the game as a young man and loved it. His father was lawyer and Congressman Robert McKnight, while his mother Elizabeth was a member of the well-heeled and land-owning Denny family. His brother, Woodruff, is likely the "McKnight" who appeared at second base and in right field for the Enterprise club during the summer of 1865. Denny McKnight wasn't blessed with the skill of his brother, or Al Pratt, so instead focused his efforts on managing teams. He became an organizer and a director of the Allegheny Base Ball Club, which played their games at Union Park in that city. It lay south of Pennsylvania Avenue, alongside the Pittsburgh, Fort Wayne and Chicago Railroad. His mother's family provided the land. By the mid–1870s, as professional baseball was spreading, McKnight and his associates felt it was time to field a professional nine to compete against other major American cities. McKnight sought membership in the new National League for its inaugural 1876 season, but his bid was rejected.[38] Undaunted, McKnight and his directors created the Alleghenys that year as a semi-professional nine and undertook an extensive series of games against such teams as the Buckeyes of Columbus, the Philadelphias, New Haven, Indianapolis, Cincinnati and the two teams in St. Louis, the Browns and Red Stockings. Allegheny won 39 games and lost 25, while tying three.

After their successful 1876 season, McKnight and several directors of other teams shunned by the National League, met to consider forming a rival professional loop that would be more open and accepting than the exclusive gentleman's club the League seemed to want to be. In all, about 50 baseball organizations expressed interest in a new, more broadly based league and early in 1877 the International Association was established. It adopted that name because it included two Canadian teams, the London Tecumsehs and Guelph Maple Leafs both from Ontario, along with Allegheny, Columbus, Rochester (New York), Lynn (Massachusetts), and Manchester (New Hampshire), among others. More clubs signed on, but declined to pay an extra fee entitling them to play for the league championship. McKnight was one of the driving forces behind the new organization and his Alleghenys led the loop throughout the Association's first campaign. In the dying days of the season, the Alleghenys lost to London, who featured curveballer Fred Goldsmith, a native of New Haven, Connecticut.[39] Suspicions grew that the Alleghenys had "sold" some games to gamblers during a late season tournament in Chicago. By 1878, they had trouble attracting disaffected fans, prompting the team to fold midway through the year.[40] The International Association lost several of its top teams, including pennant-winner Buffalo, to the National League after the 1878 season. Its sole remaining Canadian club, London, folded at the end of 1878, prompting the upstart rival loop to rename itself the National Base-Ball Association. The National League's first challenger expired after struggling to complete a dismal 1880 season.[41]

McKnight wasn't done with baseball yet, despite the failure of his first bid to put Pittsburgh in the National League. Baseball enthusiasts in Pittsburgh kept in touch with each other during the next few years and it was a tip from one of them that re-ignited McKnight's desire to field a big league team. The aforementioned Al Pratt was tending bar in Pittsburgh in October of 1881 when he overheard an intriguing conversation between two out-of-town customers: Justus Thorner, former owner of the Cincinnati Reds, which had been expelled from the National League after the 1880 season, and Cincinnati baseball writer O.P. Caylor. The two men were lamenting that no one had shown up for a meeting in Pittsburgh they had arranged to discuss forming a new major league. Upon hearing this, Pratt suggested they meet McKnight.[42] The meeting occurred October 10, along with baseball magnates Chris Von der Ahe of St. Louis and John Day of the New York Metropolitans.

Less than a month later, the American Association held its first formal meeting, attracting representatives from Louisville, Columbus, Brooklyn, Boston and Philadelphia. When the new loop hit the field the following spring it consisted of six teams: Cincinnati, Philadelphia, Louisville, Pittsburgh, St. Louis and Baltimore. McKnight was named president of the Association, which became known as the "Beer and Whiskey League" because so many team owners were brewers, distillers or saloon owners.[43] He organized a new Allegheny nine and named Pratt his manager, a position Pratt held until mid–1883 when he left to become an AA umpire. Allegheny finished as low as 10th place in 1884, but reached second in 1886 after which it joined the National League as a replacement for Kansas City. McKnight was followed as club president by William A. Nimick in 1885 and the following year McKnight was ousted as AA president amid charges of conflict of interest and dissatisfaction among team owners for his poor handling of a contentious player issue. After that, McKnight washed his hands of baseball and moved on to other ventures.[44]

The Allegheny club drew sizeable crowds to its home at Union Park, which was renamed Recreation Park in 1885. Things were off to a good start on April 30, 1887, for the National League club's season opener when the Alleghenys defeated the Chicago White Stockings, the reigning League champions, by a score of 6 to 2. A crowd of nearly 10,000 packed the park and savored the outcome. The optimism did not last, however. By the end of the century, the team had finished higher than fifth only once. Along the way, the Alleghenys became the "Pirates." In 1890, baseball players who felt they were being unfairly exploited by management, established the Players' League to compete with the National League. Many of the better Allegheny players jumped to the Players' League team in Pittsburgh, which was known as the Burghers. They included star pitchers James "Pud" Galvin, Ed Morris, and Harry Staley, along with outfielder Ned Hanlon and seven others. The Burghers and the Players' League expired after the 1890 season and seven of the defectors returned to the National League club without penalty.[45] The Burghers were gone but they left a legacy behind. The upstarts had established Exposition Park, originally a horse racing venue with 8,000 seats that lay alongside the Allegheny River, across from downtown Pittsburgh. The Alleghenys moved in.

Following the Players' League interlude, Pittsburgh management discovered a rare opportunity to land a fine player. The Philadelphia Athletics of the American Association had disbanded, but the AA claimed all its players. Through an oversight, however, infielder Louis Bierbauer was one of two who did not appear on the list of Athletics players formally claimed by the Association. Allegheny manager Ned Hanlon was dispatched to Erie, Pennsylvania, Bierbauer's hometown, in mid–January. He found the player in a fishing shack on Lake Erie and promptly signed him to a contract. The American Association protested and a hearing into the case was convened. During rancorous debate, an AA official blustered at one point: "The action of the Pittsburgh club in signing Bierbauer was piratical." The analogy stuck. In his book about the Pittsburgh Pirates, sportswriter Frederick G. Lieb observed: "Somehow, no one around the Pittsburgh club seemed ashamed, and it wasn't long before the piratical Pittsburgh club became known as the Pirates."[46] Meanwhile, a board of arbitration allowed the team to keep Bierbauer, who helped Pittsburgh to its best-ever finish, second, in 1893.

After a string of managers and presidents, W.W. Kerr and associate Phil Auten bought the Pirates from J. Palmer O'Neill in 1892. Kerr liked to be called "Captain Kerr, the Coffee King," because he had become a wealthy man in the coffee business. His sister, Mary Alice, married the founder of the Arbuckle Coffee Company, John Arbuckle, who latched onto the idea of selling bags of pre-roasted coffee in 1880. Previously, coffee drinkers had to roast their own beans, with mixed results. Kerr considered himself a self-made man and even though his post was simply that of ball club treasurer, he "lived under the illusion that he knew baseball better than anyone else in the front office," as baseball historian David Nemec has observed. At first, Kerr named William C. Temple as president but the following year assumed the post himself. "Regarded as one of the more trigger-happy and pompous owners of the 1890s, Kerr changed managers six times," Nemec said.[47] Despite the runner-up finish in 1893, the Pirates under Kerr found little success on the field, despite his revolving door for managers. In 1898, Kerr briefly turned the presidency over to baseball veteran Bill "Watty" Watkins. Watkins, the Canadian-born former owner of Indianapolis, had led the Detroit Wolverines to the National League pennant in 1887 during his long and successful career. But Kerr preferred to be top dog and ousted Watkins in 1899, returning as president. Late that same year, Kerr agreed to sell a minority share in the Pirates to Barney Dreyfuss, the owner of the struggling Louisville Colonels who had plans to merge the two teams.

* * *

The Forbes Field gates opened at noon to give first-time visitors a chance to familiarize themselves with the new baseball shrine and marvel at the view of Schenley Park, the Carnegie Institute, the University of Pittsburgh and grand homes and mansions that lay beyond the outfield fences. Among those in attendance were 40 old-time Pittsburgh players including Al Pratt, the former star pitcher and manager of the Alleghenys in 1882 and 1883. Also on hand was Forbes Field architect Charles W. Leavitt, who had been chosen by Barney Dreyfuss to design his grand baseball palace. This assignment marked a new challenge for Leavitt, a landscape engineer and designer of several public parks, horse racing tracks and large private estates. His body of work included cemeteries like Gate of Heaven Cemetery in Hawthorne, New York, where Babe Ruth would be interred years later. Forbes field would be his only baseball park.[48]

Before the dedication ceremonies, two bands entertained at either ends of the grandstand, one led by popular local musician Danny Nirella, known as "the March King," the other from the Fourteenth Regiment. Nirella, whose band and orchestra regularly performed at major society functions in Pittsburgh, proved to be a particularly popular attraction. He and his musicians would entertain fans on every opening day at Forbes Field until his death in 1956.[49] The formal dedication began at 2:30 when the two bands marched onto the field from the ends of the grandstand. They gathered at home plate and played while players and dignitaries emerged from under the grandstand. The Pirates were led by manager Fred Clarke, the Cubs by their manager, Frank Chance, while former Pittsburgh players followed "Uncle" Al Pratt onto the field. A mighty roar greeted the appearance of Pratt and the old-timers. Prominent businessmen, baseball magnates and other officials joined the gathering. Near second base, the Pirates and Cubs lined up to face each other and doffed their caps as Pratt and his contingent marched between them and took up a position beside the bands.[50] All present then marched to the massive flagpole in centerfield for the raising of Old Glory and a big pennant proclaiming "Forbes Field." The bands played "America" and then led the players back to the infield where the Cubs dropped out for batting practice and the Pirates went to their bench while dignitaries returned to their boxes. A cornet signaled Chicago to take batting practice, followed by the home team.

At 3:30 p.m., another cornet blast announced the game was about to begin. From Box 137 near the field, Pittsburgh Mayor William Magee threw the ceremonial first pitch to the city's director of public safety, John Morin. Officials participating in the event included Harry Pulliam, a longtime close associate of Barney Dreyfuss in Louisville and in Pittsburgh, who had become president of the National League. This would be among his last public appearances. Less than a month later, the deeply troubled Pulliam would die by his own hand. Other notables included Ban Johnson, president of the American League; John Heydler, secretary of the National League; August Herrmann, owner of the Cincinnati Reds and member of baseball's governing National Commission; and Charles W. Murphy, president of the visiting Chicago Cubs.[51] With the formalities out of the way, it was time for baseball.

The game pitted veteran right-handers Vic Willis for the Pirates against Ed Reulbach. Willis was in his final season with Pittsburgh and would play one more year before retiring. The Cubs hurler had led the National League in winning percentage the three previous seasons and would pitch for eight more years.

The game started poorly for the Pirates when a Willis pitch hit the leadoff batter, second baseman Johnny Evers. Then he walked leftfielder Jimmy Sheckard. Solly Hofman, the centerfielder, sacrificed to advance both runners and first baseman Chance singled to score Evers. At the time, Chance and Evers were known for their stellar work on defense,

A view of the bleachers and grandstand along the third base line of Forbes Field in its early days. The original capacity of the park was 25,000, and it was gradually expanded over the years, most significantly with a double-decked grandstand down the first base line in 1925 which raised the capacity to about 40,000 (Library of Congress).

as two thirds of the double-play combination of "Tinker-to-Evers-to-Chance" for Chicago, which was considered the best in the National League. Joe Tinker, the sure-handed shortstop, would start the play by firing to Evers at second who would quickly relay the ball to Chance at first, all with machine-like precision.

The game this day became a pitching duel with no more scoring until the bottom of the sixth inning when Pirates star shortstop Honus Wagner led off with a single. First baseman Bill Abstein sacrificed to advance "The Flying Dutchman" to second and then second baseman Dots Miller singled to score Wagner and tie the score at 1–1. In the top of the eighth, Evers singled. Sheckard attempted a sacrifice but advanced to second when Pirates third baseman Jap Barbeau threw wide to Abstein at first, and the ball went into the crowd. Hofman popped out. Chance drove a liner to second baseman Miller, who threw home to get Evers. But Pirates catcher George "Mooney" Gibson dropped the ball and Evers scored his second run of the game. The Cubs were up 2–1. Chicago third baseman Harry Steinfeldt lay down a bunt, which catcher Gibson scooped up, but rather than tag Sheckard coming home, Gibson threw to first to get Steinfeldt at first. Sheckard crossed the plate to score and the Cubs went up 3–1. In the bottom of the inning, things began to look promising for the home team. Clarke walked with one out, then Wagner flied out. Abstein popped up, but Evers mishandled the ball and Abstein was safe at first with two out. Miller then hit a ball to deep center field, drawing wide cheers from the massive crowd hoping it would clear the field of play and put the Pirates ahead. In center, Hofman tracked the ball well, but it glanced off his glove and skipped into spectators crowded behind him on the grass where they were held back by ropes. The crowd erupted as all three runners scurried home to put the Pirates up, 4–3. But veteran umpires Bob Emslie and Hank O'Day conferred about the play as the crowd continued to buzz at the sudden turn of events. In the end, however, the umpires determined the hit constituted a rule-book double because of spectator interference. Their ruling produced the expected chorus of catcalls. Clarke was allowed to score, but Abstein was sent back to third and Miller to second. The next Pittsburgh batter on whom the large throng came to pin their hopes was lefty Ham Hyatt, a rookie who was called upon to pinch-hit for right fielder Chief Wilson. But Hyatt struck out to retire the side with the score standing at 3–2 for Chicago.

The pitchers buckled down and it wasn't until the ninth inning that the Pirates again put men in scoring position, providing a final glimmer of hope for the huge throng. In the top of the inning, the first three Cubs batters were retired in order. For the Pirates, leadoff hitter Gibson drew a walk, then Alan Storke pinch-hit for Willis. Storke sacrificed to advance the speedy Blaine Durbin who was pinch-running for Gibson. Barbeau then drove a ball to second where Evers fumbled it, leaving runners on first and third with only one out. Tommy Leach flied out to Sheckard in left for the second out. Clarke then connected for a grounder to third where Steinfeldt fielded it cleanly and fired the ball in time to second to catch base-runner Jap Barbeau, despite his desperation slide. The rally ended and the game was lost, the final score 3–2 for Chicago. The Pirates had left 10 men on base and the Cubs stranded six. Pittsburgh recorded five hits to four for the Cubs. The home team had come within a whisker of sending everyone home happy. As the *Pittsburgh Post* observed, a bit grumpily: "Pittsburgh outbatted, outfielded and outclassed the world's champions in yesterday's game at Forbes Field...."[52]

It was a disappointing debut for the spectacular new venue, particularly for Dreyfuss. "What a shame we had to lose that one," he lamented after the game. "I'd have given my share of the gate to have won on this day."[53] But better days lay ahead. And Pittsburgh would have the last laugh on Chicago. At season end, the Pirates captured the National League pennant, finishing 6½ games ahead of the Cubs. It marked the fourth League pennant for the Pirates since Dreyfuss acquired the team in 1900 and began identifying and assembling talent. This season of 1909 was particularly sweet for Dreyfuss, and all of Pittsburgh, as the Pirates capped it off by winning their first World Series, downing the American League champion Detroit Tigers.

The baseball world beyond Pittsburgh was learning that Barney Dreyfuss, the one-time bank clerk in a faraway land, was becoming a formidable figure in the game. There was no folly involved.

Years later, Dreyfuss reflected on his fateful decision to make baseball his career. "I had a vision of what was coming, though I could not at the time see stadiums like Forbes Field," he said. "I saw that America was a nation of sport-loving people that liked to be out in the open. And I knew that baseball was a game of the people. It thrilled me, as an immigrant from Germany. I decided to go with the game."[54]

2

The Little Clerk, Big Dreams

Bernhard Dreyfuss was proving himself adept at numbers, a trait duly noted by his superiors at the bank where he toiled in Karlsruhe, the capital city of Baden in the German Empire. Dreyfuss, who turned 17 at the outset of 1882, was a slight lad whose hometown of Freiburg lay about 100 miles to the southwest near the upper reaches of the Rhine River. Dreyfuss, his name sometimes spelled Dreifuss, was in the midst of a three-year apprenticeship at the bank and showing promise. He was a good student and demonstrated fine attention to detail, although it was noted that on occasion he could be careless.[1]

The latter shortcoming was not unusual among young men of ambition who dreamed of futures and life beyond the smaller cities in Southwestern Germany like Karlsruhe. There were plenty of distractions. It seemed everything was changing, including the political map. Only 11 years earlier, Dreyfuss's home state of Baden, a hereditary monarchy, joined Prussia and 24 other states, kingdoms, cities and duchies to create the German Empire in 1871 led by Chancellor Otto von Bismarck and Emperor William I. This unification of 41 million German-speaking peoples (excluding Austria) into a federal state followed short but successful wars Prussia waged against Denmark, Austria and France.[2] In fast-changing Europe, Germany was urbanizing and rapidly becoming a leading industrial power. Free trade was instituted and barriers to economic growth removed, triggering an economic boom in the early 1870s when more new companies were established and more money invested than in the previous two decades.[3] Known as the "founders' years," the boom abruptly ended with a deep depression that began in 1873, with impacts that lingered into the 1890s. The new empire's economic prospects dimmed and the government, like many others in Europe, by 1879 responded with protective tariffs to shield industry and agriculture from cheap imports. The most significant tariffs were applied to iron and food grains.

The economic dislocation from the depression was profound, but so were the social consequences. During the 1870s about 600,000 people emigrated, primarily to North and South America. More than double that number emigrated the following decade. Overall, the German Empire under Bismarck was conservative in nature, but liberal on social issues, granting universal male suffrage at the outset and within a few years introducing health care and social security.[4] Bismarck did so to retain the support of the working class and keep them from supporting the socialists, whom he described as "enemies of the Reich." He instituted a policy of *kulturkampf*, which targeted socialists and German Roman Catholics, providing further impetus to emigration.

Life in the new empire was improving for adherents of the Jewish faith like young Dreyfuss, however. In Baden, Jews had been granted civil rights as early as 1818, but not equal political rights. Their fight for the right to vote was sometimes met with violent resistance. During the liberal Revolution of 1848 that swept Europe and challenged the old order, widespread anti–Jewish rioting erupted in Northern Baden. In response, full emancipation for Jews was denied. By 1862, however, local civil rights were extended to them and they were allowed to settle in the last of the duchy's cities that had previously excluded Jews, including Freiburg.

The Jewish population in Baden had risen to 24,009 by 1862. Discrimination continued, however, and when the Baden Army became part of the Prussian military, Jews held little hope of advancement within its ranks, although they were conscripted like every other German male. By the 1860s, Jews began to participate in the duchy's political life, but continued to face discrimination on many fronts.[5] At the time of his birth, Bernhard Dreyfuss, like all Jews, was required to be baptized in a Christian church. His baptism as a Lutheran was on February 26, 1865, three days after his birth.[6]

The liberal sentiment sparked by the Revolution of 1848 gradually improved the lot of the Jewish population in Germany. Beforehand, Jews were forbidden by law from owning property of any kind, although they were still subject to taxes. They could not hold any elected office and in order to survive they became peddlers, traders, middlemen and brokers. With enlightened government, Jews were allowed to become merchants, they could learn trades and become doctors and lawyers. And they could own land.

A skillful statesman, Bismarck sought to preserve peace on the continent through alliances with Russia and Austria-Hungary as territorial ambitions of some newly emerging powers became clear. Conscription was a fact of life for men across Europe as armies were raised and expanded.

There was so much for the young bank clerk Dreyfuss to ponder at the outset of the 1880s. Would the economy remain weak, limiting his chances for success in the banking industry when so many businesses had failed? What if he were called upon to bear arms for the German Empire? And if conscripted, would his prospects be limited because of his religion?

Relatives and friends had emigrated, mainly to America. Why had they sought greener pastures there? At times he must have found his work tedious and limiting. What did his future hold? There were so many questions facing the ambitious young man. He could be forgiven for daydreaming.

Dreyfuss's father, Samuel, often spoke of America where he had spent a decade before returning to Freiburg in 1861. He was not alone in emigrating to what was considered a land of freedom and opportunity by many oppressed peoples. Some friends and family had already done so. Samuel, born in 1832, had a sister, Fanny, who had married area merchant Leopold Bernheim (sometimes spelled Bernheimer) in 1844, in neighboring Ettenheim, just west of the Black Forest. Six years later, the young couple left for the United States. Joining them were Leopold's father, Leon Solomon Bernheim, and Leopold's brother, Henry, and Samuel Dreyfuss. The Bernheims and Dreyfuss settled in western Kentucky along the Ohio River, an important route for trade with the western frontier.[7] About 50 miles downstream to the west lay the Mississippi River, America's great transportation and trade artery.

Why the Bernheims and Samuel Dreyfuss selected the trading towns of Paducah and Smithland, in particular, is not known. Jewish settlement in the area was well under way by 1840, as America pushed westward and the new frontier was seen as offering more opportunity than the major East Coast cities where earlier arrivals had prospered.

Perhaps others from Baden had suggested those communities along the Ohio as particularly promising venues for traders and merchants. Samuel must have sent encouraging letters home, because within seven years his two other sisters, Jeanette and Babette, were in Paducah and married to prominent merchants there; Benjamin Weille, and Mangold Livingston, respectively. Chain migration of family members was alive and well as others from Baden moved to the area.

Samuel Dreyfuss settled in Smithland, rather than Paducah, in 1850. Paducah, strategically located at the confluence of the Ohio and Tennessee rivers had a population of 2,428, while Smithland, 20 miles to the east at the mouth of the Cumberland River, had 882 inhabitants. Both communities had easy access to the Deep South by way of the Tennessee and Cumberland rivers. Steamboats plied all the watercourses and towns like Paducah became important shipping points for slaves destined for the south. Tobacco was heavily traded and the town became known for its fine stores that supplied the steady stream of travelers passing by. The community became an important manufacturing center by the booming 1840s because of timber and the wholesale trade. It produced tobacco twists and plugs, cornmeal and flour, railroad ties, rope, cordage, barrel staves and many iron goods. Smithland, a slightly older community, was a major crossing point to Illinois and the north. It benefited from substantial trade with the south up the Cumberland River, which extended deep into Tennessee. Large amounts of beef, corn and tobacco were shipped southward.[8]

An excellent historical account of the people and communities along the lower Ohio River suggests the timing of the migration by the Bernheims, Samuel Dreyfuss, and members of their families was propitious:

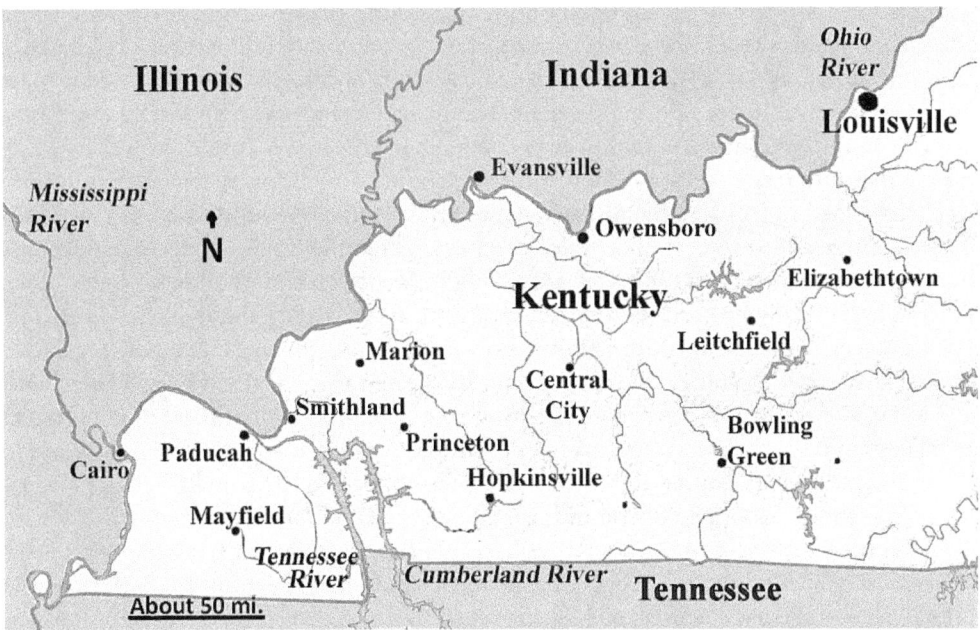

The lower Ohio Valley to which Barney Dreyfuss and his family members migrated from Germany in the mid-to-late 1800s. In Kentucky, Paducah and Smithland were centers of trade that serviced the growing areas to the west and south. Many of the newcomers to the region became merchants and wholesalers. Barney was drawn to Paducah, where his cousins operated a whiskey wholesaling business (author's creation).

The Ohio peaked as a force in regional and national development in the 1850s, when the steamboat was in its golden age and new railroads complemented river trade. Steamboats accelerated population flow, town development, commerce, manufacturing, and river improvements. Because of speed, direction of travel, and lower passenger and freight costs, farmers and merchants benefitted enormously.[9]

The Bernheims and Dreyfuss were traders and merchants: Just what the region needed. Weille and Livingston, both married to Dreyfuss sisters, did particularly well. Weille, born in Alsace, migrated to America in 1856, settled first in Smithland as did Livingston, before moving to booming Paducah where relatives were living. Weille married Jeanette Dreyfuss in 1857. Three years later, Weille partnered with Livingston to start the Star Clothing Company. Within 40 years, B. Weille and Son had become one of the leading clothing stores in Paducah, evolving into a department store.[10] Livingston, born in the village of Bingen in Baden, had apprenticed as a merchant and took up that line of work in Paducah where he married Babette Dreyfuss in 1863. His marriage to Babette lasted only two years, however. In March 1864, she was lying ill in her bedroom when a Confederate artillery shell blasted through the wall and over her bed during the Battle of Paducah when General Nathan Bedford Forest led an unsuccessful assault on the Union-held town. It was said the aunt of Barney Dreyfuss never recovered from the shock and died in confinement 13 months later, at age 25.[11] After her death, his uncle Mangold relocated to New York City where he became a knitting yarn manufacturer. He later returned to Paducah and established a dry goods and produce business along the riverfront. In time, his firm became Kentucky's largest wholesale grocery business.[12]

Paducah had been slow to grow before 1850, overshadowed by Smithland, which had a better harbor and was situated on higher ground than much of the surrounding river delta. Paducah was low-lying, prone to flooding and suffered outbreaks of malaria and other diseases. In 1851, a major fire destroyed Front Street and nearly every storehouse in town. But the coming of the railroad soon afterward, sparked significant growth.[13] Paducah found itself midway between Louisville and Memphis as well as a hub for north-south trade and it profited from trade in all directions. A Jewish community was established in Paducah by 1859 when a burial society was founded, an organization of Jewish men and women responsible for ensuring that the bodies of deceased persons of their faith are prepared for burial according to Jewish tradition. A dozen years later, the first Jewish congregation was organized. That same year, 1871, the area's first, and only Jewish mayor, Meyer Weil, a German immigrant, bank director and merchant, began two four-year terms.[14] The oldest Jewish community west of the Alleghenys was likely about 300 miles upriver in Cincinnati where a first congregation was organized in 1824 and 12 years later built its first synagogue. A benevolent society was formed there in 1838 and in 1850 the first Jewish hospital in the United States opened in Cincinnati.[15] Jews played a key role in the development of communities along the Ohio for many years.

Samuel Dreyfuss, who would father baseball executive Barney Dreyfuss years later, spent most of his time in Smithland, putting down roots there in about 1850. Precious little is known about Samuel, who turned 18 that year. His son didn't speak about him. Records show that Samuel was born in Altdorf, Baden, June 7, 1832, to Rabbi Moses Baer (Bernhard) Dreyfuss and wife Roset (Fanny) Hirsch. He had a brother, Schoeny (Samson), and sisters Jeanette, Babette and Fanny. By 1850, both his parents had passed away and Samuel decided to try his chances in the new world. He opened a business in Smithland and became a naturalized citizen. It was said some of his activity involved selling alcohol to the native population and that he prospered in so doing. Despite his success in business, he returned to Altdorf in 1860 or 1861 and went into business with his brother. Later in 1861, at the age of 29, he married Fanny Goldschmidt and the following year, daughter Rosa was born, followed by Frieda in 1863, Bernhard in 1865 and Elizabeth in 1875.

It's not known why Samuel Dreyfuss returned to Germany. He may have been homesick and unable to find a wife. Perhaps his business ran afoul of the authorities. He may have been lured back home by the gradual liberalization and extension of civil rights in Baden. Or he may have worried about his future along the Ohio as the political climate in the United States grew tense. It was feared the South might secede from the Union and armed conflict might disrupt, if not ruin, his livelihood. But Samuel had been so confident in America and its prospects that he had become a naturalized citizen, so his decision was a major reversal. One account said he was "broken in health" when he returned to Baden.[16] But it couldn't have been irreparably broken, because he lived until the age of 64, passing away in 1896. His motives remain a mystery and his son never shed light on the matter.

Samuel's son Bernhardt, soon called "Barney," was no doubt intrigued by his father's tales of life in far-off America. He knew his aunts Babette and Jeanette had moved there to begin new lives. And he would have heard about the tragic circumstances surrounding the death of Aunt Babette in the same year he was born. The young Dreyfuss no doubt peppered his American relatives with questions when they visited family in Freiburg and area.

After his primary education in Freiburg, Barney Dreyfuss studied in Karlsruhe where he began an internship with a bank. At some point in 1882, midway through his time there, the 17-year-old was contacted by a cousin, Isaac Wolfe Bernheim. Bernheim, 34, had migrated to Paducah in 1867. Isaac was the son of Leopold Bernheim and Fanny Dreyfuss, one of the sisters of Barney's father, Samuel. Isaac and his brother Bernhard were in the wholesale liquor business and needed a good bookkeeper to help them expand their Bernheim Brothers firm. "While our business was growing," Isaac Bernheim explained later, "my brother and I were reaching the stage in life where we looked for a gradual reduction of our laborious duties. We began to cast about for younger shoulders on which to place some of our increasing responsibilities."[17] One of the first candidates to spring to mind was their first cousin, Barney Dreyfuss, toiling in the bank in Karlsruhe. They offered him the position of assistant bookkeeper and he readily accepted, although it's unclear whether his father Samuel approved. Regardless, by 1882 Barney Dreyfuss was in Paducah crunching numbers in the Bernheim's whiskey business just as the brothers were expanding their operation from merely wholesaling liquor to distilling their own rye whiskey and bourbon brands.

Isaac Wolfe Bernheim played a key role in the life of Barney Dreyfuss. He would be a rock and an invaluable resource for his young cousin, probably having more impact on him than his own father. Cousin Isaac was a classic rags-to-riches success story, a man who showed his young nephew that hard work and focus could pay huge rewards in the new world. Years later, he wrote and published *The Story of the Bernheim Family*, from which much of the following account is derived.

In the fall of 1861, when he was 13, Bernheim's parents found Isaac a non-paying apprenticeship in a commercial shop in Freiburg where he swept the floors, made deliveries and learned the basics of selling, advancing over time to bookkeeping and handling money. To cover his clothing and living expenses, the slight young man was forced to find work at nights and Sundays to earn some money. He recalled his experiences in those days were not particularly pleasant, but taught him some important life lessons, primarily "to love work, to practice economy, and to be self-reliant." He then found a position as a clerk in Mannheim, about 120 miles to the north, with a salary equivalent to $11 a month, but even with the low cost of living in Germany at the time, he was barely able to get by. Young Bernheim found this job "exceedingly" unpleasant and soon began to look for something else. By August of 1865 he was employed by a wholesaler of knitted goods in Frankfurt, the financial and commercial center of southern Germany, about 50 miles north of Mannheim. His employer was disappointed he was so young and slight, having only corresponded with Bernheim before the lad showed up at his door. But the young man put his rudimentary sales skills to work, persuading the owner to give him a chance to show what he could do. It paid off for both.

Bernheim thrived in Frankfurt, his first big city, proved himself to be a valued employee and found a circle of friends. But money remained in short supply and he skipped meals so he could buy an overcoat and spare underwear. Early the following summer, the Austro-Prussian War (also known as the Seven Weeks' War) broke out and Frankfurt, not far from the scene of hostilities, saw commerce grind to a halt. Companies began laying off employees, but Bernheim was retained when three-quarters of the clerks in his firm were let go. He had made a positive impression on management in just a few months.

That same summer of 1866, two Americans appeared in Frankfurt, one of them his uncle, Mangold Livingston, who was visiting relatives in Freiburg and those in his hometown of Bingen, on the Rhine. He had become a widower after the Confederate-cannonball-induced death of his wife, Babette, Isaac's aunt. Livingston was unfamiliar with Frankfurt and found he had time to kill because his rail travel was disrupted by troop movements during the war which by July 14 reached within 25 miles of the city. He and fellow Paducahan Moses Kahn showed up at Isaac's place of work one afternoon that month. The rest of that day and all the next they canvassed a wide array of issues from the war at their doorstep to life in America and comparisons to Europe. Young Isaac was an absolute sponge and later wrote: "I had never before come in contact with real Americans, and had not had the opportunity to get information at first hand as to business conditions, business opportunities, the mode of life, customs and system of government in their great country." He had read about America and was impressed with its republican form of government. Likewise, he was impressed with his two visitors who seemed so prosperous and content. "It set me to thinking about my own future and what America could do for the young man with health, ambition and a willingness to learn," he would recall.

At the time, Uncle Mangold was involved in a business that made cotton knitting yarn in New York City. He offered young Isaac not only a position in his office but to lend him the funds to pay his way to New York. His nephew was sold on the idea and agreed to the proposition. Livingston then returned to Bingen, where he wooed and married his second wife, Amalie Friedburg and took her back to America.

Isaac's mother adamantly opposed his plan to emigrate, sowing seeds of fear in him and then, when that failed, guilt about his duties as a son. Fanny even called upon her brothers, Samuel and Samson Dreyfuss, in her bid to dissuade him. Samuel, of course, had spent about a decade in Kentucky and had become an American, but was willing to help Fanny, who had married Louis Weill after the death of her husband Leopold in 1856. But Weill died in 1865, making her a widow for a second time and leaving her feeling vulnerable. Having lost her second spouse within the past year, she couldn't bear

2. The Little Clerk, Big Dreams

to lose a son to a distant land. But Isaac was headstrong and got his way. In September, not long after the Austro-Prussian War ended, he left Frankfurt for his mother's home in Freiburg to prepare for his great adventure in America by studying English. Late in March 1867, he sailed to New York in steerage class aboard the *Hansa* from Bremerhaven. Because the food was so poor onboard, Bernheim survived—and thrived—on boiled Irish potatoes. He arrived in New York on April 7, with four dollars in his pocket. He found his uncle's establishment in the darkness that same night, but it was shuttered. The next day he returned, only to learn from Uncle Mangold the company was on the verge of bankruptcy, hit by a sudden depression in the cotton trade. The factory had been idle for weeks. There was no job for him. In addition, post–Civil-War stagnation in the labor market meant jobs everywhere were scarce. Things were looking bleak for the new arrival as he stayed with his uncle and aunt and pondered his fate.

Out of the blue, an old school chum of Livingston learned about the dilemma facing the new immigrant and offered to help. He ran a successful store in Wilkes-Barre, Pennsylvania, and offered Bernheim a job as a traveling peddler. By May, young Isaac was trudging along the back roads of Pennsylvania, selling housewares, knitting supplies, ladies' stockings, handkerchiefs and other notions. By October, he'd done well enough to acquire a horse and wagon and he extended his wares to include clothing. For the winter, he opened a small shop to display his goods in the crossroads hamlet of Overton, in the rugged country northwest of Wilkes-Barre. Business was poor but he enjoyed socializing with members of the community, attending parties and dances, shelling corn, singing and playing games and even attending Sunday school and church. Bernheim was mastering the English language and learning American customs.

As he prepared to return to the road in the spring, he learned Uncle Mangold's business had failed and he had returned to Paducah. There, he was opening a store with his brother-in-law Benjamin Weille, the husband of Bernheim's aunt Jeanette Dreyfuss. Livingston and Weille offered their nephew a position. But he hesitated because he had enjoyed his time in the Overton area so much. About the same time, however, the young peddler learned his horse had died and would be costly to replace. That clinched it. He auctioned off his remaining goods and bade farewell to Pennsylvania. By May of 1868 young Bernheim was working in the store of his uncles in Paducah as a store clerk, performing largely menial tasks. He found Paducah far ahead of Overton, with a population approaching 5,000 inhabitants. "There was neither club nor theater," he noted, however. "The town had a great many saloons, but it possessed only one beer hall." So, to discuss business and current events, shopkeepers would visit each other's establishments to socialize at the end of the work day.

Within a few months he met Moses Bloom, operator of a local wholesale liquor business with a partner, Reuben Loeb. Bernheim impressed the liquor men with his bookkeeping talents. He was hired and paid the princely sum of $40 a month. The young hire found the books of Loeb & Bloom were in terrible shape and he quickly reorganized them, delighting Bloom, in particular. In time, Bernheim was made a travelling salesman for the firm. That created an opening for a bookkeeper and Isaac wrote to his brother Bernhard back in Germany about the opportunity to come to America and replace him. The brothers were reunited early in 1870 when Bernhard joined Loeb & Bloom. Within months, the Franco-German war erupted and their mother wrote her sons saying she was so thankful they had emigrated and were safe, otherwise they would have been conscripted. She herself migrated to Paducah in 1874, just in time for Isaac's marriage to

Amanda Uri, bringing with her a young son and daughter from her second marriage. At the outset of 1872, the Bernheim brothers quit Loeb & Bloom, tired of repeated clashes with co-owner Loeb, whom they considered cunning and ignorant.

The ambitious young brothers soon afterward found a financial angel who helped them establish their own liquor wholesaling business. Elbridge Palmer, an aging, well-heeled wholesale grocer, was impressed with the integrity and plans of the hardworking brothers and invested $2,000 in their enterprise. Bernhard invested his life savings of $1,200. Palmer remained a silent partner and took one-third of the profits from Bernheim Brothers, until he withdrew three years later. The new firm managed to survive the economic crisis of 1873 that felled many businesses across the United States and it gradually expanded throughout the Ohio Valley and beyond. In 1883, Bernhard married Rosa, Dreyfuss's sister. The Bernheim Brothers firm was off to a promising start and the brothers settled into lives that were becoming comfortable for them in Paducah.

Isaac Bernheim realized that to distinguish itself, Bernheim Brothers needed to do more than simply wholesale the whiskey produced by others. He pursued new sources of choice whiskey and created new blends. Among other whiskeys, he developed a specially distilled bourbon he named "I.W. Harper." The initials were his own, but he borrowed the Anglo-Saxon surname from the late John Harper, a legendary horse breeder from the Lexington area. Harper's horses, Longfellow and Ten Broeck, were two of the most successful racehorses of the nineteenth century. Longfellow became known as "King of the Turf" after winning 13 of his 16 starts from 1870 to 1872. From 1875 to 1878, Ten Broeck won 23 of his 29 races.[18] It is not known if Isaac Bernheim was acquainted with Harper, who died in 1875, but he certainly was aware of his success. The Harper name, he felt, aside from hinting at success, was less likely to engender ethnic prejudice than his foreign-sounding Bernheim name.[19] He registered the trademark in 1879. In time, I.W. Harper became a very popular brand of bourbon, the distinctive American barrel-aged distilled whiskey made primarily from corn. Another innovation pioneered by the business-savvy Isaac Bernheim was the use of glass bottles instead of the traditional ceramic jugs and wooden casks normally used for whiskey. He realized buyers would appreciate being able to see the clarity of the Bernheim product in clear containers.[20]

Jewish immigrants controlled a disproportionate share of the whiskey trade for reasons rooted in history. By the 1880s, Louisville had become one of America's leaders in whiskey production and while only three percent of the city population was Jewish, fully a quarter of the whiskey trade was owned by them.[21] It was to Louisville that the Bernheim brothers moved when they outgrew their operation in Paducah. The whiskey trade provided unique opportunities for Jewish entrepreneurs, that were denied them elsewhere. The lucrative brewing industry was not open to them. Brewers tended to hire German Protestants because of lingering anti-Semitic prejudice they brought from Europe where brewing guilds had banned Jews. Besides, vertical integration of the beer business, with direct lines of supply from brewers to saloons, discouraged outsiders. And the wine-making industry was not attractive, because Americans had not yet developed much of a taste for the grape. Retailing or wholesaling of wine had poor prospects, even though some Jewish immigrants were familiar with that industry. For instance, Leopold Bernheim, father of the Bernheims, had been a wholesale buyer and seller of wine in Baden. In America, it was whiskey that offered the best opportunity to Jewish businessmen. And whiskeys such as bourbon, derived from corn mash, were distinctly American and so had a ready market. Jewish newcomers saw opportunity.

The need to ensure that the alcohol used in various religious observances was kosher had long required their involvement in all steps of the liquor trade, from production to distribution, and had historically given Jewish entrepreneurs a unique commercial niche. In medieval and early modern Europe, bans against Jewish ownership of farmland diverted many into intermediary market roles that included importing and exporting alcohol.[22]

After Russia took control of parts of Eastern Europe, Jews often found that the liquor business was one vocation from which they were not barred. In her book, *Jews and Booze: Becoming American in the Age of Prohibition,* Marni Davis, a Georgia State University history professor, noted that Jews "brewed, distilled, and sold all varieties of intoxicating beverages to both Jews and Gentiles since the beginning of the Diaspora."[23] An expert in ethnicity and immigration, Davis said that in Europe: "Intoxicating beverages were among the many commodities Jews trafficked as intermediaries." She said Isaac Wolfe Bernheim illustrated the trend perfectly. When he arrived in Paducah, several prominent Jews aside from Loeb and Bloom were engaged in the liquor trade, including Meyer Weil who was elected mayor in 1871. So, for the Bernheims and other members of their faith who flocked to the Ohio Valley in the 1800s, the liquor business was a logical choice for a livelihood.

Like Chinese and Italian immigrants in the nineteenth century, Jews often hired from within their own families and ethnic group, with earlier arrivals providing jobs and loans to those who came later. So it was not unusual for Jewish businessmen to hire nephews, cousins, brothers and more distant relatives. Aside from hiring his brother and nephew, Isaac Wolfe Bernheim married the daughter of one of the early Jewish investors in Bernheim Brothers.[24] Family was important.

The I.W. Harper brand was an instant success, winning gold medals in 1885 in New Orleans, in 1893 at the Chicago World's Fair, in 1900 at the Exposition Universal in Paris and in 1904 at the Louisiana Purchase Exposition. The capper came in 1907 when the celebrated bourbon also took gold at the Greater Louisville Exposition. Winning in their distillery's hometown was a coup and prompted them to bill I.W. Harper as "Gold Medal Whiskey."[25] By this time, Bernheim Brothers had become one of the largest whiskey distillers in the United States.[26]

Barney Dreyfuss arrived in Paducah in 1882, shortly after Bernheim Brothers began selling I.W. Harper bourbon and expanding their product line and territory. He held the post of assistant bookkeeper and quickly lived up to the faith his cousins placed in him. "He showed the keenest aptitude, and rapidly developed into an exceedingly valuable and trustworthy man," Isaac Bernheim recalled years later. When the Bernheim Brothers relocated to Louisville in 1888, having outgrown its quarters in Paducah, Dreyfuss was promoted to head bookkeeper and manager of credit. Two years later, the Bernheims granted him a "working interest" in the firm, making him a wealthy man.[27]

The young clerk from Freiburg was off to a grand start in a new land. He learned early on that hard work had its financial rewards in America.

Barney Dreyfuss soon found something else about America that he found irresistible.

3

A Fine Diversion

Baseball had developed a strong following in Paducah by the time Barney Dreyfuss hit town in the early 1880s.

Until 1857, the game hadn't spread far from New York, although a variation of the game was played in Massachusetts during the late 1700s. Settlers from the British Isles brought with them cricket and bat-and-ball games like rounders that are the most likely antecedents of the games taken up by Americans when they found rare moments for recreation. There was never a magic moment when the game was "invented." The story about it originating in Cooperstown, New York, in 1839 was a convenient myth created and promulgated to "prove" an American pedigree, when in fact the game evolved over time, perhaps centuries. Depictions of bat-and-ball games have been found in wall relief images from Ancient Egypt, suggesting a game, translated as "batting the ball," dates back nearly 4,500 years.[1]

The Civil War helped spread the game beyond the northeastern United States, when Union soldiers taught it to Confederates and Northerners played each other in Southern prisoner-of-war camps. The game reached the southern border state of Kentucky shortly before the opening salvos of the bloody conflict were fired by forces of Confederate General Pierre Gustave Toutant Beauregard at the Union soldiers defending Fort Sumter, South Carolina. Most often considered a southern state, Kentucky declared itself neutral early in the war, although many of its inhabitants made no secret of their sympathies for the South. There is evidence of a game played in Louisville in July of 1858 between two sides fielded by the Louisville Base Ball Club.[2] And the first box score for a game played in that city appeared in the *Louisville Democrat* on July 15.[3] Louisville was a bustling hub of commerce, with a population surpassing 68,000, when two sides picked from the Louisvilles again took to the field in July of 1860.

The game trickled down the Ohio River despite (or because of) the war. On October 21, 1866, in the town of Paducah, the local club tied a visiting nine from Cairo, Illinois, 32–32.[4] Paducah, population 4,500, had developed a strong commercial rivalry with the Illinois river delta community of 2,200 inhabitants lying 40 miles west at the confluence of the Mississippi and Ohio rivers. Their competitiveness spilled onto the baseball field and in the early years Paducah easily dominated its smaller rival, whose teams were often known as the Egyptians. In 1897, the *Paducah News* noted the two towns had been battling each other for baseball supremacy for three decades. The *News* and the *Cairo Bulletin* helped fuel the on-field rivalry. "Gloating by newspapers was as common as their claiming that bad umpiring had robbed the local team following defeats," Paducah baseball historian Randy Morgan has written.[5] Morgan discovered that reference to early games in Paducah's paper was rather spotty, but he found hints the town likely witnessed its first contests shortly before the Civil War. When peace returned, Paducah had at least one semi-professional team representing it.

Another early team was fielded a few miles upriver from Paducah in Evansville, Indiana, a community of about 12,000. On July 15, 1865, a four-inning game of "town ball" was played when the Crescent City Ball Club split into two teams under a Dr. Haas and a man named Britton. The local paper said the teams played 17 men aside for the first three innings and each added a player for the fourth. The Haas nine prevailed 69–54. "We have seldom, if ever, witnessed finer playing," gushed the *Evansville Journal,* which noted that "excitement was intense" during the last two innings.[6] The comment suggests other games predated that one, which sounds rather primitive in nature. A rematch of the same nines came a week later when the Britton side won, 77–66. It must have been less thrilling because editorial comment was missing. In 1866, the Evansville Ball Club was formed and in July of 1867, took a boat downriver to play Paducah. That same summer two more clubs arose in Evansville, the Resolutes and the Workingmen's Base Ball Club. In August, the Resolutes challenged Owensboro, Kentucky, a town of about 2,500 some 40 miles up the Ohio and defeated the Kentuckians 59–21.[7]

Baseball was flourishing in Ohio River Valley communities large and small by 1869 when the first openly professional team made history much farther upriver in Cincinnati. At the time, playing the game for money was frowned upon by followers who felt the game should remain a gentleman's pastime, untainted by the unseemly pursuit of victory. But determined to become more competitive, teams invariably found ways to compensate players under the table, or by providing a "job" in a local firm that may have entailed little or no work. They began to cast wide nets geographically in pursuit of talent. The Cincinnati Red Stockings, formed in 1866, had become a formidable club by 1869–70 when they embarked on an extended road tour, travelling more than 12,000 miles in pursuit of baseball glory for their city of 215,000. At the time, Cincinnati was often referred to as Porkopolis because of its many pig slaughterhouses. It soon became nearly as famous for baseball and in taking the game to an entirely new level. The Red Stockings, led by Harry Wright, an Englishman by way of New York, proved that money could be made from baseball, although after a winning streak of 84 games spread over two seasons, their net profit amounted to little more than pocket change.[8] The success of the Red Stockings led to the creation of the first professional baseball league, the National Association of Professional Base Ball Players, in 1871.

Downriver in Paducah, a team named the Idlewilds was attracting public attention of its own and in 1876 it was noted it had gone three years without a loss to Cairo.[9] In May of that year, the Idlewilds put an exclamation mark on the town's baseball supremacy by pummeling a hapless nine from Cairo 36 to 6.

Given the competitive environment in both commerce and in sport, Bernheim Brothers likely already had a team by 1882 when Barney Dreyfuss joined his cousins in Paducah, although it's doubtful the brothers themselves found time to play the game. They were often on the road, drumming up business far and wide and would have had trouble committing to a team even if they wanted to. As baseball fever spread, teams often consisted of members of various employee groups. Some games pitted married men against bachelors, or "fat men" against more slender lovers of the game. Occupational affinity led to competition pitting one department against another in large firms and between different businesses entirely. Bragging rights were becoming important. With several liquor distributing firms in Paducah competing with each other, it could be expected that a growing number of Bernheim employees took up bat and ball to seek glory on the diamond.

The *Paducah News* noted by late summer 1882 that baseball had gripped the town:

> The small boys of the city have the baseball craze to an alarming extent. They don't do anything but play the game and talk of nothing else but their clubs &c. [*sic*] There is, as a lad to-day informed us, not less than twenty-five juvenile clubs of ball playing in the place, with near a dozen of clubs of nearly grown boys and grown men.[10]

Paducah and the Bernheims presented the latest young immigrant from Germany with a pleasant change from the ways of the old world. The city was prospering and the Jewish community was vibrant. While the newcomer still struggled at times with the English language, he could always find someone with whom he could converse in German. Managing the books for the company was much easier and more enjoyable than the complex tasks he had performed for the bank in Karlsruhe. In later life, Dreyfuss claimed his first assignment at Bernheim Brothers was scrubbing whiskey barrels.[11] But that is doubtful and likely a harmless embellishment of his rags-to-riches story. The fact is he was very slight and was hired for his ability to deal with numbers, not for the muscles needed to wrestle heavy whiskey barrels in a warehouse. His duties as assistant bookkeeper suited his studious nature perfectly and he was far more comfortable with a ledger than with language. His memory and attention to detail soon paid dividends for the Bernheims. While Dreyfuss tended to be somewhat introverted, cousin Isaac was an extrovert who had developed into an effective salesman and leader of a company that was beginning to expand significantly.[12] When Isaac saw good work, he rewarded it. Dreyfuss was paid $20 a month to start and he needed $12 each month for board, netting him $8. He worked long hours and at night learned English. He proved himself indispensable and was soon receiving "handsome" increases every year from his appreciative cousins.[13]

Newcomer Barney Dreyfuss looked after the books for Bernheim Brothers, a whiskey business operated by his cousins in Paducah, Kentucky. The firm was a successful wholesaler of alcoholic beverages and later a distiller of fine bourbon. As a young man living along the Ohio River, Dreyfuss fell in love with the game of baseball and it was said that he played reasonably well at second base (ca. 1900, National Baseball Hall of Fame Library, Cooperstown, New York).

The pre-eminent ball team in Paducah by 1882 was the Eckford club, a popular name of the day for baseball teams. It was a salute to Henry Eckford, a famed American builder of warships that participated in the War of 1812. The Eckfords travelled widely along the Ohio and Mississippi rivers and in August played the Reds down the Mississippi in Memphis, winning one game and losing another.[14] Later that month, they challenged the Vogels in Louisville for a purse of $100.[15] The result of that game is not known. The Cairo newspaper remained unimpressed with the Eckfords, however, claiming Paducah had bolstered its roster with a pitcher and catcher from Evansville and Louisville, adding "without these professionals in the most important position in the ring, the club would amount to little or nothing."[16] The paper attributed Paducah's previous successes to imported professionals, dismissing the abilities of its hometown talent. The *Paducah News* fired back at accusations from Cairo that professionals had been added to the Eckford lineup. The *News* said two young men from Evansville, who were skilled ballplayers, had taken jobs at a shingle factory in Paducah and joined the team. The two additions were not professionals, the paper insisted, and Cairo had no right to dictate who joined Paducah's roster. "The Eckfords," it added sarcastically, "would much rather the Cairo boys would import seven or eight good players in order to make the game more interesting.... If you want to play, say so; or shut up."[17]

Games against rival Cairo were well-attended and Paducah usually prevailed. The Eckfords soon developed ambitions beyond their backyard. Late in the season, Paducah and Memphis played in each other's ballpark and in both cases the visiting team won. In August 1883, the Eckfords travelled by covered barge 40 miles down the winding Ohio River to Cairo with "a large company of citizens including ladies." Paducah lost that contest 7–3 and the *Cairo Bulletin* crowed: "It appears that this year the Eckfords depended entirely upon their home talent as Cairo did, and the result is that last year's success did not follow it," the *Bulletin* said. "The [Paducah] boys played very well indeed; they made several brilliant dashes, but they are certainly no match for Cairo's crack nine. If they would stand any chance of winning here, they will have to trot out a professional or two again."[18]

Losing to Cairo and the dig from its local organ must have stung the baseball cranks in Paducah, leaving them determined to recapture past glory. Before the playing season ended, Paducah salvaged some pride in a well-attended game by surviving a three-run barrage in the ninth inning to down the pesky Cairo club 9–4.[19] Paducah had so often dominated Cairo in preceding years that even the *Bulletin* acknowledged it, sometimes in odd ways. In a brief news item about a Paducah grand jury returning four times as many indictments as its counterpart in Cairo, the *Bulletin* was moved to admit, albeit cheekily: "Cairo can lay it over Paducah in everything but baseball and criminals."[20]

Before that 1882 season ended, a stock company was being formed to enclose the Trimble baseball grounds in Paducah and "organize a club of picked players from Evansville and this place, and enter what is known as the Southern base ball league, to which a number of good clubs belong," reported the *News*.[21] It would appear nothing came of the league idea.

Baseball had become a source of pride in Paducah and defeat did not rest lightly on the shoulders of its residents. Had Barney glanced out any window of the Bernheim Brothers business on North Second Street he may have seen the game being played by boys and men that originally may have seemed odd to his European eyes. Or he may have passed impromptu games during the short walk to his living quarters with relatives on Ninth Street. He may have followed the exploits of the Eckfords in the newspapers.

Barney never spoke about any "eureka moment" for him in baseball, but he had plenty of exposure to it. One account, often repeated, was that his interest in the game was medically induced. Dreyfuss was supposedly feeling stress from long hours at his new job and a doctor ordered him to consider outdoor pastimes such as baseball. But that prescription was more likely made later in Louisville where he moved with the rapidly expanding Bernheim operation and assumed much more onerous duties. Regardless of where that doctor practiced and prescribed, Barney Dreyfuss contracted a case of baseball fever not long after arriving in America.

"Baseball was so active in Paducah that Barney Dreyfuss became captivated," Paducah native and historian Jeff Youngblood has written. "He had no problem finding games to play, but a German immigrant working his way into the local clique was certainly a challenge." Despite his shy nature and slight build, he was keen to play, trying every position before settling for second base where it was said he performed respectably.[22] Years later, Dreyfuss told a newspaper reporter in Paducah he'd never seen baseball before arriving in town. Once there, however, he immersed himself in it, learned the game and studied its peculiar language. Whether it was the numbers associated with the game that attracted him, or simply an opportunity to get out of the office for awhile, Dreyfuss was hooked. He played recreationally and when that failed to satisfy his newfound passion, he began organizing teams, initially with players from Bernheim Brothers and later fielding semi-professionals he scouted from the area.[23]

By 1884, Barney Dreyfuss dramatically increased his involvement in baseball. That year, he managed his first team representing Paducah.[24] Details are few, but it appears he assembled a semi-professional nine of locals and imports and he may have played second base alongside them for a time.[25] Among the new faces appearing in Paducah were brothers George and Will Dovey, from Central City, Kentucky, 90 miles to the east, where their family owned a coal mine. The Doveys played a variety of infield positions, while George also pitched and Will caught for him. The brothers, 22 and 30 respectively, had played for Central City for a couple of seasons and appeared with Evansville, Owensboro and Louisville teams during the early 1880s. They may have appeared with Paducah as early as 1882 when the *Cairo Bulletin* mentioned the opposition fielded "professionals from Evansville and Louisville."[26] George played under the name "Colby" and Will as "Dayton," likely to hide their true identities because of parental disapproval about time spent away from the family's struggling coal operation. Playing under an assumed name was not uncommon in a day when baseball was seen by some families as a needless distraction from honest work. George showed particular promise as a pitcher and might have made it to the professional game. During one late August game in 1884, he struck out 15 batters while playing for Central City.[27] In recounting George's long baseball career many years later, the *Evansville Press* reported that George Dovey met Dreyfuss in 1884 when "they" organized the Paducah team.[28]

Aside from his talent, George Dovey would have shared firsthand knowledge he gleaned from baseball teams upriver and how they operated. And he may have been in Paducah for reasons aside from just baseball. One account said the Dovey Coal Mine had an agency in Paducah (from which it may have shipped its product), while another said George attended a business college in town.[29] Regardless, George Dovey and Barney Dreyfuss shared a love of baseball, developed great respect for each other and became lifelong friends. In 1906, when Dovey and another brother, John, purchased the Boston Beaneaters of the National League, Barney Dreyfuss, then owner of the Pittsburgh

Pirates, helped them deal with the League and find investors. By then, Dovey and Dreyfuss had graduated to become powerful figures in the National League, far removed from the dusty diamonds of the Ohio Valley.

During that 1884 season, the Paducah Eckfords continued to challenge teams from tiny Cairo, to Memphis, Tennessee (population 35,000), and elsewhere across the region, hoping to recapture bragging rights as one of the crack clubs along the Ohio. On August 24, however, Cairo unexpectedly trounced Paducah 37–9. This was considered unacceptable in Paducah and within days, team management, likely including Dreyfuss, acted. The *Cairo Bulletin* reported that the Eckfords had retained the service of four professional players, two from Evansville and two from Louisville (the Dovey brothers likely among the four). The paper insisted, by contrast, that Cairo employed no professionals whatsoever.[30] A few days later, however, the *Bulletin* admitted that a pitcher and catcher from Murpheysboro in southern Illinois had materially aided the Cairo nine in the game. The paper also reported that stock was being issued for a "permanent" baseball association (meaning professional) which hoped to acquire suitable grounds with seating for 1,000 fans.[31] Of the shellacking administered by Cairo on the 24th, the *Paducah News* complained the umpiring was biased and that only two Cairo residents played on its team, the rest were imports, including a professional pitcher and catcher from St. Louis. The Cairo paper rejected those "surmises and gross mis-statements," insisting Paducah's defeat "was due entirely to their great inferiority as players."[32] The trash talk in newspapers along the Ohio remained alive and well. The Paducah nine ended August with a tough 11–10 loss before 600 spectators in Memphis to a team also known as the Eckfords. A few days later they again were defeated by Cairo, this time by a score of 12–6. The Cairo newspaper kept up its partisanship and complained the Paducah roster now included several professionals from Louisville.[33] For Barney Dreyfuss, his first season running a team must have been a disappointment. But better days lay ahead.

By 1885, Dreyfuss and other lovers of the game in Paducah decided the time had come to field a fully professional, or at the very least, a very strong semi-professional team. That meant finding talent and raising money to pay the players and defray expenses. Dreyfuss, along with his newfound lieutenant in baseball, George Dovey, began to pursue suitable players. A new Paducah Base Ball Association was established and began selling shares at $50 apiece and Dreyfuss acted as secretary of the new organization. One such share in the new ball club, signed by him, Certificate number 17, was unearthed years later and can be found in the Baseball Hall of Fame in Cooperstown. It bears the date of May 23, 1885, and was issued to A.M. Laevison.[34] It is not known how many shares were sold in total.

The new season got off to a rough start when Paducah was whitewashed by Memphis, 22–0, on June 7. Paducah found itself completely outclassed by a new professional team, the Cotton Nine, its base runners reaching third only once and second just twice. The reporter for the *Memphis Appeal* provided little detail because the game was "too laughable."[35] No box score was provided, so the rosters are unknown. A clue can be found elsewhere in the same newspaper which carried listings of recent arrivals at the Peabody Hotel, including the Paducah baseball club. Thirteen names were listed, among them Barney Dreyfuss, "Colby," and "Dayton."[36] This was one of the few times they appeared in print together, even if the Doveys were using assumed names. The performance of the Paducahans gradually improved, attributable no doubt to the two Central City imports. On July 5, 1885, they defeated Cairo 8–6 and the next day travelled 20 miles southwest to

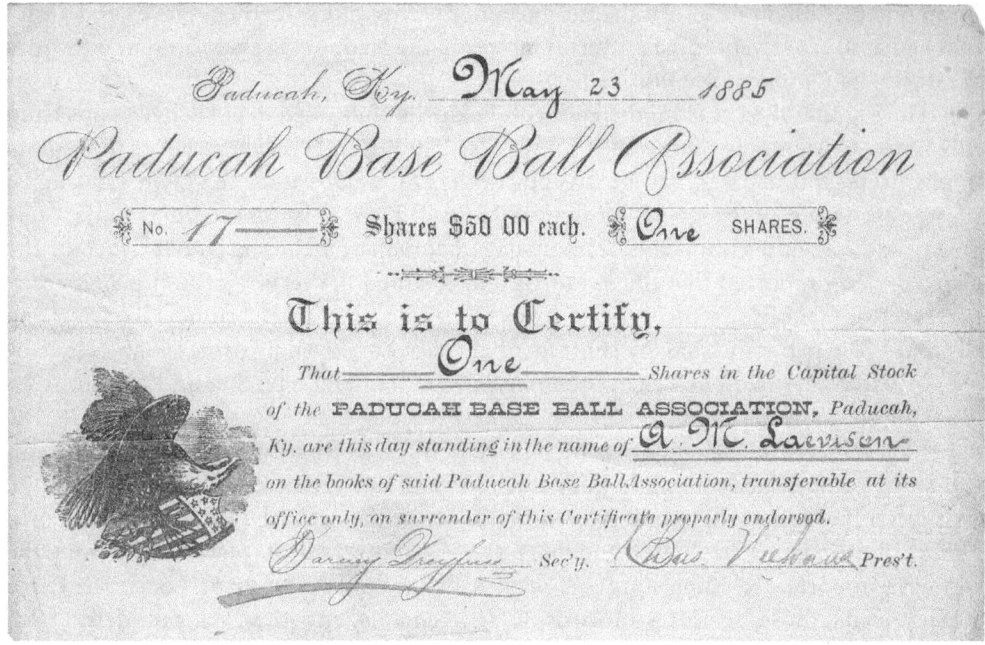

Not long after arriving in Paducah in 1882, Barney Dreyfuss became active in baseball and began managing local teams, demonstrating real talent in the latter capacity. In 1885, he helped organize a semi-professional team and signed this stock certificate as secretary of the club (National Baseball Hall of Fame Library, Cooperstown, New York).

edge Charleston, Missouri 8–7. Downriver in Memphis, the local paper noted: "The town has gone clean daft over baseball."[37] The game was spreading throughout the South.

The Doveys continued to appear occasionally with the Central City team and in advance of an August 8 game against Owensboro, the *Owensboro Messenger* noted Central City was "procuring a strong battery, the Dovey Bros., who have been playing this season in the Paducah club—a nine, by the way, who have downed every amateur club in the Mississippi valley."[38]

Despite the scouting of Barney Dreyfuss and the solid play of the Doveys, Cairo again prevailed over Paducah in the season series between the towns, taking the coveted "solid silver ball" at the end of 1885.[39] Talks were underway late that year about establishing a league for the entire area to replace the rather haphazard system of arranging games. A formal schedule would be used to determine a champion. A Blue Grass League was established in 1885 and by early 1887 discussions were underway to establish an Indiana-Kentucky League with teams from Paducah, Cairo, Evansville, Terre Haute, Indiana, and Henderson, Kentucky.[40]

The 1886 season produced more disappointment for Paducah, although by now the Dovey brothers were no longer hiding their identities. Their names appeared in the box scores of an August 16 game in which Cairo downed Paducah 5–2 before 500 cranks, despite the losers being "reinforced by material from Louisville."[41] George Dovey played shortstop but went hitless and made two errors. Will was at second and scored one of Paducah's runs and recorded a single error. The Doveys continued to appear on the roster of some Louisville teams, but not the professional Eclipse nine. The Eclipse, renamed the Colonels, were members of the American Association for the loop's entire history from 1882 to 1891.

At some point, word of the play by the Doveys in Louisville attracted the attention of St. Louis Browns owner Chris Von Der Ahe and his manager Charlie Comiskey. The pair travelled to Louisville in a bid to sign the brothers to the Browns, the AA champions from 1885 to 1888. A Louisville newspaper years later described Comiskey sitting down with Will Dovey while Von Der Ahe set his sights on George. Comiskey reached some sort of deal with Will, which may have been scotched later by Von Der Ahe. There is no record of Will ever appearing in a league game with the Browns. He was given a tryout with the Louisville Colonels in 1886, who promptly farmed him out to Fort Wayne, Indiana. Then, after playing a season in Binghamton, New York, Will retired from the professional game.[42]

The mercurial Von Der Ahe was close to reaching a deal with George during that meeting in Louisville, but grew suspicious the younger Dovey was not acting in good faith and might jump to another some other team for better money. Von Der Ahe angrily stormed off back to St. Louis with Comiskey in tow and George remained in Louisville.[43] The Dovey brothers struggled to keep Dovey Coal Mines operating when their parents left them in charge and returned to their home in Pennsylvania. The mine, three miles south of Central City at Mercer Station, was susceptible to flooding, a situation linked to underground rivers in Mammoth Cave, a few miles to the southeast. The strain of business may have been too much for Will, who committed suicide in 1899.[44] The mine was sold soon afterward and its new owners filed for bankruptcy in 1911.[45] George Dovey, meanwhile, never married and moved first to Cleveland and then St. Louis where he became successful in the streetcar business.

Meanwhile, the Bernheim brothers worked diligently to expand their operation in Paducah, invariably putting business ahead of pleasure and even family commitments. Isaac would act as a travelling salesman through an area that grew to include the South, the West and Northwest. When he returned home, younger brother Bernhard hit the road to replace him. The firm was expanded with an investment from Isaac's father-in-law Nathan M. Uri and for a time was known as Bernheim Brothers and Uri. By 1888, after a year of deliberation, the brothers felt the town could no longer accommodate their rate of growth. It was particularly tough for Isaac to consider a move since his heart was in Paducah, his friends were there, his mother had moved to town and his six children were all born there. Following an inventory in January, the brothers realized they had to move, choosing Louisville "which at that time was one of the great distributing centers of the country for fine whiskies."[46]

On April 1, Bernheim Brothers opened in a large new building on Main Street between First and Second streets. They invested heavily in Pleasure Ridge Distillery, presumably to provide additional product.[47] "The policy of increasing our trade with the increase in our capital was adhered to," Isaac wrote later. "We engaged more travelling men as we needed them, and soon our business expanded from Maine to Texas and from New York to California."[48] The move to Louisville and the distillery purchase proved immediately profitable. By 1890, sales for Bernheim Brothers reached about $2 million and it was considered the "largest whisky house in Kentucky."[49] The I.W. Harper premium brand of bourbon had been joined by another strong seller, Old Continental. By then, the Bernheims had 22 travelling salesmen who travelled as far afield as Mexico and South America. One hundred cases of I.W. Harper were being shipped to Chile by 1897 when total sales had risen to $3 million and Bernheim Brothers was described as "the largest whisky house in the world."[50]

Barney Dreyfuss's duties increased as he became credit manager and then was granted a sizeable interest, reported to be one-tenth of the firm he helped build. The *Louisville Courier-Journal* traced the rise of the Bernheim Brothers operation and Dreyfuss's role in it in a lengthy article during 1897, the same year they opened a state-of-art distillery to make their own product. "And in all this immense business," it concluded, "the firm has lost little. This is due to Mr. Dreyfus [sic]. He has the financial conditions of firms on the end of his tongue, and he receives twice as many reports from Bradstreet and Dunn as any other Louisville concern." It was clear the young credit manager was keeping close tabs on businesses the same way he did later on baseball players with his "dope book." At age 23, Barney Dreyfuss was becoming a wealthy man like his cousins and living the American dream. Before he left Paducah, he became a naturalized U.S. citizen, just as his father had done so many years earlier.[51]

Dreyfuss was busier than ever with Bernheim Brothers in their large new quarters in Louisville, working six long days every week. It may have been at this point, rather than back in Paducah, that he sought medical assistance while feeling the effects of overwork. A doctor suggested the 23-year-old get more fresh air and exercise and his co-workers concurred.[52] Dreyfuss needed little encouragement to heed the advice and was soon heavily involved in baseball in Louisville. He couldn't have asked for more. By that time, Louisville had become a significant hotbed of amateur and professional baseball.

When it came to the game he had embraced, Barney Dreyfuss was in the right place at the right time.

4

Louisville

With its long history as a minor league baseball city, it may surprise some followers of the game to learn Louisville made significant contributions at the big league level.

The Kentucky city is where the notion of the National League was born in a bar and it fielded major league teams for 20 years before the beginning of the twentieth century. Late in 1877, Louisville's second year in the National League, a game-fixing scheme by four of its players to pad their wallets and please gamblers was uncovered, prompting Louisville to resign from the League. The four were banned from baseball for life and the words "Louisville" and "scandal" became forever linked. Four decades later "Black Sox" and Chicago were added to the lexicon for the same reason. After a four-year absence from top-tier baseball, Louisville became a founding member of the American Association in 1882 and remained there until the league expired in 1891. It then returned to the National League. For many years, baseball historians believed the first black major leaguer, Moses Fleetwood Walker, made his debut in Louisville in 1884, thereby breaking the color barrier in baseball. The same year, amateur player Bud Hillerich, who made bats for himself in his father's woodworking shop, began supplying other players. They were instantly popular and the Louisville Slugger was born. Louisville's team, the Eclipse, renamed the Colonels in 1885, set a record for baseball futility in 1889, losing a still-standing record of 26 consecutive games. Amazingly, they rebounded the very next year to capture the American Association pennant. Also in 1889, Louisville players staged the first strike in baseball. During its tenure in the majors, Louisville introduced star players such as future Hall of Famers Honus Wagner, Fred Clarke, Rube Waddell and Jimmy Collins, along with Pete Browning, Guy Hecker, Deacon Phillippe and Tommy Leach. Baseball historian Philip Von Borries has touted Louisville as a unique city with a "big-time baseball tradition and history." He drew support for his assertion from American Association chronicler Bill O'Neal, who has written: "Few cities can claim as rich a baseball heritage as Louisville."[1] Not to be outdone, acclaimed baseball historian David Nemec chimed in, calling it "one of America's greatest baseball cities."[2]

Louisville's first organized baseball club took to the field in 1858, playing on a vacant lot at the northwest corner of Fourth and Breckinridge streets, south of downtown. Before the summer was out, another local club, the Phoenix, was competing with the Louisville Base Ball Club. When Civil War guns fell silent in 1865, two new teams were formed, the Eagles and the Eclipse, the latter likely named after an iconic and successful Kentucky thoroughbred racehorse. On July 19 that summer, the first game was played according to standardized, modern rules, including nine innings and nine men aside, a first west of the Alleghenies in a field at Nineteenth and Duncan streets northwest of the city core. It pitted the Eagles against the Nashville Cumberlands, the former winning,

22–5. By 1869 and 1870, Louisville was playing the powerful Cincinnati Red Stockings from 135 miles up the Ohio River. And losing. Badly. The worst rout came April 21, 1870, when Cincinnati humiliated the Eagles 94–7.

The Louisville Olympics, the city's fifth organized nine, was fielded in 1871. They played west of downtown at 28th and Elliott streets on a lot that by the end of the decade was taken over by the Eclipse, who improved it, renamed it Eclipse Park and used it for their games in the American Association. During the 1870s, several more ball clubs were established in the west end of Louisville, a working-class part of town with many inhabitants of German and Irish descent.[3] The game was morphing from a gentleman's pursuit into one for the masses.

Sometime during 1875, Louisville got wind of plans by Chicago baseball magnate William Hulbert, owner of the White Stockings, to chart a new course for baseball outside the National Association of Professional Base Ball Players. Hulbert was fed up with rowdiness, gambling, drunkenness, and lack of respect for player contracts, among other issues, that plagued the first professional league during its five-year run. Organized gambling was a scourge within the National Association and in ballparks everywhere. Cranks freely bet on games, but stayed home if they felt their team was in the thrall of gamblers. The situation had become so bad that local officials posted signs at some ballparks with warnings such as: "NO GAME BETWEEN THESE TWO TEAMS IS TO BE TRUSTED."[4]

A secret meeting to discuss a new option devised by Hulbert was held in Louisville on December 16 and 17, 1875, in a small back room at Al Kolb's Oyster and Liquor Bar on West Liberty Street. It included representatives of professional baseball clubs from Chicago, St. Louis, Cincinnati and Louisville whose discussion led to plans to form a new league. Those attending agreed to approach four eastern teams, Boston, Hartford, Philadelphia and the Mutual Club of New York to join them in a new eight-team professional loop to challenge the struggling National Association. Aside from widespread gambling and drunkenness, the old Association was marked by a failure of teams to play games that had been scheduled and by "revolving" (players who disregarded contracts to jump to clubs for more money). It was also uncompetitive, Boston having won the last four of its five pennant races. Stung by his clashes with Boston and Philadelphia teams over players, Hulbert wanted to create an entirely new league led by hard-headed capitalists able to put the game on a sound financial footing, rather than players, who controlled the NA and had demonstrated little organizational or business sense. It would be a league of baseball *clubs,* not of ball *players.* Hulbert sought a ban on Sunday games, on alcohol and on gambling, and he was determined to establish respect for scheduled games and for umpires. He was a moralist, but also a realist. Had his Chicago club remained in the National Association, it might have been expelled because Hulbert had tried to sign for 1876 Boston's "Big Four" of Al Spalding, Deacon White, Ross Barnes and Cal McVey while the 1875 season was still under way. There was likely going to be a price to pay for such tampering outside the approved signing period.

Representing Louisville at the pivotal meeting in the city was Charles E. Chase, an executive in the wholesale liquor and distillery firm E.H. Chase and Company. Chase would become vice-president of the Louisville Grays while the president was Walter N. Haldeman, publisher of the *Louisville Courier-Journal.* The two men were the principal investors in the team.[5]

At the conclusion of that seminal gathering in Louisville, Chicago's Hulbert and St. Louis owner Charles A. Fowle were directed to meet the four eastern clubs February 2 in New York and persuade them to join the four western cities in an eight-team loop. Hulbert and Fowle were given power to act and they succeeded brilliantly. The easterners agreed. The beginning of the National League is often cited as February 2, 1876, in New York, but baseball historian Harold Seymour acknowledged the die was cast several weeks earlier in the unlikely venue of a Kentucky city along the Ohio River. "Louisville, therefore, was the real birthplace of the National League, not New York City," he argued.[6] The creation of the National League was the death knell for the National Association.

On April 25, 1876, the Louisville Grays lost their National League home opener to Chicago 4–0, before 6,000 cranks at their ballpark at St. James Court, just south of downtown. The visiting White Stockings, accompanied by owner Hulbert, featured veteran pitcher Al Spalding, heavy hitter Ross Barnes and slick first baseman Cap Anson. On the roster for the Grays were effective right-hander Jimmy Devlin, shortstop Chick Fulmer and manager/outfielder Jack Chapman. The visitors scored single tallies in the second, third, fourth and seventh innings as Spalding held the home club scoreless. Despite the disappointing result for the local cranks, the *Louisville Courier-Journal* hailed the whitewash as "The Finest Game of Base Ball Ever Witnessed in Louisville," in one of its seven headline decks. It argued the Grays had acquitted themselves well, considering they faced the powerful Chicago nine, an opponent it termed "the most expensive in the land. The individual players command, in some instances, salaries which seem almost fabulous."[7]

The Grays finished their first season with 30 wins and 36 losses, good for fifth place. Devlin pitched all but one of Louisville's games, compiling 30 wins and 35 losses. Chicago pitcher Al Spalding, meanwhile, won 47 and lost 12 as his White Stockings captured the inaugural National League pennant, finishing six games ahead of Hartford and St. Louis. And only Chicago turned a profit for the season, slightly more than $37,000.[8] Meanwhile, Louisville had done its part to help put baseball on a solid new footing and root out gambling. During the season, it expelled substitute outfielder George Bechtel for throwing a game and trying to bribe his fellow teammates to help him "sell" future games for gamblers.

Things were not rosy in Louisville as far as Devlin was concerned. He traveled at his own expense to the winter meeting of the League, held December 6 in Cleveland, to seek his release from the Grays. He argued management had failed to comply with conditions of his contract. Louisville vice-president Charles E. Chase soundly rejected that assertion at the gathering. The board of the League sided with Chase and instructed Devlin to withdraw his appeal. He did so and a disappointed Devlin then slipped away, still tied to the Grays against his wishes. His was one of several player appeals considered by the board in Cleveland, "all of which were either dismissed or settled in favor of the owners, setting a pattern of one-sided behavior that would persist for nearly a century."[9] Hulbert and his fellow magnates were determined to show who was in control now. Henceforth, players were merely employees. Devlin's pronounced unhappiness in Louisville would linger and may have been a factor in his behavior the following season.

The National League was back for 1877, reduced to six teams after expelling New York and Philadelphia for failing to complete their full schedule of games late the previous season. Unlike 1876, the new campaign would feature a real pennant race, although it would become known as the only one in major league history proven to have been rigged.[10] And Louisville was right in the thick of it.

The Chicago White Stockings did not repeat as the League powerhouse. Catcher Deacon White was playing first base for Boston and Al Spalding's decision to abandon pitching in favor of newly acquired hurler George Bradley and switch to first base did not work well. Meanwhile, hitter Ross Barnes struggled with the rule change that no longer considered a struck ball that began fair but rolled foul, to be considered fair. He had mastered the technique to good effect, but elimination of the "fair-foul" rule lessened his contribution to the team. This weakening of Chicago left Boston and Louisville as the top contenders. The Red Caps retained most of their crack roster from the old National Association and added Hartford ace Tommy Bond to their lineup. Boston was good, but Louisville just a bit better. Devlin pitched every inning of all 60 games that season and performed well, despite any lingering misgivings about management, as did new Grays captain and outfielder George Hall. Louisville took an early lead in the pennant race and by August 13 were 4.5 games ahead of Boston, with a winning percentage approaching .700.[11]

Four days later, the Grays began their last eastern road trip of the season in a comfortable position, needing to win only half their remaining games to clinch the title. Initial losses to Boston and Hartford were considered minor setbacks, but further unexpected ones began to pile up. On August 21 in Hartford, the then-third-place Dark Blues whitewashed the Grays 7–0, the first time all year Louisville had been shut out. Suspicions arose when it was learned gamblers had favored Hartford that day over league-leader Louisville. The Grays fell out of first place during a three-game series in Boston when they were swept by the Red Caps. Then, on the eve of two more games scheduled against Hartford, Grays vice-president Chase received a troubling telegram one morning at breakfast. "Watch your men," it said.[12] It came from an unknown individual in Hoboken, New Jersey, saying that Hartford was again favored in the upcoming contests and that something was wrong with his Louisville players. Chase disregarded the warning as the handiwork of some troublemaker, but when he learned the Grays lost 6–3, he sent a message of concern to manager Jack Chapman asking why he had substituted Al Nichols for regular third baseman Bill Hague. Chapman replied that captain Hall wanted Nichols to appear before his hometown crowd in Brooklyn where the game was played. Satisfied, Chase dropped the matter, but grew alarmed again when he received another anonymous telegram saying there was crooked play going on as Nichols, Hall and Devlin made numerous costly errors. He immediately wired Chapman to bench Hall. The road trip ended with losses of 1–0, 3–2, and 6–2 to last-place Cincinnati. When they returned home, the Grays were in second place, five games behind Boston. John A. Haldeman, the baseball writer for the *Louisville Courier-Journal*, and son of the paper's owner and club president Walter Haldeman, smelled something amiss in recent developments. He accused Hall and Devlin of crooked play, prompting League president William Hulbert to order Chase to investigate and root out any wrongdoing he found. Devlin and Hall denied everything, but sportswriter Haldeman found that Devlin, Hall and Nichols, with the likely connivance of shortstop Bill Craver, had arranged with gamblers to throw games. Devlin confessed he had played "carelessly" and that he and Hall took money to lose exhibition games, but not scheduled ones. Nichols said nothing and Craver insisted he was innocent despite a personal history of game-throwing behavior. Chase seized telegrams that showed Devlin, Hall and Nichols had indeed sold scheduled games, receiving no more than $500 from gamblers. Craver was considered guilty by association, despite the lack of firm evidence against him. Regardless, on October 30, Hulbert banned all four players from professional baseball for life.[13] He was determined to set an example and stamp out the scourge of gambling, a cancer which had persisted despite the best efforts of Hulbert and his fellow owners.

Louisville baseball historian Bob Bailey carefully examined the play of the four players based on accounts and box scores during Louisville's swoon, looking for definitive proof of deliberate bad play. He noted that fielding errors were common in the game at the time when catching gloves were just beginning to appear, so finding clear evidence of a fix was "problematic." Bailey carefully studied Devlin's record in particular, acknowledging that earned runs are hard to discern in some box scores. He found that before the fateful eastern trip, Devlin allowed an average of 5.05 runs per game. That dropped to 4.75. And during the final 10 games of the season in which Devlin won 35 games in all, it dropped further, to 3.77. Bailey said he could find no evidence of "funny business" in those numbers. Another complicating factor was the situation with Cincinnati. Bailey said the sudden departure and later reappearance of the financially troubled Red Stockings during the season meant standings published while the season was still under way were sometimes unclear. In the end, the Boston Red Caps won the pennant by seven games or by three games, depending whether Cincinnati games were included in the official standings. At the end of his analysis, however, Bailey had little doubt that Devlin, Hall and Nichols threw games that season. He was not as certain about Craver, despite a previous record of doing so. But Bailey noted that crooked play by the Grays may not have cost Louisville the pennant at all. A late surge by Boston, with 20 wins and just one loss from August 17 until the end of the season "may have swayed the standings beyond what the Louisville Four did."[14]

Despite the scandal, the National League did not eject or otherwise penalize Louisville and the city was included in early plans for 1878. However, the directors of the Grays met on March 7, 1878, to review the situation and voted to notify the league they were resigning. The *New York Clipper* explained their decision this way: "The dishonesty which was proven in last year's team has in a great measure disgusted the public with the game, and the directors thought it advisable to retire from the business for at least one season." It added there were rumors afloat that several gentlemen in the city had already raised $5,000 to field a "very strong" professional team for 1879.[15] Nothing materialized from that bit of intelligence, however. So for now, at least, Louisville's time among the top baseball cities in America was over.

St. Louis also dropped out of the League, believing it couldn't field a competitive nine in 1878 without Devlin and Hall, whom the Brown Stockings had signed for the upcoming season, but were now banned from the game.[16] Aside from the Louisville gambling scandal, which tarnished baseball, Hulbert and his fellow magnates were struggling to turn a profit. All six clubs finished the season in the red. St. Louis lost an estimated $8,000; Chicago, $6,000; Hartford, $2,500; Boston, $2,230.85; and Louisville, $2,000. Cincinnati had disbanded entirely because of its money woes. "The Louisville scandal proved to be the icing on the cake for a terrible season," it has been said.[17] Meanwhile, Craver continued to insist on his innocence, Nichols and Hall slipped into obscurity and Devlin constantly begged for reinstatement, without success. A winner of 65 games in just two National League seasons, Devlin struggled with poverty and died in 1883 at the age of 34.

Interest in baseball waned in Louisville during 1878 when, for the first time in five years, there was no professional team. Some Louisvillians may have felt shame because of the betting scandal and resented having the city's name sullied, while others may have been angry, feeling that gamblers had snatched away the National League pennant from their team. Despite concerted efforts by organized baseball to stamp out gambling, it remained widespread among those who attended games. Upon suspecting a fix was in, cranks who liked to place their wagers at the ballpark stated away and attendance suffered. In the rival International Association, established in 1877 to challenge the National League, its two top teams, London (Ontario) Tecumsehs and Pittsburgh Alleghenys were both plagued in 1878 by rumors of "sold" games. In both cities, this led to sharp declines in attendance and revenue needed to pay players and produce returns for investors. The Alleghenys collapsed in mid-season, while the Tecumsehs struggled to complete their 1878 schedule after releasing their professionals late in August.[18][19]

Amateur and semi-professional baseball continued in Louisville, but press coverage was scant. About the only bright spot for cranks was the play of the Eclipse club, which had been established in the West End to challenge the Olympics and eventually took over their ballpark. In 1878, the Eclipse played a reconstituted Grays nine, which retained no one from the professional team of the previous year. The Eclipse won five of their six contests. By 1879, the Eclipse had become the best nine in the city and were crowned state champions. Among their opponents were teams from Cincinnati, New Orleans, Cleveland, Akron, St. Louis, Philadelphia and Brooklyn. This success began to bring fans back to the ballpark. The Eclipse were helped in large measure by some local young players on their roster who had grown up a few blocks apart and learned the game in their neighborhood. Among them were several members of the Reccius family, which has been described as "the first family of Louisville baseball." They became saviors of the game during a dark era for baseball in the city.[20]

William Reccius (pronounced "REX-e-us") was born in Germany in 1848 and migrated to the United States with his parents when he was six. Brothers John, Phil and Frank were born in Louisville in 1859, 1862, and 1864 respectively. The Reccius boys took to baseball and played it in the streets of their west-end working-class district. Among those joining in was neighbor Louis Rogers "Pete" Browning, born in Louisville in 1861. Also from the neighborhood came Jimmy "Chicken" Wolf, born a year later, who, like Browning and the Reccius boys, showed great promise at the game. Billy Reccius learned the trade of machinist, but in 1873 opened a toy and sporting goods store downtown on Third Avenue. It was said that when Albert Goodwill Spalding and his brother Walter opened their sporting goods business in Chicago early in 1876, that Billy Reccius was among their first customers. Reccius constantly needed baseball equipment for the Eclipse who were becoming one of the top semi-professional teams. Under his leadership, the team produced several future major leaguers from Louisville natives, including Pete Browning, Jimmy "Chicken" Wolf, Fred "Dandelion" Pfeffer and Reccius' younger brothers John and Phil. Originally, Billy Reccius was the pitcher, but by 1878 at age 30, he began to focus more on managing the Eclipse. The team, for which eccentric star and heavy hitter Pete Browning first suited up in 1877, two months before he turned 16, attracted not only a local following but a national reputation as it traveled widely from Boston to Cleveland, Indianapolis, St. Louis, Cincinnati, New Orleans and elsewhere. John Reccius became a reliable pitcher and outfielder during Louisville's first two seasons in the American Association, while younger brother Phil, primarily a third baseman, spent eight years in the AA with Louisville, Cleveland and Rochester. Billy Reccius had quit playing and was a co-owner of the Eclipse when it entered the American Association in 1882. He personally held the lease on the grounds of Eclipse Park. The Eclipse club reorganized as a stock company in 1881, selling shares to fund its operations, with Billy Reccius as treasurer, malt dealer J.W. Pank as president and businessman Frank Carroll as vice-president. With the new funds, the Eclipse began playing out-of-town teams almost exclusively, a move that was not popular with the local teams it had traditionally played.[21]

Pete Browning was the star of the baseball show in Louisville, helping to carry the city of about 120,000 through the four years it languished without a professional league team. A gifted natural athlete and youngest of eight children, six-footer Browning was plagued by mastoiditis, an inflammation of the mastoid bone behind the ears, which robbed him of his hearing. It was a painful condition and led him to abuse alcohol to dull the pain. He had two operations, which brought only temporary relief. Browning hated school and was illiterate, likely because of his many absences and hearing problem. But he could hit a ball better than anyone else in Louisville and became a drawing card for the Eclipse. Known as "The Gladiator" by fans, his eccentricities were many and endeared him even more to followers of the team. Browning was originally a pitcher who became an infielder. But he was moved to the outfield because of his fear of being spiked on the base paths. For the same reason he refused to slide. In the field, he had "hands of stone," according to baseball historian Von Borries, but his hitting more than made up for that shortcoming. Browning developed a habit of staring into the sun to "improve his 'lamps' [eyes]." And he hoarded "retired" bats to which he had assigned Biblical names but felt they no longer had hits in them. Never married, he stored his wooden retirees in his mother's basement, reportedly more than 200 of them.[22] He was constantly on the lookout for promising new lumber. Despite his poor behavior attributable to drink, club officials were unwilling to deal harshly with their star who helped them win games and drew fans to the park. Browning was an acknowledged standout when the Eclipse joined the American Association in 1882. That year he won the batting crown, the first ever for a rookie. He remained one of the top batters during his 13 years in the major leagues, compiling a lifetime batting average of .341, twelfth highest in the history of the game. It remained above .300 for seven consecutive seasons and in 1887, it reached .402. Browning held league batting titles three times, in 1882 and 1885 in the American Association and in 1890 with the Players' League.

Browning's batting prowess and search for bats containing hits led to one of baseball's enduring myths that persists, despite no evidence whatsoever to support it. The story goes this way. Early in the 1884 season he was in a hitting slump and one day he broke his bat. After the game, an avid young sandlot player named John A. "Bud" Hillerich, who'd been watching the game, offered to make Browning a new one in his father's wood-turning shop, where the young lad crafted bats for himself. The shop mainly produced butter churns, bedposts and axe handles at the time. Young Hillerich worked through the night to produce a bat to Browning's specifications, supposedly. The Gladiator liked his new weapon, especially how it performed the next day when he collected three hits to end his slump. It was said this marked the birth of the iconic Louisville Slugger bat. Nice story, that. But just as Abner Doubleday never once mentioned he invented baseball in Cooperstown in 1839, or anywhere, at any time, Browning never spoke about any connection with the iconic bat. Louisville baseball historian Bob Bailey dissembled the Browning myth in *The Baseball Research Journal*, attributing the story to an overzealous public relations man for Hillerich and Bradsby who first shared it in the firm's *Famous Slugger Yearbook* of 1939. Bailey believes young Bud Hillerich gave a bat he'd made to a young player who may have been hoping to make the 1884 Louisville team. When other players saw Hillerich's handiwork they were impressed and insisted he make more for

them. The bats were first known as Hillerich bats, then Falls City Sluggers, before the name Louisville Slugger was trademarked in 1894.[23]

During Louisville's time away from the bright lights of major league ball, its fan base gradually returned, with as many as 3,000 spectators drawn to Eclipse Park. But not everything was positive. An ugly incident arose late in the 1881. On August 21, the opposition was the White Sewing Machine Company of Cleveland whose best player, catcher Moses Fleetwood Walker, was not allowed to play because he was Black.

The *Louisville Courier-Journal* referred to him as a "quadroon," a term applied at the time to someone who was only one-quarter African American. That day, the crowd was anxious to see Walker, whose fame as an outstanding catcher was spreading. Chants of "Walker, Walker" greeted him when he passed the grandstand during pre-game warm-ups. The welcome surprised him because that same morning at the St. Cloud Hotel, management refused to let him have breakfast with the team because of his color. Wary, Walker had to be coaxed to acknowledge the cheers. He had just learned the Eclipse management and some players were unhappy with his appearance at the park and he didn't want to antagonize them further. "He still hesitated, but finally threw off his coat and vest and stepped out to catch a ball or two and feel the bases. He made several brilliant throws and fine catches while the game waited," the paper reported.[24] Clearly the crowd wanted to see Walker perform, but Louisville pitcher John Reccius and second baseman Fred Pfeffer walked off the field, refusing to play when it appeared Cleveland was about to insert Walker into the game in the second inning. "The objection of the Eclipse players was too much, and Walker was compelled to retire. When it was seen that he was not to play, the crowd heartily and very properly hissed the Eclipse club," the *Courier-Journal* noted. The home team had threatened to cancel the game if Walker played, so Cleveland relented. The move cost the visitors dearly. Without their star catcher, they lost 6–3.

The Louisville newspaper was unhappy at the incident, noting the controversy "caused considerable comment of an unfavorable nature upon the conduct of the Eclipse Club." Walker, it said, "has played against other League clubs and in many games with other white clubs, without protest." A sub-headline on the paper's account of the game read: "An Uncalled for Exhibition of Prejudice on the Field Towards a Quadroon." If the reporting was complete and accurate, it's noteworthy the crowd seemed more liberal and accepting of a Black man than the Louisville players and management. But Louisville baseball historian Bob Bailey thinks the crowd was likely hostile, a fact ignored by the paper. "We need to remember that the *Courier-Journal* was edited by Henry Waterson, whose journalistic career after the Civil War promoted reconciliation of North and South and some reconciliation between the races. His views were liberal for the time and the views of the paper today continue that tradition...." Bailey suggests Waterson's views likely influenced how stories were reported.[25]

Walker was not the first African American to play baseball at its highest level, or even the first Black in major league ball. In 1878, Bud Fowler appeared as a pitcher for Lynn, Massachusetts, of the International Association, a professional loop established

Opposite: **Barney Dreyfuss moved with the Bernheim Brothers firm to Louisville in 1888. At the time, Louisville was a member of the American Association and Pete Browning was one of the stars of the Louisville Eclipse, later renamed the Colonels. Browning's batting prowess earned him the nickname "The Gladiator." He is often wrongly associated with development of the famous Louisville Slugger bat by that city's woodworking firm of Hillerich and Bradsby (Library of Congress).**

to challenge the National League, but to this day still not designated a major league, despite compelling reasons to do so. So Fowler is considered the first Black to play "organized baseball." It turns out the first black to play in a recognized major league was William Edward White, rather than Walker. An accomplished player at Brown University, White played one game for the Providence Grays in 1879, then a member of the National League, thereby earning the distinction that for so long had been accorded Walker. White was inserted into the lineup at first base when regular Grays first-bagger Joe Start broke a finger on his left hand.[26] White played well, hitting a single in four at-bats, stole two bases, scored one run, played without error and registered 12 putouts. Providence defeated Cleveland 5–3 that day. Despite his solid play, White's entire major league career consisted of that single game. His distinction earned that day as a Black man was overlooked because it was believed he was white. And he insisted he was. But, his father was white and his mother was his father's domestic servant, a mulatto. It is only recently that baseball historian Peter Morris found White described in U.S. Census records as mulatto. So to him, because of one game, goes the distinction of being the first Black to play in major league ball, not Walker. Given the situation with White, Fleet Walker is carefully described today as the "first openly Black player" in the majors. He, too, was mulatto, with one Black grandparent, but never passed himself off as anything else.

Walker returned to Louisville for opening day, May 1, 1884, with the American Association's Toledo Blue Stockings, for whom he also caught. That day Walker played, but not well. His battery mate was former Eclipse pitcher Tony Mullane who disliked him. Walker went 0-for-3 at the plate, with four errors and two passed balls. Toledo lost 5–1. The audience, the *Courier-Journal* reported "was a large one and very orderly." The paper made no mention of any signs of prejudice, but one of its competitors demonstrated some. The *Louisville Commercial* reported: "Toledo's defeat was all on account of a coon." And back in Toledo, the *Blade* reported Walker had been "hissed and otherwise insulted … because he was colored."[27] Walker sat out the second game in the series, but returned for the third when he recorded his first big-league hit. Later that month, Louisville appeared in Toledo for a series and the crowd hurled abuse at the visitors for the treatment Walker had received in Louisville, likely based on the account in the *Blade*. After appearing in 42 games that year for Toledo, Walker's major league career came to an end. Race remained a divisive issue for six more decades in baseball, the color barrier not finally broken until 1947 by Jackie Robinson with the Brooklyn Dodgers.

About a month after Walker's first appearance in Louisville in 1881, talk translated into action among cities in the Midwest about the need for another major league to challenge the eight-team National League. Meetings were held in Philadelphia and Pittsburgh, where it was decided to hold a founding meeting for the new American Association November 2 in Cincinnati. Louisville sent Eclipse president J.H. Pank and treasurer William Reccius to the gathering which attracted representatives from host Cincinnati, as well as Pittsburgh, St. Louis, New York, Brooklyn and Philadelphia. Denny McKnight of Allegheny (Pittsburgh) was elected president, while Pank became vice-president. Discussions went well and in April, the American Association fielded six teams: Louisville, Cincinnati, St. Louis, Philadelphia, Pittsburgh and Baltimore, while the National League returned with eight.

The new loop soon became known as the "Beer and Whiskey League," because four team owners were associated with brewing, distilling or saloon-keeping. The AA charged 25 cents admission (half that of League teams), offered alcohol in its ballparks and played games on Sundays, both measures intended to attract more working class and blue collar cranks. The new model for baseball proved successful. As historian David Nemec put it in his acclaimed *The Beer & Whiskey League,* the new baseball magnates felt good about their decision that very first season when Cincinnati took the pennant and Louisville placed third. The AA had defied the skeptics, and "was the first professional league, major or minor, to finish its schedule in its initial season without any franchise transfers or casualties," Nemec said.[28] The American Association would last for 10 seasons, during which Louisville changed its name to the Colonels. They finished generally in the middle of the pack, making them a second division club, often out of the pennant race as early as July 4. They placed dead last in 1889 with 27 wins and 111 losses, setting a record for futility by losing a record 26 consecutive games. The following year, they bounced back to capture the AA pennant with 88 wins and 44 losses. The Colonels made baseball history by going from worst to first in a single season.

Louisville had returned to the major leagues in 1882 after a four-year hiatus during which baseball was resurrected and star players emerged who would soon make significant contributions to the professional game. Big league ball was reborn in one of America's great baseball cities after a false start and new chapters in its history were about to be written.

That same year, some 330 miles down the winding Ohio River, a significant future contributor to the professional game was just getting settled in Paducah. Barney Dreyfuss, a newcomer from Germany and future Louisvillian, was falling in love with a game he had never before seen and which he would help transform.

5

Buying In

Barney Dreyfuss and the Bernheims relocated to Louisville just in time to catch the beginning of the 1888 season for the Colonels. The team's followers were no doubt hoping for better things on the diamond from a club that finished the previous season in fourth place in the eight-team American Association, for the second year in a row. Their best finish in the AA was third, four years earlier. Louisville had never contended the way the old 1877 club did when supporters felt it was robbed of the National League title by gamblers and thrown games.

The Colonels were unable to perform well consistently and fan support fluctuated because there is no substitute for winning to attract fans to the ballpark. Their biggest problem lay behind the scenes. The team, it has been said, was "chronically undercapitalized."[1] Management was unwilling or unable to attract the best players because so little was in the treasury. And little was done to develop talent, leaving the team to languish in the middle of the standings during the 1880s. By the end of the decade, the total capitalization of the club amounted to a bit less than $20,000, well below its competitors and in some cases half that of the more successful clubs. Louisville simply could not compete in bidding wars for good players.

Ownership was a significant part of the problem as well. Distillery executive J.H. Pank was president of the Eclipse for the team's first two years in the American Association. But by early 1884 he was at loggerheads with his fellow directors. In a lawsuit filed against him related to a $600 gambling debt he'd incurred, it was alleged he owed his fellow directors $700. They refused to let him resign his post until he paid them back. In court documents it was revealed the Eclipse lost more than $400 during 1883.[2] Pank denied any wrongdoing but directors felt otherwise and let him go, likely never getting their $700. He was replaced by Will Jackson, Jr., a lawyer and member of the Kentucky state legislature. Jackson was a popular politician and may have been spreading himself rather thin. Club management under the tenure of Jackson and his successors has been described as rather cloudy by historian David Nemec, "a problem that would plague the franchise until 1899 when Louisville finally left the major league scene."[3] Jackson lasted only a year, during which time the club was believed to have broken even.[4] He was replaced in 1885 by another lawyer, Zach Phelps, who was president when the club retired the Eclipse name and became the Colonels. W.L. Lyons, a city financial broker and newly elected Louisville councilman took the helm of the club early in 1888. None of the directors who acquired shares in the club was known to have particularly deep pockets which, because of poor gate revenue, left them unable and unwilling to incur losses.

Lyons lasted only a few months, replaced as president by furniture dealer Mordecai Davidson, who had been a director for nearly six years and had acquired most of the shares issued by the club. Following a meeting on June 6, it was announced that Lyons and other directors had resigned and that Davidson was in charge. He had clashed with directors who wanted to strengthen the Colonels by selling off four players and hiring a completely new infield. Davidson insisted that was too much of a gamble and the underperforming foursome should be pushed to play better.[5] A Union Army veteran, Davidson had been secretary-treasurer of the ball club and he brought a taste for discipline along with a businessman's perspective to his new post. Of Davidson, 44, the *Louisville Courier-Journal* said: "He is a young business man of force and character, and thoroughly understands base ball, both as a sport and as a business. He is personally popular with the players...."[6] Davidson would be put to the test on both the on-field and business aspects of the team and the players came to despise him. Within days, the new president relieved manager John "Kick" Kelly, who had piloted the Colonels to 10 wins and 29 losses. Davidson took over managing duties, winning one of three games before Louisville utility player John Kerins was hired for the job. Kerins was sacked after three wins and four losses and Davidson resumed managing for the rest of the season.

Former president Lyons had promised 1888 would be the year the Colonels became a contender and long-suffering fans hoped he was right. Their home opener was against Cincinnati on April 28, when about 3,000 of them saw the Colonels win 6–4. The next day, 7,000 were at Eclipse Park, including 1,500 who travelled from Cincinnati, when the Reds won, 8–3. But a crowd of only 500 saw the visitors win 6–5 on April 30. Attendance was best on Sundays, such as July 15 when Philadelphia downed the Louisvilles 11–5 before 4,500 cranks. By October, games against Cincinnati drew as few as 400 and 500 spectators and losses continued for the home club. Dwindling fan support hurt the box office and president Davidson kept a tight rein on the club's purse strings. In November it was admitted the team "made but little money" during the 1888 campaign but no details were provided.[7] As manager, Davidson led the club to 35 wins and 54 losses in all. The Colonels finished in seventh place, their worst showing yet, with a record of 48–87.

An avid fan of the game, Barney Dreyfuss likely went to Eclipse Park as often as possible during the season while he and the Bernheims settled into their new quarters. He may have been itching to become involved with the American Association team, but that would have to wait. The whiskey business came first and president Davidson was firmly in control of the Colonels for the time being.

Davidson faced a difficult situation in his bid to turn around club fortunes. Baseball historian Bob Bailey put his dilemma this way:

> His tight-fisted approach toward players and club fiscal management was not merely a reflection of a robber baron mentality. It was well-grounded in the reality that the Louisville club was pitifully undercapitalized and operated by a group of owners that, while individually comfortable financially, did not possess personal wealth sufficient to build a contending squad.[8]

The Louisville club president began taking steps to improve the financial picture during the off-season. In January, Davidson announced he would no longer advance players any money until they earned it. Traditionally, managers provided players some funds before opening day to tide them over the winter months. Davidson said that practice was a mistake. From now on, they were to report for work April 1 and would receive their first pay on April 15, not a day before. He added, ominously, that each player would be paid on the 15th of each month "provided none of them are fined for drunkenness or indifferent playing."[9] Fines would become a flashpoint between Davidson and the players. Meanwhile, rumors were afloat that Davidson was trying to unload the team that off-season. It was reported he owned more than 300 shares in the club, representing 60 percent of all stock, and had been in talks with "two well-known business men."[10] Nothing came from this and Davidson remained in charge on opening day 1889 for what would become a history-making season—but not in any way he would have wanted. In the meantime, he had hired Dude Esterbrook as manager, an eight-year veteran who had played first base the previous season for Indianapolis. This left the determined president free to focus his efforts on turning around finances.

On opening day at home, April 17, a crowd of 2,000 saw Kansas City defeat the Colonels 7–4. The following day, half as many cranks were on hand when the Cowboys again prevailed, this time 8–6. The Colonels lost twice more before Kansas City left town. Two losses to St. Louis came before Louisville had its first win of the season, 17–7, against the Browns on April 23. It hadn't been a promising start. On their first road trip, the Colonels lost eight of 10 games. Things were looking grim. Davidson was travelling with the team and by the end of May found himself behind on the team payroll. Davidson had reduced the Colonels to 11 men to cut costs and manager Esterbrook was tapped as a substitute player. Davidson disdained what he viewed as poor behavior and a lackadaisical attitude by any Colonel. Even more, he hated losing money. So he began fining players to address both issues. He levied fines of $25 for every in-game error committed by players, adding more if they objected. At the time, the average ballplayer earned about $1,400 for an entire season and by May the club president bragged he had already imposed fines totaling $1,435. His players were upset and some found themselves without any paycheck at all and Davidson claiming they owed money to *him*. A losing streak began May 22 at home against Baltimore. Esterbrook had been replaced as team manager by right fielder Jimmy "Chicken" Wolf after winning two games and losing eight. Fans and the press began blaming Davidson for the sorry record when the managing change did little to improve things. "The Louisville Base-ball Club under its present incompetent management has reached the state of a nuisance," the *Louisville Courier-Journal* complained June 12, adding the team had been "losing game after game until it has become a disgrace to the city it started out to represent." Davidson, it said, was trying to move some home games to Cincinnati and Philadelphia in a bid to improve gate receipts, which would "ultimately result in the ruin of the Louisville club." And it appeared another attempt was under way to buy the club, the paper said.[11]

On June 13, the Colonels arrived in Baltimore for a four-game series with the fifth-place Orioles. Louisville had lost 18 straight games at that point, with a record of eight wins and 38 losses. Davidson announced each of his players would be fined $25, no matter how well they played. With that, he took a train to New York City, where the American Association gathered to consider the Louisville situation and Davidson's actions. Learning that his players were threatening to go on strike, Davidson left behind a note at their hotel warning that if they failed to show at the ballpark for Friday's game each would face a $100 fine. Only six of the Colonels showed up. Six didn't, walking out in the first-ever strike in baseball. They were Pete Browning, pitcher Guy Hecker, catcher Paul Cook, second baseman Dan Shannon, pitcher Red Ehret and third baseman Harry Raymond. Three semi-professional players from Baltimore were found by new manager Wolf to complete the Louisville roster.

That same night, Davidson, accompanied by American Association president Wheeler C. Wikoff, arrived in Baltimore. The Association backed Davidson and Wikoff announced any form of rebellion would leave players open to even bigger fines and blacklisting forever from baseball. Emboldened, Davidson docked Friday's no-shows $100 apiece. A doubleheader planned for Saturday in Baltimore was cut short when rain returned after five innings of the first matchup, but it was considered complete and Louisville lost its 20th consecutive game by a score of 4–2. On Monday a doubleheader was played and Louisville lost both games. All its players showed up, however. Their strike was over. Baltimore manager Bill Barnie had persuaded the angry Colonels to retake the field and file a formal grievance about their treatment directly with the Association.[12] Davidson imposed no more fines. Back home, the *Courier-Journal* reported that "Davidson's Disaffected Daisies" had returned to work, but the paper blasted the club president for his actions, especially when he refused to buy train tickets so his players could return to Louisville. "If Mr. Davidson has any consideration for the people of Louisville, he should sell the club upon its arrival in this city," the paper declared.[13] Back in town, Davidson insisted he fined his men because their careless play had cost the team too many games on their eastern road trip. "I studied their play carefully, and saw that something must be done to liven them up so that we could win a few games," he said. Davidson admitted that during his talks with American Association directors he sought financial help for his team.[14]

In Louisville, fresh from a 0–21 road trip, team losses continued. More trouble was brewing when players found their pay packets missing significant amounts of money because of the fines. Only three players received the money owed them. Pitcher Guy Hecker was considered relatively lucky because his pay amounted to $1.95. Several were told they owed Davidson money, including Browning who learned Davidson wanted $325 because of fines accumulated for his poor behavior. "All the players were indignant at the treatment they had received, and several of them may refuse to play today," the *Courier-Journal* reported on June 22.[15] Meanwhile, Davidson was again in talks with local parties said to be interested in the club. He wanted $9,000 and rejected an offer of $7,500. Meanwhile, the Colonels lost their 25th consecutive game, 7–6, to St. Louis, before 300 spectators. Their 3–2 defeat by the Browns, which came after 11 innings on June 22 was their 26th consecutive loss. The following day the historic record of futility came to an end and the Colonels finally tasted victory, downing St. Louis 7–3.

By early July, Davidson gave up trying to find a buyer and surrendered the club to the American Association. The newspaper fretted that if something positive didn't happen within 10 days, Louisville would lose the franchise forever. A group of local gentlemen had offered $5,000 to keep the club in the city. Asked why he had given up, Davidson was blunt: "I have exhausted all my resources, and I am necessarily compelled to take such a step, although I regret it exceedingly." He said the $5,000 offered him would not even cover his indebtedness. Meanwhile, the players were hurting financially, having missed three pay days by then. They could not even afford to wash their uniforms and had been forced to borrow money from Kansas City and St. Louis players.[16]

On July 4, a syndicate of 10 stockholders acquired the club for an undisclosed sum that supposedly equaled Davidson's indebtedness.[17] Directors of the American Association gathered in Louisville to ratify the sale and consider grievances filed by the players who argued the fines imposed on them were unfair. The $100 levies on the six players who refused to take the field in Baltimore were upheld. So, too, was a $100 fine on Browning for misbehaving in Brooklyn. But the AA reduced the total amount owing from $1,435 to $735, saying some of the financial penalties were "unjustly and arbitrarily imposed."[18] Meanwhile, railroad executive Lawrence S. Parsons assumed the presidency of the club.

By August, second baseman Dan Shannon relieved manager Chicken Wolf, who had compiled a 14–51 record. Shannon continued the losing tradition, piloting the team to 10 wins and 46 losses before Jack Chapman replaced him. Chapman had successfully managed the Louisville Grays in 1876 and 1877. In his return, Chapman recorded a single win and six losses. Veterans Hecker and Browning were released before season's end when the final record of the Colonels stood at 27 wins and 111 losses. It marked the first time a major league team had lost more than 100 games in a season. Many of those defeats had been close, however. During the 26-game losing streak, seven games were lost by a single run. The Colonels' streak of futility in 1889 remains unbroken to this day. While the Colonels displayed average offense, they had been undermined by woeful fielding and pitching. Louisville placed dead last in the eight-team American Association, 28½ games behind seventh-place Kansas City and 66½ behind pennant winner Brooklyn. The new shareholders in Louisville could be forgiven for wondering what they had gotten themselves into, although buying into an American Association team hadn't been a costly proposition.

Jack Chapman proved to be an invaluable addition. He had wide contacts throughout the baseball world and began tapping into them as he added new faces to the roster for 1890. He received unexpected help as he set about to improve his cellar-dwellers. The Players' League was established by players upset at salary limitations they faced and the reserve clause that bound them to teams until those teams disposed of them. The situation was likened to slavery by some of the rebels. Both measures had been introduced by owners to curb costs that rose when players were free to offer their services to the highest bidder. The reserve clause had been a factor in the establishment of the Union Association in 1884, but that league, which simply ignored it, vanished after a single season. The impact of the Players' League on Louisville was a weakening of the other members of the American Association. The new league signed more than a quarter of the players on AA team reserve lists, with St. Louis, Baltimore and the Philadelphia Athletics hit hardest. Louisville lost five players, but none of them was considered much of a loss.[19] Pete Browning had been suspended late in the 1889 season for drunkenness and signed with the Cleveland Infants of the Players' League, where his .373 batting average during 1890 produced his last batting crown. Browning later returned to Louisville briefly after stints with other clubs, his major league career ending in 1894. Aside from the thinning out of its teams because of the latest upstart league, the AA's first-place and fourth-place clubs, Brooklyn and Cincinnati, jumped to the National League for 1890. As bad as this was for the American Association overall, this was good news for Louisville, which was about to field a younger team under the veteran Chapman.

The 1890 season marked a complete turnaround for the Colonels. They had such a fast start that they were in first place after two weeks and picked up the nickname "Cyclones." In late March, a tornado had struck Louisville causing millions in property damage and claiming more than 100 lives. The team arranged a benefit game for the victims of what was called a cyclone, but the event was snowed out. Their new name acknowledged the whirlwind pace at which they were blowing away the competition.[20] Reality set in after several weeks, however, and they slipped to fourth by June, nine games back of the first-place Athletics. But 12 straight wins during a 20-game home stand in July catapulted them back to first. The team amassed a .660 winning percentage by the end of August and was 6½ games up on second-place St. Louis. In September, Louisville won 17 games and lost eight to claim the AA pennant on September 20 at home, taking both ends of a doubleheader from Philadelphia, 22–4 and 10–0 before 3,743 fans. The following day, a Sunday, Eclipse

Park was packed with 8,267 happy fans who saw the Cyclones again down Philadelphia in another doubleheader, 12–4 and 16–3, the latter game called on account of darkness after seven innings. This Cinderella season marked the first time a team had gone from worst to first in a single year. Louisville finished with an 88–44 record, a 61-game improvement from their disastrous 1889 campaign. Their run production had increased 30 percent while across the league it had declined 11 percent. Pitching was solid, too. Louisville hurlers surrendered the least runs in the Association, reduced their walks issued by nearly 40 percent from the previous season and cut their earned run average by more than two runs a game. Scott Stratton had 34 wins and Red Ehret notched 25.

As winners of the AA pennant, Louisville faced the National League champion Brooklyn Bridegrooms in the World's Series. Brooklyn had jumped from the American Association, so the championship would pit the previous year's AA cellar dwellers against its champions. Louisville dropped the first two games of the seven-game series at home. Following a game-three tie, Louisville took game four before leaving Eclipse Park. In Brooklyn, the Bridegrooms won game five at Washington Park, but Louisville came back to win the sixth and seventh games. That seventh meeting, on October 28, left the teams in a 3–3 tie for the series, but the weather turned miserable and crowds were thin. The teams decided to leave the series tied and spoke of resuming it the following spring, but nothing materialized from that. This marked the last contest in the early World's Series between the American Association and the National League, established in 1884 to determine overall baseball supremacy.

Louisville's principal owner throughout 1890 and into early 1891 was Lawrence Parsons, who oversaw a recapitalization of the club as president. He insisted the club lost money in 1890, but stockholders accused him of careless business practices, perhaps verging on criminal. In March of 1891, Louisville was reorganized and funds advanced to it by some large stockholders. By August, Parsons departed, supposedly because his railroad bosses were unhappy at his involvement in the professional game, and he left behind a trail of litigation that took months to resolve.[21] He was replaced by prominent local physician T. Hunt Stucky, an avid baseball enthusiast and longtime shareholder and director. Stucky was no judge of playing talent, however, leaving that important task to others, with disappointing results. He had his hands full as the club continued to struggle financially, despite its newfound success on the field. The club was put up for sale in November of 1891 at public auction in a move intended to satisfy a bank mortgage. It was sold for $6,359 to a group headed by local businessmen Larry Gatto and Fred Drexler, Jr., that also included Stucky. Drexler soon faced public and press criticism for secrecy surrounding the ball club's business affairs and for failing to take steps to improve the on-field product.

Sometime during the ongoing turmoil, Barney Dreyfuss began buying shares, likely at depressed prices. He dipped into his savings and may have borrowed funds from the Bernheim brothers.[22] Despite the financial struggles of the team and its poor record, Dreyfuss believed it was a wise investment. Others were not so certain. But when it came to baseball, the accounts receivable manager for Bernheim Brothers remained an optimist. He continued adding to his holdings over time. Dreyfuss believed that prudent spending by him and by the team could produce good quality baseball and attract fans so desperately needed to improve the bottom line. He had been successful in the whiskey business and he was supremely confident lessons he learned there could be applied to the game he had grown to love and make it profitable. He wanted to be part of another success story.

The Players' League expired in January 1891 after just one season. Some of its teams were left in such a poor state financially they couldn't meet late-season payrolls. Losses were significant. It has been estimated that across the three leagues, the total easily reached $250,000, possibly as high as $500,000.[23] The American Association suffered more than the National League, which sensed its rival's vulnerability and began to lure its players and franchises. This prompted the Association to reply in kind, by withdrawing from the National Agreement, which had governed such matters since 1883. Many players who had deserted to the Players' League were welcomed back by their original teams, despite earlier threats of expulsion. But competition for their services from the teams still standing only increased player pay, thereby reducing baseball's profitability in those cities.

Meanwhile Louisville, once again known as the Colonels, crashed back to earth with a thud while other teams in the American Association rebuilt. The team finished eighth in the nine-team Association race with 53 wins and 84 losses, 40 games back of pennant winner Boston Reds. In December, it was announced the American Association was about to disband and four of its teams, St. Louis, Washington, Baltimore and Louisville would join the National League, expanding it to 12 teams. There was some opposition to Louisville, one of the weaker clubs, with an unsuccessful bid to admit Buffalo in its stead.[24] The remaining Association clubs in Boston, Philadelphia, Columbus, Milwaukee and a new club in Chicago were bought out for about $130,000 in total, with their debt assumed by the League to be paid off from future gate proceeds. In the merger it was agreed that Sunday games could be played, but no team would be compelled to play that day. It was a bid to appease National League teams, many of whom still opposed Sunday play. Also, each club could decide on its own whether to serve alcoholic drinks in its park.[25] The Association was gone, but its practices like Sunday play and sale of alcohol that helped it succeed for so long would continue.

By 1892, Barney Dreyfuss owned enough stock to become a director and he was re-elected to the post the following year. He attracted his first notice in the press for his connection to the Colonels midway through the 1892 campaign.

"'Barnie' Driefus, the well-known crank, who managed and owned the Paducah Club for two years, is the man who deserves credit for securing Al Macfarland. He is after several other players for the Louisvilles."[26]

The newspaper would soon learn the correct spelling of the new director's name, while still describing him as a fan. The player referred to was actually Alex McFarlan, 22, a second baseman and right fielder who looked promising. But he played only 14 games with the Colonels and was released without making much impact. His entire major league career consisted of those 14 games. Just as the *Courier-Journal* would get better at spelling the name of the new club director, Dreyfuss would get better at identifying baseball talent. Much better.

Aside from his growing interest in the Colonels, Dreyfuss was president and secretary-treasurer of the City Base-Ball League, which consisted of four teams fielded by leading Louisville businesses including Bernheim Brothers. All games were played in Eclipse Park, the home park of the Colonels. It is not known if Dreyfuss played for the Bernheims in that league, but there was a report of him appearing in a game that pitted the city's wholesale whiskey dealers against the whiskey brokers during 1894 when he was 29. The teams that day were augmented by players from the City League and the game took place on the Colonels' home field. Thomas Batman, secretary of the Colonels, a distiller, appeared on the field along with Dreyfuss and several of their business associates.

Batman, 41, it was reported, played third base in unconventional style. He "tried unsuccessfully to stop all the balls that came his way with his feet," while Dreyfuss and the others "tried to play, and derived considerable amusement from the trial." No further details of play were provided. A crowd similar in size to those traditionally drawn to weekday games of the Colonels witnessed proceedings.[27]

For 1892, the National League had become a monopoly with a real chance to pay dividends to the capitalists who controlled teams. It was the era of big trusts in business and baseball now reflected that economic reality. Baseball historians Harold Seymour and Dorothy Seymour Mills said the monopoly was undisguised now, citing a *Sporting News* opinion that the situation "enabled the magnates to do about as they please without let or hindrance." A newspaper put it this way: "'There is probably no business—unless it is the gas office—that is conducted more in the Vanderbilt-public-be-damned principle than baseball.'"[28] This was a reference to cunning railroad and shipping tycoon Cornelius Vanderbilt, one of the richest men in American history. As the only game in town when it came to big league baseball, the National League began cutting costs to ensure profitability which had been so elusive. But financial woes and declining attendance plagued teams throughout 1892. By season's end, when the Boston Beaneaters claimed the pennant, it was reported by League president Nick Young that total losses reached $100,000. He insisted "baseball must in future be conducted on a purely business basis" if owners ever hoped to turn a profit.[29] No numbers were revealed for Louisville, but it was clear the club continued to struggle. One of the measures adopted by League magnates to reduce spending was to cap player salaries, an informal limit set at $2,400 for the 1890s.

Outside cities hoping to join the League sometimes eyed the struggles of Louisville as a possible opening for them. "In what seemed liked an annual tradition, Louisville was on shaky financial footing and occupied a tenuous position within the League," it has been said.[30] Even worse, in early 1893 Louisville had no home park, because Eclipse Park burned to the ground late in the 1892 season in a blaze attributed to arson.[31] Rumors emanating from Indianapolis said Louisville would disband and that baseball promoters in the Indiana capital, as well as in Buffalo and Milwaukee were poised to replace the League's weakest link. The crisis passed when principal Louisville shareholder J. George Ruckstuhl purchased land for a new ballpark just south of the old one for a reported $35,500.[32] He vowed Louisville was in the League to stay. The 1893 season began in the remnants of the old park before the team moved into its new home, also named Eclipse Park, later known as League Park. The new facility was mainly wood in construction and served until late in the 1899 season when it, too, was destroyed by fire, this one caused by a lightning strike.

After a disappointing 1892 campaign, 1893 marked a turnaround for baseball. Attendance improved in most National League cities, particularly in Chicago and New York. The pitching distance was set at 60 feet, six inches, ending years of tweaking the distance in a bid to find the right balance between hitting and pitching. The Boston Beaneaters captured the pennant for the second year in a row and Louisville limped to an 11th place finish, second last in the loop, with a record of 50–75. President Nick Young reported at the fall meeting of League magnates that the "season now closed has been a grand one financially for the League for every club has shown a decided improvement over last season, and the consequence is that every one has a balance to their credit." It was estimated New York, Philadelphia and Pittsburgh had each turned a profit of $50,000. The League was doing so well it erased the $130,000 debt it incurred to "retire" the five former American Association clubs.[33] It is not known what reports Louisville shared with the League, if any, but it was later revealed the Colonels didn't turn a profit until 1895, the club's first in six years.[34] By then, Barney Dreyfuss was secretary-treasurer and a bright young man named Harry Pulliam was completing his first year as the club's financial manager.

The Panic of 1893 was a sharp economic downturn that began midway through the year when the Reading Railroad went into receivership, leading to the failure of hundreds of banks and railroad-dependent businesses across the United States. Thousands of businesses were ruined, and unemployment hit four million Americans. Compounding the misery, an agricultural depression gripped the West and South. The recession lingered and the economy did not rebound until 1897.[35] These were tough days to make money in baseball. Despite the ongoing criticism he faced from fans and the newspapers, Fred Drexler was returned as president at the Louisville baseball club's annual meeting in December, when several directors were listed, including a "B. Dreyfus." The paper was getting closer on Barney's name.[36]

The 1894 season was yet another struggle for the club. On the field, the Colonels won only 36 games while losing 94, good for 12th and last place in the National League, 54 games behind the pennant-winning Baltimore Orioles. At a meeting of directors, it was revealed club revenue was $25,000 less than during the money-losing 1893 season. No amount was disclosed.[37]

Fans were growing tired of losing teams and directors remained unhappy at losing money. Even the *Louisville Courier-Journal*, which usually boosted the club, was growing grumpy. Within days of the last game, it noted the 1894 campaign had cost the club $103,700 "and was a very poor article for the price. The club jealously guards the secret of the amount of its losses."[38] President Stucky steadfastly refused to reveal how much income the club earned, admitting, however, "a loss of some thousands of dollars."[39]

At the outset of 1895, director Dreyfuss recommended the club hire Harry Pulliam, the new city editor of the *Louisville Commercial*. The move was intended to improve club fortunes because Pulliam was assigned the task of carefully monitoring income and expense. The son of a tobacco farmer, he had graduated from the University of Virginia law school before entering journalism and working for some papers in California before returning home to Louisville. Pulliam had covered the Colonels for the *Commercial* and drew praise for his knowledge of baseball. Full of nervous energy, he was a likeable workaholic, able to persuade people to pull together, such as the news-gathering team at the *Commercial*. A confirmed bachelor, Pulliam was a flashy, if eccentric dresser, with a penchant for stylish hats. A reporter once described his fashion sense this way: "all the colors of the rainbow were utilized by him in the color scheme of his fancy waistcoats."[40] Charming and a gifted storyteller, he had many friends, was focused, and able to prioritize and undertake many tasks. His integrity and honesty were beyond reproach. He and Dreyfuss had met through baseball and became good friends. Barney persuaded his fellow directors to give Pulliam the newly created post of financial manager of the team. Pulliam, about to turn 26, accepted the challenge and took a six-month leave of absence from the *Commercial.rcial*.[41]

Pulliam soon produced an improvement in club finances. His efforts to find playing talent, however, would prove more challenging than he could have imagined. But he was now working alongside Barney Dreyfuss who scoured the sporting press and other sources looking for leads on players and entering their names and accomplishments in his "dope book." The two men would forge a partnership that would produce success for them while leading to significant changes in professional baseball. Their work had just begun.

6

"I am tired of losing so much money...."

Sporting Life magazine took note of the hiring of Harry Pulliam, saying this was a wise move for the struggling Louisville franchise because of the newspaperman's knowledge of baseball. It went on:

> His appointment will also give genuine pleasure to the newspaper boys, and it is believed it will do more real good for the game in Louisville than any step that could have been taken. The club is sadly in need of some one to work up local interest. It is believed that Mr. Pulliam is the very person to do this, and when he takes charge of the financial end of the club you may look for a boom.[1]

Pulliam was barely settled into his job when the *Louisville Courier-Journal* reported that the baseball club had narrowly averted bankruptcy the previous summer of 1894. T. Hunt Stucky, who had been returned as president, had been forced to borrow $4,000 from the National League with the loan secured by a mortgage registered on the franchise. By the time of Pulliam's appointment, however, half the money had been repaid.[2]

In early April, the club's new business manager opened an office in the Columbia Building downtown, which would become the headquarters of the team. Pulliam announced he would accompany the Colonels on their road trips to keep a close eye on spending and income. He was trying to engineer some deals to acquire players but was finding that more difficult than expected. For a team with limited funds, baseball's reserve clause was problematic. Wealthy clubs could reserve (control) as many as 32 players, although active rosters generally had 16 to 20. That meant as many as another 16 of their men were tied up and off-limits for teams looking to improve. So Pulliam had to focus on finding unproven players with raw talent.[3] It was hard luring them to the perennial cellar-dwelling Louisville team. During team travels, Pulliam would quietly slip away to see players he had been alerted to, giving many of them an opportunity. In all, 40 players appeared in a Colonels uniform during 1895, five of whom lasted only a single game. Seven of their 15 pitchers failed to register a win.

The Colonels weren't completely bereft of talent. Louisville native Nathaniel Frederick "Dandelion" Pfeffer had been with the team since 1892 and was a topnotch second baseman. Before joining the Colonels he had played with the powerful Chicago White Stockings teams of Cap Anson. Pfeffer was a key member of the vaunted Chicago infield dubbed the "Stone Wall," but he was past his prime and appeared in only 11 games with Louisville before moving on to New York and then back to Chicago in the next two years. Fred Clarke was the star of Louisville and a future Hall of Famer. He was discovered by Barney Dreyfuss early in 1894, playing for the Savannah Modocs of the

Southern Association. The talent of the teenager from Winterset, Iowa, drew the attention of *Sporting Life* which said he played a "phenomenal game, both in the field and at the bat." Dreyfuss, always on the lookout for talent, noted this reference and put Clarke in his "dope book." By midseason, as the year-old Southern loop struggled, the Louisville secretary-treasurer learned that Clarke was hitting .311 with 54 games under his belt. Dreyfuss arranged a business trip to Memphis where Savannah was playing. There, he saw the heavy-hitting left fielder take over as catcher when the regular receiver took ill. Clarke was by far the best player on a Savannah club so broke its manager, John McCloskey, couldn't buy train tickets to return home. Dreyfuss came up with a solution. He gave McCloskey $200 for rail fare in exchange for the contract of Clarke. The 21-year-old Clarke joined the Colonels lineup right away and in his first game belted four singles and a triple against a strong Phillies team. The future Hall-of-Famer was off to a great start. Aside from being a fine hitter, he was a good left fielder and an aggressive base runner. In Clarke, Dreyfuss found a fierce competitor.

Unfortunately, in his early days as a Colonel, Clarke developed some bad habits from hanging around with his teammates, who were fond of drinking and womanizing. It began to affect his play and Dreyfuss became concerned enough to take him aside for a chat in his office. "He didn't lecture me," Clarke recalled years later. "He merely said: 'Fred, you know if a man goes into any kind of business and neglects it, it will surely go to the dogs.'" With that, Dreyfuss strode out of the office and left the young man to reflect on his words. Clarke did, and the next day returned and promised to do better. "I do not think any employer ever gave a young player better counsel," Clarke said.[4] A special bond developed between the two men in a baseball relationship that would last for many years.

Once the 1894 season ended, Dreyfuss hired Clarke's old Savannah manager McCloskey to replace Bill Barnie.[5] During 1895, Clarke had 96 runs and a batting average of .347 to lead the team. Dan Brouthers, 37, a five-time batting champion and solid first baseman played in 24 games in his only season as a Colonel. Another Hall of Famer, Brouthers was in the twilight of his career. Third baseman Jimmy Collins, 25, appeared in 96 games, his only season with Louisville and his first in the major leagues. He, too, would make it to Cooperstown. Other notables were solid shortstop Jack Glasscock and pitcher Gus Weyhing.

After a close race for the 1895 pennant, the powerful Baltimore Orioles claimed it for the second year in a row, fending off the troublesome Cleveland Spiders. With 35 wins and 96 losses, the Colonels again finished 12th and last, this time 52½ games back of the Orioles. About the only good news was that Louisville hadn't lost money, which the *Courier-Journal* felt was worthy of celebrating:

> All the debts have been paid and a nice cash balance is on the credit side of Secretary Dreyfus' books. This is the first season the club has made any money in six years. It is also the first season the Louisville Club employed a financial manager. Mr. Pulliam has filled the position with credit to himself and profit to the club. Before this season the finances of the club were looked after in a loose sort of way. Small sums were lost or overlooked here and there, and the aggregate at the end of the year invariably left the club in debt.[6]

Pulliam, it noted, was always at the entrance gates for home and away games to ensure the Colonels received their fair share of the ticket sales and he was always arranging exhibition games "wherever a few dollars could be picked up." Pulliam was constantly trying to negotiate better than the posted rates for rail travel and hotel rooms. The paper acknowledged he was "handicapped by a losing team," but was invariably kind and obliging in his dealings with other clubs. He made many friends among the Eastern clubs where before Louisville had none. The paper's recap of the season suggested there had been "too much experimenting with young players" and it should have hired more experienced men. Pulliam's efforts to improve the League's doormat team was noticed in Pittsburgh where the *Pittsburgh Press* commented on the financial turnaround. "Much of the credit for the Louisville club's financial success belongs to Harry Pulliam, a bright young newspaper man of Louisville." It described him as having "a hard row to hoe at the start … he made capital out of their misfortune by telling such thrilling hard luck stories that fans all over the country began to sympathize with the unfortunates, and before the season was over the colonels had good rooters in every town of the league circuit."[7] Pulliam had proven to be a good fit for the Colonels and the experiment of putting him in charge of club finances had paid off. He had found his calling in baseball and never returned to the newspaper business.

At the annual meeting of directors in late December, Pulliam was praised and his post made permanent. Directors were pleased with the financial picture but remained coy about any profit turned. Barney Dreyfuss was returned as secretary-treasurer and revealed only that "a comfortable profit had been realized last year." The amount was not believed to be large. Dreyfuss and president Stucky were congratulated for the young players they had signed and directors decided to retain manager John McCloskey and fund some minor improvements to Eclipse Park.[8]

The enthusiasm about the financial picture and Pulliam's promotional efforts for the Colonels produced dividends on opening day, April 16, 1896, when a crowd of 10,000 jammed Eclipse Park. "Never before in the history of the game had such a crowd witnessed a ball game in this city," the *Louisville Courier-Journal* reported.[9] At 1 p.m., a large parade began at the Louisville Hotel and carried a large procession to the ballpark. Barney Dreyfuss was master of ceremonies for the parade, which was led by Eichorn's Band playing on a large wagon, followed by the visiting Chicago team, now known as "Anson's Colts," then the Colonels, directors and officers of the two clubs and, finally, baseball editors and reporters from Chicago and Louisville papers. Eclipse Park was filled with people who could get away from their jobs this Thursday, including politicians, ministers, priests and the 100-member "Rooters Club." The entire city council was on hand when Mayor George D. Todd and Colonels president T. Hunt Stucky strode to the mound where Todd was introduced to umpire Stump Weidman and then delivered the ceremonial first pitch. The celebration of baseball's return for another season was marred only by the result of the game. Chicago won the close contest 4–2. It was an impressive start for yet another season at a time when many observers were wondering how much longer Louisville could remain a major league city.

For 1896, things were little changed in the National League. The Baltimore Orioles claimed the pennant for the third year in a row and Louisville finished last for the third straight time, 53 games back, at 38–93. A low point came during a three-game series in late June at home against the Cleveland Spiders. The Spiders were one game out of first place, behind Baltimore. Louisville was already in the basement, 22½ games behind Cleveland. The Spiders were led by manager Patsy Tebeau, an abrasive character who had turned the club into one of the rowdiest and most aggressive teams in the League. Louisville was considered a gentlemanly club by comparison. Umpire for the series, Stump Weidman, had played nine years in the major leagues as a pitcher and outfielder. This was his one and only season as an arbiter. The Spiders won the first game, 8–3, while bulldozing a rather meek Weidman. During the third inning Cleveland argued over one of Weidman's calls and outfielder Jesse Burkett became so irate he grabbed him by the shoulders and shook him hard. Another Spider physically pushed Weidman who took the abuse and continued. The following day, Weidman was apparently fearful of Tebeau and his men, making several calls against the Colonels that drew the ire of 1,000 spectators. "It was a battle royal from start to finish, and it was as full of fight and rowdyism as it was possible for a game to be," reported the *Courier-Journal*. "The main cause of it all is that Mr. Weidman has no more business umpiring a game of ball than a six-year-old boy."[10]

Louisville manager Bill McGunnigle, who had just replaced McCloskey, realized the umpire was unable to control the Spiders who, led by Tebeau, relied heavily on intimidation. So McGunnigle urged his men to adopt similar belligerent tactics. The Colonels began to argue every call. Tebeau continued threatening the umpire and getting his way. "Just wait. I'll get you," he warned Weidman at one point. The game was tied 4–4 after nine innings and it was growing dark. The crowd urged Weidman to call the game, happy to settle for a tie with the high-flying Spiders. Tebeau insisted Weidman continue into the tenth and he complied. The Colonels decided to delay as much as possible to force Weidman to call the game as darkness gathered. The Spiders hit two singles, then Chippy McGarr launched a Bill Hill offering over the left-field fence to put the visitors up 7–4. Jimmy McAleer then homered to make it 8–4. Louisville declined to make easy outs in order to extend the inning and force Weidman's hand, so the Spiders deliberately struck out to retire themselves. When the Colonels came to bat in the bottom of the inning, down by four runs, they moved even more slowly, hoping the game would be called and revert to the 4–4 score after nine innings. "The game at this point was a howling farce. People all over the stands were yelling that they could not see the ball and begging the umpire to call the game," the *Courier-Journal* said. But Tebeau demanded Weidman continue the game, so he did.

In the bottom of the tenth, Colonels batters killed more time by sweeping off home plate and picking imaginary bugs from their uniforms. As it grew ever darker, Cleveland pitcher Nig Cuppy managed to fill the bases. By now, Weidman was merely guessing at the location of pitches and midway through the at-bat of Bill Hassamaer, he finally called the game. Irate, the Spiders converged on Weidman. Center fielder Jimmy McAleer aimed a punch at his head but Weidman dodged and it struck his left shoulder. "This blow was the signal for the riot," the newspaper said. Seeing this altercation, about 300 fans tumbled out of the stands and charged at the Spiders, among them local welterweight boxer Tom Lansing and six private police officers. By the time they joined the melee, Weidman had been struck by several Cleveland players. Lansing found and confronted McAleer and knocked him down with a hard blow. McAleer crawled away from the altercation on hands and knees, but managed to find a baseball bat he used to strike a stout young man who relied on a cane. In retaliation, the younger man wielded his cane to deliver a "resounding whack" to McAleer's head, prompting the player to scurry to refuge at his team's bench. Private policemen struggled to bring order to the scene. Spider left fielder Jesse Burkett was punched in the mouth by a fan and then the crowd formed a circle to let Lansing have a go at him. Face-to-face with a professional pugilist, the ballplayer fled. Louisville manager McGunnigle and the private police officers did their best to protect the Spiders as they boarded their team carriage "surrounded by a jeering, howling crowd of some 200 boys and men." The mob followed their getaway vehicle, hurling stones and insults at the players who cowered on its floor.

The next day was wet and while the teams waited to play a game that was ultimately rained out, eight Spiders were arrested on charges of breaching the peace and brought before a local judge. Tebeau was fined $100, McAleer and Ed McKean $75 each and Burkett $50. Charges against other players were dismissed. As they left town with a win and a tie and somewhat poorer, the Spiders found themselves in a virtual tie with Baltimore in the standings.

In October, club secretary-treasurer Barney Dreyfuss announced Louisville had turned a profit of about $5,000 during the season, an amount reported as "remarkable for a tail-end organization. The directors attribute this fact to Financial Agent Pulliam's excellent management of financial affairs." President Stucky said he was prepared to step down and be replaced by someone who could travel with the club. Harry Pulliam was touted as the perfect candidate and expressed interest.[11] Just before the annual meeting in early January, Stucky formally retired, expressing regret his medical practice prevented him from taking a more hands-on approach to leading the team. He was praised for providing "clean base-ball," his distaste for rowdyism and a willingness to make concessions in the interest of team harmony.[12] Pulliam was named president and manager of off-field operations. He was granted the power to sign and release players at his own discretion "and will run things to suit himself. He has long wanted a chance to be in absolute control, and this was given him…."[13] Directors also gave Pulliam $10,000 to do with as he saw fit and to help him lure players to Louisville. They announced cash awards for the team's top players in various categories along with team bonuses that rose with the final standing of the club. A total of $9,000 was available if the Colonels won the pennant. "Somebody must have administered a hyperdermic [hypodermic] injection of liberality into the directors' arms," the *Courier-Journal* was moved to remark. The willingness to spend money was a strong vote of confidence in their young new president. So it was particularly noteworthy, when Dreyfuss presented revised numbers in his annual report showing the club had actually lost money on the season, despite his earlier assertion of profit. No reason was given for the turnaround. Attendance of 119,000 provided only enough revenue to pay off several outstanding debts.

For 1897, the National League was determined to crack down on rowdyism and abuse of umpires. The ballpark riot in Louisville the previous June when the Spiders visited was far from an isolated incident. Baltimore and Cleveland relied on a roughhouse style of play and umpires were hard to find because of the shabby treatment they received. Two years earlier, 59 umpires had been used and League president Nick Young was forced to hire arbiters unseen or rely on former major leaguers with no umpiring experience at all (like Stump Weidman). The only solution devised by Young for the new season was to allow umpires to fine players $5 if they deliberately defaced or discolored a ball that was in play. Predictably, rowdyism continued.[14]

The 1897 season also saw the Baltimore Orioles knocked off their three-year perch as League champions by the Boston Beaneaters. Meanwhile, Louisville improved to 11th place, 23½ games ahead of the even more hapless St. Louis Browns, who managed to win only 29 games and lose 102. Baltimore's failure to repeat was attributed to internal dissension and injuries. Boston, won 93 games, while compiling an impressive 22–2 record in June.

The season produced yet another painful episode for the Louisville team which demonstrated dramatically that work remained to be done. On June 29 in Chicago, they lost 36–7, establishing an all-time record for most runs scored by a winning team. The humiliation came during a road trip when Louisville went 7–17. "Awful Work," headlined the *Louisville Courier-Journal* of the showing, which came just after second baseman Jim Rogers was replaced as manager by left fielder Fred Clarke. The newspaper highlighted the injuries afflicting the Colonels, including that of president Pulliam, saying he was "sick at heart."[15] The *Chicago Tribune* called the game "a farce" which featured "laughable errors by the Kentuckians." Louisville pitchers Chick Frazer and Jim Jones were pounded for 30 hits. "The crowd which came out was more than repaid for its visit," the *Tribune* said, "for a more spectacularly weird exhibition of the national game was never given."[16]

Fred Clarke became manager midway through the 1897 season at age 24, becoming one of the youngest managers to lead a professional team. He managed from his left field position and soon proved to be an able leader and trusted lieutenant for Dreyfuss. He'd amass 1,602 wins as a manager, spanning 19 seasons, in which he also played. Clarke led by example and was able to instill good morale among his players who tended to be loyal to him. He expected his men to be combative while on the diamond, but gentlemen away from the ballpark. Clarke did not accept mental mistakes and could be critical of players who made them.[17] His loyalty to Dreyfuss prompted him to decline offers made by other teams who appreciated his leadership abilities.

The positive news for Louisville in 1897 was the acquisition of two key players, Honus Wagner and Rube Waddell, both of them future Hall of Famers. Pulliam with his

Following the collapse of the American Association after the 1891 season, the Louisville Colonels joined the National League and never finished better than ninth. In 1897, they finished 11th of the 12 teams in the League. That same season, they acquired future star Honus Wagner. In this image of the Colonels, player-manager Fred Clarke is third from the left in middle row, Wagner is fourth from left, beside him (National Baseball Hall of Fame Library, Cooperstown, New York).

war chest of $10,000 was finding it hard to spend money when players were unable to leave their teams or unwilling to sign with such a chronically underperforming one. His charm and powers of persuasion could only go so far. As a scout he nearly missed landing 23-year-old Johannes Wagner, who would become one of the biggest fish in baseball.

A few years earlier Pulliam had befriended a Louisville ballplayer named Claude McFarlan and extended him some favor. In early 1897, McFarlan was an outfielder for Norfolk in the Atlantic League and that May first saw Johannes Wagner playing for rival Paterson, New Jersey. Wagner had been signed by Paterson co-owner Ed Barrow. In six games between the two teams Johannes Wagner, batting cleanup, homered twice and belted two triples and a double. McFarlan was impressed and penned a letter to Pulliam touting the bow-legged and awkward-looking third baseman from Carnegie, Pennsylvania, just west of Pittsburgh. Wagner, 23, was not built like many ballplayers. He was five-feet-eleven and approaching 200 pounds, with a barrel chest, massive shoulders, arms and hands and he appeared ungainly. Still, McFarlan was impressed with both Wagner's bat and his glove. McFarlan received no reply from Pulliam to his scouting report and fired off another letter. When that was ignored, he sent off a series of "collect" telegrams to Pulliam. After the eighth, Pulliam finally replied, asking McFarlan to stop pestering him and complaining the "collect" telegrams were bankrupting the club. Pulliam's blistering retort came in a very lengthy telegram he sent to McFarlan on a "collect" basis to get back at the player.[18] McFarlan was not deterred, anxious to both improve the fortunes of his hometown team and to repay Pulliam. He finally persuaded the stubborn Pulliam to see Wagner during the next eastern road trip by Louisville. When Pulliam and the Colonels were staying in New York during that trip, the persistent McFarlan was playing in nearby Newark. He finally talked Pulliam and third baseman Fred Clarke, soon to be named manager, into slipping over to Paterson on June 6 to see Wagner in a game against Hartford. Other team owners and scouts were in the crowd of 3,000 that day when Wagner had two hits, a stolen base and three putouts. But Pulliam and Clarke left unimpressed. The former then telegraphed McFarlan: "Saw your miracle play today. Don't bother me any more about him. Whatever gave you the idea that anybody with such gates-ajar legs can play baseball? I'm sending this collect, darn your hide. Let it be a lesson to you. It's lovely weather we are having, is it not?"[19]

Pulliam's reaction was not universal. On June 12, new Pittsburgh manager Patsy Donovan went to Paterson in a bid to sign the bulky Pennsylvanian. He offered the team $1,500 for Wagner's contract but management refused. Meanwhile, Wagner caught fire. On July 1, he homered twice and stole two bases. Two days later he belted another homer. On July 5 he went 3-for-4 with a double and the next day hit for the cycle, going 4-for-4. On July 11, he connected for two triples and two doubles in an 11–5 defeat of McFarlan's Norfolk club. Wagner's hitting helped him win the Atlantic League batting title with an average of .375, while his fielding average stood at a credible .898.[20] He was the lone bright spot on a Paterson team that was struggling on the field and at the box office. After watching Wagner play several more times, Pulliam began to understand McFarlan's enthusiasm for the awkward-looking third baseman and made an offer for him that was rejected by Paterson president Charles McKee.

By mid–July, as the woes for the Paterson team mounted, McKee and Barrow were willing to consider offers for their star. Pittsburgh was already negotiating and willing to pay $2,000 for Wagner when Dreyfuss came up with $2,100 and an infielder to seal the deal.[21] Pulliam was so pleased with the new acquisition he joined him on the train ride to Louisville, with a stop along the way at Wagner's home in Carnegie. On July 19, Wagner made his big-league debut in center field against Washington. He made an immediate impact in Louisville, adjusting easily to the National League, although he was not used to being an outfielder and made a number of errors. Third base was occupied by Billy Clingman, so his familiar spot was not available to the rookie. In 61 games with the Colonels, Wagner played 53 games in the outfield and nine at second base. He hit .335 and stole 22 bases.[22] One of the worst teams in the National League had scored a coup, landing a player who would become one of the biggest stars in baseball. Wagner's acquisition by the Colonels led to his story and likeness being featured on the front page of the August 28 edition of *Sporting News* which dubbed him "one of the finds of the season" and predicted he would become a star in the National League. And if Claude McFarlan hadn't finally worn down Harry Pulliam, Wagner would have been signed by someone else. Johannes Wagner became known as Honus (pronounced "HAW-ness") Wagner and would be a huge asset for Pulliam and Barney Dreyfuss in their upcoming baseball exploits.

The other future Hall of Famer signed that season was southpaw pitcher George Edward "Rube" Waddell, 20, a Pennsylvanian from Butler County, just north of Pittsburgh. A hulking six-foot-one and nearly 200 pounds, he had the emotional maturity of a child.[23] He played for teams near his home and before Harry Pulliam found him had already earned his hayseed nickname for the simple pleasure he derived from fishing, playing marbles with street kids, chasing fire trucks, fighting fires, and eccentric behavior on and off the field. During a spring training game with Louisville on Easter Sunday, Waddell was struck by an egg tossed by a spectator that landed on the top of his head. "You couldn't faze that guy, though," his team-mate Tommy Leach recalled many years later. "He's the only guy I know who appreciated a thing like that. So he showed them how good he was by calling in the outfield and striking out the side."[24] Waddell's antics became the stuff of legend and made him a crowd favorite, but baseball historian Bill James has suggested he may have suffered from a personality disorder, autism, attention deficit disorder or even a developmental disability. Regardless, Waddell was a fearsome pitcher. His excellent fastball and curveballs were made even more effective by pinpoint control. In his 13-year major league career he won 193 games and struck out nearly three batters for every one he walked, compiling 2,316 strikeouts in all. He'd become one of the top left-handed pitchers in major league history.

The story goes that after spending the winter of 1896–97 on the family farm in Butler County, Waddell decided he'd like to play for Youngstown, Ohio, in the Interstate League. He applied to them but was rejected as too slow. Out of the blue, in late March or early April, he received an offer from the Pittsburgh Pirates, who a year earlier wanted nothing to do with him. A new manager, Patsy Donovan, had taken over from catcher and manager Connie Mack. Donovan sought new talent and some scouts suggested Waddell. Donovan had heard about him and asked the big lefty to join the club for breakfast one morning. A voracious eater, Waddell didn't have to be asked twice and joined the club at the appointed time and place. The Irish-born Donovan was becoming known as a fine judge of talent and for his quiet dignity and commitment to the work ethic. He wanted to know more about the big pitcher and had him sit beside him. The bizarre story of what happened next is related by Waddell biographer Alan H. Levy:

> No one knows exactly what Waddell said or did that morning while sitting over breakfast next to Donovan, but it must have been offensive. For immediately after breakfast, before he had even seen Waddell throw a single ball, Donovan released him outright. Baseball people

commonly refer to a brief stint in the majors as "a cup of coffee." Never was such an experience more literally so than Rube's touch with the Pittsburgh Pirates in the spring of 1897. Full bellied, but empty handed, Rube trudged back to Butler.[25]

Later that season, Waddell was pitching for Evans City, a community near his home. He also pitched for Homestead, a steel-making community just east of Pittsburgh, sometimes appearing in exhibition games against travelling Philadelphia and Pittsburgh clubs, when he caught the attention of scouts. At the end of the month Louisville signed him for $500.[26]

With his start late in the season, Waddell appeared in two games, with a no-decision and a win, striking out five in 14 innings. Pulliam and Dreyfuss concluded the big lefty needed more seasoning and for 1898 assigned him to Detroit in the Western League. He pitched nine games there before getting into a fight over a fine imposed for repeatedly missing practices and he quit. Waddell pitched a few games in the nearby Ontario cities of Windsor and Chatham before returning to Homestead. In 1899, he was with Columbus in the Western League, where he enjoyed success, picking up 26 wins and 8 losses there and in Grand Rapids. He rejoined Louisville for the last month of the 1899 season, winning 7 games and losing 2 in his 10 appearances. Like Honus Wagner, Rube Waddell would become an important cog in the plans of Pulliam and Dreyfuss.

Friends and admirers of Pulliam announced late in September they were nominating him as a candidate for representative in the Kentucky state legislature for the eighth and ninth wards of Louisville. The busy baseball manager, who had always been

This pass, good for free admission to the Polo Grounds in New York, was issued to Barney Dreyfuss by Giants' owner Andrew Freedman for the 1897 season. In the corridors of power of the National League, Dreyfuss and Freedman were often at odds. The ornate pass has been passed down through the Dreyfuss family since then (Len Martin).

interested in politics, won the subsequent election and served for two years. During that time, he and Dreyfuss would have their hands full with baseball intrigue. But, adept at time management, Pulliam was able to represent Louisville in Frankfort where he introduced a bill intended to protect cardinals, which were being captured and skinned for their plumage or sold abroad.[27]

The annual meeting of the Louisville ball club was held in late December when Barney Dreyfuss tendered his resignation, replaced as secretary-treasurer by brewer Charles P. Dehler, who had been vice-president. T. Hunt Stucky replaced Dehler in the vice presidential post. Directors stoutly denied the resignation of Dreyfuss had been sought. President Pulliam demanded the newspapers "state emphatically that Mr. B. Dreyfuss resigned of his own accord—that his business as a whiskey merchant was too pressing for him to continue to assume the additional duties of secretary and treasurer of the ball club."[28] Dreyfuss retained his growing number of shares and would remain a director. The *Courier-Journal* predicted the election of Dehler would be welcomed by baseball writers because he had demonstrated a willingness to share "baseball news or gossip." Dreyfuss, it complained, "usually appeared as a sort of self constituted society for the suppression of news." Barney was up to something, the paper may have sensed. It was probably correct.

Pulliam, whose favorite saying was "take nothing for granted in baseball," reported he didn't expect many roster changes for the upcoming season and wouldn't disclose financial results, other than that they were "perfectly satisfactory to the directors."

A month later, director Dreyfuss made headlines with a move that might be construed as a power play to take control of the team. He claimed he was owed $8,000 by the team for funds he had advanced to keep the Colonels afloat. He wanted that money now, or the 16,000 shares still held in the club treasury. That was half of all club shares and together with those he already owned, they would give him majority control. The *Courier-Journal* carried a *Sporting Life* report saying that differences among stockholders had arisen and "will likely result in one person securing a controlling interest in the club's stock, and consequently permitting that one person to dictate the club's policy." The individual was not named, but it was further noted "if you hear that President Pulliam has become the owner of a majority of the club's stock, you will know that the expected has happened, and Mr. Pulliam is representing a certain well-known man long prominently identified with the club."[29] There was no mystery man to the Louisville paper, which hinted Dreyfuss was conniving with Pulliam. After a secret meeting of directors, it was reported that Dreyfuss settled for an undisclosed sum of money rather than the shares he sought. For his part, Dreyfuss insisted everything was "entirely harmonious" among directors. Dreyfuss, it was reported, was responsible for "coming to the rescue of the club and helping it out of sundry tight places." Directors insisted they had no plans for any change in management.[30] The intrigue didn't interfere with plans for a new season. Dreyfuss may not have acquired control of the club through shares, but his man Pulliam was head of the organization and could be counted on for support.

Despite saying earlier he expected few new players, by early April Pulliam was signing men expected to make the Colonels appreciably stronger in the capable hands of returning manager Fred Clarke. He added more as the season progressed. Among them were Tommy Leach, Dummy Hoy and Topsy Hartsel. Leach was found by Dreyfuss in August after he was cut by New York. A utility player, Leach only appeared in three games but the future star would pay big dividends with his play for Dreyfuss in years to come. Hoy, a deaf mute, was a veteran outfielder who possessed both a strong glove and bat. He played 148 games. Hartsel, a left-handed lead-off batter and outfielder, joined the Colonels late in the season for his major league debut. The three were among the top players secured by Pulliam and Dreyfuss that season. Several more were farmed out to give Clarke a season-starting roster of 18.[31]

Dreams for a better season in Louisville were soon dashed. By the end of May, the Colonels were in 10th place, already 16½ games back of first-place Cincinnati. By June 30, they languished in 12th. A month later they were 11th. After a July road trip in which they lost 12 of 18 games, carping began. "Prodigal Sons Return To-Day," the *Courier-Journal* derisively headlined the team's return. The newspaper said it had always supported the Colonels but the tradition of losing was becoming too much to bear. Louisvillians, it said, had hoped the team would bring credit to the city, noting "it has gone on year after year hoping for good results which never came, and the Colonels landed near the last hole with disgusting regularity." It pinned the blame on president Pulliam and his "unwise move" of keeping Clarke as manager.

> Even Mr. Pulliam's friends, and lots of them, for he is exceedingly popular, are now persuaded that he made a mistake when he accepted the position of President of the Colonels. The truth is Mr. Pulliam does not know the game of base-ball. He has a penchant for signing whole bundles of youngsters, and then dispersing them. This is one of the most glaring faults of the organization. Louisville will never have a team that will advertise the city to advantage until the gentlemen who control the management buy players, etc., gather together men who know how to play base-ball ....[32]

That assessment had to rankle both Pulliam and his partner-in-baseball Barney Dreyfuss. The Colonels were losing goodwill in the community and a friendly and sympathetic press was necessary if there was any hope for the future. Some rare optimism broke out in September when the team finally began to pull together to become one of the hottest teams in the League, winning 18 of 24 games with a chance to catch eighth-place Pittsburgh. But that effort ultimately fell short. The Boston Beaneaters took the pennant and Louisville finished in ninth place, 33 games back, with a record of 70 wins and 81 losses. It marked a substantial improvement from recent years for the Colonels, their win total the highest since the 88 won in their stunning last-to-first 1890 season. Honus Wagner batted .299, but Fred Clarke led the Colonels with .307 and Hoy followed with .304.

By late 1898, directors of the Louisville franchise, which had long been rumored to be for sale, received an offer from Detroit interests who were seeking that city's return to the National League. The Detroit Wolverines were League members from 1881 to 1888 and had taken the pennant in 1887, but had trouble drawing fans because of the League ban on Sunday play at the time and the franchise was sold to Cleveland. G.A. Vanderbeck, owner of Detroit's team in the Western League reportedly offered $35,000. Louisville directors initially wanted $60,000 but dropped that to $50,000, which Vanderbeck rejected as still too steep. It was learned Louisville had lost $13,000 during the season just past and that directors Dr. Stucky, brewer Dehler, Dreyfuss and saloon-keeper Casper Hammer, described as "practically the sole owners" of the club, had been forced to dig into their pockets to cover expenses. The loss was the greatest in club history and as usual the amount involved was not released. Much of it was attributed to Louisville's being a poor draw on the road when gate receipts fell far short of club needs. Proceeds were particularly bad in Brooklyn and New York where operating expenses for the Colonels amounted to $300 a day. One game in New York drew only 100 spectators. The *Courier-Journal* said the 1898 season had been a poor one financially for many

National League teams, blaming rowdy players as "the principal cause for shrunken gate receipts."³³

Barney Dreyfuss granted a rare interview with the newspaper, saying he couldn't predict whether the Detroit bid would succeed:

> I will say, however, that I am tired of losing so much money every year. Nothing would please me better than if we could keep the team here, but we cannot stand the strain, and I don't think any small set of men could. If more of us were interested financially it would be different. We are seriously considering the Detroit matter…. All of us want to get out if we can do so without losing much money.

Dreyfuss, who had become the voice of the team, said he planned to attend the upcoming meeting of National League owners in New York with secretary-treasurer Dehler and president Pulliam. Meanwhile, Vanderbeck upped his offer to $42,000, warning if Louisville wouldn't sell, he'd pursue the Cleveland franchise, for which it was rumored he'd be willing to pay $75,000.³⁴ Dreyfuss replied the offer was still too low, but it was for the directors to decide. He wanted nothing less than $50,000. Dreyfuss said the club debt totaled about $34,000 and he wanted to make money on the transaction.³⁵ The directors rejected the offer, even after Vanderbeck sweetened it to $46,500.

About this time, it was noted that Dreyfuss "has been conducting the affairs of the organization" likely because of the extent of his share holdings as well as his closeness with club president Pulliam. The indebtedness of the club was actually $36,000, but he refused to sell unsold stock in the club treasury just to keep it going. Dreyfuss said it was a bad investment because Louisville would be expelled from the League in December of 1902 with the expiration of the National Agreement, the 10-year working arrangement for its 12 member clubs. He said he expected Washington and Baltimore would also be expelled when the League contracted to eight clubs from 12. "Let it be distinctly understood that we directors are not trying to work any con game on the public," he said. Dreyfuss was not willing to sink any more of his money into the club and said he had dissuaded Isaac Bernheim at Bernheim Brothers from investing. Dreyfuss said he still hoped Detroit would buy the Colonels and he would do his best to persuade League magnates to accept that course of action. He knew unanimous approval would be needed, but Chicago owner Jim Hart and Indianapolis owner John T. Brush were already objecting.³⁶ Hart and Brush may have been aware of Vanderbeck's growing reputation for brashness and deceit in his business dealings. Or they simply wanted to shrink the League. On the latter, they were not alone.

National League magnates gathered in New York City on December 13 when president Nick Young was authorized to develop an 1899 schedule for 12 teams, even though it was clearly understood by all present that "the long-term fate of certain NL franchises had been foreordained."³⁷ There was still discussion about contracting to eight teams. A day later, Detroit's Vanderbeck announced he was no longer interested in Louisville. He acquired no team at all and Detroit remained in the Western League, which soon became the American League.

At the very end of the month, Barney Dreyfuss was grinning like a Cheshire cat, despite the collapse of Detroit's interest. He had just returned from a trip east but when he was buttonholed by a newspaper reporter about his dramatic change of mood, he refused to provide any explanation.

Clearly, something was afoot.

7

1899: One Door Closes...

At a special meeting of directors of the Louisville Base-Ball Club, secretary-treasurer Dreyfuss announced that the National League was willing to buy the franchise and that New York and Philadelphia were offering good money for several of the best Colonels. The directors suddenly had plenty to consider at the dawn of 1899.

The League's offer was not revealed and was contingent on two other developments. The first was whether the owners of Cleveland were able buy the bankrupt St. Louis Browns from a court-appointed receiver. The second was completion of an expected merger of Baltimore and Brooklyn. If both came to pass, the League would buy out the weak Louisville and Washington franchises, shrinking the loop from twelve to eight teams.

Andrew Freedman, the notoriously abrasive and tight-fisted owner of the New York Giants had offered $16,000 for Louisville outfielders Fred Clarke and Charlie Dexter. Freedman added another $4,000 for pitcher Bert Cunningham, winner of 28 games in 1898, the ace of the Colonels pitching staff. The Philadelphia Phillies wanted Clarke, Dexter, catcher Malachi Kittridge, pitcher Bill Magee and third baseman Billy Clingman.[1] It was believed that selling off four or five of the Louisville players could produce $25,000 for club coffers to which directors had contributed when funds were short. Late in 1898, for instance, Dreyfuss lent the treasury $6,000 to cover player salaries.[2] "Whether the Louisville stockholders will decide to dispose of these players and thereby realize some ready cash, which they say they sorely need, is a question which will not be answered until the annual meeting this week," the *Courier-Journal* reported on January 1. Dreyfuss was unsure whether his fellow directors were willing to sell some of the best talent. "As for myself, I do not feel like letting Clarke go, because he has infused life and ginger into the team and his services are practically invaluable," he said of his player-manager. Dreyfuss felt Freedman had suggested some trades which were not in the best interests of Louisville, although Dreyfuss believed a stronger New York team would be good for the League and improve profits for all teams.

Dreyfuss said the League's push to contract to eight members was alive and well and depended on the sale of the St. Louis franchise, a matter still before the courts in that city. In Cleveland, where the Spiders drew few fans despite on-field success, owner Frank Robison was trying to buy the Browns and transfer his team to St. Louis. If successful, that would pave the way for creation of an eight-team circuit. Dreyfuss said the League was willing to pay the price sought by Louisville for the Colonels, an amount he refused to disclose, although *Sporting Life* put it well above $50,000.[3] "It is enough to set us all even and is not too much for the League to give," he said. The *Courier-Journal* said directors had recently complained they lost $13,500 on the 1898 season and seemed anxious to get out. The Colonels remained a poor draw on the road, a major factor in their losses which, many months later, were estimated at closer to $23,000.[4]

By late January, a court in St. Louis approved the sale of the Browns after a long legal battle waged by their owner Chris von der Ahe. A receiver was empowered to hold an auction. It wasn't until mid–March, however, that the sale was completed to a local lumber dealer not known for his interest in baseball. It turns out he was acting as an agent of Robison in Cleveland, whose acquisition of St. Louis was readily accepted by the League. In the meantime, Dreyfuss and his directors in Louisville had undergone a change of heart once they assessed the various offers before them. They decided to reject them all and focus on increasing the value of the franchise during the upcoming season. Selling off players would have produced quick cash but significantly reduce the amount directors would receive for a hollowed-out franchise. Besides, the upcoming season looked promising given the strong finish of the club in 1898. Early in January, Dreyfuss announced a sale of stock in the ball club to the public. About $34,000 in shares were available, he said, and $2,000 worth was quickly snapped up. Some of the big stockholders had already decided to increase their holdings, he said, because they believed it to be a wise investment. Dreyfuss himself purchased $3,800 of stock from former club president Fred Drexler.[5] "If the stock was worthless we would not want it ourselves, and as we intend to take more of it this is a pretty good sign that we think it a good investment," Dreyfuss said. The directors held $16,000 worth of stock in total and several lent further funds to the club to cover salaries and meet expenses.[6] Within a matter of days secretary-treasurer Dreyfuss admitted sales had fallen flat. He conceded "the outlook is most discouraging," and that selling shares "is the hardest work I have ever tackled." Despite this disappointment, Dreyfuss continued signing players for the upcoming season. By the end of January, the stock sale was pronounced a flop and was halted. "We have not sold enough stock to do us any good," one director lamented. That unnamed director, most likely Dreyfuss, went on to say "the Colonels will stay here…. We have made all plans for the campaign, and we will not consider any offer for the club now."[7]

Barney Dreyfuss's role as leader of the Louisville Base-Ball Club was formalized February 16 with his election as president. Harry Pulliam replaced him as secretary-treasurer and Charles Dehler became vice president. The public was told the move was made at the request of Pulliam. "Mr. Dreyfuss will conduct the affairs of the club simply because he is financially interested to a large extent, and, besides is ill and his physicians have recommended that he travel about as much as possible."[8] Here was yet another story promulgated about Dreyfuss, his stress, and his doctors, a variation of those told about his being prescribed fresh air and outdoor activity in Paducah and Louisville which led him to baseball.

About this time, Dreyfuss reduced his role at the Bernheim Brothers distillery and warehouse. Some sources say he quit entirely, but news accounts late into the year reveal he continued to work outside the ball club. For instance, it was reported he was unable clear his business schedule in Louisville late in March to attend an important meeting of the National League.[9] That gathering was to finalize the schedule, an important issue for Louisville, and his absence would prove critical. But his other business was apparently more pressing than baseball. Then, shortly after the season ended, he was reported in Pittsburgh "on liquor business."[10] That was reinforced in mid–November when *Sporting Life* said he would not winter in Louisville "but it is likely that he will spend the winter in New York city, having charge of the New York interests of the firm of Bernheim Bros.…"[11] Dreyfuss may have grown tired of being cooped up in an office with ledgers and paperwork and frustrated he couldn't focus his energies on transforming the Colonels into a successful operation. Especially after he and his associates had sunk so much money into the club. So it's likely he took a leave of absence from the distillery and then agreed to represent Bernheim Brothers in a less-confining capacity. Regardless, his greater involvement in the team and plans to travel with it drew kudos from his friend Pulliam who said Dreyfuss "will make an admirable head for the team. He is liberal, conscientious and a fine business man. He will treat the players right, and is bound to succeed."[12] Pulliam, who held no shares, had been willing to surrender the club presidency for some time. It is likely he and Dreyfuss had carefully orchestrated the move.

Late in February it was announced that Baltimore and Brooklyn had consolidated into one team and the same was likely for Cleveland and St. Louis. Dreyfuss vowed that Louisville "is in the National League to stay. I will not sell my franchise now for any price."[13] He had taken to calling Louisville "my franchise," reflecting his near-absolute control of the team. The new president said he once wanted to sell but the situation had changed. "I have made arrangements to take a long vacation, and will give my personal attention to my club all the season." That latter comment begs the question, a vacation from what or where? It tends to reinforce the notion he was granted some sort of leave from Bernheim Brothers. Dreyfuss added that "my players" would report for spring training in Georgia and all but two of them had already signed contracts.

Dreyfuss and Pulliam attended the National League meeting in New York City from February 28 to March 2 where a draft schedule was presented but final approval deferred until March 15, the day after it was expected Cleveland owner Frank Robison would acquire the St. Louis club at auction. Dreyfuss was optimistic about the new season and encouraged the owners of Eclipse Park to add 1,000 seats to the grandstand and 1,200 to the bleachers. His sunny outlook was apparently contagious because it was reported that betting money in Louisville backed the Colonels to take the League pennant, a surprising turn of events.[14]

The players reported to Louisville and left for spring training in Thomasville, Georgia, on March 18. Pitcher Deacon Phillippe was among the last to sign a contract, waiting until appearing in Thomasville to do so. Phillippe, a native of Virginia, had played two seasons with Minneapolis in the Western League, where the big right-hander caught the attention of Dreyfuss, likely in the pages of *Sporting Life* or *Sporting News*. He was drafted and Dreyfuss offered him $1,200 for the upcoming season. Phillippe felt his services were worth more than that and sent the contract back unsigned. He returned to his farm in South Dakota, saying he could earn more by organizing an independent team there. Dreyfuss wouldn't let his quarry go. He told Phillippe he was the worst-looking pitcher he had ever bought for Louisville, and reminded him of a game the previous season in Kansas when Phillippe surrendered 26 runs. When he wanted a player, Dreyfuss didn't give up and wanted him to moderate his financial expectations. Soon afterward, Phillippe's barn burned down and he suddenly needed money. If he wanted to play professional baseball Phillippe realized he had to sign with Louisville, who held his rights. Dreyfuss spotted his opportunity. "Sign with me and you will never regret it," he promised Phillippe, but adamantly refusing to increase his offer. Reluctantly, the pitcher agreed, but delayed doing so as long as possible. He didn't regret it, as Dreyfuss predicted. Phillippe spent most of his major league career playing for Pittsburgh and after his first four years *Sporting News* pronounced him one of the most prosperous players in the National League.[15] Another player in camp had jumped at the chance to play for Louisville. During 1898, Tommy Leach had been given a two-week trial by the New York Giants, but was returned to his Auburn team. Giants owner Andrew Freedman explained: "We don't take midgets on the Giants." Leach was five-foot-six and weighed barely 150 pounds, about the same stature as Louisville owner Dreyfuss, who found Freedman's discard and signed the 20-year-old for $650. Leach appeared in only three games for Louisville before season end. He was thrilled to be back with the club again for 1899, but after a shaky start was demoted to Worcester for six weeks. Leach was a solid utility player, most often playing third base or second and eventually developed into a power hitter and star in the League. He continued to play for Dreyfuss until 1912.[16] Such was the loyalty Dreyfuss could engender in players like Clarke, Wagner, Phillippe and Leach because of his fair dealing.

On March 24, the National League reconvened in New York to finalize the playing schedule with opening day less than a month away. Dreyfuss could not attend, citing pressing business elsewhere. To represent Louisville interests at the gathering he enlisted Boston Beaneaters president Arthur Soden. That was a mistake.

Dreyfuss had seen an early draft of the schedule a few weeks earlier and everything suited him. So he wasn't surprised by a report from the scheduling meeting that Louisville fared "exceptionally well," by getting its allotment of Sunday dates on which it heavily relied to fill club coffers.[17] That was a misrepresentation. To his chagrin, Dreyfuss soon discovered Louisville had actually been stripped of 11 Sunday games, a move that would cost his club more than $16,000 in revenue. Those valuable dates were allocated to Cincinnati, Chicago, Cleveland and St. Louis and replaced by weekday doubleheaders for Louisville. Only six Sunday games were allotted for the Colonels. Dreyfuss smelled rats and placed the blame squarely on Cincinnati's Brush, Chicago president James Hart and Frank Robison, the new owner in St. Louis, who was still head of Cleveland. "There was a conspiracy to defraud the Louisville Club, and this is a criminal charge," Dreyfuss thundered. "I didn't know I was associated with a gang of assassins."[18] *Sporting News* reported the trickery was orchestrated by Cincinnati and Chicago to punish Louisville for Dreyfuss's ingratitude after they provided him six players on reasonable terms. The publication quoted Chicago president Hart insisting Dreyfuss had been "offensive" to the Western clubs.[19] For his part, Soden had utterly failed Louisville, relying on assurances from Robison that no changes had been made from the earlier draft.

Col. John I. Rogers, president of Philadelphia, said he would stand behind Louisville, telling Dreyfuss: "It is an attempt to freeze you out." Rogers then told a newspaper reporter: "These conspirators in the National League are certainly going farther than I thought they would dare go. Mind you, I say conspirators, and I mean it." Rogers said they were deliberately trying to bankrupt Louisville and force it out, along with Washington, to achieve an eight-team circuit. "It is too outrageous to be condoned. Still this is only a sample of the dirty work that has been going on in the League in recent years ... affairs in the National League are in a frightfully bad shape at the present time. The Brush faction seems determined to bring about the disintegration of the National League."[20]

Opposite: **Honus Wagner, the shortstop and slugger who joined the Louisville Colonels in 1897, was among the players who went to Pittsburgh in 1900 with Barney Dreyfuss. Dreyfuss took the top talent from Louisville to strengthen the Pirates into whom he bought so he could stay in baseball (Library of Congress).**

Dreyfuss complained about the treatment given Louisville in letters to all League owners and newspapers in their cities. He said either a mistake had been made or unfair punishment had been inflicted on his club. He noted the preliminary draft schedule had allocated Louisville six Sunday games on the road and 11 at home. That was changed to remove all Sunday road games and five of those at home. He said replacing the lost Sunday dates with weekday doubleheaders meant "our business prospects are almost entirely destroyed." He said it was well known throughout baseball that Louisville is a "Sunday town," unlike many other cities. In the 1890s, only Louisville, Chicago, St. Louis and Cincinnati played League baseball on Sunday. The Eastern clubs refused to do so. Dreyfuss urged his fellow magnates to contact League president Nick Young to have him adopt the version originally presented.[21] Dreyfuss then headed off to Washington to plead his case directly with Young. Aside from support from Rogers, Dreyfuss was backed by Boston president Soden, New York president Andrew Freedman, Pittsburgh president W.W. Kerr, and Brooklyn owner Ferdinand Abell. Allying himself with Eastern clubs did not endear him to the Western clubs with which Louisville traditionally voted.

Initially, Brush wouldn't talk about what had happened, other than to say he strongly supported reducing the League from twelve to eight teams. But it was generally understood that he, Hart, Robison and Soden supported retaining weak clubs in Baltimore and Cleveland only until Washington and Louisville could be driven out.[22] Later, however, Brush said he and Dreyfuss had clashed two years earlier over a player and Dreyfuss vowed he would fight everything proposed by Brush from then on. Removing Louisville's Sunday games was a form of pay back. president Hart in Chicago was even more blunt, telling the *Chicago Tribune*: "the Louisville club was deprived of its Sunday games purposely and with malice aforethought, and that we did it for the benefit of baseball as a blow to Freedmanism, and that we are glad we did it and will do it again whenever we get a chance."[23] He and Brush were annoyed with Dreyfuss for aligning with the Eastern clubs. For his part, Freedman, whose name was becoming associated with self-interest in baseball, said he was "disgusted" at the change affecting Louisville. He supported changing the schedule, adding "the New York Club won't be a party to any trickery." Freedman said he supported contraction of the League but wanted it done fairly by buying its weaker clubs, rather than by "freezing them out."

Andrew Freedman had become a polarizing figure among club owners. He'd been the majority owner of the New York Giants since 1895 and was known for his arrogance, bad temper and short fuse. He made a fortune in real estate and the ball club was merely his plaything and distraction from business. He didn't need to make money from the Giants like his fellow magnates, so he didn't invest much in his team. Consequently, the Giants weren't particularly competitive when the League needed the most populous city in America to attract large crowds and strong revenue for the benefit of all. Except for a third-place finish in 1897, Freedman's Giants generally finished around seventh. Few of his fellow owners could abide the man they found abrasive and most often difficult. By the time of the Louisville schedule debate, Freedman was still stewing about the League's response to an anti–Semitic slur hurled at him by player Ducky Holmes during a late 1898 game against Baltimore. Holmes, a former Giant, was ordered suspended by the League for the remainder of the season, producing outcry from players and *Sporting Life*. Holmes' lawyer obtained an injunction that returned Holmes to left field for the Orioles, prompting Freedman to play the remainder of New York's games under protest. His fellow magnates sided with the player, saying Holmes' suspension was illegal because he had never been given a hearing. Freedman resented that stance and vowed revenge. He was determined to teach his fellow owners a lesson by fielding non-competitive teams to hurt everyone's bottom line. In New York, fans didn't respond well and stayed away in droves as the Giants slipped to a 10th place finish in 1899. Freedman bragged about his unwillingness to find good players as his plan unfolded and he began to boycott League meetings until owners acted against Holmes. Freedman agreed with his fellow owners on one key thing, however, that the League should ultimately be reduced to eight teams. But he bitterly opposed allowing syndicates to own more than one team. This led to his clash with the faction led by Brush and Hart who were engineering the consolidation of Baltimore with Brooklyn and Cleveland with St. Louis. Brush had become the leader of the anti–Freedman faction. The bad feelings lingered into early 1900 when a truce of sorts was achieved and Freedman said he'd begin acquiring better players to improve his franchise and thereby boost League revenues.[24] But for now, the League remained split between the Brush and Freedman factions.

Barney Dreyfuss was left scrambling to save the season for Louisville. He was hoping to enlist Washington and Baltimore to help him persuade the League to reinstate the original schedule. He found additional support from *Sporting Life,* which urged the League "to find a way of righting the wrong done the harassed Louisville Club…." It went on:

> To permit Louisville's present ruinous schedule to stand is to set a momentous precedent for punishing, to the verge of confiscation, real or fancied disloyalty to any party or faction. To admit such a doctrine is virtually to place the rights and property of every club at the mercy of any temporarily dominant faction. Can the League afford to thus add to the instability of base ball as a business?[25]

The sporting publication claimed Dreyfuss was being made to pay for his objection to the "scheme of Robison, Hart and Brush to get the St. Louis franchise."[26] The controversy raged into early April with harsh words exchanged between Louisville and members of the Brush faction. Dreyfuss received legal advice about seeking an injunction against the League under "co-partnership" law to keep it from using the contentious schedule.[27] He continued to woo Brooklyn, Washington and Baltimore for support. Meanwhile, the days left before the beginning of the season were dwindling. Dreyfuss demanded League magnates vote on his appeal by April 6, or he would initiate legal action. In Philadelphia, Phillies owner Rogers opined Louisville had a good case to take to court.[28] Meanwhile, Brush in Cincinnati vowed no quarter—or Sundays—would be given. The magnates gathered in Chicago on April 10 where Dreyfuss was at his persuasive best and succeeded in getting some Sunday dates reinstated, despite Brush. Two days later, the *Courier-Journal* reported Dreyfuss was a much happier man. "The Louisville Club gets back most of the Sunday dates it was robbed of; there has been a revision of the schedule, and everybody connected with the Louisville Club is gloriously happy." The paper noted there were now enough Sundays for Louisville "to keep the wolf from the door." Dreyfuss was anxious to mend bridges and began attributing the schedule controversy to "a complete misunderstanding. I want to say that everything is all right now. The best of feeling prevails between all concerned." He said Brush and Hart had met Louisville "half way" and he appreciated their willingness to do so.[29] The 1899 season was already proving to be controversial and teams had yet to take the field.

On April 14, opening day, Chicago, known as the Orphans for a second year, were the visitors at Eclipse Park for a game that attracted 10,000 fans. The Colonels roster was the same as that fielded on the final day of the 1898 season, with Fred Clarke as lead-off batter and Honus Wagner batting cleanup. Orphans pitcher Clark Griffith allowed a Louisville run in the bottom of the first but then buckled down and proved too much for the Colonels who couldn't score again. Louisville pitcher Bert Cunningham had a bad day, allowing 15 runs on 15 hits, while fielding errors abounded.

Despite the high hopes of Dreyfuss and the long-suffering fans in Louisville, the new season soon began to look much like so many others, despite the talent on the team. By May 19, the Colonels were in eighth place, 9½ games behind the stacked St. Louis club, renamed the Perfectos by Robison. By then, Louisville was last in attendance, having drawn 26,000 to Eclipse Park and 25,000 on the road. The figures for St. Louis were nearly triple that. The hollowed-out Spiders in Cleveland attracted only 3,179 at home by that date, but 55,762 on the road, for total attendance nearly 8,000 greater than the Colonels.[30] Bad weather had plagued Louisville's spring training and the pitchers, in particular, were slow to find their form. Shortstop Billy Clingman was injured early in the campaign, upsetting the chemistry of the infield where Wagner was still being moved around. Then right fielder Charlie Dexter became ill. Dissension broke out with catcher Malachi Kittridge a major contributor. Dreyfuss, who travelled with the team, released him after 46 games.

Rookie pitcher Deacon Phillippe provided an early season highlight when he threw a no-hitter on May 25 against New York in his seventh major league outing. No Giant was able to get beyond second base in Phillippe's masterful performance which the *Louisville Courier-Journal* called "as good a game as was ever pitched."[31] Louisville won 7–0. The six-foot right-hander struck out only one batter, but scored a run and stole a base in blanking the eighth-place Giants. All this came two days after Phillippe's 27th birthday. His fastball and curves showed great control, it was said. In his debut season, Phillippe, whose name was often mangled in press reports, won 21 games and lost 17, with an earned-run average of 3.17.

Another highlight came June 16 during a four-game series at Eclipse Park against St. Louis, who had just slipped to third place from its early season perch atop the League. The Perfectos consisted of the best players Robison had moved to St. Louis from Cleveland and the stacked team was performing well, as had been expected. They had won the first two games of the series in Louisville and for the third contest they tapped former Cleveland Spider Cy Young to pitch. Just two weeks earlier, the right-handed future Hall of Famer collected his 250th victory. Louisville had lost six games in a row when they took the field that day before a crowd of only 300 and gave the ball to righty Bert Cunningham. The Colonels were not getting along among themselves and *Sporting Life* had reported Dreyfuss was "thoroughly disgusted" with their play and contemplating changes. About this time, he signed "Chief" Zimmer, a sturdy 38-year-old veteran catcher with a good bat who had been released by the Spiders after 20 games. Zimmer didn't smoke or drink and did not swear, traits admired by Dreyfuss, a non-smoker and light drinker. The team owner insisted his teams deport themselves in a gentlemanly fashion and he liked what he saw in Zimmer.[32] St. Louis jumped out to an early 2–0 lead in the first inning, but Louisville replied with three runs in the second. The Perfectos plated three more runs in the third and two in the fifth before the Colonels scored three times in the bottom of the sixth, capitalizing on a throwing error by Young. St. Louis crossed the plate three times in the top of the seventh and added single runs in the eighth and ninth innings to lead 12–6. Expecting yet another loss, about half the Louisville crowd had wandered off.

What happened next was completely unexpected and the fans who remained were richly rewarded by the turn of events in the bottom of the ninth. Dummy Hoy and Fred Clarke flied out to left field as the Colonels appeared to be breathing their last. But Charlie Dexter drove a Young offering to right field for a single. He was followed by Honus Wagner who belted another single, this one to center. Claude Ritchey followed with a single to right field to score Dexter and advance Wagner to third. Walt Woods connected for a high popup that dropped unmolested between third base and home plate. Young, third baseman Lave Cross and catcher Jack O'Connor couldn't agree on who should field it. During their confusion, Wagner began yelling as he ran home to make the score 12–8. Dave Wills doubled on a short fly to left field, scoring Ritchey and Woods. "How the little crowd did roar," the *Courier-Journal* said. Then yet-to-be-released Kittridge singled to right, scoring Wills. Topsy Hartsel was installed to pinch-run for Kittridge as the crowd came to life with the Colonels trailing by just a run. Cunningham helped his cause by singling to third base where the ball was mishandled by Cross. Dummy Hoy was deliberately walked to load the bases and the tension mounted. Clarke then drove a Young offering to left field, tying the game to a chorus of cheers. Dexter drove a ball to third base where Cross fielded it cleanly and threw to second base to catch Clarke, forcing the game into extra innings. On the inning-ending play, Clarke slid hard into "Cupid" Childs at second, apparently hoping to shake the ball loose and sending Childs flying. The second baseman came up swinging at Clarke and umpire Jim McDonald and shortstop Bobby Wallace intervened, while not far away combative St. Louis manager Patsy Tebeau punched an unruly spectator who had been calling him names throughout the game. That confrontation drew police just as other occupants of the bleachers tried to join the fray. Tensions were high.

St. Louis was held scoreless in the top of the tenth. Wagner led off for Louisville in the bottom and collected his fifth hit of the game, driving a single past Wallace at short. Wagner then stole second. Ritchey tried to advance him but struck out on three bunt attempts. Walt Woods flied out to Harry Blake in center field to make it two out. Wagner stole third as Young delivered to Dave Wills, who drove the ball to second base where Childs fumbled it and an alert Wagner sprinted home. The Colonels won the game 13–12 to the delight of the few fans still on hand. Perfecto catcher O'Connor was so angry at the improbable turn of events that he threw the game ball out of the park and it struck a distillery building across the street.[33] The local newspaper went on at length describing the chain of events that gave Louisville their come-from-behind victory, concluding: "A team that can finish like the Colonels finished yesterday can play winning ball." Up to that point, however, winning was not common.

The Perfectos recovered the following day to whitewash the Colonels 7–0, but the improbable Wagner-led victory over Cy Young played a role in turning around the season for Louisville. By June 20, they had just 16 wins with 38 losses, but for the rest of the way they went 59–39, setting a torrid pace. Just as the Colonels were beginning to attract attention for their winning ways, the team suffered a serious blow.

On August 12, Eclipse Park, now often referred to as League Park, was heavily damaged during an electrical storm. About 3 a.m. some live wires crossed in the Western Union press box, setting the grandstand ablaze. Most of it was reduced to rubble, but the bleachers, box office and entrance were saved. The loss was set at $12,000, only partly covered by insurance. Charles Dehler, vice-president of the ball club, was one of the owners of the park which was erected in 1893 to replace the earlier Eclipse Park lost to arson.[34]

Dehler said he needed to confer with Dreyfuss, who was in Brooklyn with the Colonels, before deciding whether to install temporary seating or some sort of replacement structure.

Temporary stands were installed, but they proved uncomfortable and fans stayed away, so after a 12-game home stand concluded on September 2, Dreyfuss announced the team would play all its remaining 38 games on the road. That final game in the charred park was memorable. The opposition was Washington, a team even worse than Louisville and similarly targeted for extinction by National League magnates. The Colonels won, 25–4, driving Senators pitcher Bill Dinneen out of the pitching box in the fourth inning after he had surrendered fourteen runs, three of them homers. Dinneen switched positions with right fielder Buck Freeman who gave up 11 runs and three more homers. The game was called after eight innings because the Senators had to catch a train. "The people laughed out loud all during the eight innings of play," the *Courier-Journal* reported. "It served as a fitting windup to the local baseball season."[35]

Sporting News said the Louisville decision to install "circus seats of the cheapest kind" had been a mistake and resulted in poor attendance. It accused Dreyfuss and his fellow directors of pocketing the insurance money instead of investing in better seats. Such cynical moves by management showed the club would not be back in 1900, it charged. Meanwhile, the *Courier-Journal* complained: "The club has deserted the city for foreign and apparently greener fields." The newspaper didn't believe club assertions neither the players nor the club were for sale, that a new grandstand would be built, or that the Colonels would return for 1900. The team, it said, "deserts the city because the public would not sit for hours on hard benches in a broiling sun. The spectators, or the city, as you will, are not at fault. The desertion of the team is due to bunglesome management and nothing else; to a penny-wise and pound-foolish policy."[36]

Stung by the criticism, club secretary Harry Pulliam issued a statement defending Dreyfuss. He said the club president could have moved the team out of town immediately after the fire, but instead chose to remain and tried to accommodate fans with temporary seating. Philadelphia, Pulliam said, had made an attractive offer to play host for Louisville games. Instead, Dreyfuss gave a "fair trial" to the temporary seats but lost money on every game. "There is no reason to attribute any ulterior motives to the club officials," Pulliam said. "They are simply doing the best they can under the circumstances. The only reason for the transfer is the destruction of the grand stand." He stressed that neither the team nor its players were for sale, that a new grandstand would be erected, and that the Colonels would be back for 1900. He went on to defend Dreyfuss, saying: "He has never made anything out of baseball, and is a sportsman in the fullest sense of the word." The *Courier-Journal* reported the club lost $200 a day to play at its damaged park and that Dreyfuss could fetch $30,000 to $35,000 by selling Wagner, Clarke, Cunningham, Phillippe, Dexter, Leach and pitcher Pete Dowling. The value of the franchise was estimated at $25,000 to $30,000.[37]

The Colonels played at a blistering .690 clip throughout September, but ended the season two games below .500 with a record of 75 wins and 77 losses, good for its second consecutive ninth-place finish. The Colonels were helped substantially in their late-season turnaround by Rube Waddell, called up from Grand Rapids and Columbus where he had been sent early on. The big lefty won seven of the nine games in which he started as a Colonel while striking out 44 with an earned run average of 3.08. On October 2 in Chicago, the eccentric Waddell openly mocked opposition batters as he struck out 13 of them in a 6–1, eight-inning victory, relying on "bewildering speed and curves." He allowed only three singles. The *Chicago Tribune* reported that Waddell "laughed all through the contest, and he and his backwoods catcher, [Tacks] Latimer, jabbered and taunted the victims as they filed in a hopeless procession from the bench to the plate and back again."[38] Waddell's late-season heroics landed his image on the front page of *Sporting Life* a few days later. Dreyfuss admitted he had made a mistake in farming out the oddball hurler early in the season because he might have helped Louisville finish even higher in the standings.

In early October, National League president Nick Young reported all teams cleared a profit for the season.[39] About the same time, Dreyfuss admitted he was now willing to sell the Louisville franchise, but not for anything less than $75,000. And he was unwilling to commit to next season in the city. He said the team was $5,000 ahead of expenses before the fire, but began to lose money afterward. Weeks later he revealed the club profit on the season was a paltry $300.[40] Dreyfuss complained about the lack of patronage and that the team was underappreciated by Louisvillians.[41] The Colonels fared better than three other National League teams in 1899, despite the grandstand fire. At home, 109,319 attended games while on the road 222,145 fans watched the Colonels play for a total season attendance of 331,464. In figures released by the National League, only New York, Washington and Cleveland drew smaller crowds at 305,068, 291,013 and 270,405, respectively. Cleveland, with its roster of left-over players, attracted only 6,088 spectators in total to its home games.

It was becoming clear there would be no outcry from either Louisvillians or the newspapers if the Colonels disbanded or decamped for permanently greener pastures. Barney Dreyfuss came to realize that and was already working on another plan, this one a blockbuster. He was determined to prove professional baseball that he enjoyed so much could be a money-making venture.

8

...Another Door Opens: The Colonels and a Captain

French Lick Springs, Indiana, is not normally associated with baseball. The resort based on mineral springs is about 75 miles west of Louisville and by the late 1800s was attracting wealthy and notable guests seeking relief from gout, rheumatism and even alcoholism. It was here after the 1899 baseball season it was learned the Pittsburgh club of the National League was for sale. The source was guest John T. Brush, the crusty owner of the Cincinnati Reds, and two stories emerged about whom he told. Years later, sportswriter Fred Lieb said Brush invited Barney Dreyfuss to the resort and revealed Pittsburgh owner W.W. Kerr was discussing a possible sale to former Pirates manager William "Watty" Watkins. Brush said he'd been involved with Watkins at some point but had backed out and thought this presented an opportunity for Dreyfuss.[1] A contemporaneous press account, however, said Brush and Harry Pulliam were among the guests at the health resort and that Brush asked Pulliam why his baseball partner Dreyfuss hadn't pursued Pittsburgh. An excited Pulliam immediately placed a long-distance telephone call to Dreyfuss to share what he had learned.[2] Barney Dreyfuss soon swung into action, knowing he could count on his collaborator Pulliam.

William Warren Kerr turned 52 in 1899. He and partner Phil Auten, of Chicago, had been shareholders in the Pittsburgh Burghers of the ill-fated Players' League of 1890. Afterward, the two men began acquiring shares in the Pirates and soon gained control of the club. Pittsburgh's best finish was second, in 1893, but the rest of the time remained a second division club in the 12-team circuit. The Pirates placed seventh or eighth usually, although they reached sixth in 1896 under manager Connie Mack. Auten was a silent partner of the meddlesome and wealthy Kerr, of whom it was said, "made changing managers seem as routine as changing shirts."[3] He was notorious for a short temper and his insistence on being called "Captain Kerr, the Coffee King." A top executive at the Arbuckle Coffee Company, he fired six managers during his time with the Pirates, including Watty Watkins, who had led the Detroit Wolverines to the National League pennant and the world's championship over St. Louis in 1887. Watkins became manager for Pittsburgh in 1898 and Kerr also named him president, telling others he was retiring from baseball. But Watkins soon smelled the coffee and resigned the following May after a 7–15 start, replaced by Patsy Donovan who had managed the club before Watkins arrived. Regardless of manager or whomever he named president, Kerr invariably pulled all the strings in Pittsburgh and continued to do so. After Watkins departed, Kerr reclaimed the presidency. During the 1899 campaign Pittsburgh added some promising rookies to an otherwise rather ordinary lineup; spitballer Jack Chesbro and Clarence "Ginger"

Beaumont, a speedy outfielder with a good bat. Kerr was still trying to field a winning club, but was growing weary at his inability to succeed in that quest amid the glare of publicity.[4]

By the time of the revelation at French Lick Springs, Watkins was still talking to Kerr about acquiring shares in Pittsburgh on behalf of some interests in Indianapolis, where the Canadian-born Watkins made his baseball headquarters and fielded professional teams. He had been encouraged by Brush to look at acquiring Pittsburgh although the crusty Cincinnati magnate had backed out of any direct involvement. Watkins continued talks with Kerr for parties he declined to identify. On October 24, the *Pittsburgh Press* reported Kerr was selling the club and had already rejected offers he felt were too low.[5] Reports of Watkins meeting with Kerr and Auten and his frequent visits to Pittsburgh during October filled the newspapers in Pittsburgh. Watkins obtained an option to acquire stock in the ball club but he and Kerr couldn't agree on certain details. On October 26, after two hours of talks in his office, Kerr declared the deal was off.[6] The option he granted Watkins had expired at noon and their discussion ended after that deadline passed. If Watkins wanted to make another offer, he could, Kerr said. The newspapers reported Kerr and Auten sought cash for their shares, but Watkins preferred to extend payment for up to two years. This suggested Watkins' partners were not particularly wealthy.

Watkins returned to Indianapolis, but before leaving town he met Barney Dreyfuss at the train depot, apparently by pre-arrangement. The pair held secret talks with Kerr, from which Watkins left early to catch his train. The new discussions were deemed "unsatisfactory" and afterward Kerr announced the sale was off entirely and he'd remain president of the club.[7] A couple of days later, Watkins broke his silence about his October 26 one-on-one chat with Kerr when he stopped in Detroit on his way to his farm near Port Huron: "I had an option on the club at noon Friday. I had ready $5,000 in cash as a forfeit. I saw Mr. Kerr during the forenoon, and we talked until after noon. Then ... he informed me that my option had expired. I do not think he had any serious intention of selling at all."[8]

Watkins refused to reveal the amount he had offered Kerr and left Pittsburgh "in a bad humor," it was reported, but he wouldn't rule out a return.[9] Given Kerr's declaration he wasn't selling, the presence of Dreyfuss was attributed to other baseball business, likely the signing of Honus Wagner and Pat Flaherty, both of whom lived in Carnegie, just west of the city. The truth soon emerged. On October 29, the *Louisville Courier-Journal* reported Dreyfuss had bought the Pittsburgh franchise and would merge the Pirates with Louisville, fielding the best players from the two clubs. Harry Pulliam would act as treasurer and manager.[10] Rumors were rampant as Dreyfuss held talks with Kerr and was granted an option to purchase shares that expired on November 4. Kerr's partner Auten arrived from Chicago as negotiations continued. One newspaper story said Cincinnati's Brush was behind Dreyfuss, but other reports said Dreyfuss had sufficient funds of his own and had backers in Louisville. Kerr was seeking $75,000 for the team, it was said. The *Pittsburgh Press* saw fit to introduce Dreyfuss to its readers as "thoroughly posted on baseball affairs and has more practical knowledge of the players than any other magnate. All the deals which he has made have turned out well ... [he] is not afraid to spend money to get a good player."[11] Meanwhile, Dreyfuss declined to explain his presence in Pittsburgh or confirm any discussions were under way with Kerr and Auten. But he confided in Wagner and word quickly spread.[12] It was reported a deal had been reached with a price tag of $70,000 and several conditions.

J. Earl Wagner, owner of the Washington Senators, whose club like Louisville's was targeted for elimination by the National League, chimed in to say he'd been speaking to Dreyfuss and confirmed Pittsburgh could be Barney's for $70,000. "The Pittsburgh franchise is one of the most valuable in the league. On an investment of $70,000 Dreyfuss should realize $20,000 clean profit next season with the team he will give Pittsburgh," the Washington magnate opined.[13] Dreyfuss returned to Louisville where he soon conceded he was negotiating to buy the Pittsburgh franchise. He said Kerr owned $85,000 of the $100,000 in capital stock and it would "take a considerable sum to buy him out." Dreyfuss said he was selling his Louisville stock to raise funds and he expected the Louisville franchise to fetch from $10,000 to $12,000. He borrowed money from his cousins, the Bernheims, to whom he would again turn in another year to help him increase his stake to become sole owner.[14] He sounded optimistic. "Pittsburgh is a good ball town and with the team I can place there money will undoubtedly be made," Dreyfuss said.[15] While the suspense dragged on, Dreyfuss was asked if Harry Pulliam would remain with him. "He certainly will," he replied without hesitating. "I regard Mr. Pulliam as a most excellent baseball man, thoroughly honest and consistent, and if there is a Louisville team next year he will be with it."[16] *Sporting Life* explained their relationship this way: "Barney Dreyfuss has a high regard for Colonel Pulliam as a general all-around hustler and promoter of enthusiasm."[17] The two men had become virtually inseparable through their shared love of baseball and a determination to make it a paying proposition. Sometime earlier, both Dreyfuss and Pulliam had been named Kentucky Colonels, an honorary title conferred by the state governor to recognize noteworthy accomplishments and service to community. So here, in Pittsburgh, the two Colonels were dealing with a man who liked to be known as "Captain."

The sale was set to close on November 4 and it was reported Dreyfuss brought the Louisville club lawyer and the necessary funds to Pittsburgh to sign the necessary papers. But a hitch developed. Dreyfuss, always careful in business, wanted Kerr to assume full responsibility for any outstanding liabilities and debts incurred by the club. But the Captain balked, citing advice from his own lawyer not to sign a document dealing with that issue. "All I asked was for reasonable protection," Dreyfuss insisted afterward.[18] Disappointed, he returned to Louisville, saying he had lost "a considerable sum" by converting securities into cash to come up with the funds needed to close the deal. The amount of his loss was later said to be $1,300. Dreyfuss said there would be no further offer made and that Louisville would remain in the League.[19] It appeared the Captain was vacillating again, just as he had with Watkins. "President Kerr stated last night that he was through for good with accepting options for the club. He did not expect another buyer to bob up," the *Pittsburgh Post* reported November 5.[20] *Sporting Life* castigated Kerr for extending Dreyfuss "the same shabby treatment" he gave Watkins and said Dreyfuss was entitled to protect himself by insisting Kerr accept responsibility for club debts and liabilities.

Later in November a secret meeting of National League owners was convened in New York, where they discussed contracting to eight teams and increase competition by ending cross ownership, or syndicate control of more than one team. Outside the gathering, Kerr conceded he was willing to sell stock to Dreyfuss in exchange for the best Louisville players, but he was not interested in selling him enough shares to control the Pittsburgh franchise.[21] Reports surfaced that Kerr wanted out of baseball entirely, however, and wanted to retire as president of the Pirates, but his chosen successor had declined the post. And it was said Dreyfuss also planned to retire from the game. Rumors

8. ...Another Door Opens: The Colonels and a Captain

and speculation continued to swirl in advance of the National League's formal winter meeting December 12. The issue of contraction was again expected to be on the agenda, as was the knotty issue of how to deal with Louisville, Washington, Cleveland and Baltimore. Meanwhile, newspapers were reporting the rise of a new rival for the National League, the American League, in which baseball men from Louisville had expressed some interest.[22]

Several weeks earlier Dreyfuss and Pulliam had paid a visit to Chicago where owner Jim Hart was interested in acquiring some players from Louisville. Hart and Pulliam had developed a good relationship, although Dreyfuss and Hart remained rather wary of each other. The Louisville men let Hart make his pitch, but they concluded that even his best offer was insultingly low and they returned home.[23]

On October 31, Dreyfuss sold all his shares in the Louisville club to his fellow directors and Pulliam was elected president to replace him. In Pittsburgh, Dreyfuss and Kerr had hoped to reach a deal more palatable to National League owners than that concluded between Cleveland and St. Louis which generated opposition to cross-ownership of franchises, known as syndication. "Consolidation" was the term favored by Kerr and Dreyfuss.

On the morning of December 8, after two weeks of discussion, a deal was reached. The Pittsburgh papers focused on what the Pirates were getting, noting that for $25,000 Kerr obtained the best players on Louisville, including Fred Clarke who would become manager. They included pitchers Deacon Phillippe, Rube Waddell and Jack Chesbro, along with second baseman Claude Ritchey, catcher Chief Zimmer, utility player Tommy Leach and the versatile Honus Wagner. Lesser Pirates would be transferred to Louisville to replace them.[24] Dreyfuss had acted as a sort of middleman to help Louisville (where he still had pull, as well as associate Pulliam) unload players and Pittsburgh improve its roster while he was negotiating for shares. He'd become president of Pittsburgh, while Kerr and Auten retained just enough shares to keep control. Dreyfuss obtained his half-interest in the club for $47,000 in cash, it was revealed several months later by Francis C. Richter in *Sporting Life*.[25] The deal met with approval in Pittsburgh and some resignation in Louisville. The *Pittsburgh Post* editorialized: "This is a big deal in the baseball world, and it is commendable. Even now there are enthusiasts who are certain that the latest move is the correct one, and that Pittsburgh will be at the head during the next season."[26] In Louisville, principal shareholder Dr. T. Hunt Stucky admitted the team had lost a total of $72,000 in seven seasons, only once turning a profit. Stucky said he hoped the club would be purchased, otherwise it would continue as an independent operation at much lower cost. The *Louisville Courier-Journal* suggested if owners could fetch $20,000 for the franchise, Louisville might enter the Western League.[27] Dreyfuss, the new Pittsburgh magnate, remained in the Smoky City a few days to tidy up details there. The Louisville newspaper described him "as happy over the recent baseball transaction as the man who finds a dime in one of his old vests." It continued:

> "Just as soon as this meeting is over," he said tonight, "I will hasten to Louisville, pack my trunk, take my wife and babies and hustle back to Pittsburgh. I like the town and expect to remain there. I think we have a chance for the pennant next year. At any rate first division is certain, and by the addition of Sunday baseball by the Pittsburgh club we are sure to make money. Without meaning any disrespect to Louisville or to my recent copartners in the Colonels, I will say I am glad I am out of the Louisville Club. If they play there next year, I hope they will make money."

Player and manager Fred Clarke developed a very close relationship with Barney Dreyfuss during their many years in Louisville and Pittsburgh. He was rewarded handsomely by the diminutive owner for his on-field success, his leadership and his loyalty (Library of Congress).

Dreyfuss, usually better at diplomacy, was preoccupied with the upcoming League meeting in New York where he was expecting positive response to his purchase and a decision on the fate of the Louisville franchise.

This was a big move for Barney, whose life had changed appreciably since his arrival in Louisville nearly 12 years earlier. Aside from being a wealthy man he was now a husband and a father. During a train trip to a springtime music festival in Cincinnati in the early 1890s, the bachelor in his late '20s met a smiling, slim young woman named Florence Wolf, seven years younger than he. The youngest of 13 children in a Louisville family, Florence was a trained pianist and shared Dreyfuss's love of music. Their chance meeting led to romance and then marriage in 1894 when he was 29 and she was 22.[28] Two years later, son Samuel was born, named after Dreyfuss's father. In 1898, daughter Eleanor arrived. When Dreyfuss relocated to Pittsburgh, his children were toddlers.

At the National League's meeting in New York from December 12 to 16, Harry Pulliam announced Louisville was willing to relinquish its franchise and the Robison brothers promised to fold their Cleveland club. To assess what further contraction might be possible, a committee was established to recommend next steps to the next League meeting.[29] Washington and Baltimore remained alive for the time being. During discussion, Dreyfuss strongly supported contraction to eight teams to ensure profitability for all remaining franchises and suggested establishing a board to appraise the value of the weakest teams and buy them out.[30]

As 1899 drew to a close, Louisville correspondent John J. Saunders wrote in *Sporting Life* that the remaining investors in the Louisville club were hoping the National League would purchase the franchise for $12,500. He also described the mood in town. "In so far as Louisville for 1900 is concerned not much thought is being given to it. It seems most likely we are out of the League, and few seem to regret even that condition of affairs and the lethargy concerning next year's prospects isn't a good indication of extensive profits in a baseball investment in Louisville." After 20 years as a major league baseball town, Louisville was about to be relegated to history and no one seemed upset at the prospect.

* * *

The city to which the Dreyfuss family moved at the outset of 1900 was far different from Louisville, the latter having stagnated somewhat as it was surpassed as a trading center by Cincinnati and as a transportation hub by Chicago. Since 1880, when its population of 123,758 ranked it 16th in the nation, Louisville had grown to 205,000 but slipped to 18th. Among those cities now surpassing it was Pittsburgh, America's 11th largest metropolis with nearly a half million inhabitants when combined with Allegheny City lying just across the Allegheny River. Exposition Park, the home of the Pirates since 1891, was located in Allegheny City, which would be annexed in 1909. The Pittsburgh region was dotted with steel mills, ironworks and refineries which fueled its economy but dirtied the air, producing the nickname "Smoky City." The city provided Dreyfuss a much larger palette to prove baseball could be a profitable and successful venture.

The National League met again in New York from March 7 to 9 for one of the more significant gatherings of baseball magnates ever held. In a bid to end hostilities with New York owner Andrew Freedman for the good of all concerned, they rescinded the $1,000 fine levied on Freedman for his reaction to the League's failure to act on the anti–Semitic slur uttered by Baltimore player Ducky Holmes. And at the suggestion of Barney Dreyfuss, the owners agreed to reimburse Freedman the $15,000 in annual rent he was paying to tie up Manhattan Field to keep baseball competitors out the country's largest city. Team owners agreed to buy out the four weak links in the League in a bid to become a profitable eight-team circuit. Washington would be paid $39,000 for its entire operation and Baltimore $30,000 for its franchise, while the club reserved the right to dispose of its players for additional money. Cleveland would get $25,000 for the team and its grounds, while Louisville would receive only $10,000. The League, however, would assume Louisville's large debt, believed to be about $104,000.[31] The formal resignation of all four clubs was then accepted and League president Nick Young was asked to develop a schedule for an eight-team loop.

On another front, magnates didn't seem overly worried about Ban Johnson, who had rechristened the Western League as the American League with plans to install teams in Chicago and Cleveland. National League owners had been working on a plan for their own minor league to provide opportunities for smaller cities, but it had collapsed.[32] Perhaps it was because of their preoccupation with that plan, arrogance, or a feeling Johnson couldn't seriously challenge the League. Johnson was warned that the National Agreement, with its territorial protections, precluded his establishing teams in Chicago and Cleveland. Johnson was a formidable force they would soon realize was as arrogant and driven as any of them. The 36-year-old former sportswriter had been president of the Western League since 1893 where he had been successful by clamping down on the rowdiness which still plagued the National League. By 1897 his circuit, with teams in cities like Milwaukee, St. Paul and Kansas City, drew one million fans with several franchises outperforming National League clubs.[33] Within days of that meeting of National League magnates in New York, it was announced the American League would place a team in Chicago, despite their warnings. Johnson had reached an agreement with Jim Hart, owner of the National League's Chicago Orphans, to do so. Hart insisted Johnson abide by the National Agreement and not put another club in a National League city for five years, that he not schedule game dates to conflict with Hart's team, and that he operate in the south end of Chicago, home to many of the city's stockyards.[34] As part of the deal, apparently intended to curry favor with the National League, Johnson also agreed to buy the Cleveland ballpark from the League for $10,000. The new American League team in Chicago would be known as the White Stockings. Johnson had arranged an American League presence in both Chicago and Cleveland, which he intended to include in an eight-team loop with Milwaukee, Detroit, Indianapolis, Buffalo, Minneapolis and Kansas City. Louisville, once rumored as a potential member, was not included.

The Pirates held spring training in Thomasville, Georgia, where the Colonels had trained, and by early April they moved north for exhibition games in Memphis, Louisville and Dayton on their way to St. Louis for an April 19 season opener. About 10 days were spent in Louisville as the Pirates played intra-squad games, and with the remnants of the Colonels and other teams. Given the exit of Dreyfuss just a few months earlier, the protracted stay in Louisville was an interesting decision. In one game against Louisville, the Pirates lent the local club several of its best players and still prevailed 16–4. Only 100 spectators witnessed the mismatch. A close game was held April 4 when Pittsburgh defeated Rochester 19–10, scoring 11 runs in the ninth inning to down the reigning Eastern League champions.[35]

Crowds remained light during their stay in Louisville and the total Pirates gate amounted to less than $200, a surprise for Dreyfuss who had allocated $4,000 for spring training.[36] It was reported, however, the poor revenue wasn't causing him any grief. "He says he planted $16,000 for baseball in the Kentucky town and is willing to sink more to get the Pirates in shape for the championship season."[37] A Pittsburgh reporter noted that local baseball writers "are not throwing many bouquets at the Pirates" and were overlooking good play and focusing instead on "defects."[38] Another reporter asked Harry Pulliam about the reception his club had met in Louisville, to which he replied:

8. ...Another Door Opens: The Colonels and a Captain

The town is awfully sore on Barney Dreyfuss for taking the team away from there. The people there actually believe that Barney made a bad business move. They claim that there would have been more money in the game had he transferred the Pittsburgh team to Louisville. Very few could be induced to witness the games, and the few that did go out could see nothing good, except for the performance of the one [former] Louisville player [Tommy Leach].[39]

The Pirates opened their 1900 season in St. Louis against the newly christened Cardinals on April 19. Pittsburgh wore new blue-gray uniforms, with navy blue sweaters, stockings and collars, while St. Louis featured red togs that prompted their new name. The Pirates fielded the following lineup: leadoff hitter Ginger Beaumont, the center fielder; manager Fred Clarke in left; Jimmy Williams, the third baseman; Honus Wagner, the right fielder; Bones Ely, the short stop; Claude Ritchey, the second baseman; Pop Dillon at first; Chief Zimmer the catcher; with right-hander Sam Leever at the bottom of the order.

The game attracted 12,000 fans who saw their team blank the visitors 3–0. Aside from losing the game, Pittsburgh pitcher Sam Leever split open a finger and was sidelined. The Pirates' home opener came April 26 against Cincinnati when 11,000 fans, a local record, crammed into Exposition Park. Additional seating for 2,500 had been installed by the optimistic Dreyfuss but it proved inadequate and some fans were forced to stand in roped-off areas of the outfield. Rube Waddell started for the Pirates but he fooled few batters and his teammates displayed plenty of rust. In the sixth inning, Waddell was replaced by Jack Chesbro. Noodles Hahn kept Pirates batters in check and the Reds led throughout the game. With Pittsburgh playing poorly, 3,000 to 4,000 fans left the park. They missed an exciting finish. Going into the bottom of the ninth inning Cincinnati was winning 12–4. The crowd erupted as the Pirates scored seven runs, falling one short of tying the game.[40]

By the end of May, Pittsburgh was in fourth place, with 20 wins, trailing Philadelphia, Brooklyn, and St. Louis. Their play was uninspiring, however, especially from a team many observers predicted would be among the best that year. Honus Wagner, however, was on fire. Through 31 games he hit a League-leading .463, with 23 extra-base hits and only three strikeouts. He played well in right field and also when asked to occupy first and third base. The pitching staff performed solidly early in the season. Deacon Phillippe was 13–6 by the middle of July, while left-hander Jesse Tannehill was 11–4. Sam Leever and Rube Waddell also delivered strong performances when needed.[41] On June 19, southpaw Waddell was outstanding when the Pirates faced Chicago in the Windy City. He and Orphans hurler Clark Griffith each pitched 13 scoreless innings. Both future Hall of Famers were sharp. Waddell's speed and fast curves were countered by the devastatingly slow curves from Griffith. In the 14th inning, Waddell had two outs and two strikes on former Pirate Billy Clingman, but walked him, bringing Griffith to the plate. The Chicago hurler connected for a double to score Clingman for a 1–0 Orphans victory. Waddell had struck out 12 batters, five more than Griffith in the test of endurance.[42]

Waddell was always testing his manager Clarke who was a stickler for proper behavior, one of the many reasons Dreyfuss valued his manager so highly. Discipline was important to both men in their quest for success in baseball. Neither permitted rowdy behavior on the diamond or loose behavior away from it. Waddell, however, was a challenge and completely irresponsible, taking off on a whim and missing practice. His late-night antics were beginning to affect his performance. Clarke confronted the impulsive big lefty, but his lectures did no good. Clarke learned Waddell was playing ball every evening in front of his boarding house in the Oakland area of Pittsburgh with businessmen, and had hurt his hand while playing catcher. The manager snapped. "We all loved Rube," Clarke explained later. "But I knew I couldn't stay manager long if I let him take French leave [absence without permission] whenever he wanted. During one of his absences I went to Barney Dreyfuss and said: 'Life is too short to monkey around with this guy. Suspend him and mail him his check.'"[43] On July 7, Clarke suspended Waddell indefinitely without pay and relayed his decision to Dreyfuss who backed him up.[44] Waddell began playing with semi-professional teams in Western Pennsylvania before Connie Mack, manager of Milwaukee in the American League, persuaded him to go west on the understanding Waddell could be recalled at any time by the Pirates. In Milwaukee, Waddell won 10 games in a little more than a month, including both ends of a 22-inning doubleheader in Chicago on August 19.[45] That day, he had agreed to pitch both games if Mack would give him some time off. Milwaukee won the first contest, a 17-inning game, by a score of 3–2, and Waddell shut out the Brewers 1–0 in the second game, shortened to five innings because of darkness. Mack, one of the few managers able to understand and curb the excesses of the talented Waddell, was suitably impressed. Mack may have pulled out some of his hair, however, when he saw a *Sporting Life* report about his hurler. It said a Milwaukee-area dairy barn was struck by lightning and caught fire shortly before Waddell arrived on the scene and found the farmers "standing idly around." He promptly took charge and organized them to help save 40 cows, wagons, buggies, machinery and other items to reduce the loss. "'Rube' was badly burned on one hand while saving a wagon."[46]

Meanwhile, Wagner continued to demonstrate his hitting prowess, although by the end of June his batting average had dropped to .400. In August it reached .489 for the season during an 18-game hitting streak. Three days after that run, he started a 17-game streak and then another 11-game stretch in September. The Pirates and former Colonels began to gel by late July and were a game back of second-place Philadelphia. By mid–August they reached second and remained there until the end of the month, trailing the red-hot Brooklyn Superbas, formerly known as the Bridegrooms, by seven games. By September 1, *Sporting Life* reported: "Pittsburg continues to put out larger crowds than any city in the country. The profits to the Pittsburgh Club this year will be the largest in the history of the organization."[47] That prediction no doubt put a smile on the face of club president Dreyfuss and his secretary-treasurer Pulliam.

Waddell was recalled by the Pirates at the outset of September to bolster Clarke's pitching staff in the run for the pennant. By September 25, the Pirates were playing well as Brooklyn faltered. Dreyfuss was thrilled at the performance of the team and offered his players a bonus of $1,000 if they reached first, predicting once there they would not be dislodged. "The amount he has not given out even to the players themselves, but he will be liberal," said one report. "'I don't care for any more money,' he says, 'this season I've got money back for the year, and now I would like to win a little glory. That's the reason I want that flag.'" He also promised a $500 bonus if the team held onto second place.[48] By September 30, however, the Pirates had slipped to four games back as they dropped four of five games to lowly Cincinnati. On October 11, Waddell set a season record of 12 strikeouts in a 2–1 victory over Chicago, while allowing only five hits. The Pirates concluded their season by winning five of their last seven games to finish 4½ games behind Brooklyn, with a record of 79–60. Brooklyn's amalgamation with Baltimore had proven even more successful than the Pittsburgh-Louisville "consolidation." Three former Baltimore pitchers, Frank Kitson, Harry Howell and Joe McGinnity played a big role in winning games for the Superbas. Pittsburgh had done well, but with a better start to the season might have realized Barney Dreyfuss's dream of a National League pennant.

Individual performances by the Pirates had been impressive. Wagner had the top League batting average at .381 and best slugging average at .573. He collected the most total bases with 302, had the third best runs batted in at 100, third most hits at 201, was fifth in on-base percentage at .434 and tied for fifth with 38 stolen bases. He had been an offensive juggernaut. On the pitching side, Tannehill and Phillippe tied for second-most wins with 20, and Waddell was second in strikeouts with 130 despite his abbreviated season. He also had the lowest earned-run average at 2.37, and he and Phillippe finished 1–2 in baserunners allowed in nine innings.

Dreyfuss wasn't satisfied with second place. He wanted more. He knew his team had won 11 of their 19 meetings with Brooklyn during the season and believed they could do so again. He challenged Brooklyn's manager Ned Hanlon to a five-game post-season series in Pittsburgh to settle bragging rights about which team was actually superior. Surprisingly, Hanlon agreed and the *Pittsburgh Chronicle-Herald* donated a silver cup, valued at $500, to be awarded the champion. On October 15, the series began at Exposition Park before a disappointing crowd of 4,000. Led by the strong pitching of McGinnity and Kitson, Brooklyn took the first two games. Deacon Phillippe blanked the visitors 10–0 in game three in an impressive outing. McGinnity, the 29-year-old submarining right-hander whose 28 wins (with only 8 losses) during the season led the League, was given the ball again for game four on October 19. He led the Superbas to a 6–1 win over Pirates hurler Leever, who was relieved by Waddell, to take what was billed as the "baseball championship of the world."[49] The crowd for the final game was 2,335 and the series produced $3,000, evenly split between the two teams. The victorious Superbas gave the *Chronicle-Herald* trophy to McGinnity in recognition of his outstanding contributions to the club. For the Pirates, Wagner had been solid, batting .400 with two stolen bases.

It had been an impressive first season in Pittsburgh for Barney Dreyfuss and Harry Pulliam. The team cleared $43,000, the best-ever financial result for any Pittsburgh club.[50] The Smoky City was a serious contender in baseball, a testament to their shrewd acquisitions, trades and the complex deal that brought the best of the Colonels up the Ohio River. And better days seemed to lie just around the corner.

9

Success at Last

Much of the credit for the strong showing by the Pirates in 1900 was given to Barney Dreyfuss and his able lieutenant Harry Pulliam. Aside from the on-field success, the club's profits of $43,000 exceeded all other teams in the National League.[1] The praise for the new 35-year-old president apparently didn't sit well with Captain Kerr who had spent a decade trying to achieve what the little Kentucky Colonel had accomplished in a single season. Together, Kerr and his partner Phil Auten still held control of the team, with 501 of the 1,000 shares that had been issued. Dreyfuss owned 473, making him the largest single shareholder.

Kerr felt he'd made a mistake surrendering control of the Pirates and decided to oust the successful interloper. He sought to be acknowledged not only as Captain Kerr the Coffee King, but as the undisputed "king" of baseball in Pittsburgh. His ego would allow nothing less. While Kerr awaited the club's annual meeting in January, when he planned to vote Dreyfuss out, he and Auten devised a plan to also rid themselves of Pulliam. Auten made it known he was unhappy with Pulliam and wanted his nephew Frank Balliet to become secretary-treasurer, a job Balliet had held in the past. Pulliam felt obliged to resign, a fact first made known on December 15.[2] A few days later, just before Christmas, Pulliam told a reporter who found him in New York that he didn't know what his future held, but he appreciated his time in Pittsburgh and his baseball partner.

> Mr. Dreyfuss made a strong fight for me to hold my place—a fight, I might say, that I did not want him to make, but he wanted me to stay and I could not prevent his fighting for me. Barney stuck to me like a man and when I left he pressed his personal check for $500 in my hand as his appreciation for my efforts and his regards for me. I appreciate Barney's stand for me.[3]

Dreyfuss, as always, didn't intend to go down without a fight. He realized that he too was being targeted and looked for backers, sometimes finding them in unexpected quarters. *Sporting Life* remarked it was odd his reward for success would be his removal. "It rarely happens that a corporation makes a change in its executive head after a successful season ... from the standpoint of results, Mr. Dreyfuss deserves endorsement."[4] As the story circulated that he might soon be gone, newspapers predicted Dreyfuss and his "right bower" Pulliam wouldn't be unemployed for long. Both Andrew Freedman in New York and Frank Robison in St. Louis were said to be interested in hiring them.[5] The Pittsburgh club, known legally as the Pittsburgh Athletic Association, had been incorporated in New Jersey and the annual meeting was set for January 12 in Jersey City. It was widely expected Dreyfuss would be terminated at that time. If he survived, however, he planned to retain Pulliam, whose resignation had not yet been accepted officially.[6]

As the shareholders convened, D.I. Heyman, a lawyer from Louisville who held 10 shares and represented Dreyfuss, asserted the meeting was illegal. He said under New Jersey law, shareholders needed 20 days' advance notice of any such meeting. This requirement had not been met. "President Dreyfuss ruled that the point was well taken, and ordered an adjournment," it was reported.[7] Kerr and Auten were enraged. Their plan to depose him quickly had failed and the fight was on. Kerr hired lawyer Norman L. Rowe to act on behalf of the majority of Pittsburgh shareholders whom he insisted wanted Dreyfuss out. Within days, Rowe asked a judge to order a business meeting be held to deal with a president "who is charged with mismanagement." The judge refused to act, however, and Rowe was directed to return to court on February 19 when a panel of judges would consider the request.[8] This bought Dreyfuss some valuable time. "I am not fighting," he insisted, "the other people are doing that. I am fulfilling the duties of my office and am saying nothing." He said if forced to fight, he would. "The world loves a fighter and hates a quitter," Dreyfuss said, adding he'd respond at the proper time and place, adding ominously: "There is plenty of dirty linen to wash."[9]

The papers were full of stories about the squabble and who sided with whom and why. Meanwhile, behind the scenes Dreyfuss quietly canvassed potential investors who might be willing to help him buy out Kerr and Auten. The Coffee King and his partner soon grew weary of fighting and were likely concerned some sort of "dirty linen" might be exposed, so they offered to buy out Dreyfuss. But he flatly refused, insisting he was a buyer, not a seller. Kerr and Auten replied with a price they felt he'd never be able to accept, but Dreyfuss called their bluff and accepted, confident in his newfound investors. On February 18, the day before the fight was due in court, the *Pittsburgh Press* carried the scoop: a deal had been struck giving Dreyfuss control of the club. Kerr and Auten were out. Dreyfuss was joined by new investors who included the manager of the *Press*, Oliver Hershman, and W.K. Schoepf, general manager of the Consolidated Traction Company. The trio paid $66,150 for the shares held by Kerr and Auten.[10] Dreyfuss would remain as president, with Schoepf becoming vice-president and Harry Pulliam back as secretary-treasurer. Kerr and Auten dropped the court challenge. It was later learned Barney paid $35,000 for the additional shares he bought to gain control of the club.[11] The doughty Kentucky Colonel had won another battle, a bit less than two years after fending off the National League's attempt to squeeze the life out of his old Louisville club by stealing its Sunday dates. Many more battles lay ahead and he wouldn't shrink from any of them.

Barney Dreyfuss and other League magnates faced two serious challenges as they considered plans for the 1901 season. Players were growing militant and organizing to confront owners about their treatment, while the American League and Ban Johnson were becoming aggressive and threatening the League's monopoly.

Players had organized the Protective Association of Professional Baseball Players the previous June and begun demanding better treatment from club owners. Chief Zimmer, Dreyfuss's aging catcher, had been named president. The association was particularly upset at the practice of owners farming out players to other clubs without the player's consent, a move which often meant a cut in salary. Because of the reserve clause, they couldn't escape the clutches of owners until the owners agreed. There were fears the players might strike to back their demands, which included some limitations on the despised reserve clause itself. The players assured owners their intentions were not radical, but the magnates grew alarmed.

A meeting was held between association leaders and owners in December of 1900 at which the players pledged to help stamp out rowdyism, a move which had won wide public acceptance for Johnson's American League that year. The players sought a limit on suspensions, club payment of their medical bills for injuries, establishment of an arbitration process to settle disputes and release from their contracts 10 days after owners violated any terms in them. The players said they did not intend to wage war and promised not to deal with the American League until the National League considered their demands.[12] The owners gave the demands short shrift, however, one declaring they would "destroy the National League." With that, the talks were over and the players promptly met Johnson who was receptive to all their ideas.[13]

Sensing an opportunity to lure players while National League owners were preoccupied with internal disputes, the hard-driving Johnson declared on January 28, 1901, that the American League was a major league. He waived the longstanding salary cap of $2,400 and began ignoring existing contracts, the latter move clearly illegal. He easily attracted dozens of players who had played on National League teams. The hardest hit clubs were in the East. Players who jumped to the new circuit included stars like Cy Young, Nap Lajoic, John McGraw, Clark Griffith, Jimmy Collins and Hugh Duffy.[14] AL teams would take the field in Milwaukee, Cleveland, Washington, Baltimore, Detroit, Philadelphia, Boston and Chicago. The last three would go head-to-head with National League teams (and draw more fans than each of them).

Barney Dreyfuss wasn't overly worried about losing players to Johnson's upstart league. He believed the soon-to-expire National Agreement, under which the National League operated, would limit the AL's ability to compete. Most importantly, Dreyfuss felt he remained on good terms with most of his players throughout the time-consuming battle with Kerr and Auten. By early March he had obtained personal service agreements, or signed contracts, with nearly all them.[15] A notable exception was Jimmy Williams, who jumped to the new American League club in Baltimore. Williams had second thoughts after a few weeks and said he'd return to Pittsburgh if Dreyfuss would protect him from any legal action Baltimore might bring against him. Stung by Williams' defection, Dreyfuss refused. He was particularly incensed about how he'd lost his third baseman. Williams lived in Denver and Dreyfuss had sent him train fare to get to training camp in Hot Springs, Arkansas. Baltimore manager John McGraw intercepted Williams somewhere along the way, took him off the train and signed him for his Orioles.[16] Dreyfuss would have nothing further to do with the player and filled his position at third with Tommy Leach. Meanwhile, Honus Wagner was offered a sum estimated at as high as $20,000 to join the American League's Chicago club, but he declined, remaining loyal to the Pittsburgh owner. On March 6, Wagner signed with the Pirates for about $4,000, a nice raise.

Like other players, Wagner had been limited to the maximum permitted salary of $2,400, the cap imposed by National League owners. That cap was blown off by the arrival of the American League. Similarly, pitcher Jack Chesbro was pursued by the Boston Americans but also opted to remain a Pirate. With the exception of Williams, the team roster for 1901 would resemble that from 1900.[17] Johnson and American League owners also had been after Fred Clarke, Deacon Phillippe and Tommy Leach. It was suspected that shortstop Bones Ely was acting for the new league and relaying information about his teammates. Aside from trying to protect his players, Dreyfuss sought to guard his franchise from inroads by the American League, by renting land adjacent to Exposition Park and much older Recreation Park, several blocks to the north. He also tied up other potential sites for a baseball park in Pittsburgh, at a cost of $15,000 a year.[18] There had been rumors in the papers that Detroit was looking to move to the Smoky City.

Dreyfuss's treatment of players helped him withstand the pilfering of them by American league owners. Other teams did not fare nearly as well and may have learned a lesson from the Pittsburgh owner. "The respect and generosity with which the Pirate organization had treated its players was a major factor in keeping the Pirates intact for the 1901 season and the remainder of the baseball wars," Wagner biographer Arthur D. Hittner observed.[19] Dreyfuss had developed a bond with his men while waging war against petty tyrants locally and against the League intent on forcing him from the game he loved so much. If Dreyfuss was your friend, you knew it. If he was your enemy, you quickly learned he was a tough adversary.

Sportswriter Fred Lieb noted that Dreyfuss, unlike most of his players, drank very little and did not smoke. "He wasn't too easy to get along with, and at times could be severe, dominating, critical and stubborn," Lieb said. Some of his men found him difficult, while others befriended him. "He was also a relentless fighter. In debates in the National League council halls, his fellow club owners often accused him of being arbitrary, unreasonable and obstinate. 'Barney, you're like a bulldog,' Charles Ebbets, former Brooklyn president, once told him. 'You get hold of something, and you never let go.'"[20]

A more intimate picture of Dreyfuss was painted by Honus Wagner in a serialized telling of his life and career carried in newspapers across America in 1924. Wagner described him as a famous fan and as just one of the guys:

> He was the only club owner I ever knew who was just as rabid a fan as any rooter in the grand stand. He got in the game first as a fan and not merely to start a new business, as a lot of people think.
>
> So much has been said of Barney Dreyfuss as a wise baseball owner, a smart trader and a man who understands every angle of the baseball business that few know of him as a fan. Barney has calmed down in his later days and can take the games as they come without getting excited.
>
> Mr. Dreyfuss would travel with the team, mix up with the players and engage in any of their games, their amusements. He would mix up in practical jokes and give and take. But, above all things, he was crazy to see his ball club win.[21]

If Dreyfuss couldn't join his players on the field, he clearly enjoyed playing with them when away from it. They came to understand that for him baseball was more than just a business, that he truly loved the game and he absolutely hated losing. It was easy to grow attached to an owner like that during an era when most owners were ruthless capitalists focused on the bottom line, viewing players merely as tools to achieve profit.

Pittsburgh opened at home on April 27 in a ballpark that was part quagmire. Exposition Park, lying alongside the Allegheny River, had been inundated with floodwaters a few days earlier and was still drying out in the bright sunshine when 10,000 turned out to see the Pirates take on the St. Louis Cardinals. Both teams battled the conditions as much as each other. The infield was in good condition, but water covered part of right field. An area near the fence was described as a "frog pond" and mud was everywhere. It was agreed by the managers that any ball landing in the right-field water would be considered an automatic double. The Cardinals exploited that nicely, with five splashdowns there, but the home team "did not land one in the coveted slime."[22] The visitors managed 12 hits off Pirates hurler Jesse Tannehill and won the game 7–2. Barney Dreyfuss would remain irritated at his club's flood-prone home park for which he had just signed a six-year lease. He realized a new park was needed but put off the hunt for new grounds until another day.

Exposition Park on Pittsburgh's North Side, across from downtown, is where the Pirates were playing when Barney Dreyfuss acquired the club in 1900. It had been their home for nine years. Prone to flooding and located in a gritty part of town, the park presented constant headaches for Dreyfuss. This image is from a few years later, by which time the Pirates had relocated to their new home in the Oakland district (Library of Congress).

In the meantime, he had to endure the nickname the local press bestowed on center-right field: "Lake Dreyfuss."[23]

It was widely expected Pittsburgh would be the class of the League because reigning champions Brooklyn had lost ace Joe McGinnity to Baltimore in the American League. But the Pirates, becoming known as the Buccaneers, or "Bucs," and sometimes as the "Corsairs," had a slow start. After losing his first two games, Rube Waddell was released, considerably reducing the stress on manager Fred Clarke. Waddell was picked up by Connie Mack, manager of the Philadelphia Athletics, whose team went on to capture American League pennants in 1902 and 1905. The Pirates languished in fourth place late in May and into June. Bones Ely, the suspected American League spy, was released after 65 games and was also hired by Mack in Philadelphia. Chief Zimmer, now 40, struggled at the plate, with a .220 batting average in 69 games, but he remained strong defensively. Manager Clarke gently coaxed the best out of his men and by June 12 the Pirates reached first place, edging past the unexpectedly strong New York Giants, then kept ahead of Philadelphia to win the pennant by 7½ games. Their record was 90–49. Brooklyn finished third, 9½ games back. New York ended in familiar territory, seventh. An outstanding Christy Mathewson, playing in his first full season, won 20 games for the Giants and would play a key role in New York's success that lay ahead. Clarke batted .324 while Wagner hit .353, alternating among four positions before settling at shortstop where he'd shine for the rest of his career. Wagner continued to be a terror on the base paths, stealing home twice June 20 during a Jack Chesbro 7–0 shutout of the Giants. In that game, Wagner collected four hits. For the season, Deacon Phillippe had 22 wins and Chesbro 21.

Barney Dreyfuss had finally won it all. Ably assisted by his "right bower" Harry Pulliam, the little bookkeeper from Freiburg, Germany, had reached the pinnacle of success in baseball by dint of determination and hard work. He couldn't be happier. The fans were thrilled as well and a trophy was presented to him by the Railroad Men of Pittsburgh to mark the accomplishment.

Sporting Life hailed the Pirates winning the pennant as "the most gratifying and popular occurrence in the National League for nearly a decade...." Pittsburgh, it said, played good and consistent ball without resorting to the rowdyism and umpire-baiting employed by other teams, and "because of the universal esteem in which the Pittsburg club's square sportsman president, Mr. Barney Dreyfuss, is held." It liked the fact that after several years being held by Eastern teams, the NL pennant had gone West, for the good of the loop.[24] A week later, the same publication featured short profiles of Dreyfuss and Pulliam, along with the players. Of Dreyfuss, it said: "He is shrewd, able, liberal and a true sportsman. Of all the League magnates he is the most popular with press and public." It added that because his players like him so much "the American League has been unable to make any inroads on his team." Pulliam was credited with rolling up "unprecedented" profits for Pittsburgh in the season just ended. "Mr. Pulliam is so diplomatic as to remain popular with all of the magnates of the National League, and that is saying a great deal, considering the conflicting interests abounding in that organization."[25] In *Spalding's Guide,* editor Henry Chadwick said the success of Pittsburgh in 1901 "was mainly due to the pluck, energy and unwonted liberality of financial expenditure in securing a winning team for his club which marked the work of its enterprising and persevering president, Mr. Dreyfuss."[26]

There was no post-season competition this year, other than a few games with local clubs, and the team settled for a lavish banquet hosted by Dreyfuss at the Schenley Hotel late in October. William C. Temple, a former president and part-owner of the Pittsburgh club, acted as toastmaster. When Dreyfuss was called upon to speak he assured the large audience more success would come. "Everybody who was on the team this year has been retained, and will stick with us."[27] Soon afterward, he quietly distributed bonus checks to his players, anxious to avoid publicity. It was said they amounted to a total of $2,000 and came on top of money earned from post-season games, an October 4 field-day benefit at Exposition Park and their share of souvenir and photograph sales.[28]

The season had been a good one for the National League overall, with attendance reaching 1.9 million. It outdrew the American League, which operated in smaller cities, by about 250,000.[29] Both circuits had profited, Pittsburgh making a tidy profit while some other NL clubs lost money.[30] American League owners were in good spirits and their winter meeting saw little conflict as they approved the transfer of the Milwaukee franchise to St. Louis. Their collegial mood was in sharp contrast to the National League meeting in December, one of the more conflict-infused gatherings in recent times. Pressing business included the election of a new president because the term of Nick Young had expired. Also on tap was consideration of a plan to reorganize the League into a trust, a scheme promoted by John T. Brush of Cincinnati and Andrew Freedman of New York, both of whom, ironically, had previously opposed syndicate (or cross) ownership, during baseball contraction discussions. They found support from Boston's Arthur Soden and Frank Robison of St. Louis. Brush and Freedman said they wanted to improve the competitiveness of the League, dominated as it was by three clubs, a chronic situation that impaired profits. Under their plan, all clubs would be consolidated into one body with shares then issued to individual clubs. The trust would be administered by a Board of Regents selected by stockholders and it would have complete control over League business, including hiring managers for each club, licensing players and placing them wherever deemed appropriate. The trust was also touted as a means of fending off competition from the American League.[31] Dreyfuss and three other magnates were not sold on the plan. The Pittsburgh owner saw it as a personal attack because he feared money would be siphoned from his profitable franchise into money-losing ones. Into this controversy stepped former pitching star and Chicago president Albert Goodwill Spalding, who years earlier had proposed a trust-like organization for the League in a bid to pursue elusive profits, but his plan had gone nowhere.

Spalding no longer favored any such arrangement and argued passionately against the Brush-Freedman trust plan, saying it would be the death knell for the League. Barney Dreyfuss nominated Spalding for president to replace the ineffective Nick Young, but magnates were deadlocked through 25 votes. When the Brush-Freedman faction "bolted" from one session, the remaining delegates voted in Spalding. The freshly installed president told the press he was determined to protect the League from Freedman and would only continue as president if Freedman left. "He must be wiped off the baseball map. On his record in baseball, and I speak only of his baseball record, I openly and publicly charge Andrew Freedman with being a traitor and a marplot [one who destroys a plan through meddling]. He has done more to ruin baseball than any other four forces that ever existed in the history of the game."[32] In retaliation, Freedman initiated legal action against the League for the vote on Spalding. The turmoil prompted the *Boston Globe* to say team owners had put their organization "in a position to be pitied by all lovers of the national game. Split in two, it has the most bitter kind of a fight on hand that will drag along through the winter and finally drive some of the parties out of the business." The comment was prophetic. The following summer, Freedman announced he was leaving the game and selling control of the Giants to Brush. The deal was finalized at the club's annual meeting later. Even before Freedman left, the trust plan died for lack of support. "If the Freedman plan had succeeded, I would have wanted no more of baseball," Dreyfuss declared.[33] Spalding's presidency continued despite the legal challenge to his election, but in early April he stepped aside when a judge ruled his election was invalid. He was replaced by an executive committee headed by Brush, which would oversee League business until another candidate could be found. With all its internal strife and leadership turmoil, the National League had little appetite to wage war with its unexpectedly successful and determined rival, the American League, which was unified behind its hard-driving president Ban Johnson.

As Dreyfuss prepared for the 1902 season, he was again heartened that he lost no players to Johnson's upstart circuit, putting the Bucs in a position to repeat their pennant-winning performance of the previous year. To the roster he added catcher Harry Smith and short-stop Wid Conroy, both of whom he lured from American League teams, Philadelphia and Milwaukee, respectively. The Pittsburgh home opener was April 22, preceded by a procession through the streets and raising the 1901 pennant at Exposition

Park to the delight of 15,000 fans. Spectators were not disappointed as the Pirates scored their fourth consecutive victory, downing Cincinnati 4–3, having just swept a three-game series in St. Louis. The victories kept coming, with 15 in their first 17 games. At the end of May, they were 30–6, a comfortable 7½ games ahead of Brooklyn.

Fred Clarke later called the 1902 Pirates the greatest ball club he ever led.[34] Pittsburgh baseball historian Ronald T. Waldo has concurred, calling them "the first true powerhouse team of the 20th century ... [who] rightfully earned their place as one of the top teams in baseball's long, rich history."[35] They walked away with the pennant, fully 27½ games ahead of runner-up Brooklyn. Pittsburgh won 103 games and lost only 36, the best record in baseball history up to that point, with a winning percentage of .741. Pittsburgh had a better start than in previous seasons, reaching first place by late April and never looking back. The predations of the American League on Pittsburgh's major competitors weakened them and helped the Bucs to their second-straight championship. The Pirates were led by the hot bats of Ginger Beaumont, Honus Wagner and Fred Clarke, who batted .357, .330 and .316 respectively. Beaumont was the League batting champion. Pitching was also solid, if not exceptional. Righty Chesbro topped the League with 28 wins, while lefty Tannehill and righty Phillippe each registered 20. Newcomer Ed Doheny, a southpaw acquired in mid-season 1901 from New York, was next with 16 wins. Meanwhile, diminutive third baseman and reliable slugger Tommy Leach led the circuit in home runs, with six. Dreyfuss's men had again made him proud.

As the most successful team in the National League and featuring some of its best players, the Pirates became a target for Ban Johnson and the American League who tried to establish his league's legitimacy by luring players with fatter paychecks. The 1902 Pirates were a great team and part of their success came from their swagger. Several players developed egos, however, which made them vulnerable to flattery and left them with an inflated sense of self-worth. This was fertile ground for Johnson and his raiders. Dreyfuss endured one aggravation after another sparked by the aggressive younger circuit throughout the 1902 season. In early June, a mischievous rumor out of St. Louis said Wagner and backup catcher Jack O'Connor were jumping to the Browns in that city. The story was denied by Wagner, Dreyfuss and Pulliam.[36] Others rumors followed. Ban Johnson supposedly wanted Pittsburgh to jump to the American League, and was talking to Dreyfuss about buying the club. There was little truth to the stories obviously intended to boost the AL at the expense of its older rival. Pulliam grew weary of having to correct the record and in July told the press:

> You can state positively for the Pittsburgh management that it is done for all time with Ban Johnson and his colleagues. Under no circumstances will we form an alliance with the American League interests. The Pittsburgh club has been and will be loyal to the National organization. We cannot subscribe to a cut-throat policy, and for that reason, if no other, we would necessarily reject any overture from the American League.[37]

The aggressive Johnson wasn't giving up. He befriended Pirate Jack O'Connor, upon whom he came to rely for inside information on the team and to make contacts with players. Realizing a welcome mat did not exist for him in Pittsburgh, Johnson undertook what Dreyfuss later ridiculed as a "gum shoe mission." On August 20, Johnson and his vice-president, Charles W. Somers, launched a clandestine bid for Pittsburgh players. The AL men arrived by train from Cleveland and went to the Hotel Lincoln. There, Somers registered as "J. A. Benham of Saginaw, Michigan," while Johnson kept out of sight and then joined Somers in their room. They met with several members of the Pirates brought by O'Connor. Johnson offered them attractive contracts for a team he said the AL would establish in Pittsburgh for 1903. Meanwhile, Dreyfuss and Pulliam had been tipped something was afoot and rushed to the hotel to confront the American League honchos. Somehow, word they were on their way reached the interlopers. Somers fled abruptly, leaving Johnson to escape by way of a freight elevator while hiding among garbage cans. The pair reunited on the train out of town. The episode did nothing to improve Dreyfuss's view of Johnson or his league. The moment he learned of O'Connor's role in the caper, Dreyfuss released him, explaining: "I will not stand for any treachery or disloyalty from anybody while in my employ. No player can be a stool pigeon for the American League and draw salary from the Pittsburgh Club at the same time."[38]

Johnson was not done trying to filch talent from the Bucs. A few days after the failed "gum shoe" mission, Johnson paid a visit to Worcester, Massachusetts, where first baseman Kitty Bransfield was recovering from a leg injury suffered that same month. Bransfield had already agreed to a contract with Dreyfuss for the next season, but had not yet signed it.[39] Dreyfuss had learned from sources that Johnson was after Bransfield and sent Harry Pulliam to see the infielder and ensure his loyalty. On his way to Worcester, Pulliam discovered he was on the same train as Johnson. He sneaked out of his overnight berth to Johnson's where he found the American League president's shoes and hid them, according to one story. In the morning, Pulliam had a dandy head start for Bransfield's place that meant Johnson would again come up empty-handed.[40]

He learned pitchers Jesse Tannehill and Jack Chesbro, whose excessive salary demands he had rejected, had also signed American League contracts for 1903 and several more Pirates were likely to do so. Talk of a franchise in Pittsburgh eventually fizzled, with a suggestion it might be resurrected the following year. Chesbro, Tannehill, O'Connor and Conroy were instead assigned to the franchise being transferred from Baltimore to New York. Tommy Leach joined them, but had second thoughts. He returned the money and told Dreyfuss he preferred to remain in Pittsburgh. Barney retained a soft spot for the little slugger and agreed to keep him. Wagner stayed loyal to Dreyfuss despite lucrative offers he received during the season. "The National League is good enough for me and the treatment I have received from the Pittsburgh club is such that I have no desire to go elsewhere," he explained. "We have had the best there is in the land under Mr. Dreyfuss and I am going to stick by him."[41] Wagner biographer Arthur D. Hittner doubted the star was completely altruistic, saying: "That he opted to stay with Pittsburgh was probably attributable as much to his love for Carnegie [his nearby hometown] as to his genuine loyalty to Dreyfuss, Pulliam and Clarke."[42]

During the season, Exposition Park continued to exasperate the Pittsburgh owner. On July 4, the city held its largest-ever Independence Day celebrations with guests who included President Theodore Roosevelt. About 600,000 watched the parade in which Roosevelt was featured. He gave a speech at Schenley Park and attended a banquet, but did not see the game at Exposition Park. Had he done so, he would have needed rubber boots because it was waterlogged from recent rain. Crowds of more than 10,000 attended each game of the holiday doubleheader against second-place Brooklyn. Playing conditions for the first game were poor because city sewers had backed up, leaving water that was ankle-deep in right and center fields. In the first game, the Dodgers were blanked 3–0. Water continued to rise and by the second game it was knee-deep in the outfield, but the game went on. A ground rule was adopted that any fair ball landing in water would be ruled a single. In the ninth inning, center fielder Beaumont thrilled the crowd when he stretched high in the air to catch a two-out fly ball and plunged into the lake surrounding him.[43]

Dreyfuss had considered other possible venues for a ball field, but planned to take his time to get it right. He had five more years to run on his lease with the Pittsburgh and Western Railroad, a division of the Baltimore & Ohio system. So it came as a surprise that fall when the railroad announced it wanted to expand its freight yards onto the site and was seeking a municipal ordinance to do so. This would leave the Pirates homeless. Rumors suggested that once the Pirates were evicted from Exposition Park they might be replaced there by an American League team in a bit of skullduggery. Dreyfuss tried to sound nonplussed about any potential competition. "There is not room here for two clubs and the best way to settle the matter once and for all is to have a fight," he said, adding, "I will devote my time to trying to improve the team, which will win or lose the fight for popular approval."[44] Either the railroad changed its mind or the ordinance wasn't granted, because Dreyfuss and his Pirates remained at their Exposition Park home until 1909.

Sporting Life reported Pittsburgh had been the most lucrative National League franchise during 1902, followed by New York, Chicago and St. Louis. It provided no specific numbers as it noted Brooklyn broke even, while Boston and Philadelphia were "heavy losers."[45] In attendance, Pittsburgh attracted 243,826 fans, placing third behind New York and Chicago. Overall, National League attendance reached 1.68 million, down about 240,000 from 1901, while the American League reported 2.2 million, an increase of more than 500,000. Stories persisted, however, that the new league exaggerated attendance figures at some parks to boost public perception of its acceptance.

A post-season series was devised in which the Bucs played a team of all-star players from the American League, called the "All Americans." The stars included pitcher Cy Young of Boston, leader of his league with 32 wins, who led his team to the pennant, along with Cleveland infielder Nap Lajoie, holder of the American loop's batting crown with an average of .378. Aside from some additional bragging rights, the post-season test was expected to be a lucrative venture for everyone. On the eve of it, however, Dreyfuss released the trio of Chesbro, Tannehill and outfielder Lefty Davis, as punishment for their having signed contracts for 1903 with Johnson and company. Spitballer Chesbro, his 28-game winner, begged to participate, but Dreyfuss stood firm. He relied on Sam Leever and Deacon Phillippe to carry the pitching load in the series that began October 7 in Pittsburgh. The Pirates won the first game 4–3, despite a strong effort by Young. The next day, they whitewashed the All Americans 8–0 as Phillippe allowed only three hits. The series moved to Cleveland where a scoreless tie was called after 11 innings. A fourth game was held the following day and the all-stars picked up their only win, 1–0, with Young earning the shutout. Pittsburgh took the honors in what editor Francis C. Richter in *Sporting Life* called "the nearest approach to a world's championship this fall."[46]

This marked the close of another gratifying season for Dreyfuss, Pulliam, the Pirates and baseball fans in Pittsburgh. The on-field campaign had again been won and he'd need to replace his two top pitchers to win a third pennant, but Dreyfuss was already working on that. In the meantime, more battles loomed in the corridors of power in the National League.

For those hostilities, Barney Dreyfuss was also ready.

10

1903: Making History

Stories that the American League planned to install a franchise in Pittsburgh continued to appear in newspapers that fall of 1902, in the prelude to the National League meeting on December 9. Ban Johnson said it made sense to have AL teams in both Pittsburgh and New York. A group of businessmen led by Charles J. Pedder and including Coffee King W.W. Kerr and his partner Phil Auten, had supposedly lined up investors and found a suitable site for ball grounds in the West Oakland area of the city. Kerr and Austen regretted their sale to Dreyfuss and wanted back into the game, this time as competitors. It was rumored the new group would acquire the Detroit franchise and transfer it to the Smoky City. Publicly, Dreyfuss again scoffed at the notion of a competitor, saying Pittsburgh couldn't support two major league teams. "I wouldn't lift a finger to stop them," he told the *Pittsburgh Press*. "I know that if they do come in there'll be a funeral later on and we'll be the pallbearers."[1] But if he had to fight, he would.

In mid–November Ban Johnson said his league was proceeding with its plans for a franchise in New York to challenge the National League Giants and he thought it best to defer considering any move into Pittsburgh for at least another year. Detroit would stay put and the focus was on New York.[2] Despite Johnson's stance, stories continued to circulate that the Pirates might still face an American League challenger for 1903. By early December, Johnson's vice-president, Charles Somers, said he favored Pittsburgh for a new franchise after he was lobbied by Pedder and his group.[3] Plans for Pittsburgh were shelved, however, when the American League owners met and took no action. Their priority was potentially lucrative New York and the task of finding suitable grounds there. They succeeded and the franchise would become the New York Yankees.

The sale of controlling interest in the New York Giants by Andrew Freedman to Cincinnati's John T. Brush was formally approved at New York's annual meeting. Brush paid about $200,000, much of it raised from selling his Cincinnati franchise to local interests. Freedman was out of baseball for good, much to the relief of fans, observers, scribes and other owners. Brush had already hired as his manager John McGraw, a move that annoyed Ban Johnson who had suspended McGraw as manager of the American League's Baltimore Orioles for rowdy play by his team. The best Orioles had been lured to New York to reunite with McGraw. Johnson retaliated by taking over the carcass of the Baltimore franchise and moving it to New York to compete with Brush's Giants.

With Freedman out of the picture, Dreyfuss had an opportunity to expand his influence in the National League where he had assumed the role of schedule maker, doing his best to be fair to all teams in allocating holidays, and ensuring schedules made sense and that needless (and costly) travel was minimized. He and Harry Pulliam made a point of getting to know August "Garry" Herrmann, the new president in Cincinnati. Herrmann, whose partners included Cincinnati Mayor Julius Fleischmann, paid $150,000 for his share of the Reds.[4] The Pittsburgh men felt Herrmann might become a valuable ally for them in upcoming business, particularly in their newfound effort to promote a peace treaty between the rival leagues. Pulliam and Dreyfuss wanted mutual respect for player contracts to end the raiding by Johnson and Brush and travelled widely to line up support among National League owners.[5] Pulliam conferred with Johnson and several of his American League magnates in New York, although no one was willing to reveal the topic discussed.[6]

On the eve of the December 9 National League meeting, a report said Dreyfuss planned to "cut a large figure" at the gathering. "Barney has a scheme, details of which are kept as secret as the key to cipher code of the secret service department," it added. He had spent time in Cincinnati with then visited Jim Hart in Chicago before returning to Cincinnati. It was speculated his agenda included promoting the election of former Pirates owner W.C. Temple as National League president and that he opposed plans by John T. Brush to establish an executive board. Dreyfuss had already lined up support from Cincinnati, Chicago, Philadelphia and Brooklyn to oppose the Brush plan.[7] At the League meeting, Herrmann's suite proved to be a popular gathering place. He was lobbied there by both the Brush and Dreyfuss factions as he tried to feel his way as a newly christened League magnate. Frank Robison, usually a supporter of Brush, announced he was tired of losing money and was inclined to try supporting the successful Dreyfuss in League politics.[8] For his part, Herrmann eventually sided with Dreyfuss.

League magnates adopted the latest playing schedule developed by Dreyfuss for 1903, which included Sunday dates for the first time in history for Philadelphia and Boston. The question of electing a new president to replace Al Spalding then arose. W.C. Temple of Pittsburgh had decided he didn't want the job after all and neither did former player John Montgomery Ward. The magnates then unanimously elected Harry Pulliam. "I am for Pulliam," Herrmann, the new Cincinnati president declared. "because he likes everybody and everybody likes him." Pulliam's charm offensive had succeeded. Chicago president Jim Hart joked: "We had to weaken Pittsburgh so we took its most valuable man."[9] As for Dreyfuss, he was restrained, saying, "I am sorry to lose Harry, but the League needed him." Upon seeing his friend elected, however, it was said Dreyfuss had wept.[10] Pulliam insisted he would not assume the post if the vote was not unanimous. Even John T. Brush, who originally opposed him, backed the dapper and personable Pulliam who began brokering a peace deal between the League and its upstart rival. Dreyfuss said Pulliam was just what the league needed at that moment in history. "Barney Dreyfuss realized that two leagues existing in harmony was the best solution to insure that baseball had a long, healthy life," it has been said.[11] A peace accord would help his Pittsburgh franchise continue to prosper. He knew Harry Pulliam had the people skills necessary to reconcile the warring factions.

There was a grudging consensus among the National League owners that peace talks should be considered with the American League on the eve of its move into New York. Herrmann sent a letter to Ban Johnson proposing discussions begin in Cincinnati, aimed at ending the baseball war. The Cincinnati owner and Johnson were well known to each other, Johnson having been a sportswriter and editor for a Cincinnati newspaper for nearly a decade ending in 1895 when his baseball duties became onerous. The two men had often socialized. Dreyfuss and Herrmann would play a key role on behalf of the National League in the talks that soon followed.[12] Both sides had grown tired of fighting so the discussion proved successful. The older loop agreed to recognize the American League as a legitimate, and equal, major league. Outstanding disputes surrounding players were resolved and the leagues agreed to respect each other's contracts. The American League would proceed with its plans for a team in New York, the Highlanders, but not establish one in Pittsburgh, suggesting Dreyfuss had been persuasive. Brush was unhappy he'd face new competition but that Dreyfuss would not. He wanted the lucrative metropolis to himself and resented the obvious clout now wielded by Dreyfuss. "That Dreyfuss is a smart fellow," Brush complained. "It's all right for me to have to buck an American League club on Manhattan Island, so long as he is saved any opposition in Pittsburgh."[13] At one point, Brush pursued a court injunction to prevent Pulliam and the league from ratifying the deal. But once he was allowed to vent his feelings in a minority report, he abandoned a fight he was bound to lose. As part of the agreement, a three-member National Commission was established to oversee the two leagues, chaired by Herrmann along with the presidents of both circuits. It would focus on carrying out terms of the new National Agreement, dealing with the interaction with minor leagues and enforcement of player fines and suspensions. Thus ended what baseball historian Ronald T. Waldo dubbed "one of the most stubborn fights in baseball history."[14] Dreyfuss had played a key role in the peace deal achieved by his trusted friend Pulliam. The Pittsburgh magnate had won yet another war, his friend Harry was now president, and Dreyfuss's influence over his fellow magnates had grown with the departure of Freedman and the reduced influence of Brush.

Political battles were one thing, but ensuring continued success for the Pirates on the field and at the box office remained vitally important. As usual, Dreyfuss began signing players early in the off-season and was praised for his use of option clauses to extend one-year contracts an extra year. *Sporting News* described it as a "sensible policy" to make contracts legally and morally binding for a second year.[15] His immediate need was for pitchers to replace Chesbro and Tannehill who together had won 48 games for the Bucs in 1902. Fred Clarke had used basically five pitchers during that season, but a dozen would see action in 1903. Bill "Brickyard" Kennedy, a right-hander formerly of the Giants was signed and would deliver a 9–6 season, performing below expectations. To find more pitching, Dreyfuss turned once again to his "dope book" to find talent mentioned in sporting publications, newspapers or by his network of contacts. He signed Cy Falkenberg, from the University of Illinois, Bucky Veil, from Bucknell University who was playing semi-pro ball in Altoona where Dreyfuss found him, and Irvin "Kaiser" Wilhelm from the Southern Association.[16] All were right-handers but the most successful of them, Veil and Wilhelm, won only five games. Leever and Phillippe were back and would post 25 wins apiece. Leever would have the lowest earned run average in the League at 2.06 and highest winning percentage (.781). Aside from the pitching staff, the rest of the roster from 1902 remained largely intact.

One of the last daring raids for players before the peace accord was signed between the two major leagues involved Honus Wagner. Pitcher Clark Griffith had been named manager of the New York Highlanders for 1903 and was on the hunt for talent. He set his sights on Wagner and, armed with a wad of American League money, was determined to sign the Pittsburgh star. In his syndicated life story published many years later in *Sporting News,* Wagner described Griffith arriving in his hometown during a snowstorm.

Griff didn't know me and I was driving along the snowy streets in Carnegie in my sleigh. I saw a man trying to buck the drifts and I stopped and asked if I could help. He said he was Clark Griffith and he was looking for Honus Wagner.

I told him I was Wagner, but he almost didn't believe me. I finally convinced him when I stepped out of the sleigh and showed him my bow legs, my trademark. That clinched my identity.

I took Griff to my home and he gave me his proposition, saying he was prepared to offer me $20,000 to sign for one year. I was making $3,000 with Pittsburgh and $20,000 seemed like a lot of money. I told Griff I didn't think there was that much money in the world. He calmly pulled out 20 $1,000 bills and I must admit it was tempting. But I told Griff I was perfectly satisfied where I was and that Barney Dreyfuss had treated me fine.

Later, when Barney heard the story, He came out to see me. He always used to say the American Leaguers made their offers in stage money, but this was the real thing.[17]

Wagner and Dreyfuss enjoyed a special relationship over the course of their 21 years together in Louisville and Pittsburgh. In the newspaper series about his life, Wagner explained why he wouldn't desert Dreyfuss for more money. "Barney Dreyfuss was one of the smartest baseball men in my time and my truly great friend." He said they never had a contract dispute. "He'd call me up in the winter and say my contract was ready. I'd come downtown to Pittsburgh and he'd hand me a blank contract, telling me to fill in my own figures. But I always signed a blank contract." Wagner said he never worried what number Dreyfuss would insert and seldom knew the actual amount until he received his first paycheck in the spring. "I knew he was fair and a square shooter. He always treated me fine and I never had any complaints." Wagner's sentiments were shared by many other Pirates, so there were relatively few defections or salary disputes.

The lineup for 1903 was Wagner at shortstop, Kitty Bransfield at first base, Claude Ritchey at second, Tommy Leach at third, Fred Clarke in left field, Ginger Beaumont in center, and Jimmy Sebring, added to the roster late in 1902, in right. Behind the plate, catching duties were shared by Eddie Phelps and Harry Smith. The Pirates opened the 140-game season on the road in Cincinnati where they swept four games from the Reds. Then it was home to Pittsburgh for their April 21 opener against the St. Louis Cardinals. Exposition Park was crammed with a record-setting crowd of 18,000 with about 3,000 fans standing in the outfield behind ropes. The National League pennant for 1902 was raised and new League president Harry Pulliam, a familiar face, was guest of honor. Deacon Phillippe had a poor outing and was replaced by newcomer Falkenberg in the sixth inning. The Bucs scored two runs in the bottom of the ninth but it wasn't enough to catch the Cardinals who won 9–8.

Wagner started the season with a bang, hitting everything in sight, his batting average reaching .429 after the first 10 games before tapering off. Jimmy Sebring, the new right fielder, endeared himself to fans on April 23 at Exposition Park when his speed and daring saw him turn two long hits into inside-the-park homers against the Cardinals. The Pirates slipped from first place to second, then third where they were lodged from mid–May to mid–June. Strong hitting compensated for weaker pitching this season, with Wagner, Beaumont, Clarke and Leach providing much of the offense. During a game in May against Cincinnati at Exposition Park, Wagner unsuccessfully tried to steal second base and collided with second baseman Jack Morrissey who claimed Wagner was trying to spike him. The two men tangled as Cincinnati players surrounded them and threatened Wagner. The umpire ejected the Pittsburgh star and League president Pulliam suspended him for three games after seeing the umpire's game report, a move that drew no protest from Pulliam's former team.[18] Later that same month, Pulliam suspended new Pirates hurler Doheny for three games for inciting the crowd in New York when Pittsburgh defeated the Giants 3–2 in a tightly contested game. Doheny struck two Giant batters in the back with pitches and later threw his bat toward the catcher who was chasing his infield pop-up. The crowd erupted and a police escort was needed to get the increasingly unstable Doheny out of the park. Pulliam had promised to show no favoritism as League president and he was living up to that.

During the first week of June while Pittsburgh occupied third place, their pitchers rolled off six consecutive shutout victories, a major league record, all at Exposition Park. The whitewashes came to an end, but the wins kept coming. The Bucs won 15 straight games, including the six shutouts, which propelled them to first, a position they would not relinquish for the rest of the campaign.

An ugly incident occurred June 26 in New York that strained relations between Pirates president Dreyfuss and League president Pulliam. Fred Clarke was brutally beaten by Giants catcher Frank Bowerman before the game. The pair got into an argument that turned physical in a deserted office where Clarke was left battered and bruised. The Giants won the game 8–2 behind the arm of Christy Mathewson. Fred Knowles, the club secretary for the Giants apologized for the incident but Dreyfuss wasn't satisfied. Furious, he demanded Pulliam take action against New York. But Pulliam refused to get involved, angering his old associate even more. The day after the assault on Clarke, the Pirates earned some revenge on the field, winning 4–2, with the winning run scored, ironically, by the bruised Clarke. The crowd that day was the largest ever to witness a baseball game: 32,240.[19] The high-flying Pirates invariably drew well in New York, which provided a big boost for the bottom line of both clubs and the League.

Pittsburgh was pursued by New York, whose Mathewson always seemed to best Wagner and company, and by Chicago, but both challengers fell short. The improvement of New York under John McGraw during his second year as Giants manager was dramatic. One of his former Baltimore players, Roger Bresnahan, batted .350 and his former Orioles pitcher Joe McGinnity had 31 wins, one more than Mathewson. The Giants finished 6½ games back of Pittsburgh and did well at the gate despite the new competition from the Highlanders. New Giants owner John T. Brush was a happy man, although he hid it well.

The Pirates were League champions for the third year in a row. Wagner returned as the League batting champion with a .355 average, Clarke was just behind with .351, Beaumont had .341 and Tommy Leach, .298. Even pitcher Brickyard Kennedy contributed to the offence, with an average of .362 in his 58 at-bats. Pitching hadn't been quite as strong as in 1902, but Leever and Phillipe managed 25 wins, followed by Doheny with 16. The latter hurler was a tragic case. Doheny was plagued by demons. He had won 16 games for the Bucs in 1902 and was on track to do even better in 1903, but after a 12–6 start his behavior grew increasingly bizarre. He clashed with some of his teammates and believed detectives were following him. He left the team without permission in late July amid reports he was not well. After a few weeks at home in Massachusetts he returned and improved his record to 16–8 before his mental issues again overwhelmed him in late September. He was granted a leave of absence by Clarke and Dreyfuss and was taken back to Massachusetts and placed in the care of a doctor.[20]

After the season ended, Pulliam said profits amassed during the season were "simply enormous." New York's came to $100,000, while Pittsburgh's increased to $60,000 and

Chicago reported $50,000.[21] Both the revenue and attendance for New York were the best in the history of that city, Pulliam noted. Despite the fact three of its eight clubs failed to make money, the new president gushed that "the old National League is now in better shape financially than at any time in its history."[22] Dreyfuss played a key role in the turnaround and while some of his fellow owners might resent his success, he had become a powerful figure in baseball, less than five years after some of them tried to force him out of the game he loved.[23]

Barney Dreyfuss was always looking ahead and he welcomed the opportunity to play the first-ever pennant-winners of the American League, the Boston Pilgrims, most often known as the Boston Americans. As soon as it became apparent the Pirates and Americans were likely to win their respective titles, baseball writers began suggesting they meet in a post-season series to determine a "world's championship." The Americans, led by 28-game winner Cy Young, had taken the AL pennant by 14½ games over Connie Mack's Athletics. His fellow hurlers Bill Dinneen and "Long Tom" Hughes had 21 and 20 wins respectively. Boston was led by manager Jimmy Collins, a stand-out third baseman and future Hall of Famer. The team's top batter was Patsy Dougherty with an average of .331 while power hitter Buck Freeman led the AL with 13 home runs and 104 runs batted in.

As early as August 10, American League president Ban Johnson was talking about seeing Boston and Pittsburgh, then comfortably leading their leagues, face each other in a post-season series. He said he had faith in Collins and his boys "holding their own" against the National League champions.[24] At the National League, president Harry Pulliam felt a post-season series would not only cement the peace agreement between the two leagues but draw spectators to see a battle for baseball superiority. In New York, however, John T. Brush said he'd never let the Giants play the "invaders" in a post-season series. "I am not in sympathy with the American League or its methods and will refuse to aid

A game played at Exposition Park in about 1904. The park was situated alongside the Allegheny River, which often overflowed its banks, and near the steel mills and foundries of Pittsburgh, which fouled the air. It didn't take long for club owner Barney Dreyfuss to pursue a new home, eventually settling in Oakland, three miles east of downtown (Library of Congress).

them in the advertising they are looking to get out of a series with us." Besides, he said, the public "will be satiated with baseball and be glad of a rest" by end of regular season play.[25] Barney Dreyfuss had no such reticence and he and Boston president Henry Killilea were having exploratory talks by early September.[26] Killilea, a former part-owner of the Milwaukee Brewers, had helped Johnson establish the American League and in early 1902, Killilea headed a group that paid about $60,000 to purchase the Boston club from Charles Somers. A hiccup came September 14 when it was reported Pittsburgh might be unable to play a post-season series. "The crippled condition of the Pirates, and the peculiar actions of pitcher Eddie Doheny, are said to make it doubtful whether the series will be played."[27] Wagner injured his finger and then his knee, missing several games late in the season. Several other players including Fred Clarke, Ginger Beaumont and Tommy Leach were recovering from injuries. Sam Leever hurt his pitching arm while skeet shooting and would see only limited duty. Doheny remained at home, so the pitching ranks were rather thin for a team considering post-season play. But Dreyfuss couldn't resist seeking glory as "world champions" and his talks continued with Killilea, despite the outspoken reservations of magnates like Brush. The National League champions were expected to prevail, but if the American League won, it would gain the credibility Johnson desperately sought. There was a risk, but Dreyfuss was willing to take it. He felt it would be good for baseball.

On September 16, Dreyfuss and Killilea agreed to a best-of-nine series beginning October 1 in Boston with three games, then to Pittsburgh for four and back to Boston for the final two games, if needed. The agreement specifically stated the series could not be called off and that only players who were on their club roster as of September 1 could participate. Receipts from the series would be divided equally. Umpires were to be Hank O'Day of the National League and Tom Connolly of the American League.[28] Trouble soon loomed when the Boston players threatened to strike. Killilea, a lawyer who still lived in Milwaukee, had contracts with his players that expired September 30. They wanted their club's entire share of projected proceeds from the series or they would walk out. Anxious to proceed, Killilea extended all player contracts two weeks and said he'd split with them the club's share of receipts from the series. Contracts for the Pirates expired October 15 and Dreyfuss and Clarke promised players they'd receive the entire Pittsburgh proceeds from the series if they won.[29]

With preliminaries out of the way, it was time to play for a world championship, the first since the final National League-American Association post-season tilt in 1890, when Louisville met Brooklyn. No champion was declared back then because the series ended in a 3-3 tie due to bad weather. The previous year, the NL's New York Giants had downed the AA's Brooklyn Bridegrooms. So no team could claim the honor of world champions since the Giants of 1889.

October 1 was a warm and sunny Thursday when the series opened at Boston's Huntington Avenue grounds. The crowd of 16,000 far exceeded the park capacity of 9,000 and fans were allowed into roped-off areas of the outfield. Deacon Phillippe faced Cy Young in the much-anticipated opener. Phillippe prevailed, striking out 10 Boston batters as the Bucs went up 7-0 before weakening in the seventh inning and giving up two runs. Boston added another in the ninth, but the visitors came away with a convincing 7-3 victory. The following day, before 9,415 fans, Sam Leever, still nursing his sore arm, took the mound for the Pirates, facing off against Bill Dinneen. Boston's Patsy Dougherty scored an inside-the-park homer in the first inning, his first of two home runs that day.

Bucky Veil replaced Leever early on and did well but Dinneen threw a three-hit shutout as he faced 29 batters, two over the minimum. He struck out 11 Pirates and the Americans won 3–0. Game Three was on Saturday when 18,801 fans flocked to the park, the largest crowd of the series. Spectators more than 20 deep were held back by ropes in the outfield and hits into their midst were deemed ground-rule doubles. Phillippe was back on the mound and the Pirates won 4–2. Game Four was scheduled for Monday in Pittsburgh but it was rained out so the series didn't resume until Tuesday, October 6, when an unexpectedly light crowd of 7,600 appeared at Exposition Park. Fred Clarke took advantage of the extra time off to again turn to Phillippe who faced Dinneen. Neither pitcher was particularly effective, Phillippe allowing nine hits and Dinneen 12. For six innings the game was close and either team could have prevailed. The Pirates, leading 2–1, scored three runs in the seventh when Beaumont and Leach tripled. Then Boston replied with three runs in the top of the ninth to come within a run of the Pirates, but a tired Phillippe held on. He left the tying run on base in the ninth as Pittsburgh won 5–4 for a 3–1 lead in games. His admirers, and there were many that day, rushed onto the field, hoisted Phillippe on their shoulders and paraded him around the park. This marked a high point in the series for Pittsburgh which needed just two more victories to claim the world championship.

Game Five was October 7 when a crowd of 12,322 filled Exposition Park. Hits into the crowd standing behind the outfielders were considered ground-rule triples. Boston exploited that fully as they faced aging Brickyard Kennedy on the mound. Cy Young was back for Boston and the game remained scoreless for five innings. Young managed to strand some of the best Pirates that day on base, while allowing six hits in all. Kennedy had a bad sixth, giving up six runs while behind him Wagner, Clarke and Leach made uncharacteristic errors. Four more Boston runs crossed the plate in the seventh when Gus Thompson (2–2 on the season in five appearances) relieved Kennedy and the Americans rolled to a lopsided 11–2 win. Kennedy and Thompson had surrendered 13 hits in all, including five triples into the crowd. Boston finally had its second win. Kennedy's disappointing appearance was his last game as a professional. It was his 36th birthday.

For Game Six, Clarke went with sore-armed Leever against Dinneen in a rematch of game two. Despite his bad wing, Leever pitched reasonably well and both pitchers allowed 10 hits. But Boston's hitting came in timely bunches and the visitors won 6–3 to tie the series. The cold weather seemed to hurt the Bucs more than Boston as more errors were made by the Pirates. Because of the cold, the seventh game was postponed a day to Saturday, October 10. The delay again helped Phillippe, the ace of the series for Pittsburgh. This final game at Exposition Park attracted 17,038 fans praying for another Phillippe victory, 5,000 beyond the park's official capacity. Beforehand, Phillippe's admirers gave him a diamond stickpin along with their thanks. As sportswriter Fred Lieb suggested, the thoughtful gift may have jinxed Phillippe. He was up against Cy Young again and this time the Boston hurler bested him, the Americans winning 7–3 to lead the series. Again, Boston batters took advantage of the ground rule that hits into the crowd standing behind the outfielders were considered triples, doing so five times this particular chilly afternoon.

The Pirates still held out faint hope southpaw Doheny might return to their lineup and Clarke had sent his uniform to his home in Andover, Massachusetts, to let him know his teammates were thinking of him. But the pitcher misunderstood the gesture completely, thinking it meant his career had come to an end. After the Pirates lost at home on October 10, he became agitated and his doctor and male nurse were summoned by his wife. Doheny blamed the doctor for keeping him out of the big series. The nurse was able to calm him, but suddenly Doheny lashed out, savagely knocking him unconscious with a cast iron stove leg. Doheny was taken into custody by police. He wasn't going anywhere but to an asylum.[30] Barney Dreyfuss expressed sorrow to Doheny's wife at the tragic turn of events. "We lose a great pitcher in him," he said. "I was in hopes he would come around all right for next season. Doheny I considered as good a left-hander as there is in the country when he was in condition."[31] Doheny died in a state mental hospital 13 years later.

Rain delayed Game Eight in Boston until October 13, a Tuesday when only 7,455 fans appeared at the Huntington Avenue grounds. The overworked Phillippe was called on again by Clarke and he faced Dinneen. Phillippe established an all-time record for starts in a world series, with five. He pitched decently but Dinneen was at the top of his game, allowing only four hits compared to eight by Phillippe. Dinneen's speed and sharp-breaking curves fooled Pirate batters. Behind Phillippe, the defense was poor with three errors committed to none for Boston. Clarke had hurt his leg in the last game in Pittsburgh and Wagner, mired in a hitting slump and limping because of his injured knee, managed his first hit in 14 times at bat. During the eight games his batting average was .222. The game was scoreless until the bottom of the fourth when Boston plated two runs, adding another in the sixth as Dinneen kept Pittsburgh off the score sheet. Wagner, his woes persisting, ended the game by striking out. The Americans won, 3–0, making history by claiming the title of first modern "world series" champions.

Aside from offering congratulations, manager Clarke had little to say about the heartbreaking loss. Barney Dreyfuss was gracious, saying Boston won on merit, adding, however, "I wish we had had our full string of pitchers. I say this, not to detract, but in simple justice to my own. I am so proud of them as if they had won every game of the series."[32]

In *Sporting Life,* editor Francis C. Richter observed the lame arm of Leever and departure of Doheny had left Pittsburgh "practically pitcherless" and the Pirates could have been forgiven for declining to play. Regardless of who won the series, Richter said, baseball had been the big winner and "the public is bound to hail both teams as the very best exemplars of the one great, clean and honest national sport. In all respects has the great world's series been a credit to and good thing for the game of base ball."[33]

Back in Pittsburgh, Dreyfuss demonstrated his pride in his men in a tangible way. He donated his owner's share of series receipts to the pool of money allocated to them. Each Pirate received a check for $1,316. In Boston, by contrast, Killilea kept his club owner's share of $6,699.65 and each of his players received $1,182. So players on the second-best team pocketed about $150 more than the victors.[34] "The boys deserved it," Dreyfuss told Fred Clarke. "They've won three pennants for me, and stuck by me during the American League raids. I'm glad to do it." Clarke himself was doing well financially and within weeks signed a three-year contract at $7,500 a year, making him one of the best-paid men in baseball.[35] And he was already receiving a share of club profits thanks to the enlightened and grateful Dreyfuss. Such generous gestures as those were unheard of at the time and only endeared the Pittsburgh owner all the more to his men. In return, when the players gathered to collect their checks they presented Dreyfuss with a stopwatch inscribed with all their names. Then they burst out singing "For He's a Jolly Good Fellow." They didn't forget Clarke, presenting him with a watch chain and charm.

The post-season series for baseball bragging rights had been a disappointment for Barney Dreyfuss, his players and the fans in Pittsburgh. The owner had come so close to being able to claim his club as champions of the world. Overall, however, the 1903 campaign had been a success by drawing good crowds and good press and it showed the two major leagues could get along.

But would a "world's championship" become a regular feature of baseball? History had been made when the two leagues reached a peace accord and it seemed smooth sailing lay ahead. But some of Dreyfuss's colleagues who controlled the game had other thoughts and soon all the hard work and innovations he pioneered would come under assault.

11

Riding High in the First Division: 1904 to 1908

The National League's winter meeting was convened December 8 and 9, 1903, in New York when the peace agreement with the American League was ratified and Harry Pulliam was returned as president. He was formally granted powers that allowed him to fine and suspend players for disorderly conduct on the field and to ban players from baseball who had "jumped" their contracts.[1] The NL owners also adopted a rule that seemed to undermine the peace accord, suggesting the baseball marriage wasn't an entirely amicable one. No National League club would be permitted to trade any player to an American League team without the unanimous approval of all National League clubs. The *Chicago Tribune* complained this "knocks in the head" a scheme of free trading espoused by NL's Western team delegates.

National League magnates may have been licking their wounds following the loss of Dreyfuss's Pirates to the upstart Boston Americans and were determined to reassert their supremacy and clout. Delegates considered lengthening the 140-game-long season of the past four years to 154. Given their pecuniary interests, it seemed logical the move was made to earn more money. But no secret was made about the true intention—to thwart any further post-season play with the American League. The season would open April 15 and close October 15 when it was believed that cold weather would preclude further play. The move surprised chief schedule maker Barney Dreyfuss, who fully expected the "world's championship" series would continue every fall. Also caught short was Cincinnati president Garry Herrmann who preferred a shorter season to avoid playing in cold weather.[2] As a relative newcomer, Herrmann was open-minded and bore no longstanding grudge against any challenge to the primacy of the National League. He was fine with playing against the junior loop. But there was little he could do. The World Series of 1903 was considered by most of his fellow magnates to be a voluntary arrangement between Pittsburgh and Boston, rather than something obligatory.

Aside from the hatred of the American League retained by New York president John T. Brush and his manager John McGraw, other team representatives agreed there was no benefit to letting the rival league showcase its teams and possibly win again. The *Chicago Tribune* put it this way: "The American League clubs made such a good showing against the National League this fall, winning in almost every case where rival clubs met, that the effect on the public was not relished by the National League men."[3] The longer season was approved and Dreyfuss directed to devise a schedule with 154 games, a length of season that would survive for nearly 60 years.

The American League met December 17 in Chicago and hotly debated the 154-game schedule plan which White Sox president Charles Comiskey decried as "one of the biggest mistakes ever made in baseball." He said it appeared National League owners had "bowed down" to New York's Brush who feared having to play his in-city rivals, the Highlanders. But Comiskey admitted there was nothing the American League could do but comply.[4] As the two leagues began to work together, American League president Ban Johnson saw why the National League had given the thankless job of scheduling to Dreyfuss. "How can you beat a guy like that?," Johnson marveled. "'He pulls out a schedule as soon as he gets to a meeting. If you object to that he produces a second. Finally, he will come up with a third one. Invariably, with a few minor changes, it will be just to both leagues."[5]

The 1904 season was the story of John McGraw and his New York Giants. When he joined the club in 1902 it was mired in last place. By 1903, he managed it to a second-place finish, 6½ games back of Pittsburgh. McGraw, known as "Little Napoleon" would become one of the most powerful characters in baseball who always found a way to get the most out of his players. As both a player and manager, McGraw favored speed, strategy and guile, rather than heavy hitting, a perfect approach in the deadball era. He was a solid third baseman, but a bad knee forced him to end his playing career in 1903 and focus on managing. McGraw, who wasn't above cheating on occasion, also helped develop the hit-and-run play, the "squeeze play" and other innovations. He was a tough disciplinarian whose managing tools included insulting and taunting his own players and starting fights with other managers and umpires.[6] Barney Dreyfuss shuddered at McGraw's aggressive tactics, which he felt turned off fans and sullied the game. McGraw, a future Hall of Famer, was both feared and hated, but he ensured his players were paid well, about the only aspect of the game where he and Dreyfuss concurred. Most of all, McGraw got results.

"I have the strongest team I have ever led into a pennant race," the New York manager told a correspondent for *Sporting Life* shortly before the season began. "I ought to come in first, but I don't want to go on record as predicting that—the game is too uncertain."[7] McGraw successfully piloted the Giants to a first-place finish, a comfortable 13 games ahead of the Chicago Cubs. His Giants were fast out of the gate and by season's end had amassed 106 wins to 47 losses, setting a major league winning record. "Iron Man" Joe McGinnity won 35 games and Christy Mathewson collected 33. The Pirates, meanwhile, were beset by illness that felled Deacon Phillippe, who won only 10 games. A bad leg hobbled Fred Clarke, limiting him to 72 games. Honus Wagner stayed reasonably healthy and managed to take his second straight batting crown with a .349 batting average. Pittsburgh had a poor session of spring training in unseasonably cold Hot Springs, Arkansas. Pitching, bolstered by newcomers Patsy Flaherty, Mike Lynch, Charlie Case, and others, was underwhelming and the Pirates lost 12 of their first 17 games, leaving the League champions a half game out of last place. During July, Clarke injured his arm and Wagner replaced him as on-field captain. But the Flying Dutchman lacked Clarke's people skills and got into a nasty confrontation with Pirates outfielder Jimmy Sebring about his lackadaisical play. Teammates had to step in when their heated exchange turned to blows. Dreyfuss gave Sebring a lecture and within a week traded him to Cincinnati.[8]

During July and August, injuries wrought havoc on the Bucs. Phillippe was sidelined for nearly two months with an eye infection, Clarke, his arm recovered, was out even longer with a severely infected leg and catcher Eddie Phelps was idled after being beaned. A freak accident in Philadelphia hurt two players when a rear wheel of a carriage

11. Riding High in the First Division: 1904 to 1908

transporting 14 Pirates collapsed.[9] There was some light amidst the gloom, however. On August 16 at the Polo Grounds, the Pirates took both games of a doubleheader against McGraw's high-flying Giants, 7–2 and 4–1, with Flaherty and Lynch pitching well. "The two games of yesterday showed Pittsburgh playing the game in rings around New York," reported the *Pittsburgh Press.* At one point, Tommy Leach acted as captain with Clarke and Wagner injured, prompting Dreyfuss to shoulder Clarke's task of hunting for new talent and replacing injured players. He engineered trades like one that disposed of Jimmy Sebring and brought Moose McCormick from New York to replace him in the outfield. Sportswriter Ralph S. Davis marveled at the Pittsburgh owner's unwavering optimism despite all the challenges he faced. "Take the ordinary club owner and pile on him the amount of sheer tough luck that has fallen to the lot of the little Pittsburgher this season, and it would drive him to distraction ... [but] he still comes up smiling and undaunted."[10]

The 1904 season ended with Pittsburgh in fourth place, 19 games back of New York, but Giants owner Brush stuck to his guns by refusing to play a post-season world's series. At one point during the season when they were riding high, his new rivals the American League Highlanders challenged the Giants to a best-of-seven series. So, too, did Boston, who took the AL pennant by 1½ games, proposing a best-of-five series. On October 14, however, Brush startled his fellow owners with an abrupt about-face. He advised National League president Harry Pulliam he would support a post-season series in subsequent years, but only if the terms and conditions were formally adopted beforehand. He wanted to see spelled out clearly in advance all details such as number of games, player pay, the split of proceeds, umpiring and other matters, rather than rely on last-minute negotiation.[11] Brush suggested that winning players receive 75 percent of proceeds, and the losers 25 percent. His decision was hailed by *Sporting Life,* which called it "a concession to press demands and public sentiment that deserves commendation, though it is rather tardy.... If adopted it would make a world's championship series an annual compulsory event."[12] With Brush now onside, at its December 14 meeting the League endorsed an annual post-season series with the American League beginning in 1905 to determine "the championship of the world."

Barney Dreyfuss likely had an indirect role in Brush's change of heart. He headed the scheduling committee for the League and some time earlier had promised American League owners a post-season series in 1904. He felt badly it wouldn't pit the two league champions against each other. So he came up with a plan to have his fourth-place Bucs play the Cleveland Naps, fourth-place finishers in the American League. The Cleveland club was now named after their all-star second baseman, Napoleon "Nap" Lajoie. The series was expected to focus on Lajoie's performance and that of Pirates slugger Honus Wagner. At age 30, both future Hall of Famers were in their prime. Newspapers said they were fairly evenly matched in both fielding and hitting during the best-of-five series that began in Cleveland. Wagner and Lajoie led their leagues with batting averages of .349 and .376 respectively. In the first game October 10, Wagner connected for a two-run homer. Cleveland tied the game, but rain ended it. The following day, Sam Leever pitched the Pirates to a 7–4 win. Game three was at Exposition Park on October 12, a 14-inning

Opposite: John McGraw, player and manager for the New York Giants, was known as "Little Napoleon" for his aggressive tactics and leadership on the ball field. His teams were successful because he could get the most out of his players. Over the years, he often bested Barney Dreyfuss and his Pirates. He and Dreyfuss feuded for years (Library of Congress).

marathon that was tied when called on account of darkness. A day later, Cleveland won 3–2. On October 14, Naps' pitcher Otto Hess allowed only two Pittsburgh hits and Cleveland won the game 4–1 to take the series.

The contests between the Pirates and Naps hadn't produced large crowds or receipts, but the sporting press, the public and players seemed to think it was worthwhile. Dreyfuss, co-originator of the modern inter-league series, certainly did. He was gratified when the other National League owners voted unanimously to make it an annual event. The change of mind by New York's John T. Brush, despite his distaste for the American League, may simply have been his belated acknowledgment that post-season play was inevitable so it should be formalized. Dreyfuss, with his season-ending challenges in 1903 and 1904 had been instrumental in getting Brush and the League to accept a feature that for future generations would become the very symbol of the battle for baseball supremacy.

Early in the off-season, Dreyfuss traded away first baseman Kitty Bransfield. He'd been solid at first base for four years and in 1902 the career .270 hitter had batted a healthy .305. But by 1904 he had slumped to .223. It was apparent Bransfield was struggling with personal problems as well and Dreyfuss felt the time had come to replace him. The Pittsburgh owner consulted his "dope book" and began tapping his network of scouts to fill the void. He traded Bransfield and two other players to Philadelphia for Del Howard, who would prove merely adequate in 90 games at first base while batting .292. The deal to rid himself of Bransfield was dubbed by sportswriter Fred Lieb "one of Barney's worst moves … the trade proved one of Pittsburgh's sourest deals." One player after another was tried at first for more than a decade as the usually shrewd judge of talent Dreyfuss struggled to find a regular and reliable first baseman.[13] Dreyfuss picked up speedy outfielder Otis Clymer from Buffalo, who would bat .296, and Bill Clancy from Ed Barrow's Montreal club. Clancy would hit .229 in 56 appearances in the outfield and at first. Also acquired was veteran catcher Henry "Heinie" Peitz from Cincinnati in exchange for Ed Phelps.

The 1905 version of the Pirates was appreciably stronger than the team fielded the previous season, winning five of their first six games, landing them in first place. The New York Giants soon passed them, however, and once they reached first on April 23 McGraw's men never looked back. McGraw considered the Pirates his major challenge and it didn't take long for the teams to tangle. On May 20, Pittsburgh appeared at the Polo Grounds before 20,000 fans in a game that revealed the bitterness between the two teams. Early in the contest, which the Giants won 5–4, McGraw began abusing Pirates pitcher Mike Lynch, calling him a quitter in foul language. Fred Clarke jumped to defend his player and confronted McGraw in a heated argument that threatened to erupt into fisticuffs. The umpire separated the two managers and ordered McGraw from the field, but the wily Giants skipper continued to direct his players through a knothole beside their bench. At the press gate that same day, McGraw shouted "Hey, Barney," and hurled insults at the startled Dreyfuss, challenging him to bet $10,000 on that day's game and insinuating he owed gambling debts. The Pittsburgh owner was offended by the obscenities and accusation and immediately filed a complaint with National League president Harry Pulliam.[14] A few days later, Pulliam fined McGraw $150 and suspended him for 15 days. Pulliam also made public the complaint lodged by Dreyfuss, which only further enraged McGraw and Giants owner Brush. Pulliam's actions were upheld by National League owners. But, gratuitously, they added some criticism of Dreyfuss noting his "undignified conduct in engaging in a public altercation with a manager." The Pirates owner, who prized restraint at the ballpark and had avoided returning McGraw's insults that day, was mortified. Why was he being cited when he had done nothing wrong?, he fumed. He was further stung when McGraw's taunt of "Hey, Barney," continued to be hurled at him by fans, writers and players whenever he joined the team in New York, Chicago and other cities.[15] McGraw and his Giants had managed to get under the skin of the Pittsburgh owner the way few others could.

On June 7, the Giants visited Exposition Park for the first time that season. Pittsburgh was in second place, eight games back of New York. McGraw was surprisingly well behaved as each team won two games, the final played Saturday before 15,500 spectators and won 5–0 by the visitors whose "Dummy" Taylor earned the shutout. Just before that final game, Giants owner Brush, who had avoided the Pittsburgh owner all series long, spotted Dreyfuss in front of the club office and proffered his hand, saying: "Come Barney, let us shake hands … there is no use in keeping this quarrel up." Dreyfuss replied with "a withering glance," refused to shake Brush's hand and said what he thought of Brush's support for McGraw in the earlier episode. Then, as the *Pittsburgh Gazette* put it delicately, "after bidding him to go to a place where overcoats would be a needless bit of wearing apparel, the Pirates' owner turned on his heel and walked into the grandstand."[16]

That same month of June, Barney Dreyfuss made one of his wisest acquisitions ever. His injured backstop Harry Smith was acting as a scout for the team when he spotted hard-hitting 24-year-old catcher on Edward Barrow's struggling Montreal Royals Eastern League during a game in New Jersey. Burly George Gibson hailed from London, Ontario, midway between Detroit and Buffalo, but on the Canadian side of Lake Erie. He was hitting .290 for the Royals in 41 games and was solid defensively. Dreyfuss paid Barrow $2,500 to acquire Gibson who would struggle in his first season as a Pirate, with a disappointing average of .178 in 46 games played. Gibson's hitting would gradually improve. His greatest strengths were his strong arm and amazing durability. Dreyfuss and Clarke were impressed by his defense and were patient with him, hoping his bat would come around. By 1907, Gibson appeared in 110 games as catcher, then 140 in 1908 and 150 in 1909. During the latter season, he played 134 of those games in succession to set a National League record. Gibson would become the greatest all-time catcher in Pittsburgh history and after his 14-year playing career ended, Dreyfuss brought him back to manage for two separate stints. When Gibson signed with Dreyfuss that day in 1905, however, he became the fifth catcher for the club. Walking into the Bucs dressing room for the first time, Gibson cut an impressive figure, just shy of six feet tall and 190 pounds. Honus Wagner spotted the newcomer and shouted out "Here comes Hackenschmidt," a reference to a successful wrestler of the day. The nickname "Hack" was hung on him, even though he'd been called "Mooney" since his days playing sandlot ball in his native London.[17] Within a few months of making one of his worst deals in baseball, Dreyfuss signed Gibson to conclude one of his best.

The Giants were 9½ games in the lead of the National League by early August when they returned to Exposition Park. The four-game series demonstrated that hard feelings persisted between the teams. In the second contest, won by Pittsburgh 10–4, to end a 13-game Giants winning streak, fisticuffs were narrowly averted. During the third inning, New York first baseman Dan McGann slid hard into third base where Dave Brain took offense. The angry third baseman went after McGann and had to be physically restrained. During the same game, Dreyfuss was attacked in his grandstand box in a bizarre incident that some newspapers claimed occurred because he tried to stop a young man in clerical

Canadian catcher George "Mooney" Gibson began his career with the Pirates in 1905 when Barney Dreyfuss acquired him from the Montreal Royals. The rugged receiver was among the best players Dreyfuss ever signed, and the two men became close. In later years, Dreyfuss named Gibson as Pirates' manager on two separate occasions (Library of Congress).

garb from rooting for the Giants. The attacker had supposedly bet on New York and mistook Dreyfuss for a man who owed him money.[18] He became abusive and punched the startled magnate in the eye before police could pull him away. The Pirates owner, offended at the man's language and upset at the blow, pressed a charge of assault. The following morning in police court the assailant, identified as "Father Welsh," apologized to him; Barney then asked the charge be dropped. But because the story about him trying to muzzle a New York fan had been so widely disseminated, the Pirates owner felt compelled to set the record straight. He said his attacker was "not in condition yesterday to know what he was doing," a suggestion the priest was inebriated. Dreyfuss went on:

The statement that I denied Father Welsh the privilege of rooting for New York is absolutely untrue and does me an injustice. He did not root for New York yesterday when he invaded my box and used insulting language in the presence of myself and friends, among whom were several ladies.

I believe he said last night he wagered $5 upon the result, but he did not express a preference for either team while in my presence, and when I was forced to call a policeman to have him removed, I did not know which team he wanted to win.[19]

Relations were so strained between Pittsburgh and New York that the last thing Dreyfuss wanted was McGraw and Brush thinking he had silenced one of their supporters. He strongly disliked the Giants owner and manager, but he valued all fans of the game. As an owner, he knew only too well they paid the bills.

Pittsburgh made up some ground on New York during the dog days of August but fell back when the Giants regained their stride, relying on strong hitting and pitching. Pittsburgh finished second, nine games back and Wagner was dethroned as batting champ by Cincinnati's Cy Seymour who batted .377. Pittsburgh's winningest pitchers were the reliable Deacon Phillippe and Sam Leaver with 20 wins each, and Mike Lynch with 17.

In the post-season matchup, becoming known as the "world's series," pitching was excellent by hurlers for both the Giants and the Philadelphia Athletics of Connie Mack. New York was well rested, but the Athletics were tired after edging out the Chicago White Sox by two games to claim the American League pennant. Mathewson shone for the Giants, shutting out Philadelphia three times as New York took the seven-game series four games to one. Being crowned world champions no doubt pleased John McGraw and John T. Brush, neither of whom had any use for Ban Johnson and his American League. The Giants victory only enhanced their smug feeling of superiority.

Barney was still nursing a grudge against Harry Pulliam as he and the new Pittsburgh secretary Will Locke, former sports editor of the *Pittsburgh Press,* prepared for the National League winter meeting December 12 to 14. Pulliam had convened the special meeting of directors to consider Dreyfuss's complaint about New York's McGraw that led to Barney's own censure for "undignified conduct." The peeved Pittsburgh owner snubbed his old partner Pulliam in June and they hadn't spoken since. Likewise, John T. Brush, the Giants owner gave Pulliam the cold shoulder and muttered about deposing him. Brush insisted he wasn't motivated by the suspension and fine of his manager, but because Pulliam was doing a poor job. Dreyfuss swallowed his pride and decided to support Pulliam for another term, nominating him when the magnates gathered. Brush surprised Chicago's Jim Hart, a friend of Pulliam, by nominating the Cubs owner for the post. Embarrassed, Hart declined and Pulliam was returned for another year on a 6–2 vote.[20] Hart announced he had sold controlling interest of his club to Charles W. Murphy, a former baseball writer and publicist for the Giants. Hart was likely glad to be done with the devious Brush and the strain of League politics. Pulliam was granted expanded powers to determine the length of suspensions and the severity of fines when he disciplined players as the magnates continued their efforts to stamp out player rowdiness. Johnson's better-behaved American League was drawing praise and fans.

Pulliam reported National League total attendance was just shy of two million with its best revenue ever. Magnates were advised the $125,000 debt incurred to reduce the loop to eight teams in 1900 had been cleared from the books.[21] The baseball business that struggled to make ends meet when Barney Dreyfuss joined it was now an ongoing concern and the Pirates president derived some satisfaction from having played a role in that.

For the 1906 campaign, Dreyfuss's acquisition of a player left many observers scratching their heads and wondering if he had lost his eye for talent. Veteran right-hander Vic Willis, who turned 30 in April, came from Boston where had a 151–147 record during his eight seasons there. But Willis had led the National League in losses for the past two years, recording 29 of them in 1905 with only 12 wins, handicapped by the poor Beaneater defense behind him. Ownership cut his $4,500 salary to $2,400 for 1906 and he was unhappy. Some owners might have concluded Willis was over the hill and avoided him, but not Dreyfuss. He acquired him in a swap for three Pirates, his third baseman Dave Brain, first baseman Del Howard and pitcher Vive Lindaman. Dreyfuss also restored Willis' 1905 salary.[22] He felt there were more wins in the future for the aging hurler and was soon proved right. The newcomer showed his gratitude by pitching three straight shutouts early in the season and won 23 games. Willis won 21 more games in 1907, 23 in 1908 and 22 again in 1909. His sweeping curveball, deceptive fastball and durability through 13 major league seasons earned him a place in the Hall of Fame.

With a reliable cash flow established, Dreyfuss made several improvements to Exposition Park. The park was fully enclosed, a new grandstand was erected and the playing surface raised three feet in a bid to keep it above future floodwaters. A crowd of 17,036 flocked to the park for opening day April 17, 1906, when Cincinnati and the Bucs found themselves tied 2–2 in the twelfth inning. Rookie first baseman Joe Nealon launched a drive over the head of Reds' center fielder Cy Seymour to score Honus Wagner and win the game.

In early May, Cincinnati owner Garry Herrmann placed on waivers Ed Phelps, his backup catcher the previous season. Phelps had played for Pittsburgh in 1902 and 1903, helping them win the pennant and then the World Series where he played in all eight games. Dreyfuss remembered him as a fine receiver, who hit well and had speed on the base paths, but the owner let him go for lackadaisical play on occasion. Dreyfuss already had two catchers, but was looking to improve team offense. Before the 10-day waiver waiting period expired, however, Herrmann sold Phelps to Boston. On the tenth day of that waiver period, however, Phelps signed with Dreyfuss. Herrmann was in a pickle. As chairman of the National Commission he would be expected to rule on any dispute about where Phelps should ultimately go. He'd have to rule on his own conduct. The conflict of interest situation was Herrmann's first crisis as Commission chair. For his part, the Cincinnati owner claimed that Phelps agreed to be sold to Boston and the player had accepted half of the purchase price. But Phelps insisted he never agreed to be sold to Boston. Dreyfuss, already angry at this turn of events, grew incensed when he learned within a week that Herrmann had wagered $6,000 the Pirates wouldn't win the National League pennant that year. Herrmann insisted his bet was made in jest, but insiders suggested it was made while he was under the influence of alcohol. Herrmann found himself forced to recognize Phelps' contract with Dreyfuss.[23] Once close on what they felt was good for the game of baseball, Dreyfuss and Herrmann would have further clashes and their relationship would grow sour.

The story of the 1906 season was all about Chicago, its National League Cubs and their cross-town rivals the American League White Sox. New Cubs president Charles W. Murphy replaced manager Frank Selee with first baseman Frank Chance during the previous season in what proved to be a wise move. Aside from being a good leader, Chance was part of the renowned Tinker-to-Evers-to-Chance infield double-play combination that eventually landed Chance, second baseman Johnny Evers and shortstop Joe Tinker in baseball's Hall of Fame. At the weak-hitting White Sox, manager Fielder Jones was able to draw the best out of his men. Both teams fought for first place throughout the season, drawing large crowds in the Windy City, producing the top attendance figures in both leagues. The Cubs won 116 games, topping the Giants' record of 106 from 1904. The White Sox, despite the lowest batting average in the AL, relied on pitching and defense to win 93 games. Much to the delight of the fans in Chicago, their two teams met in the world's series, which was won by the White Sox.

The Pirates had their struggles during the season, but by July 4 reached second, 2½ games behind the Cubs, their guests at Exposition Park for a six-game series. The first game of an Independence Day doubleheader produced a record crowd of more than 20,000. Chicago's Mordecai "Three Finger" Brown was up against Pirate "Lefty" Leifield, a side-armer, in a hotly contested game. Brown picked up his nickname after losing most of his index finger and maiming his thumb and two other fingers on his pitching hand in a childhood accident on a farm. He also threw with a sidearm motion, his grip producing an almost unhittable sinking curveball. Brown threw a one-hitter for a 1–0 Chicago shutout. When the Cubs left town, they'd won four of the five games played, three of them shutouts. In mid–August, the Pirates appeared at the Polo Grounds for five games and lost all of them, victimized by strong New York pitching. The Bucs' slump continued into September, but they held onto third place. Wagner injured his leg sliding into second base in Cincinnati and was used sparingly. New York held onto second place and by season end the Cubs were 20 games ahead of them. The Pirates were 23½ games back of Chicago. Wagner claimed the National League batting title for the fourth time, with an average of .339. Pittsburgh's catcher Gibson appeared in 81 games but his hitting was an anemic .178. but his strong play behind the plate kept him on the roster. Gibson's time to shine would soon arrive.

The 1907 season was another successful one for Frank Chance and his Cubs, who won 107 games, only nine less than in 1906. The Tinker-to-Evers-to-Chance infield combination, to which third baseman Harry Steinfeldt also contributed, gave the Cubs solid defense. Orvie Overall won 23 games, followed by Three Finger Brown with 20 and Carl Lundgren with 18. By early summer it was generally conceded Chicago would recapture the National League pennant, the only question being by what margin. The Pirates finished in second, 17 games back. Dreyfuss made some changes, releasing second baseman Claude Ritchey who had been around since their days in Louisville (along with two others) and replaced him with Ed Abbaticchio, one of the first major league players of Italian descent. Abbaticchio, 30, his surname sometimes shortened to Abby, was acquired from Boston, now owned by Barney's old friends George and John Dovey. George and his late brother Will had played for Barney's team in Paducah during the mid–1880s, sometimes under assumed names to avoid detection by their disapproving parents. George, from nearby Central City, Kentucky, was a fine shortstop. After Will died as a young man, George Dovey stayed in touch with Dreyfuss and when the Doveys considered buying the Boston franchise from longtime owner Arthur Soden, the Pittsburgh magnate encouraged them and helped find financing. It is suspected he may have secretly acquired a stake in the club. The Doveys paid $75,000 and assumed a $200,000 mortgage on the South End Grounds in October of 1906. The Beaneaters soon became known as the Doves. Under their ownership, the club that was short on talent finished seventh, but attendance rose 42 percent during 1907.[24] With old friend George Dovey joining the ownership ranks of the National League, the influence of Barney Dreyfuss was growing. Boston's previous owner Soden had often sided with Freedman and Brush during various skirmishes, so his departure was welcomed by Dreyfuss and other owners.

The New York Giants finished fourth, four games back of Philadelphia, pleasing Dreyfuss. "I didn't win the pennant," he said, "but I am happy that two Pennsylvania clubs finished ahead of New York's Muggsy McGraw."[25] He knew full well that McGraw detested being called "Muggsy." In the world's series, the Cubs faced Detroit, which had finished a game and a half ahead of Connie Mack's Philadelphia Athletics. The Tigers were led by the bats of Ty Cobb and Sam Crawford, while their pitchers "Wild Bill" Donovan and Ed Killian each had 25 victories in the regular season. Chicago prevailed in the post-season clash, taking four straight from Detroit after a first-game tie. Cubs pitching effectively subdued Cobb and Crawford, who batted .200 and .238, respectively.

The Pirates of 1907 had been strong offensively, with a team batting average of .254 and the most stolen bases with 264. Wagner stole 61 of them despite having reached the age of 33. Leach collected 43, Clarke 37 and newcomer Abbaticchio 35. Abby proved to be a fine addition, appearing in 147 games in which he walked 65 times and had 130 hits. Wagner took his fifth batting title with a .350 average, while Leach placed fourth, with .303. Willis won 21 games and lost 11 to lead Pirates pitchers, followed by Lefty Leifield with 20–16. Veterans Leever and Phillippe were 14–9 and 14–11, respectively.

The normally astute Dreyfuss missed a grand opportunity that season that might have changed Pirate history. One of his salesman friends alerted him to a young pitcher from Kansas, a semi-professional who was dominating mining town teams out in Idaho. The big 19-year-old right-hander was averaging 20 strikeouts a game and seldom surrendered more than three hits, the salesman enthused. He offered to bring the young man east if Barney would cover transportation and expenses. Ordinarily, the Pittsburgh owner would have gambled and sent the money, but he felt the salesman's praise was excessive and he grew wary. Dreyfuss declined and missed a chance to sign the hard-throwing lad named Walter Johnson. Johnson signed his first big league contract with the Washington Senators and went on to win 417 games in the American League, second most in baseball history, behind only Cy Young who won 511. Johnson was among the first inductees into baseball's Hall of Fame. He remained with the Senators for his entire career that lasted until 1927. Meanwhile, Mooney Gibson continued his strong work behind the plate and became Clarke's go-to catcher. The durable Gibson appeared in 113 games and his bat was slowly coming around, with a .220 average.

In February 1908, Honus Wagner turned 34 and chronic rheumatism was afflicting his right arm and shoulder. He consulted his doctor and decided it was time to retire. Fred Clarke saw it as a bluff, telling a Pittsburgh newspaper that Wagner always talked this way before the season, and he expected him to sign yet another contract.[26] Wagner missed the entire training camp in Hot Springs and didn't sign until the season was four games old after Dreyfuss relented to his demand for a $10,000 contract. This was twice his reported salary of 1907 and $4,000 more than the highest offer Dreyfuss had made him. Wagner insisted later he really had intended to retire and open a garage in his hometown, but the Pirates contract was too hard to resist.[27] He'd enjoy a stellar season, earning every penny in his fat new contract.

The National League featured a tight race in which Pittsburgh, Chicago and New York led at various times, the Pirates doing so briefly in late June and early July. They caught the Cubs again later in July and held onto first for 36 days. The Giants had a poor start but by September were perched in first while Chicago and the Bucs alternated in second. Ultimately, the Pirates finished tied for second with New York, a single game back as the Cubs again took the pennant. For Pittsburgh, the ongoing weakness at first base continued to frustrate Dreyfuss and Clarke. Four players were tried there, but none could fill the shoes of Kitty Bransfield, playing that season in Philadelphia where he batted .304 for the Phillies. Wagner returned as National League batting champ, with an average of .354. He also led the league in hits with 201, in doubles with 39, triples with 19 and runs batted in with 109. He had the most stolen bases (53), total bases (308), highest on-base percentage (.415) and best slugging percentage (.542). He was a significant part of the Pirates offense. The tough-as-nails Mooney Gibson caught in 140 of the 143 games he played but his batting average remained a mediocre .228. On the mound, newcomer Nick Maddox and veteran Vic Willis topped the pitchers with 23 wins apiece. In the American League, Detroit finished a half game ahead of Cleveland and again faced the Cubs in the world's series. It took Chicago five games to down Detroit, despite the bat of Ty Cobb whose .368 average bettered his .324 clip during the season when he took the AL batting title. Orvie Overall and Three Finger Brown, winners of 15 and 29 games during the season, won the games for the world champion Cubs.

The 1908 season was a memorable one, which some observers say was the best in baseball history. *Sporting Life* described it this way:

> So grandly contested were both races, so great the excitement, so tense the interest, that in the last month of the season the entire nation became absorbed in the thrilling and nerve-racking struggle, and even the [U.S.] Presidential [election] campaign was almost completely overshadowed. High class ball was the rule in both major leagues all season long, each club in the two leagues being a factor in the struggle—else the wonderfully close races would have been impossible; the sensational individual and team performances were of almost daily occurrence.[28]

In the political race that fall, Republican William Howard Taft defeated Democrat William Jennings Bryan to take the presidency of the United States.

During the 1908 season, an incident occurred that would become famous as "Merkle's Boner." On September 23 at the Polo Grounds, the Cubs faced the Giants, the two teams then in a virtual tie for first place. Fred Merkle, 19, a utility first baseman was put into the game to replace ailing Fred Tenney, who was suffering a painful attack of lumbago. The game was tense and the fans were unruly. With two out in the bottom of the ninth inning, the score was tied 1–1 when New York batter Al Bridwell, their shortstop, connected with a pitch from Cubs lefty Jack Pfiester, driving it into center field. Merkle was standing on first base and "Moose" McCormick on third. McCormick scampered toward home with what appeared to be the winning run. As Giants fans celebrated and began streaming onto the field, Merkle decided that rather than continue running, it was more prudent to sprint to the safety of the clubhouse. Cubs' second baseman Johnny Evers realized Merkle would have been forced out at second for the third out, thereby nullifying the McCormick run. He screamed at center fielder Solly Hofman to throw him the ball. Hofman complied, but overthrew Evers, who wound up in a wrestling match for it with a fan and the Giants' Joe McGinnity, then serving as third base coach. The fan gained control and threw the ball into the stands. It disappeared from sight. Cubs manager Frank Chance demanded veteran umpire Hank O'Day call Merkle out on the play and argued the run didn't count so the game must continue. O'Day's fellow umpire that day, Bob Emslie, had missed seeing the play despite being closer to second. McGraw joined the fray to argue the run scored. O'Day ruled the run didn't count and declared the game a tie.[29] His decision was later upheld by League president Pulliam who scheduled a deciding game for October 8 at the Polo Grounds in New York. Pulliam's decision was upheld during an October 5 hearing chaired by Brooklyn's Charles Ebbets. Dreyfuss and Chicago owner Charles Murphy were disqualified from deliberations in which they were deemed to have a conflict of interest. The Pittsburgh owner was irate at being excluded from such an important decision and stormed out of the meeting room. "You will be sorry," Dreyfuss fumed, "I am through with the National League."[30] The threat was empty and he eventually calmed down. Meanwhile, a 4–2 Cubs victory in the deciding game disappointed the 40,000 spectators who flocked to the park and gave Chicago their third league championship in a row.

A nearly identical play had occurred between Chicago and Pittsburgh 19 days earlier at Exposition Park when umpire O'Day worked alone. The game was a scoreless duel between Vic Willis and Three Finger Brown after nine innings. Chicago failed to score in the top of the tenth. In the bottom of that inning, Fred Clarke singled and was advanced to second on a sacrifice by Tommy Leach. Wagner connected for a hard grounder to the right side of the infield where second baseman Johnny Evers knocked it down and threw to home plate, holding Clarke at third while Wagner scampered to second. Rookie Pirate first baseman Warren Gill was hit by a Brown pitch to load the bases. Eddie Abbaticchio struck out, but Chief Wilson singled to right center and Clarke ran home to score. As soon as Clarke crossed the plate, O'Day went to the players' bench for a drink of water. Wilson touched first and then ran for the clubhouse as fans poured onto the field. Gill ran about halfway to second before he, too, made a beeline for the clubhouse. The always alert Evers at second hollered at center fielder Jimmy Slagle for the ball. He touched the base, held the ball up and shouted "O'Day, O'Day," to claim the out on Gill. When shortstop Joe Tinker confronted the umpire, insisting Gill was out and the run was void, O'Day replied simply: "Clarke has crossed the plate." The Bucs took the game 1–0 and Cubs president Charles W. Murphy filed a protest with Harry Pulliam. Murphy said the incident showed the need for two umpires at every game.[31] His protest was disallowed, however. The similarities between the two games were striking and fortunately for him, rookie Gill escaped the notoriety that dogged Giants rookie Merkle who played 14 more years in the majors. Little did anyone know a repeat of the same controversy was so close at hand. The fact the umpire didn't see the play was important and O'Day vowed that if a similar play were to occur, he would call the runner out.[32] His opportunity to do so came sooner than he could ever have dreamed.

Midway through that memorable 1908 season, *Baseball Magazine* carried an article by Ralph S. Davis, sports reporter for the *Pittsburgh Press* who had watched Dreyfuss mature as an owner. Dreyfuss, he said, had become widely known as "one of the 'big' men in baseball, as leading club-owner in the grand old National League, as one of the best judges of a baseball player in the business.... He never misses a game played at Exposition Park, Pittsburgh, and he never fails to keep a detailed score of the contest." Davis noted the Pirates owner followed games closely from his box along the first-base line, a vantage point he preferred to being behind home plate. Dreyfuss was still an avid fan of the game and paid well to get what he wanted. "More than that, he is very liberal with the men on his payroll, and it is generally claimed that the salary list of the Pittsburgh club is always the largest in the National League."[33]

During that 1908 season, Barney Dreyfuss unveiled the latest innovation in baseball, a tarpaulin, measuring 120 feet square made from paraffined duck cloth to protect the infield during inclement weather. Fred Clarke played a key role in designing it. First displayed in May, it soon produced returns on the owner's $2,000 investment and became a model for other tarpaulin systems adopted in other ballparks.[34]

Journalist Cait Murphy wrote an entire book about the 1908 campaign, a year in which she said baseball came of age.

> Every baseball season is like a Dickens novel—a tale told in installments, until the last chapter, known as the World Series, all the loose ends are tied up and the heroes go home, tired but happy. In 1908, there are simply more chapters, more incidents, more characters, more surprises, and more drama than in any other. Six teams are in contention with two days left; in each league, the pennant is decided on the last day, the culmination of six months of hard-fought and sometimes bitter baseball.[35]

As the memorable season drew to a close, Dreyfuss was concluding a deal that would dramatically change baseball in Pittsburgh and introduce even more innovations to the game he so loved.

He'd soon be writing a new chapter in the baseball history of the Smoky City.

12

Politics, Dirty Business and Tragedy

Barney Dreyfuss made front-page news in Pittsburgh when he announced on October 17, 1908, that he was erecting a grand new baseball palace for his Pirates. "One of the Finest Baseball and Athletic Fields in the Country for Pittsburgh," proclaimed the banner headline detailing his plans in the *Pittsburgh Post* the next day.

He had acquired a seven-acre site in the fashionable Schenley Park area of Oakland, just east of downtown, where he planned to build a 25,000-seat ballpark, the biggest in baseball. His total investment would be $1 million, including the $250,000 for the land. The property was adjacent to the University of Pittsburgh which that same year shed its longstanding name of the Western University of Pennsylvania and moved from Allegheny City (Pittsburgh's North Side today) to a 43-acre site it purchased in Schenley Park. Carnegie Technical Schools was nearby and until December 1 would continue using its football field that was included in the sale to Dreyfuss. He purchased the property from the Schenley estate, whose three trustees included steel magnate and philanthropist Andrew Carnegie, the latter of whom was also a trustee for the University of Pittsburgh. It was located in the growing educational and cultural sector of a city most commonly known for its steelmaking. When Dreyfuss first moved to Pittsburgh, he lived for several years in the stately Schenley Hotel, built on the edge of the park in 1898, so he was familiar with the verdant area far removed from the city's heavy industry. His new park was just south of the hotel, which would accommodate visiting ballplayers and team officials in years to come. Carnegie and the trustees insisted the ballpark must complement the fine structures near the entrance to leafy Schenley Park, including the Carnegie Library and the Schenley Hotel. Trustees also stipulated the structure must be fireproof and that no alcoholic drinks could be served there.[1]

The site at Forbes and Bouquet streets was served by 15 different trolley lines within easy walking distance, seven of them running right along Forbes. No railroad station was more than a 15-minute ride away. Famed architect Charles W. Leavitt, Jr., was already working on preliminary plans and was reportedly pleased with the high standard of design required. His previous work focused mainly on racetracks, with Belmont Park his most notable effort. To prepare for his new assignment Leavitt spent time inspecting ballparks including the new concrete-and-steel $315,249 ornate Shibe Park that was beginning to rise in Philadelphia as a new home for the Athletics of the American League. Ground there had been broken for the 23,000-seat, two-tiered French Renaissance style park back in April. Leavitt's first-ever ballpark in Pittsburgh would be the second using concrete and steel construction and would feature many modern conveniences and innovations within a soaring three-tiered design. Elevators would take affluent patrons to exclusive boxes on the top two tiers, while wide ramps provided easy access to the stands under which a parking garage was tucked. Public telephones were available throughout. Fred Clarke designed and patented a unique tarp system to protect the infield. Dreyfuss spared little expense for a state-of-the-art facility which was described as showcasing "opulent modernity," making it unique among ballparks.[2]

This was one of the largest real estate deals in the history of the city whose population was reaching 530,000 and some wondered if Barney had bitten off more than he could chew. But he had no doubt the business of baseball had matured under his watch and such large investments could be repaid if an owner was committed to fielding a quality product. No longer was he prepared to invite the public to a wooden facility that could burn down or be flooded. He'd lost two ballparks to fire in Louisville and constantly battled floodwaters at Exposition Park which was near the red-light district in town. Besides, by providing a new facility in a better area he felt supporters would be more inclined to bring along ladies and even children. Dreyfuss was beaming when he outlined his plans to reporters:

> We hunted four years before we got possession of the best site in this or any other city. It was evident as far back as our world's series of 1903 that better accommodation would be required. Baseball, both professional and amateur, football and all other athletic sports, have progressed wonderfully in this country, but the accommodations for contestants and patrons have not kept pace. England excels us in this respect and has facilities for taking care of more than 100,000 spectators at some of its championship football games.
>
> It was impossible to build modern stands at Exposition Park because a lease could not be obtained for a term of years. Besides, we had more than a half dozen floods to contend with every year and it often happened that after spending a great deal of money on repairs all of our work was undone by a sudden flood....
>
> The new park will have as perfect drainage as can be obtained, and for the first time the Pittsburgh team will have an ideal field to play on.[3]

He promised amenities for both spectators and players would be "the best that money can command because the new park must provide, not only for the present, but also for years to come." His expectations for the park he soon named Forbes Field, were long term and prophetic. The last game was played there were on June 28, 1970, more than 4,700 games later.

Dreyfuss announced the new park would be made available for local athletic events, including baseball and football games of the University of Pittsburgh and Carnegie Technical Schools. Given the fact that site work could not begin until after December 1, he hoped it would open by early summer. The Nicola Building Company, the lead contractor, got under way two days before Christmas and the speed of the work was impressive as double shifts were instituted. With its head start in Philadelphia, Shibe Park opened in time for the 1909 season to claim honors as the first-ever concrete-and-steel stadium. Forbes Field was less than three months behind, but was much larger and even more grand than the fine new park 300 miles across Pennsylvania.

The optimism of Barney Dreyfuss came during an economic downturn following the Panic of 1907, the first serious setback for the American economy of the twentieth century. It produced a six-week run on banks and trust companies that began in October of 1907, triggered by failed speculation that led to the bankruptcy of two brokerage firms in New York. A recession was already under way at the time because of the San Francisco earthquake in 1906, whose reconstruction drew gold from the major money centers, creating a liquidity crisis. The Panic of 1907 affected the economy of the United States and the impact was felt around the world.[4] The downturn hit Pittsburgh particularly hard when many of its steel mills were shuttered and home attendance for baseball fell far below previous years. The Pittsburgh owner confirmed the drop of fan support to *Sporting Life* but declined to release specific numbers, saying only: "One has to see them to realize how much the decline reached." This prompted the publication to observe "Pittsburgh was filled with heavy-hearted and light-pursed people. They had to be contented with bulletin board games."[5] The latter was a reference to the practice by newspapers of posting scores on their windows when games were underway. Aside from Pittsburgh, the major league season of 1908 was successful financially despite the economic uncertainty and a run of bad weather. The downturn that lingered and Dreyfuss could have been forgiven for biding his time and waiting for the economy to improve. But that was not his style.

Much has been said about the Pirates owner and his willingness to invest heavily in baseball a few short years after National League teams struggled to make money and ideas were being touted such as Freedman and Brush's baseball trust to keep the game afloat. Pennsylvania baseball historian Robert C. Trumpbour noted his timing was good. "Barney Dreyfuss's investment, persistence, and vision helped baseball to retain its stature as the national pastime at a time when the entertainment landscape was rapidly changing," Trumpbour has written.[6] Yet again, when it came to baseball, Dreyfuss had a knack for sensing opportunity and pursuing it. He was ahead of the curve.

The National Commission, the three-person body which oversaw baseball from 1903 to 1920, seldom made headlines as it dealt with provisions in the National Agreement, adjudicated disputes about fines and suspensions and the relationship with minor leagues and their players. Since it was established, Cincinnati's Garry Herrmann had been chairperson, toiling alongside the presidents of the National and American leagues as they worked their way through what was often administrative drudgery. The events of late 1908 and early 1909 would raise its profile considerably. The Commission blasted into the headlines in November when Herrmann was sidelined by a sprained ankle in Cincinnati. His fellow member and American League president Ban Johnson announced in Chicago the Commission had received conclusive proof that individuals connected with the Chicago Cubs had been party to a ticket-scalping scheme at the recent world's series. The complaint came from Chicago fans who "believed they were done a great injustice in the distribution of the world's series tickets and asked the commission to investigate." Johnson wouldn't disclose any complainant or say more until Herrmann was apprised of the situation. National League president Harry Pulliam then left for Cincinnati to consult with Herrmann about next steps.[7]

Commissioners interviewed Cubs and Tigers players who claimed they were "flim-flammed out of about $500 apiece."[8] Chicago owner Charles Murphy, who challenged the right of the Commission to investigate the matter at all, was upset even further when it criticized his club. The commissioners concluded there was no "deliberate graft" or collusion between Cubs officials and scalpers. "The club is reprimanded, however, for the crude and unbusiness-like manner in which the tickets were handled, causing annoyance and disappointment to many warm supporters of the Cubs," said its report. "The sale of tickets was conducted on an amateurish plan, which caused a lot of ill feeling among the patrons of the game in Chicago."[9] By this time, Murphy was becoming despised as

The National Commission oversaw baseball from 1903 to 1920 before Kenesaw Mountain Landis became sole commissioner. In this 1913 photograph are, from left, National League president Harry Pulliam, chairman August (Garry) Herrmann of Cincinnati, American League president Ban Johnson and commission secretary J.E. Bruce (Library of Congress).

a baseball magnate, rivaling John McGraw "as the most hated man in baseball."[10] It was said Murphy had profited handsomely from selling tickets to scalpers, despite his protestations to the contrary. Murphy held a grudge against the Commission and Pulliam for allowing the investigation into his business affairs and the subsequent finding. Murphy was not alone in his displeasure. In New York, Giants owner John T. Brush was still vexed at Pulliam and the National League board of directors for their handling of the Merkle Boner affair and the order to play the October 8 game his team had lost. Brush felt his club was cheated out of the pennant and an appearance at the world's series.[11]

The National League held its winter meeting December 8–9, 1908, and no representative of New York appeared until it was extended into a third day. Brush was sulking. At the gathering, the peace agreement with the American League was formally ratified and Harry Pulliam returned as president. John Heydler, Pulliam's assistant since 1903 and league statistician, was returned as secretary-treasurer. History was made when the magnates entertained a delegation from the American League, headed by its president Ban Johnson. Representatives of both leagues expressed satisfaction with the peace treaty and spoke glowingly about the prospect of future harmony. The glad-handing and positivity after so much distrust of each other prompted *Sporting Life* editor Francis C. Richter to hail the burying of hatchets. He opined that "the larger interests of base ball were treated and conserved in a way calculated to not only preserve existing conditions and forestall or defeat any possible check to prosperity, but also keep the sport straight on the road to still greater improvement and development."[12]

The meeting was a routine affair until the last business was concluded. Then Harry Pulliam dropped a bombshell. He announced an attempt had been made to bribe umpires Bill Klem and James Johnstone during that extra game played October 8 at the Polo Grounds between Chicago and New York. Both men had filed complaints with the League, naming the person who offered the bribe and whom he claimed to represent. The revelation prompted the owners to extend their meeting a further day and urge New York owner John T. Brush to join them as an interested party. At the end of their deliberations, the League issued a formal statement to the press: "We are of the opinion that a most thorough and searching investigation of this matter be made in order to maintain the high standard and honesty of the game throughout the entire country, and if possible, to punish all persons connected with this disreputable proceeding."[13]

It was deemed "unwise" to release the names of the individuals allegedly involved. The statement added, in a bid to reassure the public: "We desire to state that none of the persons whose names are withheld at this time are in any way connected with organized baseball." Time would reveal that was a lie. Klem and Johnstone were praised for refusing the bribe and reporting the attempt and "their actions again showing to the American public the honesty and integrity of our national game." The statement was signed by all eight club owners. In October, when Pulliam first got wind of the umpire complaints and shared them with directors, Barney Dreyfuss argued the matter was serious and the umpire statements should be turned over to the local district attorney for investigation and criminal charges, if warranted.[14] He was overruled by Pulliam, however, who said Pittsburgh had an interest in the outcome of the matter because any ruling might affect its final standing with games still to play. An upset Dreyfuss was barred from further deliberations.[15] Soon afterward, he said he planned to protest the decision to order the extra game between Chicago and New York as unprecedented and wrong.[16] Dreyfuss was still annoyed at Pulliam by the time of the December meeting when a committee consisting of Brush, Brooklyn owner Charles Ebbets, Chicago's Charles Murphy, Cincinnati's Garry Herrmann and Pulliam was directed to conduct "a most thorough investigation" and pursue criminal charges if necessary. It seemed odd that Brush and Murphy were to be part of the investigation when Dreyfuss had been excluded from deliberations by Pulliam, who insisted he had a conflict. Clearly, Brush and Murphy had even greater conflicts of interest. Friction had grown between Dreyfuss and his old partner in baseball.

As for the bribery attempt, *Sporting Life* said it was believed the gamblers wanted the umpires to ensure the Giants won and that a "prominent business man of New York" was behind the offer. It said the amount offered the umpires if the Giants won the crucial game was $10,000.

Pulliam was feeling the strain of his office because of various disputes with owners now compounded by ticket-scalping and bribery scandals. He joined Ban Johnson on a trip to California during December in a bid to settle a dispute between the Pacific Coast League and an outlaw loop, the California State League. They tried to persuade both to end hostilities and join organized baseball. On his return east, Pulliam took a much-needed break to visit friends in Louisville.[17] Meanwhile, the investigation into the bribery scandal dragged on and members of the press began asking questions. "Fans are wondering what has become of the National League's Committee on Bribery," the *Louisville Courier-Journal* said about the same time Pulliam visited that city, adding, "If this committee has done anything, no one knows it."[18] Late in January, Joe Vila wrote in *Sporting News* that the public deserved answers. "Brush, who is the chairman, says nothing has been done and is inclined to ridicule the whole affair. But base ball fans are clamoring for action, and it looks to me to be very poor policy to ignore so important a matter."[19]

On the eve of a joint scheduling meeting for the National and American leagues in Cleveland late in January, Pulliam was beginning to unravel as the pressure was building. He hinted the upcoming season might be his last as president, admitting his health wasn't the best. "I have come in for more abuse than ordinarily falls to the common mortal," he complained.[20]

Pulliam's behavior was beginning to cause concern for magnates. His presence at the scheduling meeting in Cleveland proved disruptive. Dreyfuss and Charles Ebbets of Brooklyn had been assigned the difficult task of developing a schedule along with American League president Ban Johnson and secretary Robert McRoy to avoid conflicts during home games in cities where they both operated. Pulliam's absence from deliberations was noticed and Ebbets found he spent most of his time in the bar of the host hotel getting inebriated and unable to understand discussions. Later, at an evening dinner, Pulliam told "Jew stories of a respected member of the league."[21] His target was obviously Dreyfuss. Ebbets and others found this distasteful. Pulliam then refused to support the schedule developed by Dreyfuss, Ebbets and Johnson, saying they would have to work on it later at the National League office in New York. When they attended and tried to do so, he ordered them out of the office. At the owners' meeting in February, Pulliam declined to explain his complaints about the schedule, instead insisting Dreyfuss and Ebbets had been insulting toward him in Cleveland. Despite Pulliam's opposition, the owners approved the schedule they had developed. The owners retained their confidence in the work of Dreyfuss and were becoming wary of Pulliam.

Adding to Pulliam's woes were rumors that former Chicago player and manager Cap Anson was being promoted as his replacement. Anson had fallen on hard times financially and his name was raised as a potential National League president. In January, Charles Murphy of the Cubs proposed creating a position for Anson as supervisor of umpires, perhaps to get his foot in the League door. There were only about seven umpires at the time and Pulliam oversaw them as part of his regular duties. "Anson would be just the man," said Murphy. "He knows the game thoroughly and would be an impartial judge of the arbitrators' work."[22] Murphy went so far as to say if Anson wanted the job it was his. As late as early February, Anson was quoted as saying he understood umpires well and "I think I can convince Mr. Pulliam that I am the right man."[23] But Pulliam had no intention of relinquishing his oversight of the umpires, whose work he supported despite complaints from owners. Faced with insufficient support among Murphy's fellow magnates, Anson took a coaching job. But the episode did nothing to improve Murphy's standing in the eyes of the embattled president.

Pulliam's mental state continued to decline on the eve of a gathering in Chicago hosted by White Sox owner Charles Comiskey which was intended to celebrate the working relationship between the American and National leagues. A grand banquet at the Automobile Club on February 17 was described by the press as a "love feast" and would include baseball writers. Brief meetings of National League owners and those from the American League coincided with the event.

Pulliam, still irked by Murphy and Dreyfuss, took it upon himself before the gala to release some correspondence between himself and Garry Herrmann in which they discussed the Chicago owner. In one letter, Pulliam vowed if Murphy was looking for trouble, he'd be happy to comply by making a full statement about him at an upcoming meeting of newspaper writers. Another letter discussed Murphy's move to award the $10,000 bonus to his players after winning the world's series. Herrmann wrote he believed "the reason Murphy wanted to give away some of the loose change was on account of the ticket scalping case."[24] It was unclear if Herrmann was suggesting that the Chicago owner was trying to buy some goodwill in the wake of the scandal, or, more likely, that he had profited from it and thereby had "loose change" (tainted money) available to disperse. Murphy was unimpressed at Pulliam's release of the letters and boycotted the event. Dreyfuss was also absent, but Pittsburgh secretary Will Locke insisted he was ill.

Pulliam was not the only one to make mischief. Shortly before the big banquet, a story was published about the clash between Pulliam and Dreyfuss culminating in the Pirates owner being ejected from Pulliam's office in New York. Aghast, Pulliam issued a statement insinuating this "leakage" of league business came from Dreyfuss. He insisted he had ejected Dreyfuss "for a good and sufficient reason. I would do it again today if he gave me the same provocation, even if he owned all the clubs in the National League."[25] Pulliam

Barney Dreyfuss had turned his Pittsburgh Pirates into a successful and profitable franchise during the first decade of the twentieth century. He survived the contraction of the National League, helped make peace with its rival the American League, fended off syndication, and navigated the cut-throat politics of the National League. His contributions were paying off handsomely (National Baseball Hall of Fame Library, Cooperstown, New York).

said he'd been upset that the schedule proposed by Dreyfuss seemed to favor Brooklyn over Philadelphia and he stoutly denied a story being circulated it was because Dreyfuss refused to lend him $500.[26] Pulliam went on:

> I am weary and sick of the whole ugly mess, and it looks like I would get my release for although I have won all of my fights previously, I expect to lose this time because the handicap is too great. There are too many against me, but I will show the men who I think have been most unfair and unjust to me that I am a good loser.

During the banquet, Herrmann felt compelled to explain the National Commission had banned bonuses following the first world's series contest between Chicago and Detroit and had no plan to abrogate that rule, despite the plea to do so from Murphy. Herrmann said a friend of Murphy told him there would be no problem whatsoever if the owner was barred from distributing the money. Murphy was supposedly looking for a fall

12. Politics, Dirty Business and Tragedy

guy his players could blame and he could keep the money for himself. Herrmann said he was unwilling to be played like that.

Pulliam took the "love feast" in a completely unexpected direction when he rose to announce he was disgusted with baseball and was through with it. He was emotional and spoke quickly. Pulliam said he had helped Barney Dreyfuss sign a reluctant Honus Wagner before the last season and Dreyfuss had shown him no gratitude, only enmity. Pulliam bitterly assailed his long-term friend, accusing him of "intrigue, of ingratitude" and other treachery.[27] Similarly, Pulliam said he helped Charles Murphy sign Cubs manager Frank Chance to a new deal and suggested the Chicago owner was a liar. He also denounced Brush and Ebbets, accusing all four owners of conspiring to unseat him.

> My days as a baseball magnate are numbered. The National League doesn't want me for president any more. It wants to go back to the days of dealing from the bottom of the pack, hiding the cards under the table and to the days when the trademark was the gum shoe. I can't afford to quit or I would resign now from my position which pays $9,000 a year. But I will have to quit by the end of this year.[28]

So much for the "love feast." Pulliam left the attendees stunned. The airing of dirty linen before the baseball scribes prompted the National League owners to meet privately the following morning to deal with several pressing issues. They granted Pulliam, who did not attend, an indefinite leave of absence, expressing concern about his mental state. The magnates wished him well and said they hoped he'd be able to return to his post when he was up to it. John Heydler was named acting president. Chicago owner Charles Murphy apologized to Ban Johnson for remarks he had made about him and the American League. Johnson accepted. Garry Herrmann then apologized to Murphy, saying as far as he was concerned the ticket scalping issue was now "dead and buried." They shook hands. Then the committee empowered to investigate the bribery asked league owners to endorse its plan to turn over all statements and paperwork in its possession to the National Commission "for such action as they desire to take."[29] With that, the owners adjourned, hoping they had quelled the turbulence that had broken out.

Pulliam wasn't quite done. Rather than attend the meeting of the owners, he chose to issue the following statement to the press:

> I will not attend the meeting of the National League today. The reason for this is that I am not well and desire to conserve my strength. There are a lot of cheap individuals who are built like Durham bulls, who delight in nagging me to a point of desperation and then bawling me out at the top of their voices like they would some poor devil....
>
> The trouble with the so-called magnates is that, with the recent growth and popularity of the national game, they have grown money mad and want to throw sentiment henceforth to the winds. Their actions are just like those of the grasping millionaire race track owners in this country which resulted in killing American racing, the sport of kings.... The baseball magnates will kill the goose that lays the golden egg. I, for one, am willing to let them alone.[30]

Pulliam spoke about returning to California for a rest, but the magnates summoned one of his brothers from Kentucky in a bid to change his mind. But Pulliam slipped off to St. Louis despite their best efforts, then to Cincinnati where his friend Garry Herrmann persuaded him to see a doctor who suggested a long period of rest. Heeding that advice, Pulliam spent most of the winter on the west coast of Florida where many well-to-do Kentuckians had properties.[31] By early April, when he had an eye operation, he had gained back 14 pounds. Later that month, he joined Herrmann for a ball game in Cincinnati between the Reds and Pirates. In June, Pulliam was staying with another brother in Oshkosh, Wisconsin, when the National League owners gathered to consider his ongoing absence. By now, Cubs owner Murphy was openly campaigning for Cap Anson as National League president. Herrmann said he still supported Pulliam and, besides, he reminded his fellow magnates, they had promised him his job back. So the leave of absence was extended.

One of Pulliam's staunch supporters, George Dovey, owner of the Boston franchise, died suddenly at the age of 47 on June 18 from a lung hemorrhage he suffered while aboard a train crossing Ohio. Dovey had consulted his old friend Dreyfuss about some player issues and was on his way to Cincinnati at the time he was stricken. Pulliam consoled Dovey's family in Pennsylvania after which he and Dreyfuss were among the honorary pallbearers at the well-attended funeral in Philadelphia. Pulliam resumed his presidential duties in late June just in time to attend the grand opening of Forbes Field.

On April 19, the National Commission released its findings on the bribery case. It reiterated praise for umpires Klem and Johnstone for reporting the incident. The Commission refused to identify the party who had offered the bribe and said it would have prosecuted the person if it had the power to do so and with further corroboration of the umpire reports. The statement read:

> We feel, however, that in the absence of this the party charged with the offence by the umpires should not go unpunished, and for that reason we will furnish to every major league club owner the name of the person who attempted this offense, with instructions to such club owners to bar him from their respective grounds for all time to come.[32]

A few days later, *Chicago Tribune* writer Harvey Woodruff revealed the "party" was New York Giants team doctor Joseph Creamer, a close friend of manager John McGraw. Woodruff said McGraw hired Creamer to travel with the team during the 1908 season, unbeknownst to owner John T. Brush who initially refused to the pay Creamer's bill for $2,840 submitted to him at season's end. When Creamer demanded Brush put his refusal to pay in writing, Brush, sensing potential legal action, paid up. Then McGraw, likely at the behest of Brush, advised Creamer his services were no longer required.[33]

Creamer had a large medical practice and was an avid sports fan, involved with athletic clubs, boxers, bicyclists and others. Woodruff reported Creamer's friends insisted he had nothing to do with the bribery bid and that he had grounds for a lawsuit against the commission, the umpires and the Giants if they barred him from the Polo Grounds. His friends told Woodruff that Creamer had been used as a tool by the real conspirators, whom they said were three members of the New York team. The affidavits of the umpires were disclosed by Woodruff in which the bribe attempt was attributed to "a man named Dr. Creamer, official physician of the Giants." The doctor met Klem under the grandstand, with a stack of money in his right hand, when he reportedly said: "Here's $2,500 which is yours if you will give all the close decisions to the Giants and see that they win sure. You know who is behind me and you needn't be afraid of anything. You will have a good job the rest of your life." When confronted with the allegation from the affidavits, Creamer denied any involvement whatsoever, saying there was a conspiracy afoot to ruin him. "I never tried to bribe anybody in my life ," he insisted. "I have been interested in sports for nearly twenty years and nobody has ever accused me of wrongdoing before."[34]

It appeared the identity of the individuals behind Creamer might finally be disclosed at the very end of 1909. W.A. Phelon, a writer for *Sporting Life,* penned an article in the

December 18 edition about the latest in the ongoing spat between Chicago's Charles Murphy and American League president Ban Johnson. Phelon was on his way to a meeting of baseball writers when Murphy shared with the writer his latest complaints about Johnson. "Can anyone tell me what business it is of Ban Johnson's what the National League does? What has he got to say about whom the National League shall elect as president anyway?" It was apparently a reference to Johnson's outspoken opposition to former player John Montgomery Ward who was now being touted by Murphy and Brush for National League president. Johnson had warned he would never be able to work with Ward, now a lawyer. In the end, former umpire Thomas Lynch was elected president and John Heydler reverted to his role as secretary-treasurer. Johnson attended the same gathering of writers where Phelon shared with him the latest shot from the Cubs owner. Johnson "smiled grimly" and threatened to pull a skeleton out of the closet. "It is time that the Brush-Murphy combination be given a severe setback, and I am thinking of doing it in a painful way," he told Phelon.

> The umpire-bribing was hushed up by keeping the names of "the men higher up" from the press, while Dr. Creamer was made the goat—a poor fellow who at most acted only as a messenger-boy. Possibly it might jar the new combination and give the baseball world something to yowl about if I gave out those names at the coming meeting, and possibly I may do so.[35]

Despite Johnson's threat, he never publicly identified the individuals behind Creamer. It may have been leverage to persuade Murphy and others to reject Ward and choose a president with whom he could work. With that salvo, the issue of the attempted bribery died. The identity of the persons for whom Creamer acted only came to light many years later when researcher Cait Murphy carefully studied the minutes from the National League meeting of February 1909, that followed Pulliam's meltdown. The minutes revealed that Cincinnati's Garry Herrmann said Creamer admitted he was acting on behalf of three Giants. Someone had attempted to black out the names Herrmann shared with the owners, but the effort was ineffective and they could still be read. The three were manager John McGraw, pitcher Christy Mathewson and catcher Roger Bresnahan, all later inducted into the Hall of Fame for their more traditional and positive contributions to the game.[36]

Shortly before the bribery report was released, the 1909 season began. Philadelphia christened gleaming new Shibe Park on April 12 with an 8–1 victory over the Boston Red Sox, delighting the 30,000 fans attracted to the 23,000-seat facility and its environs. In Pittsburgh, Forbes Field was rising swiftly and was expected to open at the end of June.

On April 22 the Pirates played their home opener before 9,000 chilly fans at Exposition Park where mud made a mess of the outfield. Among the dignitaries on hand were Cincinnati's Garry Herrmann, whose club rallied in the ninth inning to come from behind and defeat the Bucs 7–4. The loss was disappointing but fans saw promise in newcomers Bill Abstein at first base, Jack "Dots" Miller at second and William "Jap" Barbeau at third, along with rookie pitcher Charles "Babe" Adams. Honus Wagner had skipped spring training for the second year in a row and didn't join the club until its opening series in Cincinnati. He'd anchor the infield at shortstop and wield a fearsome bat. The loss that day left Pittsburgh with four defeats against two wins, but further losses were rare once the players found their stride.

Harry Pulliam visited Herrmann in Cincinnati on July 16 to deal with routine National Commission matters when a reporter for the *Enquirer* quizzed him about several aspects of League business. "Mr. Pulliam has lost considerable weight, but otherwise his health is good," he noted. "He has good color in his face and is taking best care of himself." Pulliam chatted about the difficulty of finding good umpires, the banner year for baseball attendance and the wisdom of a new rule banning the throwing of bats when a runner starts for first base. Pulliam said he was still making his home in the New York Athletic Club and was thinking of spending some time that summer near the ocean.[37] While it would seem Pulliam had recovered from his breakdown, the public Harry was not the same as the private Harry. His friends found he was "moody, uncommunicative and lacked his usual effervescence."[38] He relied heavily on secretary-treasurer Heydler upon resuming his duties in New York. But late in July Heydler left town for a vacation in northern New York and Pulliam was left alone. The league president, it was said, "found the routine work of his office bearing down heavily on him during Mr. Heydler's absence."[39]

On July 28, Pulliam reported for work at his office in the St. James Building about 9:30 a.m. and began going through a stack of correspondence. At some point he stopped and began staring out a window. About 1 p.m. Pulliam told his stenographer he was not feeling well and left the office and went straight to his apartment at the Athletic Club. He was sitting on a sofa at 9:30 p.m. in his underwear and socks when he put a .38-caliber revolver to his right temple and fired. The bullet blew out his right eye, went through his temple and lodged in a wall. Still alive several minutes later, but in agony, he reached for the telephone, but knocked it off its cradle. That alerted the club switchboard operator something was amiss in his third-floor apartment. A staff member was dispatched about 10 p.m. and found Pulliam, blood oozing from his head and apparently unconscious. A doctor was sent for and immediately realized the wound was fatal. He asked Pulliam how he had been shot, and Pulliam gained consciousness just long enough to say: "I am not shot," before drifting away. Police arrived as he lingered near death and placed him under arrest for attempted suicide. No suicide note was found despite a search. Pulliam was is such bad shape the doctor felt it best not to move him and he remained under police guard that night as his life ebbed away. He died at 7:40 the following morning.[40] Harry Pulliam was just 40. His death made the front page of the *Louisville Courier-Journal* where he cut his teeth in baseball and met Barney Dreyfuss, and also in the Pittsburgh papers and the *New York Times*. The baseball community was in shock and flags were lowered to half-staff at ballparks.

In Cincinnati, Garry Herrmann expressed grief at losing his friend and associate, saying Pulliam "was one of the grandest characters in baseball, and one of the most lovable men in every way I ever met. He was as honest as the day is long, and a loyal and unselfish friend." In Pittsburgh, Honus Wagner wept.[41] Word of Pulliam's death hit Barney Dreyfuss hard. "The news broke me all up," he said. "I had a letter from Harry yesterday, and the tone of it was cheerful. He had nothing to worry him that I know of, and cannot account for this deed, otherwise than that his nervous temperament overcame him." He conceded that Pulliam had difficulty dealing with criticism. "Harry is one of my closest friends and the news of his untimely death fills me with grief. I can scarcely comprehend yet that it is true."[42]

National League secretary-treasurer John Heydler accompanied Pulliam's body on the train to Pittsburgh where Dreyfuss and other officials from the Pirates boarded for the trip to Louisville for the funeral and burial. Harry was laid to rest in Louisville's Cave Hill Cemetery after a funeral that attracted a huge crowd including local friends and baseball dignitaries, some of whom travelled long distances. The New York Giants were the only National League team that failed to send a representative and their manager McGraw supposedly said: ""I didn't think a bullet in the head could hurt him."[43] American League president Ban Johnson joined Heydler, Dreyfuss and John Dovey among the honorary pallbearers. Meanwhile, major league teams as well as those in Louisville and elsewhere cancelled their games that August 2 out of respect for Pulliam.[44] Afterward, directors of the National League met and established a committee consisting of Dreyfuss, Cincinnati's Herrmann and Chicago's Murphy to recommend a suitable monument for the gravesite. Heydler was elected president. It was never clearly established why Pulliam took his own life, but his biographer Mark Peavey learned Pulliam's family had a history of mental illness and his sister, Grace, took her life eight years later.[45] Among the tributes in the press to the late League president was one in the *Boston Post* that Pulliam's hometown *Louisville Courier-Journal* saw fit to reprint.

> The present prestige of baseball, at once a great industry and the most popular of American sports, is in a measure due to his unremitting efforts. Since he assumed direction of the parent major league rowdyism, once rampant, has been suppressed with an iron hand. Disputes between players, and squabbles in which umpires and players participate, still occur, but are no longer everyday features of the game.[46]

Forbes Field as seen in its early days from across the Schenley Bridge in Oakland. Barney Dreyfuss was trying to broaden the appeal of the Pirates to the middle class and to ladies by building their new home in the growing cultural and educational district of Pittsburgh (Library of Congress).

The *Post* went on to say his efforts helped transform the game to one that ladies could also enjoy once offensive behavior was largely curbed. "Unflinchingly industrious, Pulliam encountered venomous opposition" from some major league clubs, it noted. "Their efforts to undermine him preyed upon the president's mind."

On the opening day of the 1909 world's series, the National Commission met and expressed their thanks to Pulliam on an engraved card distributed to players, owners, officials and the press. It read: "This series is the fifth one under the auspices of the national commission. A year makes many changes, indeed. Harry C. Pulliam, one of the originators of these series, has passed away. His counsel in this body will be heard no more. Organized baseball never had a more zealous or devoted sponsor."[47] Pulliam's friend Garry Herrmann proposed the card be produced to express the Commission's appreciation of his work and that a similar one be produced and circulated on the opening day of each World Series when a floral wreath would also be placed on Pulliam's grave.

After a brief pause, the baseball world wagged on as Dreyfuss mourned the loss of close and longtime associates George Dovey and Pulliam. The joyous opening of his spectacular new ballpark was bracketed by the untimely deaths of two men upon whom he had relied heavily since his days in Kentucky. Fortunately for Barney Dreyfuss, better days lay just ahead.

13

Champions

After losing more games than they won during the opening days of the 1909 season, the Pirates soon began to gel and found their winning groove, powered by the best offense in all of baseball. Honus Wagner was on his way to his fourth consecutive batting crown with a .339 average while knocking in 100 runs and stealing 35 bases. Manager Fred Clarke and rookie second baseman Dots Miller were also productive, with timely contributions and averages of .287 and .279, and scoring 97 and 71 runs respectively. Tommy Leach led the league with 126 runs. Rookie Hamilton Hyatt appeared in 49 games, primarily in a pinch-hitting role where he was far more effective than at first base and in the outfield. He hit .299. On the mound, right-hander Howie Camnitz had 25 wins and 6 losses for a league-leading winning percentage of .806. His winning record tied him with Giants' ace Christy Mathewson. Veteran Vic Willis, now 33, tried to retire before the season, but Dreyfuss coaxed him back for another go round. Willis managed 22 wins and 11 losses. During one memorable stretch, he won 11 consecutive starts. Sam Leever and Deacon Phillippe contributed with eight wins apiece, four less than 27-year-old rookie right-hander Charles "Babe" Adams, who pitched mainly in relief and showed great promise.

The Pirates reached first place on May 5 and remained there all season, never seriously challenged on the way to their fourth National League pennant. On May 29, newly elected United States President William Howard Taft paid a visit to Pittsburgh, which included taking in a game at Exposition Park. A self-professed baseball fan, his retinue included his brother, Charles P. Taft, a part-owner of the Chicago Cubs, the visiting team that day. Despite his brother's connection to Chicago, Taft made no secret he was cheering for the home team, pleasing the fans near him in the crowd of 14,000. He disdained the use of an exclusive box set aside for him by Dreyfuss, insisting he wanted to sit near first base and close to the field of play. Wearing a dark gray suit and flat straw hat, Taft managed to shoehorn his bulk into a seat two rows from the field. "I want to get right down among the rooters—the baseball bugs," he explained. "The boxes are all right, but I want to mingle with those in the stand." Taft was particularly impressed by the play of Wagner who had an apparent home run declared a double by the umpire, relying on ground rules that day. "That is indeed too bad," Taft lamented as he realized what happened. Wagner, he pronounced, "is simply great." The president made no attempt to hide his enthusiasm, waving his hat several times, exclaiming, "I am with the fans and I am happy."[1] The teams were tied 3–3 after seven innings and the president had no intention of leaving. Chicago broke the game open in the top of the 11th with five runs and the Bucs lost the game, 8–3. "It was a great game and I am glad I was fortunate enough to be present," Taft said. "Yes, I am passionately fond of baseball and this recreation this afternoon has relieved me of any fatigue I may have felt from the busy day I have put in." Taft waited until the last Pittsburgh out was recorded and "was jostled and bustled like a thousand others in making his exit from the grandstand."[2] The loss to Chicago that day was one of only six for the red-hot Pirates during May when they won 20 games.

Wagner continued to excel. On June 3, the Pirates played Boston when a sooty, dark fog emanating from the city's steel mills engulfed Exposition Park, reducing visibility so much it was feared the game might be cancelled. Pittsburgh was trailing 8–1 in the fourth inning when Boston right-hander Tom McCarthy faltered, walking two Pirates when the bases were already loaded. He was pulled for Al Mattern, who struck out Clarke, giving Boston two outs. Wagner emerged from the murky haze and struggled to see the baseball that was now quite worn and almost black. He swung at the first two pitches, then connected with a third for his first home run of the season. The blast scored four runs to bring Pittsburgh within one of the Doves. In the sixth, Wagner singled to bring in another run and the Pirates tallied again in the eighth for an improbable come-from-behind 9–8 victory. On the day, Wagner batted in five runs.

The Pittsburgh shortstop was a certified star and during that 1909 season the American Tobacco Company featured his image on a new series of cards accompanying its cigarettes. Wagner objected strenuously and the printing ceased. There are two stories about why. The first was that he objected to cigarettes, then considered less publicly acceptable than the tobacco he chewed and the cigars he smoked, and he didn't want to encourage children to smoke. The second is he felt entitled to compensation for use of his image by a big company hoping to increase its profits.[3] Regardless, the print run of the "T206" Honus Wagner card was cut short, which has generated strong collector interest to this day. Only about 60 are known to have survived and some have sold at auction for more than $3 million in recent years. The modest Flying Dutchman would be amazed at the fallout and fame that followed from his simple "no."

Pittsburgh's hot streak continued into June, when they lost only three times, once at home on June 16 when the Giants' Christy Mathewson ended their 14-game winning streak. On June 28 in Cincinnati, Mooney Gibson's bat finally came alive, going 4-for-4 and leading the Pirates to a 3–2 win. By June 30, when Forbes Field opened, Wagner was hitting a torrid .411 and led in stolen bases. Pitchers Camnitz and Willis had the NL's best winning percentage with Gibson behind the plate for every game and proving to be the best defensive receiver in the League. He started every game between May 5 and October 2, shrugging off injuries that might have sidelined other catchers. By July, when pitchers preferred to walk Wagner rather than have him embarrass them, Honus grew frustrated and began chasing bad pitches. Twice he had four-game hitless stretches and his average dropped to .212 for the month. And when he reached for one outside offering, he sprained a chest muscle and was out of the lineup for two weeks. That same month, the Pirates faced the Giants at the Polo Grounds for six games and took four of them.

By September 1, Pittsburgh had won 86 games and lost 32, six-and-a-half games ahead of Chicago and 15½ up on New York. The solid play of their new iron man backstop drew attention in the press as he approached a major league record for consecutive games played. By late August even his offense had picked up and he was batting .258. In the *Pittsburgh Press* sportswriter Ralph S. Davis wrote:

> Gibson is a glutton for work. He thrives under it. Most windpaddists [archaic term for catchers] would get stale if called upon to toil as Gibson has done this season, but not so with "Hack"—he gets better every day. Gibson must be given credit for being the greatest backstop

in the business today. There is no catcher who can perform so consistently as he. His throwing to bases has been little short of marvelous, as is evidenced by the few stolen bases credited to opponents of the league leaders.[4]

On September 9 at home, Gibson set the record for consecutive games in a 3–1 win over Cincinnati, his 112th straight appearance surpassing the 111-game record set by Charlie Zimmer in 1890. The quiet Canadian was being recognized as one of the best catchers in the game and one of Barney Dreyfuss's best finds. Babe Adams was the winning Pittsburgh pitcher that day, collecting his 10th win against 3 losses.

The Pittsburgh Gazette Times praised the accomplishment of Gibson, and credited him with carefully mentoring Adams that season.

> Adams once more made himself solid with the Pittsburgh public, who thinks there is no more promising youngster in the world. Of course, the fact that old Hack Gibson gives the signals is never lost sight of. Hack is proud of the advancement of the young pitcher, and he, more than any other influence, is responsible for the order of Capt. Clarke to Adams to take his place among the regular pitchers. Adams will figure in the world's series beyond a doubt, and will have the support of every Pittsburgh fan.[5]

Gibson's consecutive-game catching streak ended at 133 when Fred Clarke left him out of the lineup on October 3. His record would last until 1944 when both Ray Mueller of Cincinnati and Frankie Hayes of the Philadelphia Athletics caught all 155 of their team's games. In the 1909 season, Gibson appeared in 150 games in all, recorded 135 hits, 36 of them for extra bases, and his batting average of .265 led all National League catchers. He threw out 52 percent of base runners trying to steal on him and his fielding percentage was .983. During September the Pirates posted a club record of 16 straight victories, led by Wagner who tripled five times and homered once during the streak. They clinched the pennant on September 28 and two days later the Detroit Tigers did the same in the American League, for their third straight year.

Dreyfuss was delighted his men had claimed their fourth pennant since 1901 and wanted to congratulate them personally. Since 1900, however, manager Fred Clarke had banned him from the player dressing room after games, regarding that space as sacrosanct and off-limits. After the pennant-clinching victory, however, Dreyfuss couldn't help himself and poked his head in the clubhouse door, asking Clarke "Can I come in?" The response was immediate. "You bet you can," his buoyant manager replied. A beaming owner then addressed the team. "I want to say that you're not only a great team but a fine bunch of fellows. I congratulate everybody."[6]

Pittsburgh took the National League pennant with a final record of 110 wins, the second-best record in League history, while losing only 42 games. In retrospect, sportswriter Fred Lieb was unsure whether the Pirates of 1909 were as great as the 1902 team, whose 103 games won came during a 140-game season for a winning percentage of .741. The 1909 club went .724 in its 154 games, with the Cubs second, 6½ games back. New York trailed by 18½ games.[7] Pittsburgh won 13 games from Chicago during the season and lost 9, while it split the 22 contests with the Giants.

The 1909 post-season championship, now widely being called the "World Series," was a much-anticipated showdown between the best players in the two leagues, Honus Wagner and Detroit's Ty Cobb. The Pittsburgh star claimed the National League batting title for the sixth time in seven years with an average of .339. He had the most runs batted in, most doubles, most total bases, best slugging percentage and top on base percentage.

The stately Schenley Hotel looms beyond the left field bleachers at Forbes Field. It was here that Barney Dreyfuss first lived when he moved to Pittsburgh. Within a decade, he built his brand new ballpark in adjacent Schenley Park. When upscale apartments were built next to the hotel in the early 1920s, he moved into them. The former hotel and apartment buildings are now incorporated into the campus of the University of Pittsburgh (Library of Congress).

He was at the peak of his career, while Cobb, 13 years younger, was just hitting his stride. The Detroit outfielder led the American League in runs, stolen bases, hits, home runs, total bases, runs batted in, batting average (.377), slugging, and on-base percentage. His 76 stolen bases more than doubled Wagner's 35. The two stars had never met but exchanged pleasantries before the first game in the series, on October 8 at Forbes Field, to the delight of press photographers. More than 29,000 fans packed the new park and 200 journalists were on hand for the much-anticipated showdown.

Both the Pirates and the Tigers were anxious to settle scores by taking the post-season honors. The Pirates lost the first Series in 1903 to Boston and the following year to Cleveland in the special series between fourth-place teams. Meanwhile, Frank Navin's Tigers had lost the last two World Series to Chicago, winning only one game in total. Clarke surprised most observers by tapping rookie Babe Adams for the pitching assignment, rather than Camnitz or Willis, winners of 25 and 22 games during the season. All his hurlers were rested but he went with Adams, his fifth most successful pitcher, who had managed 12 wins. Gibson guided him from behind the plate and caught every game in the Series. In that first game, Adams battled first-inning nerves when he walked two successive batters and allowed Detroit second baseman Jim Delahanty to single, scoring Cobb. Adams then settled down as his offense went to work. Clarke homered off 29-game winner George Mullin in the fourth inning to tie the game. His blast deep into the right-field bleachers was the longest homer ever seen at Forbes Field. The next batter was Wagner whom, some newspapers said before the Series began, the Tigers intended to "put ... out of business."[8] Mullin wasn't happy at Clarke's homer and drilled a fastball into the ribs of the Flying Dutchman as tensions escalated. In the top of the fifth inning Cobb, who had reached first on a force play, sprinted for second on an Adams pitch to Sam Crawford. Gibson fired the ball to second where Wagner scooped up the low throw and tagged Cobb as he slid into the base. American League arbiter "Silk" O'Loughlin called Cobb safe, which angered Wagner and Clarke who ran in from left field. Their howls of protest were in vain and Adams ended the inning by retiring Crawford to keep Cobb, who took three stitches to his lip from the Wagner tag, stranded at second. In the bottom of the inning, Gibson connected for a timely double to score a run and give the Pirates the lead. Wagner scored the final tally in the sixth when he doubled to left field, advanced to third on a bad throw and raced home on an infield putout. For his part, Adams didn't allow a run after the first inning in the 4–1 Pittsburgh victory.

The following day, Pittsburgh scored twice in the first inning off right-hander Wild Bill Donovan. In the second, Pirates starter Howie Camnitz allowed two singles and a double, which tied the game. The next inning, he gave up two more runs when Delahanty doubled with two men on base, prompting Clark to replace Camnitz with Vic Willis. The veteran was in the midst of his windup when Cobb took off from third, eluding Gibson at home plate with a nice hook slide. Donovan was solid that day and the final score was 7–2 for Detroit. The Series moved to Bennett Park in Detroit for Game Three on October 11. Despite rain that began shortly before game time, 18,277 fans jammed the park at Michigan and Trumbull avenues. The Bucs victimized knuckleballer Ed "Kickapoo" Summers for five runs in the first inning. Tiger errors were many and Wagner easily advanced around the bases to home, capitalizing on a throwing error and a wild pitch. In the second, two hits by Pirate batters and another Tiger error produced another run for Pittsburgh. Right-hander Nick Maddox held the Tigers at bay until the seventh inning when they plated four runs. The Pirates held on for an 8–6 win. Game Four was played on October 12 when the temperature was barely above freezing. Lefty Leifield started for Pittsburgh and was as cold as the weather, hitting Cobb in the first inning and then Delahanty in the second, when he surrendered two runs. Meanwhile, Tiger hurler Mullin shut down the visitors. In the fourth inning, Detroit collected three more runs when Leifield allowed two singles, a walk and double. Mullin shut out the Pirates on five hits and struck out 10, holding Wagner hitless for the first time in the Series. The final score was 5–0 as the teams headed back to Pittsburgh for Game Five on October 13, tied two games apiece.

The weather remained cold but the crowd of 21,706 warmed up when Clarke again sent Babe Adams to the mound at Forbes Field. The rookie had a rough beginning, giving up a home run to the lead-off batter, Tigers outfielder Davy Jones. Pittsburgh replied with a run to tie the game in the bottom of the inning, then added single tallies in the second and third. Detroit responded with two runs in the sixth on a single by Cobb and double by Crawford. In the bottom of the seventh, Clarke belted a three-run homer to center. In a repeat of game one, Tigers pitcher Summers retaliated by hitting the next batter, Wagner again, squarely in the back. The Pittsburgh star went down hard but shook off the blow and went to first base. Soon after, Wagner stole second, then third, on wild throws by catcher Charles "Boss" Schmidt and raced home to score the fourth Pittsburgh run of the inning. In the eighth, Adams surrendered a home run to Crawford but the Pirates held on to win 8–4.

The teams returned to Detroit for the sixth game, which turned out to be the most exciting contest of the Series. The Pirates scored three runs off Mullin in the first inning. At third base, George Moriarity began kicking Pittsburgh runner Tommy Leach in the shins and they exchanged several more kicks before order was restored. They had barely settled down when Wagner doubled to left, scoring Leach and Clarke. Mullin composed himself and blanked the Pirates for the next seven innings while Vic Willis was victimized for one run in the first, two more in the fourth and once in each of the fifth and sixth innings. The Tigers were ahead 5–3 going into the ninth when Pirate right fielder Chief Wilson lay down a bunt and raced to first where he collided with Tommy Jones, the first sacker. Jones fell to the ground and coughed up the ball as he slipped into unconsciousness. Dots Miller scampered home to bring the Pirates within a run of Detroit. Angry words were exchanged as Jones was carried from the field and the game continued. With none out, Bill Abstein was perched at third. Gibson grounded to Crawford, who had replaced Jones at first, and Abstein barreled home with the potential tying run. He collided hard with catcher Schmidt, gashing the backstop's right leg with his spikes. Abstein was called out and the two scuffled briefly before umpire Billy Evans intervened. Ed Abbaticchio, batting for reliever Deacon Phillippe, then struck out. Wilson decided to run on the pitch and barreled into Moriarity at third, spiking him. But Moriarity collared a throw from his catcher to make the out. The rather violent and bloody game ended with a 5–4 Tigers victory.

Detroit had won the toss to determine the site of the final game so the teams returned to Bennett Park on October 16, a Saturday afternoon, to settle the Series. Yet again, the weather was cold and skies were overcast. For the third time, Clarke gave the ball to Babe Adams, a move that showed his supreme confidence in the rookie. Rough play was again evident with more hard slides and fisticuffs. Two Tigers were injured and forced to retire from the field. Pittsburgh opened the scoring in the second inning with two runs on four walks issued by Donovan and a sacrifice fly. Mullin replaced Donovan in the fourth inning, but fared no better. The Bucs went up 4–0 on a Leach single and two walks and a two-run single by Miller. In the sixth, Leach drove a ground-rule double into the crowd standing in left center. Clarke was walked and Wagner came to bat. He was greeted with catcalls and one Tiger supporter behind that team's bench hollered loudly: "It's all right, that Dutchman has got a yellow streak."[9] Wagner responded by drilling the second pitch he saw down the left field line for a triple, to score Leach and Clarke. The throw from Davy Jones to catch Wagner at third was wild and the Flying Dutchman sprinted home for a seventh run. "I am sure that wallop gave me a better feeling than any one I ever hit," Wagner admitted years later in an autobiography that was serialized in newspapers. An inning later, Clarke was walked for the fourth time that day. He stole second and scored when Crawford missed a Miller fly to center field. Adams managed a six-hit shutout as the Pirates won 8–0 to claim their first world championship.

Barney Dreyfuss and Fred Clarke couldn't be happier. It had been a long time coming but they had finally reached the peak of baseball success. Hughie Jennings was gracious in defeat, despite Detroit losing its third straight World Series. "Mr. Clarke has one of the best teams that ever played the game," Jennings said afterward. For his part, Clarke said:

> Really I am so happy that I cannot find words to express my feelings. I have labored season after season with one object in view, and that was to see my club win a world's championship. The thought that we have succeeded and that success was accomplished by clean and pure baseball, makes me feel proud of every member of the team.[10]

For the little Pittsburgh owner, this day was one he would never forget. He had achieved his dream after so many years of trying. He had survived attempts to oust him from baseball, endured treachery from other owners and sometimes from players. He had invested heavily—emotionally and financially—in baseball to a degree few others would dare. And now he was on top of the world. He tried his best to express his feelings to a reporter this way: "If you can imagine how a person would naturally feel after he has finally secured something which he has been earnestly seeking for 10 years, then you can get some slight idea of my feelings at the present time. I never saw them play such ball as they played today."[11]

Aside from the glorious day for Dreyfuss on the field, it also marked his 15th wedding anniversary and here he was out of town on baseball business. But Florence understood her husband's other passion and sent a nice note to him in Detroit wishing that the day "would be doubly memorable" for him.[12]

The World Series was the best yet, attracting 145,807 fans, more than the past two years combined. Receipts for the seven games were also a record, totaling $188,302. The three games in Pittsburgh's big new park lured 82,885 fans, more than the total attendance in the entire World Series in 1907 or 1908.[13] Each Pirate received $1,825 and each Tiger $1,274. Dreyfuss, saddled with significant new debt for Forbes field, opted against sweetening the players' share from his own take as he did in 1903. His share this time amounted to a hefty $51,273, which helped cover the significant bills to operate his club and ballpark. Dreyfuss lamented that his old friend Harry Pulliam, who had put so much into the team, was gone. "I only wish Harry could have lived to see us celebrate our new park with a World Championship," he said.[14] Pittsburgh Mayor W.A. Magee proclaimed

The 1909 Pirates won the World Series, defeating the Detroit Tigers in seven games, to bring baseball's ultimate bragging rights to Pittsburgh and their owner Barney Dreyfuss (Library of Congress).

Monday, October 18 as a civic holiday and the Pirates would be saluted with a parade from downtown to Forbes Field. There, the players were called up to a platform to receive their World Series checks. The loudest and most prolonged cheering by the crowd was reserved for Babe Adams, the rookie hurler who had been the star of the Series with an earned-run average of a miserly 1.33.

The seventh World Series marked a high point in the career of Wagner who outplayed and out-hustled Ty Cobb. Wagner had a better batting average, .333 compared to .231, drove in six runs to Cobb's five, and stole six bases to two for Cobb. Tommy Leach had wielded the hottest bat in the Series, however, with an average of .360 with nine hits and eight runs scored. Aging Fred Clarke scored seven runs on four hits. Gibson's strong arm dissuaded or nabbed many base stealers and kept the larcenous Cobb largely in check. Gibson played every game, making 28 putouts and 10 assists with no errors.

Soon afterward, Dreyfuss summoned his star catcher to his office to ask what he was expecting in a contract for 1910. Traditionally, Gibson never signed new contracts in the fall, fearing if he were traded to a new club in the offseason he was bound by the amount specified in the contract and have no bargaining room with a new team. But Dreyfuss insisted and offered to let Gibson fill in the amount. He was determined to keep his valuable receiver. Gibson said he would sign only if Dreyfuss promised to grant him an unconditional release when he was no longer wanted. "I don't want you to sell my worn-out carcass for a lousy $1,800 after you've gotten all the good out of it," Mooney said, referring to the standard waiver fee Dreyfuss would receive (it was actually $1,500 at the time). Dreyfuss agreed to Gibson's demand and the two men shook hands on it. Gibson then signed a two-year contract at $6,000 annually.[15] Soon afterward, lost on a waiver claim was Bill Abstein, the error-prone first baseman who had struck out nine times in the series and muffed five throws. The Pirates would again be solid behind the plate, but the search for a reliable first baseman was on again.

The National League's winter meeting in December in New York would be a particularly difficult one and test the Pittsburgh owner's influence among his peers. The issue of the league presidency pitted Dreyfuss and Garry Herrmann of Cincinnati, both of whom wanted interim president John Heydler to get the post, against another faction led by Brush in New York and Murphy in Chicago who were promoting former player John Montgomery Ward. Murphy and Brush were joined by Charles Ebbets of Brooklyn in seeking a more malleable president, less inclined to back umpires in his decisions, a practice Heydler had continued from Pulliam. They sought someone "whom they can influence on this umpire question as in the old days of the National League, when it was possible for certain umpires to be barred from working in some baseball parks ... at the request of managers," said the *New York Times*.[16] Ward was someone they felt they could control. Brush was still angry at the bribery scandal when Pulliam backed his umpires to the hilt. Herrmann was particularly outspoken in his support of Heydler, however, insisting he had "given the public such great confidence in his administration" and it was in the best interests of the game that he continue. Under Heydler's tenure, Herrmann continued, "baseball was lifted to a high standard and was at the height of its prosperity."[17]

The Cincinnati owner arrived before the December 14 opening of the annual gathering in a bid to campaign for Heydler. He and Dreyfuss were joined by Boston's John Dovey and St. Louis owner Stanley Robison in backing Heydler. But they needed a fifth vote to carry the day. Dreyfuss was suspicious of Horace Fogel, the new president in Philadelphia, formerly a sportswriter, who had somehow come up with $500,000 to buy the

Phillies. It was believed the source of Fogel's money was Murphy and Charles Taft, the brother of the new U.S. president, who held shares in the Chicago franchise. Dreyfuss wanted Fogel barred from the meeting unless he disclosed the true owners of his club, but his effort failed.[18] It came as no surprise when Fogel aligned with Murphy, Brush and Ebbets to back Ward for the league presidency. The vote was split 4–4 on the presidency issue. "Heydler has been such a fine president," Dreyfuss lamented, "and when you've got a good man what's the sense in changing?" He and Herrmann were willing to give Heydler a five-year contract to end the annual wrangling over the post.[19]

Shortly before the National League conclave, American League president Ban Johnson saw fit to weigh in, repeating an earlier assertion he'd never be able to work with Ward. In 1903, Ward acted as a lawyer for a player who jumped to the American League and ever since Johnson had held Ward in contempt because of how he operated, despite a favorable outcome for the AL. He warned that Ward's election could reignite hostilities, saying: "It is certain the present good will between the leagues would be a thing of the past, and it might come to a war in the end." Ward would end harmony and be controlled by Brush and Murphy, Johnson predicted, adding "it would be suicidal to the welfare of the game." Then, in a bid to exert further pressure on Brush and Murphy, Johnson said he was prepared to name the persons behind the umpire-bribing episode at the Polo Grounds, explaining he "came into possession of considerable new evidence in the matter last summer."[20]

During the meeting, the two sides dug in on the presidency issue and stories of intrigue were circulated, including one that Herrmann and Dreyfuss would bolt to the American League if Ward became president. Under that scenario the junior circuit would increase to 10 teams for one year to accommodate them.[21] There were rumors that Murphy and Brush tried to bribe Robison to join their side by offering him topflight players to put St. Louis back in the pennant race. "Brush of New York and Murphy of Chicago are said to have made enticing offers of players to Robison if he will vote for Ward," it was reported.[22] Backroom discussions continued as it became clear the deadlock could not be resolved. Then, a startling message arrived from Johnson. He sent Herrmann a telegram following the American League meeting in New York, recanting his position about Ward, saying: "We do not wish to interfere or embarrass to the slightest degree your organization in the election of an officer." It appeared Johnson had been reined in by his owners who were anxious to avoid hostilities. Johnson's reversal shocked Herrmann and Dreyfuss and provided some comfort to the Brush-Murphy faction, but the stalemate continued. On December 18, the fourth day of proceedings, Thomas Lynch, a former umpire in the minor and major leagues, was finally elected president. He was a compromise candidate put forward by Brush when he realized Ward was a hopeless cause. The selection ended an impasse that stretched to 72 hours. Lynch's nomination was rather ironic coming from the leader of a faction unhappy that Pulliam and Heydler had so strongly supported umpires in the past. Lynch had a good reputation and was available, so he garnered support from both sides who were tired of fighting. Lynch insisted Heydler return to his post as secretary-treasurer, a move supported by owners who gave him a three-year contract. I.E. Sanborn, a writer for the *Chicago Tribune* said Lynch's election "is considered by all except the Ward adherents as a victory for the Herrmann-Dreyfuss peace faction and a practical vindication of Heydler."[23] Heydler retained an active role in League affairs in the near term and eventually became full-time president.

Cap Anson, 57, the former Chicago star and manager, had been waiting in the

Cincinnati Reds owner August (Garry) Herrmann and Barney Dreyfuss were allies as they battled less progressive National League team owners. The two men became sworn enemies as time went on, however, and Dreyfuss worked hard to oust Herrmann from his post as chairman of the National Commission, which oversaw baseball from 1903 to 1920 (Library of Congress).

wings, along with several other compromise candidates. Anson showed no reaction to the election of Lynch and promptly sought out Fogel, who by now had admitted Murphy and Brush were the money men behind him. Anson immediately applied to manage Fogel's Phillies for the upcoming season. He didn't get the job and, still desperate for money, joined the vaudeville circuit. Anson continued to dream about leading the National League until his death in 1922.[24]

The other good news for Dreyfuss from the meeting emerged before the contentious presidency arose. Fred Clarke, now 37, agreed to return to manage the Bucs in 1910, continuing his association with Dreyfuss that stretched back to 1894 in Louisville. "This will be the seventeenth year Barney and myself have been in baseball," Clarke told *Sporting Life*. "Long time, but I know that it has been a pleasurable and profitable period for me." The two-year deal, at $15,000 annually, was a $3,000 boost from 1909. The only manager earning more than Clarke was John McGraw in New York, said to be paid $17,000 a year.[25] Both Clarke and McGraw also received a share of profits from their clubs. Dreyfuss described signing Clarke as "the best possible piece of business I could have done at this meeting." For his part, Clarke scoffed at rumors he had considered retiring. "Barney Dreyfuss and I understand each other perfectly," he said. "We always treat each other fairly. I would not work in baseball for any other man, and I have had Mr. Dreyfuss's assurance every year that there will be a place with him as long as I want it."[26]

Dreyfuss had been appointed yet again to the schedule committee and won another fight at a scheduling meeting held in Pittsburgh the following month. Chicago's Murphy and Brooklyn's Ebbets were among club officials pushing to extend the 154-game schedule to 168 games but Dreyfuss was strongly opposed, arguing the season was already long enough. Ebbets touted significant financial rewards from a longer season and said 168 games should be tried as an experiment and if that didn't work out, the League could revert to 154 games.[27] At the Pittsburgh gathering, Dreyfuss won support for the status quo by promising to extend the season to October 15, but not add games.[28] All owners would have profited from a longer schedule, but Dreyfuss felt it wasn't good for the game. Financial considerations didn't shape all his decisions in baseball. For instance, he didn't allow advertising on the walls at Forbes Field when other owners used theirs to generate extra income. He thought the clutter was distracting. After Dreyfuss passed away, his family continued to ban advertising, with one minor exception. In 1943, a 32-foot-tall wooden United States Marine sergeant was placed to the right of the scoreboard along with banners promoting the sale of war bonds.

For Dreyfuss, the scheduling squabble was minor compared to his other battles, but he once again displayed his clout among League magnates.

14

Departures and Decline

During the offseason, Dreyfuss sold Vic Willis to the Cardinals, even though he had won 22 games for the Pirates in 1909. But he had clashed with manager Clarke and the owner invariably supported his manager and had little use for dissension. Willis, in whom Dreyfuss placed faith when others didn't, delivered handsomely for him. After winning only nine games for the seventh-place Cardinals in 1910, Willis was claimed on waivers by Chicago but instead chose to retire.[1]

"Our 1910 team was my biggest disappointment in baseball," Dreyfuss admitted years later to sportswriter Fred Lieb. "Never did I see a great team fold so quickly." The Pirates began well and fought for first place with the Giants, the Phillies and then the Cubs who, once they reached the top spot, remained there. New York finished 13 games back and the Pirates 17½ off the pace. Chicago had their airtight Tinker-to-Evers-to-Chance infield combination and a solid outfield. Three Finger Brown managed 25 wins and rookie Leonard "King" Cole counted 20. For the Giants, Christy Mathewson won 27 games to lead the National League, but his team was inconsistent.

A surprise for Pittsburgh was the sometimes-dismal performances by Honus Wagner defensively, although he hit .320 and tied for the league lead in hits. Babe Adams did well, winning 18 games while losing nine. But Howie Camnitz had only 12 victories, less than half his total from 1909. Lefty Leifield picked up 15 and veteran Deacon Phillippe, who was now 38, had 14. Two new faces were added to the outfield during the season, Vin Campbell and Max Carey (real name Maximilian Carnarius), a future Hall of Famer. Both showed promise and were speedsters on the base paths. Campbell, 22, hit .326 in 97 games with the Bucs. Carey, 20, a student at a Lutheran seminary and sometime shortstop, was playing for South Bend where he stole 86 bases in 96 games, earning himself a place in Dreyfuss's "dope book." He was signed by Pittsburgh in the closing days of the season.

The poor performance of the Flying Dutchman was noted early in the season. He'd been an offensive juggernaut in 1909, but clearly something was amiss. He was hitting below .300 and his fielding was subpar. Excuses were found in his injuries, a lingering cold and several slumps. He argued more with umpires than in the past, earning several ejections and suspensions and he had out-of-character clashes with teammates.[2] In *Sporting News,* Ralph S. Davis wrote that the team's "most inexcusable performances have been those by Wagner." In his harsh assessment Davis said such play "would not be excused in a bush leaguer. His fielding has been most erratic and so has his hitting." Worst of all, it seemed "he did not care how matters went." Some of Wagner's friends, Davis said, felt he spent too much time distracted by his automobile, while "less charitable" ones said he was drinking heavily. Wagner was greeted by hisses and hoots from spectators for his play and Davis couldn't imagine he would sacrifice his great career for alcohol. "I can't understand for the life of me why he hasn't been playing the game."[3]

Evidence that the problem was indeed drink came in *Sporting News* the following February when Davis noted neither Dreyfuss nor Clarke had been happy with Wagner during 1910. "It is also known that last fall Clarke and Wagner had a talk, in which the manager put it squarely up to the star on these terms, 'No booze, or no base ball.'" Wagner, Davis wrote, promised to mend his ways and things seemed to improve.[4] But his reform came too late to power the Pirates to the pennant. His batting improved by September when he was hitting at a .385 clip, but he ended the 1910 season with an average of .320, good for fifth place behind league hitting champion Sherry Magee of Philadelphia who hit .331. Wagner had his worst showing since 1898. He was tied for first in hits with Pirates third baseman Bobby Byrne with 178, but was fifth in doubles, runs batted in and in total bases.

For the fourth year in a row, Mooney Gibson played more games than any other catcher in the National League, 143. And he caught 137 would-be base stealers, more than any League backstop. His fielding percentage of .984 was the best in the league and his 203 assists led all catchers in the majors. As Wagner had faltered, the next star of the Pirates had stepped up, but it was not enough to fill the big shoes of the Flying Dutchman. Gibson's batting average was a modest .259.

In the World Series, Connie Mack's Athletics of the American League defeated the Cubs four games to one.

Dreyfuss was determined to shake things up for 1911. It was bad enough the Pirates hadn't repeated as League champions despite having more than enough talent to do so, but his team finished behind the Giants of manager John McGraw. Dreyfuss realized he had to do something to get his men, particularly Wagner, again focused on every game. He sensed it wasn't just Wagner who had been hitting the bottle. That fall, Dreyfuss announced that unless players signed contracts in which they pledged temperance, they would not be welcomed back. The idea came from Clarke who had confronted Wagner about his drinking. While some managers for other clubs were leery about imposing alcohol bans, Red Dooin quickly followed suit with the Phillies and predicted more would follow. Gibson advised Dreyfuss in a letter it was a good move. "That anti-booze contract strikes me as just right. I am heartily in accord with it and believe all the other boys will be."[5] Dreyfuss saw leadership potential in Gibson and tapped him to assist Clarke.

The whiskey business, which had made Barney Dreyfuss a wealthy man, may have feared the temperance movement that was gaining strength across North America and would eventually lead to Prohibition. But, irony be damned, if demanding his players abstain from alcohol made for better baseball, the Pittsburgh owner was all for it.

Before the 1911 season, Barney Dreyfuss parted ways with pitcher Sam Leever, who had won 194 games since joining the Pirates in 1898. Over the years, Leever had been a big contributor to the success of the Pirates and many fans were sorry to see him go. Deacon Phillippe, now 39, had been relegated mainly to relief work the previous two seasons and made three disappointing appearances in 1911 before retiring. He became manager of the Pittsburgh entry in the United States Baseball League, an outlaw league that hit the field in 1913 and played out of Exposition Park. In his honor, the club was known as the "Filipinos," and was perched atop the shaky and undercapitalized circuit when it collapsed by June.

The 1911 season would resemble the previous one for the Pirates, who again finished third, this time 14½ games out of first. The New York Giants, whose home at the Polo Grounds caught fire and was heavily damaged on April 14, reached first place in August and took the National League pennant. The Cubs finished second, 7½ games back. Lefty hurler Rube Marquard, whose contract was purchased by Giants manager John McGraw for a hefty $11,000 in 1908, began to pay dividends by winning 24 games and leading the league with 237 strikeouts. When paired with Christy Mathewson, who won 26 games, the Giants had a powerful presence on the mound.

The resurgent Giants no doubt irritated Dreyfuss, who decided to open his wallet to pursue talent as the season progressed. On July 20, he turned heads when he spent $22,500 to acquire well-regarded spitball pitcher Marty O'Toole from the American Association club in St. Paul. The amount was considered fantastic, more than twice what the Giants had paid for Marquard, whose deal had garnered headlines. To handle his spitter, Dreyfuss also purchased O'Toole's catcher, Billy Kelly, for $5,000. O'Toole had attracted widespread attention by striking out 18 batters in one game and 17 in another. Dreyfuss was determined to get him and was forced to outbid several other major league clubs. But O'Toole failed to deliver the goods for the Pirates, winning three games in 1911, then 15 in 1912, just 6 in 1913 and only one in 1914. A better acquisition was right-handed spitballer Claude Hendrix, who won four games in 10 decisions and then 24 in 1912.[6] Honus Wagner won his eighth and last batting title in 1911, with a .334 average. Fred Clarke appeared in 110 games and hit .324, while Babe Adams and Howie Camnitz registered 22 and 20 wins respectively. Vin Campbell, the outstanding rookie outfielder from 1910, held out for more money and did not join the roster until early July, appearing in only 42 games. Dreyfuss felt Campbell lacked loyalty and showed disrespect for him and the team by holding out so long. At the end of the season, he traded the speedy Campbell to Boston.[7] Connie Mack's Philadelphia Athletics won the World Series, defeating McGraw's Giants four games to two, no doubt pleasing Dreyfuss.

Another of the old-timers upon whom Dreyfuss had relied for so long also left the Pirates in 1912. After only 28 games reliable slugger Tommy Leach was traded to the Chicago Cubs along with hurler Lefty Leifield for center fielder Arthur "Solly" Hofman and pitcher King Cole, who'd won 20 games for the Cubs in 1910. Neither of the newcomers lasted long or made much of a mark. The popular Leach, 34, had been with Dreyfuss since 1898 in Louisville. He'd play four more seasons before retiring after a 19-year career and 2,156 games. His career batting average was .269 and his slugging percentage was .370. After two years in the minors, Leach returned to the Bucs in 1918 when the loss of players to the Great War created an opportunity for the 40-year-old. He played 30 games with the Pirates and managed to hit only .194. Afterward, he returned to the minors, playing until 1922, then managing and becoming a scout for the Boston Braves.[8]

Dreyfuss the businessman made a sizeable non-baseball investment during 1912 in a firm owned by his brother-in-law Edwin Welte back in Freiburg. His company, M. Welte & Sohne was becoming known for the production of innovative and complex electric-powered player pianos and player organs. Welte took over the family firm in 1900, shortly after marrying Betty Dreyfuss, Barney's younger sister. In 1912, Welte opened an American subsidiary in New York City and built a manufacturing plant in Poughkeepsie, New York, to produce the machines and their paper player rolls. Family members, including Barney Dreyfuss, invested in the new venture whose products were found in the homes of the wealthy, in palaces, in schools and on yachts. It was said one was manufactured for the *Titanic*, but arrived too late for installation. When the United

States entered the Great War, the company's property and its patents were considered assets of the enemy. They were confiscated by the American government and auctioned off and the manufacturing plant was sold.[9] Like his investments in players, not everything Dreyfuss acquired panned out as he hoped.

The 1912 season saw another strong performance by the New York Giants, who romped to the pennant 10 games ahead of Pittsburgh. The Pirates had good pitching, with their spitballer Claude Hendrix winning 24 games, two more than Howie Camnitz. Wagner missed 7 games with a sprained ankle and charley horse. He batted .324. Clarke broke a toe and didn't play at all, while pitcher Marty O'Toole was plagued by rheumatism. Outfielder Owen "Chief" Wilson hammered a league-leading 36 triples, three of them in one game, with a season batting average of .300. Boston won the World Series, four games to three, leaving the Giants as bridesmaids in the series for the second year in a row.

For 1913, Fred Clarke managed the Pirates from the bench, rather than the outfield. He was 40 and his legs were troubling him. He found it hard to stay off the field, however, and played in nine games. The team dropped to fourth and the Giants claimed their third straight pennant. Yet again, McGraw was frustrated at the World Series when Connie Mack's Athletics took the honors, four games to one. Dreyfuss was unhappy at the fourth-place finish for the Pirates and decided to make changes. He traded five of his players: Chief Wilson, infielders Dots Miller and Art Butler, third baseman Cozy Dolan, and left-handed pitcher Hank Robinson, to St. Louis for three Cardinals—Ed Konetchy, a proven first baseman and cleanup hitter, third baseman Mike Mowrey and right-handed pitcher Bob Harmon. Pittsburgh fans were unsure about the wisdom of the trade, but Dreyfuss reassured them: "At long last we again have a high-class first baseman."[10] But the Pittsburgh owner was wrong about Konetchy, who batted .249 in 1914, far below expectations.

The new Federal League was founded as a new minor loop in 1913, with teams originally in Chicago, Pittsburgh, Cleveland, Indianapolis, St. Louis and Covington, Kentucky. By August the circuit declared itself a major league and late that year defections to it were underway. Among the top players to jump was Joe Tinker, the former Cub who had been with Cincinnati. At the National Commission, Garry Herrmann was dismissive of the upstart league, saying it lacked "prosperity or prestige."[11] He promised to remain neutral if existing contracts were respected. They weren't. Nearly 50 players jumped to the Federal League from National League or American League teams, but only two of the first jumpers, pitcher Claude Hendrix and catcher Mike Simon were from the Pirates. By the time it expired in 1915, the Federal League attracted 81 major leaguers, 18 of whom broke major league contracts and 63 who ignored big league reserve clauses.[12] Federal League teams lured players by offering higher pay, which began to cause concern among the two established major leagues. Ban Johnson at the American League vowed no player from the Federal League would ever play in his loop. The upstart league did well at the turnstiles but litigation ensued over the signing of players and the Fed went to court in early 1915 hoping to have the AL and NL declared in breach of the Sherman Anti-Trust Act. It accused the two leagues of conspiring to be a monopoly. Peace talks were under way by late 1915 and the Federal League withdrew its anti-trust suit. In the settlement, Charles Weeghman, owner of the Federal team in Chicago, was allowed to purchase the National League Cubs from Charles Taft for $500,000 while in St. Louis the Terriers owner, Phil Ball bought the Browns for $525,000.[13] Other Fed team owners received cash settlements. Overall, the settlement cost the major leagues $5 million to regain their monopoly. Losses

The voice of Barney Dreyfuss had become an important one by the time National League owners met in New York late in 1913 and elected John K. Tener as president of the loop. Dreyfuss is seated at the left end of the front row (Library of Congress).

for the circuit during its brief history were estimated at from $2.5 million to as much as $10 million.

The National League entered 1914 with a new president, Pennsylvania governor John K. Tener, a former major league pitcher, picked to succeed Thomas J. Lynch who had been constantly criticized by several owners since assuming the post in 1910. Lynch discovered the sort of pressure that prompted Harry Pulliam to take his life. Tener was given a four-year contract at $25,000 a year and John A. Heydler handled daily duties until Tener's term as governor ended at the outset of 1915. One of Tener's first steps was to order Chicago's majority owner Charles Murphy to pay Johnny Evers $40,000 for dismissing the Cubs manager without providing the 10 days' notice stipulated in his long-term contract. Soon afterward, the widely disliked Murphy was forced out of the Chicago franchise when shareholder Charles Taft purchased his stock for $500,000.[14] A few months later, Weeghman became owner of the Cubs. Dreyfuss, and most other owners, were not sad to see Murphy go. The Chicago magnate had few friends in baseball and had often clashed with the Pittsburgh owner and Cincinnati's Herrmann.

For the Pirates, the 1914 season was dismal. Boston, renamed the Braves, took the National League pennant. They had been in last place as late as July 18 when it seemed the New York Giants were poised to claim their fourth straight title. The Braves featured cast-offs from other teams and managed third-best pitching overall. The Pirates finished seventh, 25½ games back, their worst finish under Dreyfuss, who was particularly upset at the performance of Ed Konetchy. Wagner hit only .252, but Gibson improved to .285, a career best. Immediately after the season, Konetchy jumped to the Pittsburgh Rebels of the Federal League. In the World Series, the Boston Braves defeated the Philadelphia Athletics four games straight.

Pittsburgh improved slightly for a fifth-place finish in 1915 when, remarkably, the 41-year-old Wagner started every game. His batting average increased slightly to .274, and he hit six home runs, 32 doubles and 17 triples. It was a different story for Fred Clarke, 42, who appeared in only one game, his last in the major leagues. He and Dreyfuss had been close for 22 years, but the team owner was upset at the failure of the Bucs to perform better. He was willing to have Clarke remain as skipper but offered him a reduced salary. Dreyfuss explained later: "Fred Clarke can't expect a first-division manager's salary when he finishes in the second division." After shaking hands with Dreyfuss, Clarke retired to his ranch in Kansas where he raised mules. "After handling ball players for many years," he explained, "handling mules should be easy."[15] Clarke had managed his ball teams to more than 1,400 victories and it was only in his last two years the Pirates had finished out of the first division.

Aside from losing Clarke, Dreyfuss missed landing one of the future stars of baseball, first baseman George Sisler, in what sportswriter Fred Lieb called "a raw deal." The Ohio native was signed as a pitcher by Branch Rickey, manager of the St. Louis Browns, upon graduating from the University of Michigan in 1915. Before attending university, Sisler had signed a minor league contract with a club in Akron, Ohio, where he had attended high school. While he was at Michigan, the Akron club sold his contract to a team in Columbus, Ohio, which then sold it to Pittsburgh. Both St. Louis and Pittsburgh claimed Sisler and the dispute went before the National Commission to be adjudicated. There, John Tener, new president of the National League, sided with Pittsburgh. Ban Johnson backed the claim of St. Louis of his American League. The deciding vote rested with Garry Herrmann, still chair of the Commission who was viewed in many quarters as too close to the American League's Johnson. The two men were known to be drinking buddies.[16] Not surprisingly, Herrmann backed St. Louis and declared the Pittsburgh contract void. He and Johnson argued that Sisler had signed his first contract while still a minor, so it was invalid. Sisler's contract with St. Louis, signed as an adult, was fine, Herrmann and Johnson ruled, over the objection of the National League's John Tener.

Dreyfuss erupted, claiming he had been robbed and complained to team owners and baseball writers across the country. He prized loyalty and he viewed Herrmann's decision as treachery. From that point on, Dreyfuss undertook a campaign to unseat Herrmann and, if that failed, to disband the Commission entirely and replace it with a new structure. As always, Dreyfuss hated losing and even went so far as to say he'd sell the Pirates because of the unfairness of losing Sisler—if he could get a good price. It was reported that former Boston Braves owner James Gaffney, who was keen to return to baseball, made an offer that fell short. The threat of selling his club may have been bluster on Dreyfuss's part but a potential sale to Gaffney caught the attention of the *New York Times.Times.*[17] Dreyfuss stayed put. At the National League annual meeting in December the Pittsburgh magnate introduced a motion to abolish the National Commission and replace it with a single man to oversee the game who had no financial interest in any team. Dreyfuss's bid failed for lack of support because Herrmann was still generally liked by most owners. Herrmann's biographer William A. Cook conceded the Sisler affair irreparably damaged the 15-year relationship between the Cincinnati owner and Dreyfuss, and "would become a question mark on the legacy of August Garry Herrmann and weaken support for him as National Commission Chairman." Cook noted that Herrmann and the commission were preoccupied with peace negotiations with the Federal League, otherwise his tenure might have come to an end at that time.[18]

For his part, Sisler's bat and fielding drew acclaim throughout his 15-year career with St. Louis and Washington and later with Boston in the National League. He won two batting titles with averages exceeding .400, he recorded 257 hits in 1920, a record unsurpassed for 84 years, and was inducted into the Hall of Fame. His presence in the Pirates lineup might have changed the fortunes of the club, which went a decade without capturing another pennant.

Replacing Fred Clarke as manager for 1916 was James "Nixey" Callahan, a former manager of the Chicago White Sox known for his impatience with player errors. Like John McGraw at the Giants, Callahan would call out his men for poor play during a game. When agitated, the former pitcher yelled at them when they fell short, peppering his language with expletives. Under his watch, the Pirates ended the season in sixth place, 29 games behind pennant-winning Brooklyn. Wagner appeared in 123 games and batted .287. The top offensive player was outfielder Max Carey, who led the league with 63 stolen bases and scored 90 runs, twice as many as Wagner. Al Mamaux was the best pitcher, winning 21 times. Barney Dreyfuss admitted he made two "painful moves" during the season, releasing Babe Adams and Mooney Gibson. Adams developed a sore shoulder and won only two games with nine losses. On August 3, the hurler who starred as a rookie in the 1909 World Series, was released to St. Joseph, Missouri, of the Class A Western League. Twelve days later he was gone. He had demanded that when Dreyfuss no longer needed him he'd be granted an unconditional release. That didn't happen. As for Gibson, Dreyfuss said he asked for waivers to comply with his catcher's wishes, but the New York Giants claimed him. "I expected to give him his unconditional freedom, and allow him to map out his own future," Dreyfuss said. "But when New York claimed him, I had to turn him over to the Giants." In so doing, Dreyfuss picked up $1,500 for the catcher (Gibson recalled it was $1,800), despite the owner's 1909 promise he wouldn't take money for releasing him. The Pirates owner praised Gibson as "one of the most faithful and hardest working players I have ever had any dealings with. It was a real pain to have to part with him."[19]

Years later, Gibson recalled the situation with bitterness. "I was furious. I went straight to the front office. 'Mr. Dreyfuss,' I said, 'you broke your promise.'" He reminded the owner he'd agreed not to sell off Gibson's "broken-down carcass." Dreyfuss, he said, "tried to offer some lame excuse" but the angry catcher strode out the door. Gibson said he called McGraw in New York and suggested the team get its money back because he had no interest in going there and was instead going home to London, Ontario. The following winter, McGraw called him there and asked him to join the Giants as a part-time player and coach, working with his pitchers. Gibson relented when McGraw sympathized with his claim about the promise the catcher said was broken by Dreyfuss. McGraw paid Gibson the waiver amount and the salary he missed in August and September from the Pirates.[20] For now, Gibson was a Giant. But Pittsburgh hadn't seen the last of the popular backstop. In retrospect, it's difficult to understand why Dreyfuss broke his commitment to Gibson. He may simply have forgotten it in the press of current business, or felt he had to abide by League rules and accept the release money from New York. But he could have turned the money over to Gibson along with an explanation. Regardless, it seemed out of character for the man who prized loyalty and believed in a man's word.

14. Departures and Decline

At the National League meeting in December of 1916, Dreyfuss again called for a replacement of the National Commission with a one-man commissioner free of financial interest in any team. He was still gunning for the Cincinnati owner who called his bluff and offered to resign if it would bring peace. But the magnates were more concerned with issues like the Great War and how it might impact baseball along with the need to rebuild public support and confidence following the bruising battle with the Federal League. There was no appetite for restructuring and Herrmann survived yet again.[21]

For the first 60 days of the 1917 season, the Pirates were mired in the League basement. The new manager, Callahan simply disappeared without telling anyone on June 30. Several days later, police found him drunk in a Philadelphia gutter. He was fired. The job of managing was assigned to Wagner for a few games before 240-pound Czech-born football player Hugo Francis Bezdek was found by Dreyfuss to replace him.[22] Bezdek piloted the Pirates to a last-place finish, 47 games back of New York who lost the World Series to the Chicago White Sox. Pitcher Al Mamaux had a poor season. He won only two games and lost 11, following two consecutive 21-win seasons. Most significantly, Honus Wagner, now 43, decided it was finally time to call it a career. Many considered him the best shortstop of all time, as he hit better than .300 in 15 consecutive seasons and stealing 723 bases in his 21-year career. During that time, he appeared in nearly 2,800 major-league games, belted 3,420 hits, 101 home runs, and drove in 1,732 runs. Wagner would be among the first inductees to the Baseball Hall of Fame. His departure was felt keenly by Dreyfuss, his teammates, and the fans of Pittsburgh who associated him with the team's glory years.

There had been grumbling in the press and among fans about the poor performance of the Pirates, who had become a second-division club after so many years as a pennant contender. Some blame was placed on the shoulders of Dreyfuss, but he soldiered on, shuffling his deck of players, ridding himself of pitchers Mamaux and the abrasive Burleigh Grimes, one of the most successful spitballers of all time. Among the better players he found was outfielder Billy Southworth, picked up mid–1918 from Birmingham. He'd bat .341. Because of the war, which America had joined in 1917, the regular season ended on September 2. Bezdek was able to lead his men to a fourth-place finish, just 1½ games back of Cincinnati and 17 games back of pennant-winning Chicago. The Cubs lost in the World Series to the Boston Red Sox. The Bucs, like many other clubs, lost some of their talent to the war effort because baseball was not deemed an "essential" service. Max Carey led the league in steals, with 58, while the Pirates' top hurler, Wilbur Cooper, managed 19 wins.

During the 1918 season, National League president John Tener resigned. His departure followed several rulings by the National Commission that seemed to favor the American League. One particularly ugly dispute was between the Boston Braves and the Philadelphia Athletics about the rights to pitcher Scott Perry.[23] Ban Johnson was a stronger personality than Commission chair Garry Herrmann and was grating on National League owners and even some magnates in his own circuit. Herrmann, it was observed in the *New York Herald*, "always was more or less under the sway of Johnson" with whom he continued to socialize.[24] And Johnson was becoming known as the "Baseball dictator" for his autocratic ways. The newspaper said the National Commission must be dissolved as part of a major housecleaning for baseball. In the same newspaper Fred Lieb broke the story that longtime critic of the commission, Barney Dreyfuss, had come up the idea of offering a new post of Commissioner of Baseball to former U.S. President William Howard Taft.[25] The Pittsburgh owner, he wrote, had spent about two weeks quietly lining up support for the idea among eastern clubs. Boston Red Sox owner Harry Frazee and Harry Hempstead, owner of the New York Giants, enthusiastically threw their support behind the Taft plan and Brooklyn owner Charles Ebbets joined them. Taft was a popular choice because of his well-established love of baseball and in 1910 he began the tradition of the American president tossing out the "first pitch" on Washington's opening day. At the end of November, Frazee and Hempstead leaked the Taft plan to the press, a move which deeply offended Dreyfuss because Taft himself had not yet been consulted.[26] Taft then pondered the offer, but on November 30 announced he was not interested in such a permanent post.[27] Frazee and Hempstead had acted without any authority in offering him the position and Johnson and his cronies would likely have blocked it anyway. Talk about replacing the Commission with a single commissioner had been under way for some time and would continue. When the National League gathered for its winter conclave in New York, Dreyfuss was undeterred, telling Lieb:

> I have been fighting for a new system of baseball government for some time and now that I am getting some people to agree with me, I am stronger for the project than ever.
>
> As far as I am concerned there is nothing personal in this fight. I know I felt I was badly treated in the Sisler matter, but that is all past and gone. I want to see baseball governed in a way that there is likely to be the least possible friction, and for that reason I strongly favor a one man commissioner with full powers.[28]

At the National League gathering, John Heydler was elected president to replace Tener and retained his position as secretary-treasurer. Because of uncertainty about how baseball would fare in the post-war environment, the magnates opted to shorten the 1919 season to 140 games. Their worries proved to be unfounded as fans flocked back to the ballparks in large numbers.

In January of 1919, both the National and American leagues formed committees to consider reforms and potential candidates for the post of baseball commissioner. Meanwhile, Garry Herrmann, chairman of the National Commission since 1903, remained on the job but his days were numbered. The Commission began devising a new system for the distribution of gate receipts from the World Series. The move was prompted by a strike threatened by players just before the recent series to protest a decision to cut their bonuses by more than 70 percent.[29]

Bezdek was back as manager of the Pirates for 1919, leading them to another fourth-place finish, winning only three more games than they lost. Hitting was poor and while outfielder Max Carey batted .307, best among the regular players, he appeared in only 66 games, plagued by boils. One of the few bright spots in the season came late, when Dreyfuss acquired rookie Charlie Grimm from Little Rock to play first base. The 20-year-old left-hander brought a banjo with him and a sense of fun as he finally solved Dreyfuss's first-base woes that dated back to 1904. Grimm batted .318 in his 14 games. The Cincinnati Reds took the National League pennant, nine games ahead of New York. In the World Series they faced the favored Chicago White Sox but the Reds won. Months later, the Series came under scrutiny for its integrity. It would be long remembered more for crooked players than for the quality of play.

Also during 1919, Barney Dreyfuss's only son, Sam, 22, graduated from Princeton University and began working in the business office of the Pirates. His father was grooming him to take over the team and by 1923 Sam, usually known as Sammy, was treasurer and in 1929 became vice-president.[30] Meanwhile, Bezdek resigned at the end of the season to become the football coach at Penn State University.

To replace Bezdek, Dreyfuss hired Mooney Gibson, a rather unexpected choice given Gibson's resentment of the Pittsburgh owner for his release in 1916. Gibson spent 1917 and 1918 with the New York Giants as a backup catcher and coach. In 1917, when New York won the pennant, he appeared in 35 games and in 1918, when the Giants finished second, only four. He worked closely with the pitchers during his time in New York, then retired at age 38. In his 14-year career, Gibson played 1,213 games, had a career batting average of .236, an impressive fielding percentage of .977 and had thrown out 48 percent of opponents who dared to steal on him. He was not about to leave baseball and jumped at an offer to manage the Toronto Maple Leafs of the International League with the encouragement of McGraw. He piloted the club to a second-place finish and was expecting to return for a second season in Ontario's capital city, 120 miles east of his home in London.

During the final month of the Leafs' campaign that ended September 14, Barney Dreyfuss began calling him about his plans for 1920.[31] Once the season ended, he offered Gibson the job of Pirates manager. Gibson was stunned at first. "Here's the man that I could have hanged, calling me up and wanting to know what I was gonna do next year," Gibson recalled in an interview late in his life with baseball author and historian Lawrence S. Ritter.[32] His old catcher reminded Dreyfuss about breaking his promise not to profit from his "carcass" by collecting a waiver fee and then failing to pay him for August and September of 1916. Gibson was in the driver's seat and Dreyfuss knew it. He agreed to pay his former catcher the waiver fee and the two months of salary. "Well, naturally, I said yes," Gibson told Ritter with a smile, noting he had already been paid the fee and salary by a sympathetic McGraw. "But Barney Dreyfuss didn't know that, and as far as I was concerned he owed it to me anyway for breaking his promise," Gibson said.[33] With that, the still-wary Gibson asked to review the Bucs roster before signing any contract and attended a Pittsburgh-Giants series at Forbes Field, unbeknownst to Dreyfuss. There, he stepped onto the field to chat with McGraw and received an unexpected standing ovation from the Pirates faithful who recognized him. In New York for a special meeting of the National League, Dreyfuss got wind of what happened and raced back to Pittsburgh. Gibson kept stalling and it wasn't until he and Dreyfuss met in Buffalo in late November that the deal was finalized and Gibson took the job Dreyfuss so desperately wanted him to accept. The one-year contract was set at $12,000, plus a bonus, depending on finish.[34]

The return of Gibson was hailed by Pittsburgh fans and the local newspapers. In the *Pittsburgh Post,* for instance, Edward F. Balinger said the hiring was a "most pleasing bit of news ... he comes not as a stranger, but more like the prodigal returning home.... He knows the game from A to Z and nobody who is personally acquainted with the big Canadian will doubt for a moment that he is qualified to take up the reins in a major league field."[35] At the *Pittsburgh Press,* Ralph S. Davis predicted Gibson would "give Pittsburgh a team that will play earnest, aggressive, up-to-date ball, and that Gibby will be able to get the very best work out of the material which is turned over to him." Davis added that Gibson's time in New York with McGraw and his ability to get along with players were important assets. "Probably no more popular player than Gibson wore a Pittsburgh uniform," he wrote.[36]

Gibson's return conjured up memories of past glories for the Pittsburgh faithful after so many disappointing seasons in recent years. The pressure was on both Gibson and Dreyfuss to right the Pirates' ship in 1920.

15

Retooling

The winter meetings of 1919 were eventful, especially in the American League where president Ban Johnson had become a divisive figure. He came under fire for suspending pitcher Carl Mays, a widely disliked player, who had walked away from the Boston Red Sox in July, saying he could no longer play there. Red Sox owner Harry Frazee traded him to the New York Yankees late that same month for two players and $40,000 in cash. Johnson feared Mays' refusal to play was a bid to get traded and undermined the reserve clause that bound players to their team. He feared it might inspire other disgruntled players to do the same. The Yankees appealed Mays' suspension in court, where a judge ruled Johnson had exceeded his authority. By now, Frazee, New York's Jacob Ruppert and Chicago's Charles Comiskey were fed up with Johnson and began agitating for his removal. The threesome constituted a majority on the American League's board of directors and a dispute soon erupted about the annual meeting in December. Johnson wanted it held in Chicago, but Ruppert insisted on New York. The Yankees owner again went to court and won.

Johnson was able to replace the directors hostile to him with more supportive owners. But Ruppert retaliated, yet again returning to court, where he claimed in a $50,000 lawsuit that Johnson had tried to drive the Yankees out of baseball by conspiring with the Giants to evict them from the Giants-owned Polo Grounds. Ruppert challenged the legitimacy of Johnson's presidency and sought to force open the American League books. The circuit was in disarray and another meeting was convened in February in Chicago where it was decided Mays could remain with the Yankees and the suspension was lifted. Johnson was stripped of his power to suspend players and issue fines. Ruppert and Clark Griffith of the Washington Senators were appointed to a new board of review, leaving Johnson as little more than a figurehead.[1]

Aside from Johnson, the National Commission, which he effectively controlled through its chairman Garry Herrmann, was also being criticized for its handling of the Mays controversy and the Scott Perry ownership fight between the Boston Braves and Philadelphia Athletics. Meantime, a part-owner of the Chicago Cubs, Albert Lasker, had devised a plan for an entirely neutral and independent body to replace the 16-year-old Commission. No owners would be allowed on it. An alternative, he suggested, was a single, powerful commissioner. The Lasker plan for independent oversight was attracting adherents, among them Barney Dreyfuss, now more than ever determined to create a single independent commissioner to guide the game.

The National League's December meeting in New York was a comparatively tame affair as owners agreed to reinstate the 154-game schedule. Out of the blue, however, Herrmann insisted Dreyfuss should no longer draw up schedules for the two leagues.

Herrmann said it was because Dreyfuss was a club owner with a vested interest in playing dates so he assigned the task to president Heydler. Herrmann was apparently good at spotting the conflict of interest in others. In himself, not so much. *Sporting News* said Dreyfuss had done an admirable job of being "fair and square" in his allocation of playing dates over the years and never favored the Pirates. But Herrmann and Dreyfuss, once allies in the business of baseball, had become enemies. "Herrmann's attitude," the publication noted, "was directly the outgrowth of the long, bitter fight between him and the Pittsburgher."[2]

Dreyfuss, as a member of the rules committee, also said it was time to ban the spitball, considered a "freak" pitch because of its erratic behavior after saliva was applied by the pitcher. He'd been campaigning against it for more than a year. Some pitchers and owners claimed they couldn't win games without it, but the Pittsburgh owner insisted it was bad for the game because it suppressed hitting. Babe Ruth had belted 29 home runs in 1919 and fans were

By midlife, Barney Dreyfuss could draw satisfaction from his success with the Pirates, financially, and on the diamond. His constant efforts to improve the game were paying dividends for owners and players alike. But he still hated losing, and he ensured his Pirates remained among the stronger teams in the National League (ca. 1920, National Baseball Hall of Fame Library, Cooperstown, New York).

clamoring for more offensive heroics. That same year a livelier ball, made from a higher grade of wool yarn around machine-wound cores replaced looser, hand-woven cores. Pitchers complained the new balls were more springy and jumped off the bat when struck. Offense improved and fans liked it, Dreyfuss argued, so why keep a pitch that tilted the delicate pitcher-hitter relationship too much in favor of the pitcher? For years, during what became known as the Deadball Era, trick pitches and a softer ball produced low game scores and few home runs. The game was being transformed into something more exciting for fans. Dreyfuss found ready support for a ban and his plan to grandfather existing spitballers but bar newcomers from using it.[3] Spitball pitching would continue in 1920, after only 17 pitchers in both leagues were permitted to use it under the grandfather clause. Burleigh Grimes relied on it until he retired in 1934, the last of his breed.[4] Yet again, Dreyfuss was looking ahead and trying to do what he felt was best for baseball and its fans. His concrete-and-steel ballpark had proven its worth and was widely copied. He was also pushing for changes in how the game governed itself and support for that was also growing. His efforts would bear fruit sooner than anyone expected.

Late in the December conclave, moments after the National League owners agreed to meet with the American League in February, Herrmann announced he was resigning from the National Commission, effective in 30 days. His decision was kept secret until the commission's annual meeting in January. There, he announced simply: "I have had enough of the present situation." He was tired of constant criticism from owners in the National League, particularly Dreyfuss, and no one seemed willing to replace him. The National Commission annual meeting was held in Cincinnati where the *Enquirer* blamed Herrmann's quitting on "malcontents." The other members of the commission, Johnson and Heydler, refused to accept his resignation and asked him to remain until the joint meeting of the two leagues on February 11. Herrmann agreed, but insisted he would not change his mind. The Cincinnati newspaper was sympathetic to him, noting, "Practically the entire opposition to Mr. Herrmann as Chairman consists of five magnates of the National League headed by Barney Dreyfuss of the Pittsburgh club."[5] The other four it identified as Charles Ebbets of Brooklyn, William Veeck of Chicago, William Baker of Philadelphia, and Branch Rickey of St. Louis. Dreyfuss had many complaints about Herrmann, chief among them was that he had become "too thick" with Johnson to properly carry out his duties as chair the commission.[6] By quitting the post he'd held since the Commission was established in 1903, Herrmann placed the governing structure of baseball under scrutiny as never before and created an opportunity for reformers such as Dreyfuss.

In December, while his decision to step down remained secret, Herrmann drew headlines with his announcement he planned to rid baseball of the scourge of gambling. The *New York Times* said Herrmann was concerned about the 1919 World Series and allegations the White Sox had thrown games to benefit his Reds. He insisted baseball officials and players would have known about any such transgression so the story was "without foundation." Of course, it was to Herrmann's benefit to adopt that position, otherwise Cincinnati's victory would remain tainted. Rather, Herrmann declared war on gambling in general. "What gambling is done in baseball starts right in ball parks," he said. "There won't be any ball park gambling next season if I can stop it, and I shall spare no efforts to stop it at the start."[7] Herrmann knew he'd be gone from the National Commission well before the season started, so his saber-rattling may have been a last-minute bid to preserve the Commission's integrity, his own, and by extension, that of his team.

In Pittsburgh, gamblers frequented Forbes Field, but not in the numbers seen in other cities. Over the years, Dreyfuss had tried to rid his park of them, but with limited success. He knew gamblers contributed to crooked play and he wanted the Bucs to stay clear of them. Besides, open betting undermined the wholesome family atmosphere he was trying to develop at his ballpark. Despite Herrmann's call for a cleanup and subsequent official efforts, betting did not disappear overnight. In Pittsburgh, uniformed police officers and those in plain clothes continued to patrol Forbes Field, nabbing anyone attempting to place bets.

Chicago White Sox owner Charles Comiskey knew gamblers had been involved in the series, even if Herrmann didn't. Comiskey had received troubling reports while the series was under way that his team was being influenced to lose to Cincinnati. White Sox officials discreetly looked into the matter and local gamblers confirmed the story, saying a $100,000 payoff had been promised to players, although far less had actually been paid. Gamblers Harry Redmon and Joe Pesch confirmed details of the scheme to Comiskey late in December.[8] He kept silent about what he learned well into the 1920 season while his team vied for first place with Cleveland and New York, finishing two games back of the Indians.

Stories about gambling and bribery were not new in baseball. An almost symbiotic relationship had existed for decades. As baseball historian Jacob Pomrenke put it so well: "This fact is indisputable: As long as there has been baseball, there has been gambling on baseball. As it grew in popularity before the Civil War, many fans [and players] found it enjoyable to be financially invested in the outcome of the game."[9] In fact, it is believed the first fixed game in baseball was September 28, 1865, when the heavily favored Mutuals of New York lost 23–11 to the Eckfords of Brooklyn. Three Mutuals players were bribed to lose that day and were later banned from the sport, although one of them was later reinstated.[10] Boxing and horse racing had lost credibility among spectators because of the influence of gamblers and some baseball club owners feared the same outcome for their game. But efforts to curb gambling in the past amounted to little more than lip service. By the early 1900s, gambling was entrenched in baseball and it was believed some of the early World Series had been affected, specifically the first one, when the Pirates lost. A gambler had offered unreceptive Boston catcher Lou Criger the handsome sum of $12,000 to call for "soft" throws from his pitchers, Criger revealed years later.[11] Many fans attracted to baseball loved betting on it. Professional gamblers understood that well and tried to profit wherever they could. At the time, wagering was widespread and bets could be placed before games or even during them, at home, in shops, in the grandstands and bleachers. It was tolerated for fear banning the practice would hurt attendance. "Betting on baseball was pervasive, an ever-present sideshow that was ignored by the three-man governing body, the National Commission," it has been noted.[12] So Herrmann's announcement was like a conversion on the road to Damascus.

Barney Dreyfuss knew full well that gambling went on in Pittsburgh, a fact that was literally in his face when he was attacked in his owner's box by inebriated gambler "Father Welsh" in 1905. That same year, Dreyfuss was insulted and taunted at the park by John McGraw, who accused him of having unpaid gambling debts. Exposition Park was located in Allegheny City, which was annexed by Pittsburgh in 1907 and gambling was prevalent there. In 1906 newly elected Allegheny City Mayor Charles Kirschler vowed to stamp out the scourge once and for all. "I intend to have a big bunch of officers at every game, and every person who places a bet on the game or on a play will be arrested," he announced. "They will be arrested every day, if necessary, until we stamp out this evil."[13] Kirschler didn't have long to act before his city was annexed and Pittsburgh apparently didn't share his zeal. Gambling continued for many years and by June of 1921 an exasperated Dreyfuss said the problem had become particularly acute and he banned professional gamblers from Forbes Field. "I am going to place men at the gates with instructions to stop every gambler who comes up. There has been a lot of gambling at the field for more than a week. I have complained to the police but they don't seem to take it seriously and now I am going to take it in my own hands."[14] It is not known how successful his efforts were.

The 1908 umpire-bribing scandal to benefit the Giants was a black eye for the game that Dreyfuss loved so much. For the time being, rumors about an attempt to fix the 1919 World Series persisted while the 1920 season got under way. Herrmann's post was left vacant at the National Commission which might otherwise have investigated.

In January, the baseball world was rocked when Babe Ruth, about to turn 25, was sold by Boston owner Harry Frazee to the New York Yankees for a mind-boggling $100,000. As part of the deal, Frazee also borrowed $300,000 from Yankees' owner Jacob Ruppert. Ruth's big bat, combined with a livelier ball and the ban on spitball pitching marked a new era of offense in baseball and the end of the Deadball Era.

Pittsburgh's new manager Mooney Gibson didn't add many new faces to the Pirates lineup for 1920 and, despite his leadership, the club again finished fourth, this time 14 games back of the pennant-winning Brooklyn Robins. Outfielder Max Carey led the league with 52 stolen bases and Babe Adams had a league-leading eight shutouts and an earned-run-average of 2.16 that trailed only Chicago's Pete Alexander. Outfielder Fred Nicholson batted .360 in 99 games. There wasn't much else to cheer the team owner or Bucs fans. Hitting was especially poor, prompting an exasperated Dreyfuss to demand an explanation from Gibson, who retorted: "I guess you just have to get me another Honus Wagner."[15] The American League's Cleveland Indians defeated Brooklyn in the World Series.

In September, Charles Comiskey's closely guarded secret about the 1919 World Series' bribery scandal leaked out unexpectedly. There had developed an unrelated controversy about a National League game several days earlier in Chicago when the Cubs were blanked 3–0 by the Phillies. Cubs president William Veeck went public with reports the game had been fixed and said he would co-operate fully with any investigation. It was said gamblers who bet on the Phillies August 31 had pocketed as much as $50,000.[16] At the time, Chicago was in third place, while Philadelphia was 22 games behind them, dead last. Whether Veeck knew crosstown rival Comiskey was sitting on his dirty little secret about the 1919 World Series is not known. But Veeck's revelation caught the attention of Ban Johnson at the American League and also that of Cook County Judge Charles A. McDonald, newly installed as top criminal judge on September 7. That very day McDonald, an avid fan of baseball, asked a grand jury to look into the Cubs-Phillies game and also "delve into the operations of baseball pools." His announcement drew cheers from members of the jury, suggesting they knew things were fishy. State Attorney Maclay Hoyne joined the fray as chief prosecutor, promising: "Every resource of the state's attorney's office will be used to uncover and bring to justice the ring of professional gamblers whose operations threatened to besmirch the one great American popular sport." The sporting press and others urged the inquiry to include the White Sox and the 1919 World Series. So, too, did the American League's Johnson, an acquaintance of the judge, who had unearthed some evidence of his own.[17] Two weeks later, on the first day of deliberations, Judge McDonald confirmed the controversy-plagued 1919 series would also be scrutinized. "We are not attempting to injure the national sport," the judge said, "but if any one is guilty of fixing games the public should know about it.... War will be waged on the small baseball pool as well as on the big betting by professional gamblers."[18] From then on, the more recent Cubs-Phillies game took a back seat to consideration of the World Series. Indictments were returned against eight Chicago players on October 29, 1920, alleging they conspired to obtain money by false pretenses. Several gamblers were also named in what had become known as the Black Sox Scandal. The trial before judge and jury began the following June. On August 2, 1921, jurors returned not-guilty findings against all accused. Students of the trial suggest jurors identified with the working-class accused rather than the supposed victim, wealthy club owner Comiskey. Historian Bill Lamb posits their finding illustrated "jury nullification," a phenomenon feared by all prosecutors when jurors take into account considerations such as feelings despite being warned by judges to consider only the evidence brought before them.[19]

The joy of the acquitted men was short-lived. The following day, Judge Kenesaw Mountain Landis, who had been elected Commissioner of Baseball eight months earlier, banned all eight from baseball for life. The men whose lives were changed forever by succumbing to temptation were ringleader Chick Gandil, Eddie Cicotte, Buck Weaver, "Shoeless" Joe Jackson, Happy Felsch, Swede Risberg, Lefty Williams and Fred McMullin. Landis was determined to clean up baseball and didn't mince words:

> Regardless of the verdict of juries, no player that throws a game, no player that entertains proposals or promises to throw a game, no player that sits in conference with a bunch of crooked gamblers, where the ways and means of throwing games are discussed, and does not promptly tell his club about it, will ever play professional baseball.[20]

Judge McDonald, who had initiated the probe of gambling in baseball, conceded he found the acquittals "disappointing," especially since Cicotte, Jackson, Williams and Felsch admitted they played roles in the bribery attempt. "But the grand jury investigation and prosecution that followed put the fear of God and the law in the hearts of crooked gamblers and shady players and has purged baseball for a generation to come," he told the *Chicago Tribune*. Some of the players, like Jackson, continued to insist on their innocence and several sought reinstatement, but none ever played again professionally. Four civil suits were later filed and all were settled out of court for undisclosed sums said to be moderate.[21] The Black Sox Scandal is considered a low point in the history of professional baseball and it shook public confidence in the game. Landis, however, was a powerful new force who intended to bring integrity back to baseball and restore that confidence. The Commissioner was helped in large measure by the heroics of Babe Ruth and the dawn of the new offensive era in baseball that lured fans to ballparks in large numbers.

Landis' appointment as Commissioner of Baseball was the result of the debate that had raged about how the game should be governed. Reformers like Dreyfuss and his fellow "malcontents" pushed the Lasker Plan for a new independent body, or individual, to oversee the game with largely unfettered powers. The resignation of Garry Herrmann meant baseball was left without a functioning National Commission, leaving major decisions to John Heydler at the National League and Ban Johnson at the American League, despite the latter's reduced powers within his own loop. There was no one to cast a deciding vote when they disagreed on important issues. The Black Sox Scandal only fueled the drive to find new leadership. It became a springboard for change and Barney Dreyfuss seized the opportunity. In early October 1920, he met with Cubs president William Veeck, White Sox owner Comiskey, and manager John McGraw of the Giants, following which they called for "an entire new deal in the way of a National Commission." An independent three-member body would have "absolute authority" and its decisions could not be reviewed, they said in a joint resolution. Dreyfuss planned to seek support for the plan from other club owners.

Word of the Dreyfuss-led initiative emerged from Chicago, a leak which dismayed the Pittsburgh owner. He then decided to explain the situation to Ralph S. Davis, the sportswriter for the *Pittsburgh Press* who also filed reports to *Sporting News*. Dreyfuss said:

> Some of us believe that only the most stringent measures at this time can save baseball, and our idea is to put the control of the game in the hands of men who will at all times be above all suspicion of even leaning toward any club or set of clubs.
>
> This tribunal, if chosen, would be absolute in its power, and would have the right, without question, to order from the sport any man, even as high as a league president, who was guilty of any move whatsoever detrimental to the best interests of baseball.

We need a tribunal of this sort which will function. The National Commission, as we have had it, has deteriorated into a joke. It has lost the respect of the public, and of baseball men themselves. It has done nothing to protect the game, and it is high time that we had an entirely new deal....

We want no baseball politics to enter into the selection or the workings of the tribunal. Petty partisanship has done much to put the game in bad repute, and it is absolutely necessary to do something that will let the public know that we are honest and on the square.[22]

By now, even National League president John Heydler was criticizing the National Commission, on which he and Ban Johnson of the American League retained their membership.[23] The names of several prominent individuals were being considered for the new governing body aside from former president William Howard Taft. They included Judge Charles McDonald, the Chicago judge who had sparked the probe into the Black Sox, U.S. Army General John Pershing, California Senator Hiram Johnson and another Chicago judge, Kenesaw Mountain Landis.

Landis, a progressive Republican, had developed a reputation as a trust-busting jurist, famously fining the Standard Oil Company $29 million (overturned on appeal) and often expressing sympathy for the underdog in cases before him, although he was unsympathetic to the radical labor movement. When three professional franchises operated in Chicago during the Federal League interlude, Landis remained impartial. He loved baseball and regularly attended games of the Cubs, the White Sox and the Whales but refused to accept free tickets. In January of 1915, the Federal League was fighting for recognition as a third major league and filed a suit in Landis' court for "relief from National and American League domination." The Feds were struggling to stay afloat and Landis chose not to render any quick decision in the case, a move that proved either wise or fortunate. The Federal League reached a peace treaty with the major leagues by the end of the year and withdrew the suit.[24] After formally dismissing it, the 49-year-old Landis said he hadn't planned to rule in favor of the upstart circuit, in any event. He explained why in the *Sporting News:* "The court's expert knowledge of baseball obtained by more than thirty years of observance of the game as a spectator convinced me that if an order had been entered it would have been, if not destructive, at least injurious to the game of baseball."[25] With that, the inveterate fan developed a reputation for saving baseball and attracted favorable attention from owners in the organized game. As early as September of 1919 he had been mentioned as the perfect candidate to clean up baseball. Soon afterward, however, he announced he was not interested in the chairmanship of the National Commission. If baseball wanted him, he wanted to work alone. The Black Sox Scandal so rocked the baseball establishment, which was operating without effective oversight, that in November of 1920 owners of the National and American leagues met in Chicago to consider the future and the indictments that had just been returned by the grand jury.

In advance of the November 8 gathering, Dreyfuss, Veeck, McGraw and their supporters sent letters to all club owners, saying it was "time for a new deal in baseball with a new governing body." The letter touted the Lasker Plan and its independent civilian tribunal as the best solution.[26] At the gathering, Landis was offered the post of first-ever Commissioner of Baseball. Most owners felt he was just what the game needed, although Ban Johnson of the American League and his "Loyal Five" group of owners disagreed. Landis was offered a lucrative seven-year contract at $50,000 a year, a significant boost from his judge's salary of $7,500 which he continued to draw until he surrendered his federal position in February of 1922. Landis told the *Chicago Tribune* he was honored to have been offered the baseball post but needed time to reflect before formally accepting it. "I, well, all I can say now is that I am a fan and love the game and admire clean sport, and that I would do everything in my power to help make baseball worthy of the name it has borne all these years as the cleanest sport we have."27

Johnson and the five American League owners backing him threatened war over the reorganization plan and sought to enlist support of the minor leagues who were then meeting in Kansas City. If Johnson and his owners weren't willing to co-operate, there was talk the National League would expand to a 12-team circuit by picking up the three AL clubs beyond Johnson's control; Boston, Chicago and New York, then add another city to be determined. In Kansas City, the minors didn't like the divisive Lasker Plan, but they disappointed Johnson by deciding to take "a neutral stand in major league rows."28 Unable to win minor league allies and unwilling to wage war over reorganization, the American League fell in line with the older circuit and all 16 team owners voted unanimously to hire Landis. On November 12, 1920, he finally accepted and any consideration of adding two side commissioners was abandoned. The judge had his control.

Landis vowed to conduct his affairs the same way he presided over cases in court, with no favors granted to either players or owners. "We have got to have a higher standard of integrity and honesty in baseball than in any other walk of life—and we are going to have it," Landis declared. "We are determined to heal the wounds suffered by the great National game and maintain the sport in the place it deserves in the heart of America."29 Landis set lofty goals for himself and for baseball. There was a new sheriff in town and his influence was immediate. Within weeks, he helped craft a new National Agreement which granted him sweeping powers and both major leagues adopted it. "Landis readily embraced these nearly dictatorial powers for almost a quarter of a century, and the owners, by and large, meekly followed along. Given the advantage of time we can see that Landis fulfilled his original mandate," baseball historian Marshall Adesman has observed.30 No team threatened to secede under Landis' watch and his penalty of lifetime bans for crooked players stands to this day. His impact on baseball cannot be underestimated.

Judge Kenesaw Mountain Landis became Commissioner of Baseball late in 1920, in part because of the campaign by Barney Dreyfuss to disband the National Commission, the ineffective overseer of the game. One of Landis's first steps was to ban from baseball members of the Chicago White Sox involved in the Black Sox Scandal of 1919 (Library of Congress).

When the Black Sox players were acquitted, he administered the strong medicine needed by an ailing game. Reformer Barney Dreyfuss with his call for reorganization of baseball, his embrace of the Lasker Plan and his influence on his peers, had played a key role in baseball getting the no-nonsense leader it needed for the next 24 years. Landis died in office in 1944 and was inducted into the Baseball Hall of Fame where his plaque reads: "His integrity and leadership established baseball in the respect, esteem and affection of the American people."

With the politics of baseball out of the way for the time being, it was back to matters on the field. For the 1921 season, Dreyfuss sought more talent for his manager Gibson and was willing to spend to get it. Ever since Honus Wagner retired, shortstop had been a problem for the Pirates, who tried nine players there with little success. Dreyfuss was impressed with Walter "Rabbit" Maranville who played that position for the Boston Braves. The 28-year-old from Springfield, Massachusetts, was only five-foot-five, had a great glove and in 1920 had batted .266 for the seventh-place Braves. Dreyfuss wanted Maranville badly and was willing to pay the price for the most colorful and best shortstop in the National League. In exchange for solid outfielders Billy Southworth and Fred Nicholson, and infielder Walter Barbare, along with $15,000, Dreyfuss acquired the fun-loving Maranville who instantly became a crowd favorite. One of his favorite stunts was the hidden-ball trick he worked with great success. The deal for Maranville showed Dreyfuss was gunning for a pennant and sportswriter Fred Lieb called it "one of the most profitable that the veteran owner ever made."[31] But Dreyfuss wasn't done. Late the previous season, he had acquired another infielder who would become among the greatest in Pirates history, Harold Joseph "Pie" Traynor, whose nickname reflected his favorite dessert. Traynor played only 17 games in 1920 and was sent to Birmingham for the first part of the 1921 season but was back with the Bucs by September. Despite his slow start, the popular third baseman remained with the Pirates until 1937 with a lifetime batting average of .320. Eleven years later he was inducted into the Hall of Fame. Other players were found for the outfield and new pitchers included rookie Whitey Glazner and Chief Moses Yellow Horse, a full-blooded Pawnee with a devastating fastball. The latter was a charming fellow who often clowned around with Rabbit Maranville, much to the consternation of Dreyfuss at times. It was a new-look Pirates team that would represent Pittsburgh in 1921, younger overall and much better defensively.

Hopes were high for the new season and the club didn't disappoint, reaching first place early on, seemingly destined for their first pennant since 1909. Newcomer Maranville, who was exceeding expectations, credited manager Gibson with the team's strong performance out of the gate. "Gibson is a great manager and a fine fellow," he said. "He's a wonder at handling men and he is endowed with as much baseball knowledge as any other manager in either of the two big leagues. The boys like him and they are going to win the pennant for him."[32] Even John McGraw was impressed with the latest version of the Pirates, which he said was the only team that stood between his Giants and the pennant. By August 24, when they appeared at the Polo Grounds for a five-game series, the Pirates were up 7½ games on New York. McGraw was determined to knock the Pirates off their perch and tried to upgrade his team with third baseman Heinie Groh acquired from Garry Herrmann in Cincinnati in a $100,000 deal. The transaction was nixed by Commissioner Landis, who ordered Groh to remain with the Reds, where he had refused to play without a big raise. Undaunted, during the last week of July, McGraw obtained hard-hitting Emil "Irish" Meusel from the Philadelphia Phillies, where the outfielder had worn out his welcome. Meusel would bat .329 for McGraw and provide a significant boost to the Giants, helping them get back in the pennant race. McGraw had to give up two players and $30,000 for Meusel who paid off for him the same way Maranville did for Dreyfuss. The series in New York started with a doubleheader when Pittsburgh lost both games. Things didn't improve as they dropped the remaining three contests before leaving town. The sweep was demoralizing for the Bucs who by Labor Day were clinging to one-game lead over the Giants. They finished the season four games behind McGraw's men, who went on to defeat the Yankees in the World Series. Dreyfuss blamed some of his club's swoon on horseplay by Maranville, banjo-playing Charlie Grimm and the prankster pair of outfielder George "Possum" Whitted and utility player Cotton Tierney. Performing well on the field were second baseman George Cutshaw, who batted .340 in his 98 appearances, while outfielder Max Carey, hit .309, and Maranville, hit .294. Wilbur Cooper won 22 games and newcomer Whitey Glazner and Babe Adams registered 14 apiece.

The 1921 season saw the Pirates involved in another innovation for baseball. On August 5, KDKA, a Pittsburgh commercial radio station, aired the first baseball game in radio history with Harold Arlin describing the action between the Pirates and the Phillies at Forbes Field. The Pirates won 8–5. Dreyfuss and St. Louis ownership remained unsure about broadcasting, however, fearing fans might opt to listen to the game on the radio rather than attend the park in person. Doubts lingered for years about the wisdom of sharing their product with profit-making radio stations. Dreyfuss banned radio microphones from Forbes Field, making exceptions only for night football and for the 1925 World Series, when WCAE, a station owned in part by the *Pittsburgh Press,* broadcast from the park.[33] At the time of his death, Dreyfuss was still trying to understand the financial implications of broadcasting and his ban remained in place. Regular radio broadcasts of Pirates games didn't begin until 1938. In Chicago, Cubs owner William Wrigley allowed regular broadcasts beginning in 1924 and in 1929 the Cincinnati Reds allowed play-by-play broadcasts of all their games.[34] The Pittsburgh owner's skepticism was not unique. Late in 1929, for instance, St. Louis Browns owner and president Phil Ball said he would raise his concerns about radio during the upcoming winter meetings of the major leagues. "Ball is in favor of forbidding the broadcasting of games on the ground that it has cost his ball club many paid admissions," the *St. Louis Post-Dispatch* reported. The Browns president said if broadcasts were to continue, station owners must pay for the privilege because they make "huge profits out of baseball." Across town, Cardinals owner Sam Breadon disagreed. He said radio broadcasts had created new fans for baseball and helped promote the game effectively. But Breadon said he was willing to see to what extent broadcasters were profiting and whether some of those profits could be directed to ball clubs.[35] At the American League meeting, Ball drew support from league president Ernest Barnard, who acknowledged teams were evenly split on the wisdom of broadcasting their games. Barnard suggested owners charge $50,000 annually, with $25,000 allocated to the home team and $25,000 to the league. "There is no reason why baseball should not share in the profits of a venture that it makes possible," he declared, since profits were healthy.[36] Owners could not agree on an appropriate course of action, however, and left the issue to individual clubs. It was becoming clear that radio broadened the fan base for all teams, whether owners appreciated that or not. Intrigued by the exploits of the players like Babe Ruth and anxious to see them in person, fans flocked to the ballpark. Radio broadcasts were becoming part of the game. For Barney Dreyfuss, this was a rare opportunity he missed to embrace a change that ultimately proved good for baseball.

The collapse of 1921 was keenly felt by Gibson and poor play continued into the next season when the Pirates were inconsistent and lacked focus. By the end of April they were in fifth place after winning seven games and losing eight. Their play improved in May when they climbed into second, 1½ games back of the Giants. June saw them lose four games to New York and three to Cincinnati, after which Dreyfuss began to second-guess his skipper, something Gibson had insisted during contract negotiations he'd never accept from the owner. Dreyfuss wanted Gibson to crack the whip with his men and abandon his "nice guy" approach. The Pirates ended June in fifth place, slipping to 10 games back of New York. In the first week of July, Gibson surprised Dreyfuss and the Pittsburgh faithful by abruptly quitting. He told players in the dressing room that he was leaving because "the club is not going as it should…. So I think I am doing what is right by stepping aside for somebody else…. Everybody on the team hustled and I want you to know I appreciate it."[37] After the game, Gibson avoided reporters and drove home to the 100-acre farm he had acquired just west of London, near Mt. Brydges, Ontario.

Dreyfuss hired Bill McKechnie, the former Pirate, to replace Gibson and he led the team to a third-place finish, eight games behind the Giants, who again defeated the Yankees in the World Series. Like those elsewhere, Bucs batters benefited from a livelier baseball. Babe Ruth clouted 35 round-trippers for the Yankees in 1922, while Rogers Hornsby of the St. Louis Cardinals led the majors with 42, Ken Williams of the crosstown Browns had 39 and Tilly Walker of the Philadelphia Athletics 37. The club batting average for the Pirates was .308, the highest in their history. Outfielders Carson Bigbee and Clyde Barnhart batted .350 and .330, respectively, while utility player Cotton Tierney hit .345 and the reliable Max Carey, .329.

Baseball had a powerful new leader at an important time in its history. A home run king was just getting established to the delight of fans in New York and far beyond. The era of offense in baseball was under way and the Pirates were again a solid first-division team with realistic hopes of another pennant.

After some troubled times in recent years, things were looking up for baseball and the Pirates.

16

Back on Top

Dreyfuss was determined to win the pennant in 1923 and continued making deals to improve the Pirates. By now he had developed a network of scouts among former players and friends who tipped him to promising talent as far away as California that he dutifully added to his "dope book." He especially wanted to bolster his pitching staff and a month after opening day he picked up veteran right-hander Lee Meadows from the Phillies. The 27-year-old had been plagued by pain in his right shoulder during 1922 and some observers thought his days on the mound were numbered. Meadows had won 12 games for the Phillies, but moving across Pennsylvania seemed to rejuvenate him and he won 16 for the Pirates. He was part of a deal that included Philadelphia infielder Johnny Rawlings in exchange for Pittsburgh pitcher Whitey Glazner and second baseman Cotton Tierney, along with $50,000. Rawlings would bat .284 in his new surroundings. Not all Dreyfuss's deals worked out so well, however. He picked up Jim Bagby from Cleveland, a righty who won 31 games for the Indians in 1920, but as a Pirate managed to win only three while losing two. A much better addition was future Hall of Famer Hazen Shirley "Kiki" Cuyler who joined the Bucs for 11 games in the outfield at the end of the season. He quickly became a crowd favorite for his hitting and would have several outstanding seasons as a Pirate.

The Bucs again finished third, 8½ games back of New York and four back of Cincinnati. Max Carey led the league with 51 stolen bases while batting .308. New third baseman Pie Traynor dazzled fans with his glove and his rifle of an arm, while batting .338 to lead the club with 12 home runs. At first base, Charlie Grimm hit .345. In all, four Pirates batted .300 or better. Right-hand curve-baller Johnny Morrison led the pitching staff with 25 wins.

Entering the 1924 season Pittsburgh was laden with talent and some observers considered the Bucs strong contenders for the pennant. But for Barney Dreyfuss it was another heartbreaker year when the team again faded late in the season and was knocked out of contention by McGraw and his Giants. To play shortstop, Dreyfuss had found Glenn Wright, whose sparkling play prompted sportswriter Chilly Davis to say he was the best at that position since Honus Wagner.[1] In his first season, Wright had 601 assists and batted .287. Two new pitchers had been added: Lefty Emil Yde, 24, who won 16 games, and righty Ray Kremer, 31, who had 18. The latter was found on the west coast by manager Bill McKechnie who'd been sent there by Dreyfuss to see some infielders about whom he'd been tipped. The Pirates got off to a slow start in 1924, climbing to fourth place in June, then reaching third in July. By early August they were in second and chasing the Giants. A three-game series at the Polo Grounds in late September sealed the Pirates' fate when the Giants swept them all. New York captured the pennant yet again, with late-surging Brooklyn 1½ games back and the Bucs three games off the pace.

Two days after the forlorn Pirates left New York's Polo Grounds, an unsuccessful attempt was made there to bribe Heinie Sand, the shortstop for visiting Philadelphia. Money was offered by Coast League rookie Jimmy O'Connell, who confessed that New York coach Cozy Dolan had put him up to it. Sand was offered $500 to go easy during a game that New York later won 5–1. The money was intended to help ensure the Giants won the pennant. This new scandal rocked baseball and Commissioner Kenesaw Mountain Landis acted quickly, placing O'Connell and Dolan on a permanent blacklist. Three Giants players were accused of complicity, but Landis acquitted them. Ban Johnson at the American League went ballistic and demanded the Giants be disqualified from the World Series and replaced by second-place Brooklyn to face Washington, his American League champions.[2] Johnson insisted nothing short of a federal inquiry was needed. Barney Dreyfuss was particularly irate, feeling the Giants were again resorting to dirty tricks to the detriment of his Pirates and to the game generally. He recalled only too well the umpire-bribing scandal of 1908 involving "Dr. Creamer" when his nemesis McGraw got off scot-free. Dreyfuss demanded the entire World Series be called off. He said he suspected McGraw was behind the scheme the moment he learned of it and urged Landis to probe deeply into the incident. "I think it is only the beginning," Dreyfuss said. "It is my opinion that O'Connell and Dolan are only the goats and that the guilt goes much further." Dreyfuss said he learned during the 1923 season that Dolan had approached Pie Traynor and encouraged him to hold out for more money from Pittsburgh, hoping he'd become dissatisfied as a Pirate and become available to the Giants. The Pittsburgh magnate complained Landis had failed to act on his complaint about player interference. When told of the comments from Johnson and Dreyfuss, Landis retorted: "these gentlemen not clothed with authority had better keep their shirts on."[3] Unimpressed with that response, Dreyfuss decided to buttonhole Landis during the World Series in Washington. The pair met by accident in an elevator at the Willard Hotel and Dreyfuss asked Landis when he could confer with him. Landis brushed him off and the Pittsburgh owner "was politely informed that the parties 'would not be in.'" Manager McKechnie was with Dreyfuss and shouted in Landis' face: "Why won't you be in?," to which the commissioner shot back: "Who are you? I have nothing to do with you."[4] Thus dismissed, the Pittsburgh duo took in the first two games of the World Series October 4 and 5 before returning home. Dreyfuss had intended to share with Landis some important information he had gleaned about the O'Donnell-Dolan matter. In *Sporting News,* Ralph S. Davis noted Dreyfuss was motivated to put Landis onto the Giants manager "due to the hatred existing between him and John McGraw." Davis added: "It is worth noting that Barney Dreyfuss was the man, who, of all others, forced Landis into office, for he personally conducted the fight against the old-style National Commission...." If Landis ever bothered to probe deeper into the affair, he told no one.

Late that same month of October the many friends of Barney Dreyfuss held a testimonial dinner to celebrate his 25 years of baseball in Pittsburgh. Davis, writing in the *Pittsburgh Press,* said recognition of the Pirates owner was well deserved because he brought topflight baseball to the Smoky City. "Very few major league clubs have had a better record over the past 25 years than the Pirates, and certainly a large portion of the credit goes to the owner of the club," he wrote. Before Dreyfuss came to town in 1899, the team never amounted to much, he said. "He is not only a good baseball man, but a keen, far-sighted business man and one who is willing to do more than his share of the general work of the league." Dreyfuss was still the main schedule-maker for the National League, he noted, and is "one of the few baseball owners who has devoted his entire life exclusively to the sport."[5]

The testimonial event was held October 25 at the William Pitt Hotel, drawing nearly 1,000 attendees, including Mayor W.A. Magee, who called Dreyfuss a "Pittsburgh institution," along with former Pennsylvania governor and short-lived president of the National League, John K. Tener. Also on hand were former manager Fred Clarke and current skipper Bill McKechnie, along with former players Honus Wagner, Deacon Phillippe and many others. Telegrams were read from those who could not attend, including Commissioner Landis who had refused to see Dreyfuss and McKechnie earlier that month. He sent a terse note simply saying he was tied up with other business. Among the more touching spoken tributes that night was that delivered by the Rev. Wallace C. Perry, pastor of First Baptist Church, who said in part: "Our baseball team is merely the extended shadow of a great personality. We are glad to pay our respects to a man who cannot be bought and who will never sell out. We admire him because he is a man of vision and a man of character."[6]

Sam Dreyfuss told the crowd he hoped to shape his life in such a way that in 25 years he'd be held in the same esteem in Pittsburgh as his father. Barney was the final speaker of the evening and struggled to find words to express his feelings on being feted, his voice breaking at times.

> A baseball club owner does have his troubles. It might be easier for him if he could at all times take into his confidence the men who patronize his club, but this is not possible. We have always tried to give Pittsburgh the best baseball possible, and I think we have succeeded in pleasing many of you in the past. Our failure to win the pennant this year was a source of deep sorrow and regret to me, but I can only say that we are still trying and that Manager McKechnie and myself are going to do our best to give Pittsburgh next year even a better outfit than that which represented the city this past season.

Dreyfuss pledged to do his best to place the sport upon "a higher plane than it now occupies and to give Pittsburgh, which I love, the finest type of player and the best possible combination of players." He then paraphrased a quote that is often attributed to Lincoln, but which cannot be verified: "I like to see a man like his town. I like to see the town like the man for the life he lives."[7] He was then presented with a silver pitcher by former National League president Tener. During the event, Dreyfuss was also given a silver cup presented by fans to mark his quarter century of baseball success in Pittsburgh.

The 1925 season improved the disposition of the Pittsburgh owner immeasurably. And that of Pittsburgh. To get to his happy place, Dreyfuss made some tough calls and sent packing some of his crowd-pleasers shortly before the winter meeting of the National League. He traded infielders Charlie Grimm and Rabbit Maranville, along with pitcher Wilbur Cooper, to the Cubs. In exchange he received good-hitting George Grantham, who played first and second, right-handed pitcher Vic Aldridge and rookie first baseman Al Niehaus. The departure of jokesters Grimm and Maranville was lamented by fans who loved their antics. But Dreyfuss had long disliked their lack of seriousness on the field. "I got rid of my banjo players," he told sportswriter Fred Lieb shortly after the deal.[8] That same year, Dreyfuss extended the double-decked grandstand into right field, bringing the capacity of Forbes field to more than 40,000. He spent $750,000 adding 12,000 seats with the towering concrete-and-steel addition that shortened the right field wall from 355 feet to 300 feet.[9]

With their revised lineup, the Pirates were a formidable powerhouse. They scored

912 runs to lead the league, 84 more than the second-best club and had a team batting average of .307. Their pitching was nicely balanced, with Lee Meadows winning 19 games, Ray Kremer, Johnny Morrison and Emil Yde each winning 17, and newcomer Aldridge picking up 15. The offense was something to behold, however. Kiki Cuyler wielded a powerful bat, collecting 220 hits and 43 doubles while his 26 triples and 144 runs scored led the league. He blasted 18 home runs and his average was .357. During the pennant drive in September, he tied a National League record with 10 consecutive hits. Cuyler's 41 stolen bases were second most in the league, behind teammate Max Carey who had 46. Carey himself batted .343, while newcomer Grantham came in with .326, followed by Clyde Barnhart at .325, Traynor at .320, catcher Earl Smith at .313 and shortstop Glenn Wright at .308. The dazzling infielder Wright also scored the first unassisted triple play in the history of the Pirates.

Dreyfuss coaxed former manager Fred Clarke out of retirement to help guide the talented 1925 club as head coach and "first lieutenant" to manager McKechnie.[10] Clarke's presence and knowledge of the game was credited for some of the Pirates' success. The Giants occupied first place early in the season, with the Bucs close behind. On June 29, Pittsburgh reached first and stayed there for all but three days until July 23, after which they could not be dislodged. They avoided the late season collapse of other years and took the pennant by 8½ games over the Giants. It marked their first League championship in 16 years. During the season, the Pirates won 12 of their 22 clashes with the Giants, delighting Dreyfuss, whose opinion of their manager McGraw remained low.

In the American League, the Washington Senators claimed the pennant for the second year in a row and were favored to repeat as World Series champions. They had the best pitching in the AL in what had been a year for hitters. Veteran Walter Johnson, now 37, could still command his fastball and had won 20 games that season. The hurler, known as "The Big Train," on whom Dreyfuss had taken a pass as a highly touted rookie in 1907, was the reason that seasoned observers expected the Senators to win. Johnson had only lost seven games all season. Stan Coveleski, 35, a spitballing right-hander, had also won 20 games while Firpo Marberry, 26, led the league with 16 saves. On defense, Washington shortstop Roger Peckinpaugh, 34, and second baseman-manager Bucky Harris, 28, anchored a tight infield. They batted .294 and .287, respectively. Overall, the Washington team was older and more experienced than the hard-hitting Pirates.

The Series opened in Pittsburgh on October 7 before a crowd of 41,723 shoehorned into Forbes Field with the help of temporary seating. Demand for tickets far exceeded seats and Dreyfuss had to refund thousands of dollars to fans who prepaid for seats, but could not be accommodated. "I'm in bad with many of our good customers for sending back their money, but I am happy that we're able to take care of so many," he said.[11] He did even better in the second and sixth games when more than 43,000 spectators were on hand. WCAE began broadcasting 20 minutes before game time, having made special arrangements with Dreyfuss, who remained uncertain about the wisdom of sharing his product for free on the airwaves. The Senators sent their ace Johnson to the mound, while McKechnie went with 19-game-winner Lee Meadows. Johnson's fastball was dancing and the Pirates struggled. He struck out 10 batters, while allowing only five hits. Meadows gave up six hits and three earned runs in eight innings before he was pulled for Johnny Morrison, whose curves didn't deceive the Senators. Washington's outfielder Joe Harris blasted a Meadows offering over the right-field fence in the second inning for a homer, while Pie Traynor did the same for the Bucs in the bottom of the fifth, with a line drive into the temporary bleachers in right. With a final score of 4–1, Washington took the first game largely because of The Big Train's masterful performance.

The next day, before Game Two began, players and fans honored pitching great Christy Mathewson, who had passed away the previous day at the age of 45. He died of tuberculosis, a legacy of his being gassed as a soldier in the Great War. At the time of his death, Mathewson was president of the National League's Boston Braves. The two teams wore mourning bands on their arms and were led to deep center field by Baseball Commissioner Landis, National League president Heydler, Dreyfuss, Mathewson's old manager John McGraw and other baseball officials. A band played "Nearer My God to Thee," as the crowd of 43,364 fell silent. The national anthem followed and the colors were raised to the top of the tall flagpole in center and then lowered slowly to half-staff.

McKechnie gave the ball to 15-game winner Vic Aldridge, while Bucky Harris went with Coveleski, the American League earned-run leader who had lost only five games all year. Coveleski was one of a diminishing number of major league pitchers still using the spitball. The game saw Pittsburgh belt two homers, one by shortstop Glenn Wright in the fourth, the other by outfielder Kiki Cuyler in the eighth. Washington's first baseman Joe Judge homered in the second inning to give the Senators a 1–0 lead. Washington managed eight hits off Aldridge and Pittsburgh seven off Coveleski. Aldridge had strong support behind him, featuring the work of Wright at shortstop and Traynor in the outfield. Coveleski was not so lucky. Peckinpaugh, played far below the expectations of a such a good player. In the first game he had made the only error recorded by a Senator and bobbled the ball twice. After Wright's homer in the fourth, the teams were deadlocked 1–1 going into the eighth inning. Aldridge retired the side and in the bottom of the inning Cuyler homered into the right-field stands, scoring himself and second baseman Eddie Moore whose infield hit had been mishandled by Peckinpaugh. Aldridge began to struggle in the ninth. With none out, he issued two walks and a single to fill the bases. Harris sent in Bobby Veach to pinch-hit and he drove in one run on a sacrifice fly to bring the Senators within a run of the Bucs. Aldridge struck out the next Senator and the inning ended with an infield put-out. The final score was 3–2 and the Series was tied as the teams left Pittsburgh.

Game Three in Washington was postponed for a day because of rain before the teams could take the field at Griffith Stadium on October 10. Shortly after noon, the Pirates were welcomed to the White House by President Calvin Coolidge, with whom they chatted and shook hands. Then everyone gathered for a photograph on the chilly and windswept White House lawn where Coolidge posed hatless despite the advice of his doctor. Later, the president and his wife attended the game. Righty Ray Kremer of the Pirates, winner of 17 games during the season, faced Alex Ferguson who had only won five for the Senators. Pittsburgh led 3–2 after six innings, but Washington picked up two runs in the bottom of the seventh for a 4–3 lead that brought the crowd of 36,495 alive. In the eighth, reliever Firpo Marberry shut down the Bucs. In the top of the ninth, controversy erupted when Pirate catcher Earl Smith connected with a Marberry offering and drove it into deep center field. Fielder Sam Rice drew a bead on the ball and jumped into the air, reaching for it as he tumbled over the fence and disappeared from view. A moment later, he emerged holding the ball aloft in his glove. Umpire Cy Rigler, who had run toward the play, declared Smith was out. Manager McKechnie and other Pirates protested vigorously, saying Rice had wrested the ball from a spectator. Rice insisted he made the catch but a fan ripped it from his glove, then returned it. The game ended in a 4–3 loss for Pittsburgh.

McKechnie protested to Commissioner Landis after the game, but Landis said it was the umpire's call, adding, "the umpire is supreme."[12] It was an umpire-supportive stance worthy of the late Harry Pulliam.

Walter Johnson returned for Game Four and was again impressive, allowing only six hits, all singles. His fastball worked to perfection and he shut down the powerful Bucs 4–0, delighting the 38,701 on hand. Lefty Emil Yde started for the Pirates but after surrendering two homers and four runs in the third inning was pulled for Johnny Morrison. During that same inning, Washington's ace Johnson suffered a charley horse running from first to second and began limping, although he was able to finish the game. The 4–0 shutout held. Babe Adams, the hero of the 1909 World Series for the Pirates, was sent to the mound in the eighth, his only appearance in the 1925 version of the fall classic.

Things were looking grim for Pittsburgh, down three games to one, as the club remained in Washington for Game Five on Columbus Day, October 12. The Pirates weren't going down without a fight and banged 13 hits off spitballer Stan Coveleski and his relievers Win Ballou, Tom Zachary and Firpo Marberry. Coveleski had poor control and took his second loss in the Series, disappointing 35,899 fans. Meanwhile, Vic Aldridge went the distance and allowed only eight Senator hits. The game was tied 2–2 after six innings, but the Pirates bats came alive in the seventh, adding two runs while the Senators replied with one. Pittsburgh added single tallies in the eighth and ninth innings to win 6–3. With that, it was back to Forbes Field for Game Six, Washington needing only one more win to take the Series.

The Bucs could take heart knowing their bats had finally come alive and, despite their precarious position, they began to believe in themselves again. Ray Kremer, loser of Game Three, faced Senator Alex Ferguson, the Game-Three winner, on October 13 when 43,810 fans packed Forbes Field, the biggest crowd to attend any game in the Series. Kremer had a rough start, surrendering a solo home run in the first inning and another run in the second before he settled down. Beginning with the last two batters in the second, he was sharp, retiring 13 successive batters. After that, only three Senators reached base. In the third inning, Clyde Barnhart and Pie Traynor scored to tie the game. Two innings later, diminutive second baseman Eddie Moore put Pittsburgh ahead 3–2 with a home run and Kremer shut down the Senators the rest of the way. The huge crowd was rewarded with an exciting come-from-behind win to tie the Series.

The seventh and deciding game was October 15 at Forbes Field when Bucky Harris sent his ace Walter Johnson back to the mound for the third time. The Big Train had won the seventh and deciding game in the 1924 World Series and Harris hoped the veteran could repeat his heroics this time out. Most of the 42,856 fans who filled the park to overflowing prayed Harris was wrong. Pirates manager McKechnie called on Vic Aldridge, winner of Game Two and Game Five to take the ball. The game had been scheduled for the previous day, but rain forced its cancellation, giving Aldridge some extra rest. Conditions weren't much better this day, however, with fog and spotty rain showers in the morning. The first pitch came during a cold drizzle that became a steady downpour in the third inning and it continued to rain for the rest of the game. Puddles were everywhere and the grounds crew spread sawdust to soak up the water and provide traction on the mound and base paths. Gasoline was burned in a bid to remove surface moisture from the infield. Pitchers were provided towels to the dry the ball and from the fifth inning on the outfielders had to peer through a heavy mist that descended on the park.

Proceedings got off to a dreadful start for the Pirates when they allowed four runs in the first inning and the Pittsburgh faithful grew silent. They knew Washington's ace had surrendered only one run in the previous 18 innings so the Bucs had dug themselves a big hole. Starter Aldridge struggled with a slippery pitching rubber, throwing two wild pitches and issuing three walks as he surrendered two runs. Aldridge retired only one Senator and was replaced by Johnny Morrison, who had pitched nearly five innings in game four, Pittsburgh's 4–0 loss. Morrison inherited three runners and two of them scored. Johnson faltered in the third inning, his feet slipping on the mound and he struggled to keep the ball dry. With three singles, a double and a stolen base, the Pirates brought in three runs. But the Senators scored twice in the top of the fourth to restore their three-run cushion, tapping Morrison for two singles and a double. Kremer came in to pitch in the fifth and kept the Senators off the score sheet until the eighth when they tallied once more. In the meantime, the Pirates scored once in the fifth and twice more in the seventh to tie the game 6–6. In the top of the eighth it began raining harder and growing dark. Peckinpaugh, who was in a 5-for-23 hitting slump, homered off Kremer into the left field bleachers to put the Senators ahead again by a single run. The Big Train remained in the game but by the bottom of the inning he was showing signs of fatigue from battling the elements. The mound was very slippery and the veteran called for more sawdust to help with his footing. With two out, Earl Smith tagged him for a double to right field and Carson Bigbee, batting for Kremer, followed up with a double to left, scoring pinch-runner Yde to tie the game. Eddie Moore was walked and it looked like the inning would end when Carey hit a hard shot to Peckinpaugh at short. But Peckinpaugh slipped in the mud trying to force Moore at second and dropped the ball, for his eighth error in the Series. The bases were now full. After fouling off several Johnson offerings, Cuyler smashed a line drive down the third base line. The players and fans thought it was a homer and bedlam broke out as the bases cleared. But the umpires, struggling with poor visibility and growing darkness, ruled it was a double and allowed only the runs scored by Bigbee and Moore. The Pirates led for the first time in the game and finished the inning without scoring again. Veteran lefty Red Oldham replaced Kremer for the ninth and retired the Senators in order, giving the Pirates a hard-fought 9–7 win and the World Series. For his part, Johnson had a miserable day, giving up 15 hits and five earned runs while striking out only three batters. For the Bucs, Carey scored three runs on four hits and Miller had three runs on one hit. Peckinpaugh set a record for futility in the Series, committing all but one of Washington's nine errors, going from his league's most valuable player to "goat" in the championship. During the Series, Carey led with a batting average of .458, ahead of Washington's Joe Harris whose .440 included three home runs.

The Pirates had shown real character to rally in what had been an exciting come-from-behind championship victory. In the crowded clubhouse afterward, manager McKechnie kissed his assistant Fred Clarke, who responded in kind. Commissioner Landis joined the celebration, as did National League president John Heydler. Landis enthusiastically shook hands with the Pirates, saying: "You are the gamest club ever to win a world's championship. I want to congratulate each and every one of you upon your fine victory. It was a great game and a great Series and you richly deserve the success that your never-say-die spirit brought you in the end."[13] Heydler was just as pumped at how the Pirates had rallied. "You are the gamest ball team I have seen in my 20 years in baseball," he said. "Always you had to come from behind to win ... now you have earned the title of the gamest of all ball clubs in the game's history as well as the world's championship title."[14] The players toasted their victory by pouring Iron City Beer over each other, but with Prohibition still in effect it was most likely the company's low-alcohol "near-beer." They also talked about their plans for their upcoming World Series checks, which would amount to $5,332. Their joy came in sharp contrast to the despair in the Senators' clubhouse, made worse afterward when American League president Ban Johnson sent young manager Bucky Harris a blistering telegram criticizing him for starting Johnson in three games and then sticking with him too long in the final one. "You put up a game fight," the League president said. "This I admire. Lost the Series for sentimental reasons. This should never occur in a World's Series."[15]

Barney Dreyfuss missed the great clubhouse celebration. He was confined to bed in his suite at the Schenley Apartments, just north of Forbes Field, having fallen ill with influenza upon his return from Washington following Game Five. His son, Sammy, was also ill. "Chilly" Doyle, sportswriter for the *Pittsburgh Gazette Times,* had an interesting item about it in his column "Chillysauce." He said the team owner had a radio receiver installed in his room so he could follow the action on WCAE. Dreyfuss couldn't bear to miss the action and temporarily shelved his misgivings about the broadcasting of Pirates games. Any positive feeling would not have lasted long, however, as Doyle noted:

> Barney's receivers went "flooey" about the first inning and from that time to the finish the president of the team had to depend on reports from the field or spontaneous shouting that carried its own story. When the bedlam of joy broke loose on top of the ninth-inning strikeout of Goose Goslin, Dreyfuss was close enough to realize what had happened.[16]

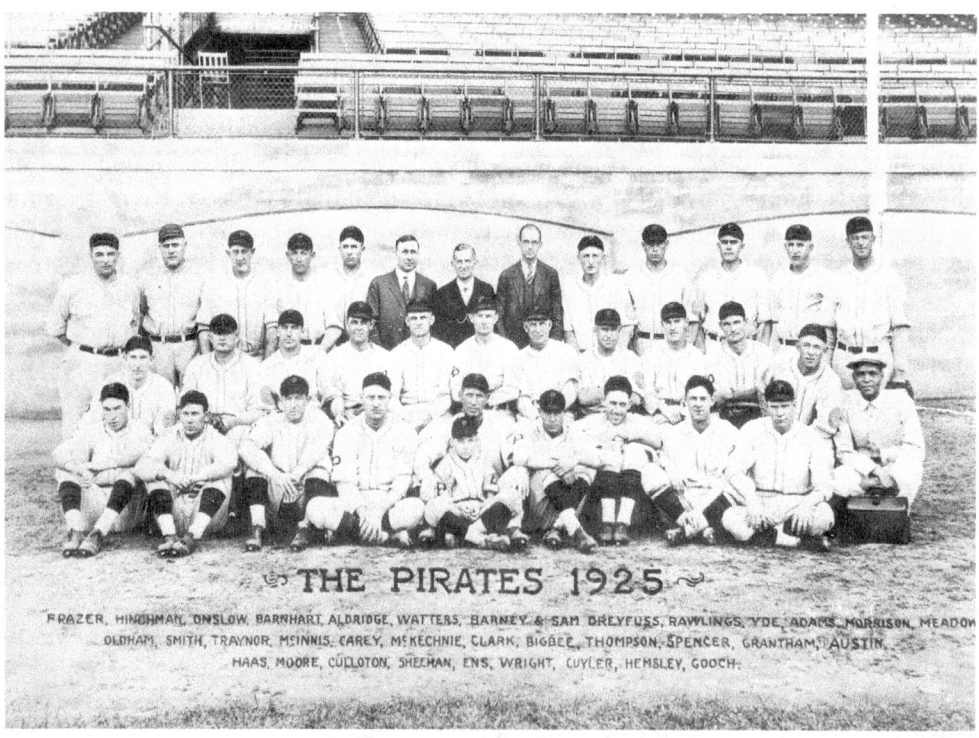

The Pirates won the 1925 World Series, the second for Barney Dreyfuss, who is pictured here in the center of the back row. To his immediate left is son, Sammy, whom he was grooming to take over the team (National Baseball Hall of Fame Library, Cooperstown, New York).

Attendance for the Series totaled 282,830 for the seven games, 18,600 less than the 1924 version between Washington and New York. But gate receipts came to a record $1.18 million, an increase of $119,039.[17] Aside from his joy at his second World Series win, Barney Dreyfuss was a winner financially. His share of proceeds came to $166,445. During a players' meeting later, controversy arose about how assistant manager and coach Fred Clarke should be treated when divvying up proceeds. Clarke, they knew, was well-set financially and was both an officer and shareholder in the club. In the end, they voted to give him $1,000, the same amount allocated to two of the club's scouts. Clarke felt insulted, however, feeling he should receive a full share like the players, and returned the check.[18]

The Pirates were widely expected to repeat their success in the 1926 season with a nearly identical roster. But it was not to be. The club started poorly and trouble developed later in the season that led to the departure of three of their stars. On the bright side, two future Hall of Famers, one of them Paul Waner, their greatest hitter since Honus Wagner, came aboard the Pirates' ship and pitcher Ray Kremer had an outstanding season. The team was among the cellar dwellers during the opening weeks of the campaign, but slowly began to regain their old form, climbing from seventh to first by June 24 and remaining there for most of the next two months. Cincinnati was playing well, but the St. Louis Cardinals were even better, allowing Pittsburgh only one win in a six-game series that began late in August. Those victories put the Cardinals on top, but the Bucs reclaimed the lead for a few days in early September. St. Louis, however, rallied to capture the pennant. The Cardinals went on to defeat the Yankees in a seven-game World Series.

Dissension in the Pirates clubhouse grew and their uneven performance, injuries, illnesses and hitting slumps combined to affect morale. Some players felt Fred Clarke had worn out his welcome. Never one for subtlety, Clarke freely offered his advice and thoughts, often spiced with salty language and sometimes with sarcasm. When first baseman George Grantham was mired in a hitting slump Clarke offered some suggestions, but Grantham wasn't interested in hearing from him. "Hey Fred, I wish you'd quit telling me things," Grantham complained at one point. But worse was to come. During a game in Boston on August 7, the Braves sent their shortstop Bob Smith to the pitcher's mound (he appeared as a pitcher in 33 games that year and won 10 of them) and Smith won the game 2–0. Clarke groused that Max Carey "isn't hitting a lick" and told manager McKechnie to find another lead-off man. McKechnie asked Clarke who he'd recommend, to which Clarke replied: "Anybody. Put in the bat boy; he can't do any worse…." Carey's pal Carson Bigbee overheard the exchange and told Carey, who resented the "bat boy" comment and complained to Babe Adams and other players. Carey's play that season had been impacted by a respiratory ailment. Some players sympathized with Carey and were so upset they talked about a player strike if Clarke didn't leave the bench. In a secret ballot, however, the players voted 18–6 to support their old coach and, after a short absence, he returned to sit alongside them. Now it was Clarke's turn to act. He demanded Dreyfuss punish the dissenters for their insubordination and he got his wish.[19] Bigbee and Adams were released unconditionally on August 13 and Carey was lost on waivers to the Brooklyn Robins.

Despite the disappointing 1926 outcome, with Pittsburgh finishing third, 4½ games back of the Cardinals, the season had some bright spots. Kiki Cuyler led the league with 35 stolen bases and Ray Kremer had 20 wins, tying him for most with three other pitchers, including teammate Lee Meadows. Kremer also had the best earned-run-average

The neighborhood surrounding Forbes Field was developed by the University of Pittsburgh over the years. In 1931, the 42-story Cathedral of Learning, a Gothic landmark, opened nearby. It provided a bird's eye view of the ballpark. To the lower left of it can be seen the former Schenley Hotel and the Schenley Apartments where Barney Dreyfuss lived at various times. This image, looking north, is from the late 1960s (Point Four Ltd.).

with 2.61 and a .769 winning percentage. Rookie outfielder Paul Waner, a 23-year-old Oklahoman, had turned heads. Waner became known for a sharp eye that kept him from swinging at bad pitches and avoid batting slumps. In his first season with the Bucs, Waner batted an impressive .336. He was found almost accidentally when the Pirates were scouting a shortstop in San Francisco. Future Hall of Famer Waner would play 20 seasons, all but five with the Pirates, leading National League hitters three times, amassing 3,152 hits and a lifetime average of .333. Also picked up during the season was a 19-year-old infielder from California, Joe Cronin, 19, found playing on San Francisco sandlots by a Pirate scout. Another future Hall of Famer, Cronin appeared in 38 games for the Bucs, mainly at second, and batted .265. Unable to fit into an already talented infield, he played only 12 games the following year before moving on. Cronin enjoyed a 20-year career with a lifetime batting average of .301 and 515 doubles.

At the end of the season, Bill McKechnie's contract was not renewed by Dreyfuss and he joined the coaching staff of the Cardinals. McKechnie was replaced by Owen "Donie" Bush, the former Tiger shortstop who had impressed Dreyfuss with his hustle during the 1909 World Series and then went on to manage teams in Washington and Indianapolis. On October 26, Fred Clarke severed his association with the Pirates, resigning all his offices and selling his shares in the club.[20] Before the season began, Dreyfuss had named him vice-president, but Clarke said he was finally done with baseball and returned to his ranch in Kansas.

Shortly before Christmas, Baseball Commissioner Kenesaw Mountain Landis made the stunning revelation he had allowed two of the game's greatest players to resign from baseball amid allegations they had fixed and bet on a game between their two teams seven years earlier. Ty Cobb, player-manager for Detroit and Tris Speaker, who held the same position with Cleveland, had placed bets on a September 25, 1919, game played in Detroit. This incident arose just before the Black Sox Scandal. It was said Cobb bet $2,000 and Speaker $1,500, while Indians right-hander Smoky Joe Wood and Tigers pitcher Dutch Leonard wagered $1,000 apiece. All placed their money on the Tigers, who, if they won that game, would finish third and qualify for a share of proceeds distributed according to a major league formula following the World Series for teams finishing as low as fourth. It was not illegal at the time for players to bet on games, but this arrangement had the hallmarks of a conspiracy. In 1926, after he had soured on Cobb and Speaker, Leonard gave American League chief Ban Johnson a letter he had received from Cobb that appeared to confirm a conspiracy. Johnson, always anxious to root out corruption and crooked players, paid Leonard $20,000 for it. A secret meeting of AL directors was held, following which Cobb and Speaker quietly resigned and were banned from any other positions in baseball.[21] Then Landis, who had little regard for Johnson, decided to look into the matter himself. In late January, the commissioner ruled Cobb and Speaker had not participated in any conspiracy and reinstated them in baseball. But neither of their clubs wanted the future Hall of Famers back.[22] Cobb was picked up the Philadelphia Athletics and Speaker by the Washington Senators. For his part, Johnson was enraged his authority had been undermined by a man he could barely tolerate. The two men clashed and Landis delivered an ultimatum: If AL owners wanted to keep Johnson, Landis would leave baseball. A future without Landis was feared far more than one without Johnson, so the owners stripped Johnson of his powers in a 7–1 vote, a move sufficient to satisfy Landis. It marked the beginning of the end for the founder and tireless champion of the American League and of clean baseball.

On July 8, a sick and embattled Johnson tendered his resignation, retiring to Indiana where he died four years later at the age of 66 from complications related to diabetes.[23] Johnson had succeeded in cleaning up the game and attracting fans to the ballpark, but he had become an autocratic czar who stayed too long. Branch Rickey, who himself had a long association with baseball, once said of Johnson: "The making or amassing of money was not part of Ban Johnson's life. He lived for the American League and the game of baseball."[24]

Johnson's positive contributions to the game were recognized by his 1937 induction into the Baseball Hall of Fame in the executive category.

Barney Dreyfuss would join him there, but not for another 71 years.

17

Last Hurrah

For the 1927 season, the Pirates introduced Lloyd Waner, Paul Waner's younger brother by three years. Paul had touted his sibling to Pittsburgh management after he was let go by the San Francisco Seals. The astute Dreyfuss purchased him for little more than train fare in 1926 and farmed him out to Columbia, South Carolina, where he batted .345 for the Comers that season. The Pittsburgh owner had developed a good relationship with Columbia team owner L.L. Propst, but had no formal affiliation agreement with the club. The Comers were left homeless when fire destroyed their home park and Dreyfuss provided the money to build a replacement, which the grateful team named Dreyfuss Field. It opened for the 1927 season, by which time the young star had graduated to the Bucs.[1] Lloyd Waner so impressed manager Donie Bush during spring training that he awarded the future Hall of Famer a spot in the outfield and made him leadoff hitter. Brother Paul batted cleanup.[2] Lloyd collected 223 hits in his rookie year, a record 198 of them singles and he batted .355. The Waners were a potent combination and made significant contributions to the success of Pittsburgh in 1927 and for many years afterward. Another wise move by Dreyfuss was hiring right-hander Carmen Hill, 31, who had appeared in 20 games for the Pirates between 1915 and 1919 and eight times with the Giants in 1922. Hill had done little to attract attention, but Dreyfuss saw potential that others had missed. Upon returning to Pittsburgh, Hill led the Pirates with 22 wins and 11 losses.

While the new additions were beginning to make significant contributions, a Pirate star for the past three seasons became disgruntled and his game suffered. Fan favorite Kiki Cuyler was batting .329 in late May when he tore ligaments in his ankle while sliding into third base. When he returned from the injury, manager Bush moved him from center field to right and made him bat second, or fifth, instead of his customary third spot. Lloyd Waner replaced him in center. Cuyler was profoundly superstitious and believed he was meant to bat third so he could drive in runs. He fought the move and the two men clashed. Tensions increased when Bush fined Cuyler $50 for failing to slide during a game against the Giants on August 6. He was benched and played only one more game, his 85th. Controversy about Cuyler persisted, with fans blaming both the manager and team owner for what they felt was shabby treatment of him.[3] Some said Dreyfuss benched him because he was still peeved that Cuyler had been a holdout in a salary dispute following the 1925 season. As always, loyalty was important to Dreyfuss and he viewed such behavior in a dim light. That explanation seemed to make sense, but sportswriter Fred Lieb said a stubborn Dreyfuss simply dug in his heels when the fans and sporting press pressured him to play Cuyler. "We're not going to let the fans, or even those fellows up in the press box, pick our lineup," the diminutive owner declared.[4] He held firm and Cuyler rode the bench.

17. Last Hurrah

The Pirates got off to a fine start, leading the National League throughout May, winning 18 games, and losing only six and occupying first place from May 22 to July 6. They were even hotter in September when they won 22 and lost nine, but didn't clinch the pennant until their second-last game, on October 1. Chicago claimed first in August, then fell off the pace. The Bucs fended off the Cardinals and Giants to take their sixth league championship with a record of 94 wins and 60 losses, 1½ games ahead of St. Louis and two up on New York. Little could the Pittsburgh faithful know it would be 33 years before the Pirates captured another National League pennant.

The New York Yankees were the baseball story of 1927 and it was Pittsburgh's bad luck to face them in the World Series. Considered by many as the greatest baseball team of all time, the Yankees were nicknamed "Murderers Row" because of their talent-laden roster. They led the American League all season, finishing with 110 wins to capture the pennant for the second year in a row. The Yankees were favored to win the series, powered by the bats of Babe Ruth, who belted 60 homers during regular play, and Lou Gehrig who hit 47. The Bronx Bombers recorded 158 home runs as a team when the only other team to exceed 100 was the Giants, with 109. Ruth collected more round-trippers himself than 12 of the 16 teams in the major leagues. New York also had stellar pitching to complement their powerful offense. The pitching staff dominated, with the lowest earned-run average in the majors, 3.20. Wilcy Moore, a 30-year-old rookie right-handed reliever posted the league's lowest earned-run-average at a miserly 2.28 and won 19 games, while Waite Hoyt won 22, lefty Herb Pennock notched 19 and Urban Shocker, 18.

The World Series proved to be a mismatch as expected and the Yankees swept the Pirates in four games. The Series began in Pittsburgh on October 5 before 41,467 fans when some members of the home team openly gasped when Ruth and Gehrig launched massive homers during batting practice. It was suggested this spooked them. Surprisingly, the Bucs outhit the Yankees in that first contest, nine to six, driving Waite Hoyt from the mound in the eighth inning. But Pittsburgh played sloppy defense, making two costly errors and Ray Kremer took the 5–4 loss. In Game Two, the Pirates scored a first-inning run on surprise Yankees starter George Pipgras, who'd won only 10 games during the season. New York scored three times in the third and plated three more in the eighth to give Pipgras a complete game 6–2 win. Vic Aldridge took the loss, disappointing the crowd of 41,634. With that, the Series moved to Yankee Stadium where more than 60,000 fans greeted their heroes. Yankees manager Miller Huggins called on 19-game winner Herb Pennock to take the mound, facing Lee Meadows. The Yankees scored twice in the first inning on Gehrig's triple to left-center field. Meanwhile, Pennock sent down every Pittsburgh batter for seven innings. In the seventh, the Yankees exploded for six runs. Lefty Mike Cvengros relieved Meadows and immediately faced Babe Ruth, who launched a drive into the right-field bleachers to score three of those six runs. The Bucs managed a single tally in the eighth to break Pennock's bid for a no-hitter, but with that, the scoring ended.

With the 8–1 victory in Game Three, the Yankees enjoyed a stranglehold on the series. For Game Four the Pirates sent 22-game winner Carmen Hill to the mound to face 19-game winner Wilcy Moore. Each team scored a run in the first inning and remained deadlocked for the next three. Ruth homered with a man on base in the fifth inning for a 3–1 Yankees lead. The Bucs picked up two runs in the seventh on a single and sacrifice fly to tie the game 3–3. They were showing some of the same never-say-die spirit that won them the 1925 Series and temporarily silenced the 57,909 fans expecting a sweep. The teams went scoreless in the eighth and in the top of the ninth the Pittsburgh batters were retired in order. Johnny Miljus, who had replaced Hill in the seventh inning, walked outfielder Earle Combs. Shortstop Mark Koenig then advanced him to second on a bunt single. Miljus threw a wild pitch and Combs, who represented the winning run, scampered to third while Koenig advanced to second. The next batter, Ruth, was walked intentionally to load the bases. Miljus then fanned first baseman Gehrig and left fielder Bob Meusel. It appeared the Pittsburgh hurler might escape a jam, but he unleashed yet another wild pitch and Combs scored to win the nail-biter for the Yankees, 4–3. For the second time in four years, the Yankees were World Champions.

Dreyfuss was bitterly disappointed at being swept four games straight when the previous three World Series had all gone the full seven games. It marked the first four-game sweep since the Boston Braves downed the Philadelphia Athletics in 1914. Even though he had mellowed somewhat as a fan, Dreyfuss still hated losing and felt humiliated his team had so poorly represented the National League. In the Pirates' dressing room afterward, the gloom was overwhelming. But Dreyfuss managed to smile as he shook the hand of his manager and patted some players on the back. "It's a tough way to lose a ball game," he lamented to Donie Bush. "Any other way but that way. I'd rather lose by a base hit." But he refused to blame Miljus for the wild pitch, saying he felt catcher Johnny Gooch had set up for a low pitch and was unprepared for the ball that arrived high and wide. "But it's all part of the game, I guess," Dreyfuss said, forcing another smile. "The best team won." Inside, the little owner was aching. For his part, Miljus, a native of Pittsburgh, was reported to be "inconsolable." He blamed himself for the wild toss that lost the Series. "Any other way but that, any way at all but that way," he kept repeating.[5] Dreyfuss wandered off to the other clubhouse where the Yankees were jubilant. He had tears in his eyes when he congratulated Colonel Jake Ruppert, the Yankees owner. Dreyfuss was downcast as he spoke to the gathered newspaper scribes about the result: "No pennant winner of one major league is good enough to win four straight from the pennant winner of the rival league."[6] Aside from the loss on the field, there were financial considerations of a short Series. Dreyfuss's share of the gate fell far short of expectations and he calculated he lost $20,000 overall, largely because of the cost of additional seating.[7] And he had to return thousands of dollars to fans holding tickets for a Game Six expected in Pittsburgh. He didn't disclose a figure, but the Yankees had already taken in $200,000 for a fifth game, all of which they had to return. Forbes Field was a smaller venue than Yankee Stadium, so for Dreyfuss the amount was significantly less. The Series produced the largest-ever pool of World Series receipts, $399,440.67. The Commissioner's office and players took the lion's share of proceeds from the first four games, under the revenue-splitting plan. New York received $167,763 and the Pirates, $111,843. Each Pittsburgh player received a check for $3,985.47 while each Yankee picked up $5,782.24. Lesser amounts were distributed to teams finishing second, third and fourth in each league, based on the proceeds-splitting protocol of the day.[8] Among the few bright spots on the field for Pittsburgh during the season that ended with such disappointment was the play of the Waners. During the post-season Series leadoff batter Lloyd scored half of Pittsburgh's 10 runs and batted 400, while Paul hit .333 and was voted the National League's most valuable player.

The Pittsburgh owner promptly signed pitcher Miljus to a new contract. "He was trying his hardest, and that is all I ask from any of my men," Dreyfuss explained.[9] Meanwhile, he began looking for a new home for disgruntled Kiki Cuyler, who rode the bench throughout the World Series. Late in November, Cuyler was traded to the Chicago Cubs.

The cheering had barely died away in Yankee Stadium when Dreyfuss had to fend off an unexpectedly virulent rumor he was selling the club to an Oklahoma oil tycoon for $3 million. He firmly dismissed the widely published story as nothing more than "hot air."[10] Now 62, the Pittsburgh owner planned to turn the team over to his son Sammy, about to turn 31, whom he'd been grooming for just that purpose.

Observers felt the two players Dreyfuss obtained from Chicago for Cuyler, infielder Earl "Sparky" Adams and outfielder Floyd "Pete" Scott, were merely average and that he came out on the short end of the deal. Some writers went so far as to call the Cuyler deal a "giveaway."[11] Dreyfuss recovered, however, when he traded pitcher Vic Aldridge to the New York Giants for aging spitballer Burleigh Grimes, who'd run afoul of manager John McGraw after a single season in Gotham. It marked Grimes' return to the Pirates, for whom he had pitched in 1916 and 1917, when he won only five games in total and lost 19. Grimes had matured to become a steady performer in Brooklyn and won 19 games for the Giants in 1927, with the third-best winning percentage among National League pitchers. That same year, Aldridge notched 15 wins for Dreyfuss. In 1928, Grimes picked up the pace for Pittsburgh, while Aldridge floundered in New York. Grimes led the League with 25 victories, and in both complete games and innings pitched. Meanwhile, Aldridge, who'd been a holdout early in the 1928 season, managed only four wins with seven losses. The deal helped Dreyfuss recoup nicely from the Cuyler "giveaway."

The Pirates led the majors in batting in 1928 with a .309 team average and six of their regulars exceeded .300. Paul Waner batted .370, second best in the League, while Pie Traynor hit .337. The team got off to a poor start, but became hot in August, winning 23 of 32 games. The Bucs cooled off again in September, finishing in fourth place, nine games back of the St. Louis Cardinals, for whom Bill McKechnie had become manager. The Cardinals faced the Yankees in the World Series and fared no better than Pittsburgh the previous year, losing four games straight as Babe Ruth batted .625 with three home runs and Lou Gehrig hit .545 with four homers. At the end of the season, Ty Cobb and Tris Speaker retired after spending the year as part-time outfielders for the Philadelphia Athletics of Connie Mack. After the 1928 season, Dreyfuss made another unpopular move that proved again he knew what he was doing. Shortstop Glenn Wright had been plagued with a sore arm during the season. Another favorite of the fans, Wright was traded to Brooklyn for two players, left-handed pitcher Jesse Petty and infielder Harry Riconda. Still ailing, Wright made only 24 appearances for the Dodgers. Riconda didn't make much of an impression in Pittsburgh and was gone after the season, but Petty won 11 games.

The Pirates improved to second place in 1929, finishing 10½ games back of Chicago. Again, hitting was solid, with a team average of .303 and six regulars hit more than .300: Pie Traynor (.356), Lloyd Waner (.353), Paul Waner (.336), Adam Comorosky (.321), George Grantham (.307) and Dick Bartell (.302). Pittsburgh was in the thick of the pennant race with Chicago and led for 37 days ending in late July, but injuries affected their play. When the Bucs struggled in August, the Cubs pulled ahead for good. During their slump, manager Donie Bush was fired, replaced by Jewel Ens, an infielder and pinch-hitter for the Pirates from 1922 to 1925. Ens led the team to 21 wins in the 35 games he was skipper. Grimes won 17 times that season, but broke a thumb on his pitching hand trying to knock down a line drive. He finished behind Ray Kremer, winner of 18 games. Newcomer Larry French, the lefty from California won seven and lost five. In Chicago, former Pirate Kiki Cuyler had a terrific season, hitting .360 and collecting a league-leading 43 stolen bases, numbers which were duly noted by his fans back in

Pittsburgh. In the five-game World Series, the Cubs lost to the Philadelphia Athletics. After the season, Barney Dreyfuss gave Jewel Ens a two-year contract, a rare move for an owner who invariably opted for one-year deals. Ens would lead the Pirates to two fifth-place finishes.

Dreyfuss was named vice-president of the National League in 1929, in recognition of his long service to the loop for which he had become the senior statesman. John Heydler, his old friend, remained firmly in control as president and Dreyfuss's appointment was largely symbolic and seen as a token of respect for his many contributions to the game. That same year, Dreyfuss appointed his son Sammy vice-president of the Pirates as the careful grooming of his successor continued. The aging owner stepped back from day-to-day operations and his son assumed a greater role in running the team.

The 1930 season opened a few months after the stock market crash and Americans found money for outings such as baseball games growing scarce so they focused their spending on essentials such as food, clothing and keeping a roof

In his later years, Barney Dreyfuss was named vice-president of the National League in recognition of his many contributions to major league baseball during more than three decades. Among them had been the thankless and complex task of devising schedules (ca. 1930, National Baseball Hall of Fame Library, Cooperstown, New York).

over their heads. Adding to the economic woes tied to the onset of the Great Depression, the Pirates were rather woeful on the field, terribly inconsistent despite their talent. Paul Waner batted .368, but brother Lloyd suffered a mystery ailment and appeared in only 68 games. Pie Traynor batted .366, George Grantham had a .324 average and Adam Comorosky hit .313. Pitcher Ray Kremer led the National League with 20 wins, while Larry French and Erv Brame recorded 17 apiece. Pittsburgh finished the year with 80 wins, good for fifth spot, 12 games back of St. Louis. Just before the season, Dreyfuss cut the $17,000 salary of Burleigh Grimes, who refused to sign a new contract and was traded to Boston. The Braves quickly traded him to St. Louis, who paid him $20,000, a princely sum at the onset of the Depression, but still far below the $80,000 salary commanded by Babe Ruth. In St. Louis, his 13 wins helped lead the Cardinals to the National League pennant, but they lost to the Philadelphia Athletics in the World Series.

Early in 1931, Sammy Dreyfuss fell ill. He was confined to bed with what doctors diagnosed as a nasty case of influenza. His condition worsened and on February 22, a day before Barney turned 66, Sammy died of pneumonia at his home. He was 34 and left behind his wife, Carolyn, and three-year-old son, Barney. His father was devastated. Havey (not Harvey) J. Boyle, sports editor of the *Pittsburgh Post-Gazette,* said the passing of the younger Dreyfuss had shocked the baseball community across the country.

"Sam Dreyfuss lived baseball from morning to night, the year round. It was his enthusiasm that made him especially capable in assisting his father in the operation of the club."[12] The *Pittsburgh Press* said Barney's chosen successor had shown real aptitude for the business of baseball. "Barney Dreyfuss pushed Pittsburgh into a place in the sun of the baseball world and won a real place in the esteem of sports lovers. Their hearts will go out to him in the calamity which has come to him."[13] *Sporting News* saluted the younger Dreyfuss for "unusual baseball acumen" and said the National League had lost "one of its most promising young executives."[14] Sportswriter Ralph S. Davis wondered aloud if Dreyfuss senior might consider selling what had become one of the most valuable properties in baseball on which he made money in all but two years he owned the club.[15] Sam had been expected to join the Pirates for their spring training in Paso Robles, California. At the same moment his funeral service was being conducted in Pittsburgh, 3,000 miles away in California the players gathered in silence in the manager's room, wearing black armbands. What would have been their first workout of training camp was canceled. Pie Traynor, the longest-serving Pirate said the death was a personal blow. "Sam was a real leader. When I came to the club in 1920, Sam made friends with me early. I took a liking to him, too, because of his enthusiasm for the game."[16]

Sportswriter Fred Lieb said Dreyfuss was grief-stricken and seemed dazed. National League president John Heydler and other team owners were among those who sought to console him and get his mind back on baseball. Dreyfuss needed help with a new season fast approaching and asked his son-in-law William Benswanger, a successful insurance man, to join him at the baseball club. Benswanger had married Barney's only daughter Eleanor, and the couple were avid pianists and music lovers. Bill was a member of the board of the Pittsburgh Symphony Orchestra and other musical organizations. Benswanger was also a Pirates fan and didn't hesitate when his father-in-law asked him to join the club.[17] The pipe-smoking, bespectacled insurance man assumed much of the day-to-day operations of the Pirates, assisted greatly by seasoned club secretary Samuel Watters.

The 1931 season was similar to the previous one, but much of the joy had left the game for Dreyfuss. His contagious, high-pitched laughter was seldom heard anymore and his dancing eyes had dimmed. His felt the loss of Sammy acutely and it was said he never really recovered from it.[18] But the business of baseball wagged on. In January, Pirates scout Art Griggs signed a young player in California who would be a significant contributor to Pittsburgh and a future Hall of Famer, although he wouldn't don a Bucs uniform until the following year. Floyd "Arky" Vaughan, a multi-sport athlete at Fullerton High School, was discovered by Griggs playing in the Orange County winter baseball league. The Pirates assigned him to Wichita of the Class A Western League for 1931, where he batted .338 with 21 home runs. Once he arrived in Pittsburgh in 1932 at age 20 he became the youngest player in the National League and batted .318 while committing a league-leading 46 errors. His defense would soon improve, and he remained in Pittsburgh until 1941 when he was traded to Brooklyn. Vaughan's career batting average of .318 as a shortstop was second only to Honus Wagner. The Yankees had also drawn a bead on Vaughan but narrowly missed signing him out west. While the new Pirate was still in Wichita, Yankees business manager Ed Barrow offered Dreyfuss $40,000 for him. The Pittsburgh owner was tempted, but told a local sportswriter if Barrow was prepared to offer that kind of money, Vaughan must be good and therefore worth keeping.[19] So Dreyfuss did, making a wise decision that paid dividends to the Pirates for a decade.

Inconsistency bedeviled Manager Ens and his men during 1931. They had a poor spring, a good July, a poor August and a hot September. The club suffered from poor play at first and second bases where several players were tried with little success. Their fifth-place finish led Dreyfuss to fire Ens. "First division Barney" couldn't abide a second division result and began considering several candidates to lead the Bucs back into contention, even before dismissing Ens. He met his old catcher Mooney Gibson and offered him the managing job on the spot. His former skipper accepted, but the two men kept the news secret until the end of November.[20]

Dreyfuss knew his old manager and friend Gibson shared his passion for "small ball" as played during the Deadball Era, in which base stealing, sacrifice bunts, and strong defense produced low-scoring games but kept fans on the edge of their seats. The two men exchanged their thoughts about the state of the game at Forbes Field during Pirates games whenever Gibson and his wife visited their son, a medical doctor who practiced in nearby Wilkinsburg.[21] Dreyfuss and Gibson wanted to return to basic baseball. The Pittsburgh owner had helped bury the spitball because it favored pitchers in the classic pitcher-hitter duel that lies at the heart of the game. But introduction of a livelier ball changed that delicate balance and led to more home runs and high-scoring games. In 1930, the National League adopted a "rabbit ball" (today it would be called "juiced") which led to higher batting averages across the board.[22] That year has been described as "the most notorious high-offense season in major league history [which] saw an average of 5.55 runs per game, the highest of the live ball era."[23] Dreyfuss disdained a game that relied so heavily on home runs. "Long hitting," he grumped, "so robbed baseball of its finer play that many games found the fans getting up and leaving at the end of the fifth or sixth inning. What was the use in staying?"[24] For Dreyfuss, baseball was more a game of nuance where each run scored was meaningful. He was a student of the game which he felt had evolved into one focused too much on big blasts, overshadowing the subtleties he enjoyed so much. He found an unlikely ally in John McGraw at the Giants, another old-timer who felt scoring was getting out of control. The National League eventually agreed the "rabbit ball" of 1930 was a mistake and for 1931 adopted a new one with a thicker cover, that was more loosely wound and had a heavier center. In late July of 1931 Barney Dreyfuss happily declared the lively ball was dead as he showed off his 40-year collection of baseballs to a newspaper reporter. He said the new ball was already proving to be a wise move. "The game today is more like old-time baseball when a run was a run," he said of the new season. By the end of 1931, the deader ball had achieved the desired impact, National League magnates learned at their winter meeting. Home runs had dropped to 493 from 892 in 1930, while total runs scored fell to 5,537 from 7,025.[25] Batting averages immediately declined across the loop, from .303 to .277 overall. Pittsburgh's .303 team average for 1930 dipped to .266, while the New York Giants, who had the best average both years, dropped from .319 to .289. The Giants' Bill Terry, who had batted a league-leading .401 in 1930 dropped to .349. The American League, where Babe Ruth, Lou Gehrig and many others relied on home runs, retained the livelier ball. It is difficult to determine how the lively ball affected attendance, however, given the onset of the Great Depression which was a factor at the turnstiles. In 1929, the National League attracted 4.93 million fans, 5.45 million in 1930 (with the lively ball), 4.58 million in 1931, and 3.84 million in 1932. The American League figures were 4.67 million in 1929, 4.69 million in 1930, and 3.88 million in 1931 and 3.13 million in 1932 while retaining the lively ball.

17. Last Hurrah

The return of Mooney Gibson to manage the Pirates came as a bit of surprise because it was thought Dreyfuss had a long list of candidates from which to choose. Gibson had left the club abruptly in 1922 to end his first managing stint in Pittsburgh, although his departure was amicable. "Modern big league history does not show any other case where a manager, once out, has returned to his old post, so in this connection Gibson scores heavily and there is an implied compliment in his being brought back," wrote Havey J. Boyle in his *Pittsburgh Post-Gazette* column. "Gibson is a happy choice."[26] The *Pittsburgh Press* understood exactly what Dreyfuss was up to. "In selecting the Canadian, Dreyfuss is thought to be attempting to capitalize on his theory that the deadening of the baseball by the National League will return the game to a basis of strategy such as was in vogue in Gibson's heyday."[27] But most of all, Dreyfuss wanted to win and knew Gibson, a key part of his 1909 World Series club, shared his passion. Edward Balinger, another *Post-Gazette* writer observed: "Gibson is back among old friends and if given proper encouragement, I believe he will be the man to lead his men out of the wilderness of the second division."[28]

His announcement of hiring Gibson was among the last public appearances for Dreyfuss, who within days was battling what was described as a heavy cold. He had planned to attend a meeting of the minor leagues in West Baden, Indiana, from December 2 to 5 with club treasurer Bill Benswanger before heading to Chicago for the National League winter meeting December 8 to 10. But Dreyfuss felt too ill to travel and confined himself to paperwork at his desk. Gibson and Benswanger attended the West Baden gathering without him. Dreyfuss still planned to travel to Chicago where he hoped to conclude some deals, but he could not shake his illness. So Gibson and Benswanger represented the team at the League gathering where, despite his absence, Dreyfuss was elected to a second one-year term as vice-president.[29]

While the National League meeting was wrapping up, a judge in Pittsburgh approved the distribution of the estate of Sammy Dreyfuss. It totaled $151,000, of which $125,000 represented the value of his 260 shares in the Pittsburgh Athletic Company, the operating entity of the Pirates. Shares in Forbes Field Company came to another $13,000 and 10 bonds in the Athletic Company were valued at $10,000. He left the bulk of his estate to his wife, Carolyn.[30]

Barney Dreyfuss was confined to bed where a doctor suggested he consult a specialist in New York City. It was becoming clear his ailment was more than a mere cold, but nothing was said publicly. Privately, he must have been concerned because on December 14 he updated his will, in which he left some money for his sisters, his grandsons and the balance to his wife Florence.[31] On December 15, he appeared "quite cheerful" when he, Florence and daughter Eleanor were driven to the East Liberty train station for the trip to New York.[32] At Mount Sinai Hospital there, X-rays revealed something the specialist felt warranted surgery and Dreyfuss agreed. On December 28, he underwent the knife but the nature of the procedure was still not disclosed. He was reported resting comfortably afterward and a second procedure followed on January 6. By now, some reports said he was suffering "a glandular infection," later amended to prostatitis.[33] Doctors pronounced themselves pleased with the surgery and the patient was resting comfortably with family members at his side. It was said it would be several weeks before he could return home. On January 29 it was reported he had taken a turn for the worse and Bill Benswanger rushed to join his wife and mother-in-law at Dreyfuss's bedside. On February 5, shortly before noon, Barney Dreyfuss died, 18 days before his 67th birthday, his death attributed to pneumonia.[34] Baseball had lost a titan, an innovator, a pioneer, a man who embraced baseball and who was still tinkering to improve the game in his final days. His death came just two weeks after that of William Wrigley, owner of the Chicago Cubs, another formidable figure in baseball.

The *New York Times* called Dreyfuss "one of organized baseball's most prominent legislative figures," a leader in many baseball wars, "in addition to gaining the distinction of being the most thoroughly schooled baseball man to be found among major league club owners."[35] Civic and business leaders in Pittsburgh, friends, former players and baseball officials paid tribute on the passing of the successful little man from Freiburg. John Heydler, president of the National League, praised a friend he had known for 35 years since Louisville, calling him "one of the bulwarks of the game.... Baseball loses its ranking leader." Former Pirates manager Bill McKechnie said Dreyfuss was "a credit to the American pastime. He was a sportsman of the highest type and it will be impossible to replace him in the baseball world." Pittsburgh manager Gibson said he regretted losing a man who had been father figure to him and "his passing is a severe blow to me. I know I am going to miss him, but his absence will cause me to work harder than ever to provide what was his foremost wish in life—a winning ball club." Honus Wagner lamented losing "a great friend.... I have nothing but praise for the way he treated me." Deacon Phillippe called him "one of the greatest figures baseball ever knew.... He was a man who always kept his word."[36] William Harridge, president of the American League said: "Barney Dreyfuss was one baseball owner who refused to allow commercialism to interfere with his ideas of how to operate a club. He was a real fan and one of sportdom's leaders."[37]

Dreyfuss was returned to Pittsburgh where the following day a steady stream of friends and associates filed past his casket at his home in the luxurious Schenley Apartments, mere steps from Forbes Field. A funeral service was held February 7 at Rodef Shalom Temple, which was filled to its capacity with more than 1,500 mourners. Honorary pallbearers consisted of a who's who of prominent figures in baseball. They included Commissioner Kenesaw Mountain Landis, National League president John Heydler, American League president William Harridge, officials from all National League clubs, former Pennsylvania governor and National League president John Tener and business and civic leaders of Pittsburgh, along with old friends. Also included were Deacon Phillippe, Honus Wagner and Jacob Ruppert, owner of the New York Yankees. The funeral service was simple and brief, presided over by rabbis Samuel H. Goldenson and B.B. Glazer. Goldenson paid tribute to Dreyfuss as a man who "elevated our national game from a mere sport to a thing of dignity, of fairness, and who by his own honesty, sincerity and fidelity to the ideals he held regarding that sport, transformed it to something worthwhile."[38] Even Commissioner Landis made a brief remark to the press before joining the procession to West View Cemetery, saying, "When I think of Barney Dreyfuss I think of integrity, fidelity—of Gibraltar." At the cemetery just west of the city, floral tributes from around the country marked the place where Dreyfuss was interred, near the grave of son Sammy who died the previous February.

Soon afterward, Florence Dreyfuss was awarded the bulk of her husband's estate including the ball club and Forbes Field. The total value of the estate was unclear initially, but a quick tally in probate court put it at $400,000 or more.[39] She became owner of the Pirates and asked Bill Benswanger to assume the role of president. He readily accepted and retained Mooney Gibson, relying on the veteran's expertise and counsel to guide the Pirate ship past the loss of its owner and navigator. Florence Dreyfuss was not the first woman to own a major league baseball club. That distinction went to Helene Britton, who

17. Last Hurrah
185

Barney Dreyfuss died in 1932, a few days shy of his 67th birthday. He'd become the senior statesman of major league baseball by that time. His funeral attracted a who's who from the baseball world. He is buried in the Dreyfuss-Benswanger family plot in West View Cemetery, just west of Pittsburgh. His stone is third from the left in this image.

His simple headstone says nothing about the significant contributions Barney Dreyfuss made to baseball (Kaitlyn Larsen).

owned the St. Louis Cardinals from 1911 to 1918, shortly before women were granted the right to vote. Britton inherited the team from her uncle, Stanley Robison, who along with her late father Frank DeHaas Robison, had owned the Cleveland Spiders then acquired the St. Louis club. A young mother with two children and a drunkard for a husband, she was forced to sell the club for financial reasons to a local investment group headed by Sam Breadon for $350,000.[40]

The Pittsburgh home opener for 1932 season was April 20, when the Pirates welcomed the World Series champion St. Louis Cardinals. More than 16,000 fans saw the Bucs blank the Cardinals 7–0 in a pitching gem by right-hander Steve Swetonic, who didn't give up a hit until two Cards had been retired in the eighth inning. Before the game, Danny Nirella and his popular bands filled Forbes Field with music, as was the custom on special occasions. At game time the musicians marched onto the diamond and led players from both teams to the center field flagpole where Old Glory was raised to the strains of The Star Spangled Banner. After a moment fluttering at the top of the pole, the flag was lowered to half-staff in tribute to Barney Dreyfuss. The Pirates wore black armbands to honor their late president and stood silently as taps were sounded to conclude the brief ceremony.

Gibson led the fifth-place club of 1931 to a second-place finish in 1932, sailing along atop the league for 44 days, but eventually finishing four games back of the Chicago Cubs. Chicago lost to the Yankees in the World Series, swept in four games straight. During the season, Gibson was helped substantially by the play of Arky Vaughan, whom he installed at shortstop and whose batting average of .318 began a decade in Pittsburgh when he never hit below .300. One of Barney Dreyfuss's last great finds was proving yet again that the little owner could identify talent. And manager Gibson fell just four games short of delivering the winner he had promised him.

18

After the Little Colonel

By 1933, Honus Wagner was 59 and itching to get back into baseball because life after the game had not been particularly successful or rewarding for him. In 1919 he and some associates had opened the Honus Wagner Sporting Goods Store on Wood Street in Pittsburgh, selling everything from guns to bicycles, and golf clubs to baseball equipment. Nine years later the store went bankrupt and Wagner lost his money. In 1925, after being urged to consider a career in politics, he launched an unsuccessful campaign for Allegheny County sheriff on the Republican ticket. Then, likely after tapping some political friends, in 1929 he was appointed assistant sergeant-at-arms for the Pennsylvania House of Representatives at Harrisburg. He found the post utterly boring and the old ball player resigned within two months. Wagner became associated with another sporting goods store in Pittsburgh, to which he lent his name and where he worked as a salesman. But he quit after a dispute about commissions. Undaunted, he then teamed up with Pirates third baseman Pie Traynor to open the Wagner-Traynor Sporting Goods Store on Liberty Avenue in 1931. The timing was poor because the Depression was deepening and within two years they were forced to shutter it, both men losing their investment. Late in 1932, Wagner applied to manage the Cincinnati Reds, but the job went to former Pirate manager Donie Bush.[1]

Bessie Wagner insisted her husband try again to get back into the game he loved. She knew how much he missed baseball and that he simply needed a nudge. At her instigation, the couple drove from their home in Carnegie a few miles to the Pirates office in downtown Pittsburgh on February 2, 1933. They told president Bill Benswanger that Honus was looking for a job with the organization, preferably as a coach. Benswanger liked the idea but left the final decision to manager Mooney Gibson. Without hesitating, Gibson welcomed his old teammate aboard and asked him to focus on coaching the infielders. Wagner was thrilled to be back in a Pirates uniform for the first time in 16 years and pledged to help Gibson any way he could.[2] The new coach was assigned to help shortstop Arky Vaughan improve his sometimes-suspect fielding. Vaughan proved to be a good student, became Wagner's protégé and the pair roomed together on road trips for the nine years Vaughan remained a Pirate.[3] Wagner stayed with the club until the end of the 1951 season after which he retired with a pension at age 77.

Coming off a second-place finish the previous year, hopes were high in Pittsburgh for 1933. Benswanger made a series of deals, acquiring former Yankees star pitcher Waite Hoyt, who'd been bouncing around several teams since leaving New York, and heavy hitter Freddie Lindstrom from the Giants. Early season play lived up to expectations and the team was in first place by the end of May, with 24 wins and 15 losses. Winning grew tougher in June, however, when they slipped to third, then reached second, just 3½ games back of the Giants. The Pirates had six future Hall of Famers on their roster: Vaughan, the Waner brothers, Traynor, Hoyt and Lindstrom, and when things didn't go well critics began blaming Gibson for mishandling his men. By July, Benswanger was publicly defending his manager who was clearly on the hot seat. "We are trying to win with the material we have," Benswanger said. "The fact that our outfield hasn't hit as we expected and some of our pitchers haven't delivered as anticipated is not Gibson's fault. No one is more disappointed than myself or Gibson that the club hasn't won more games."[4] Inconsistent pitching was a major factor in the club failing to win the National League pennant and the Pirates finished second again, five games back of the Giants.

Gibson was signed to manage for 1934, the first year Sunday games were allowed in Pittsburgh. But whenever and wherever games were played, the Pirates won too few of them to appease an increasingly restless fan base. At the end of April they were in fourth place after a lackluster start. For eight days in May they occupied first, but plunged to fifth by month-end and by mid–June were clinging to fourth, 5½ games back of League-leading New York. On Sunday, June 17, the Bucs suffered their fourth straight loss, 9–3 to the Giants and the 10,000 fans at Forbes Field that day turned on Gibson, booing him throughout the game. "Things have been going from bad to worse," the *Pittsburgh Press* groused.[5] Two days later, Bill Benswanger relieved Gibson and immediately replaced him with Pie Traynor, explaining in a brief statement: "We have been in a bad slump, much worse than we think a team of our caliber should be in, and the change is an effort to secure better results." Benswanger refused to say anything more. For his part, Gibson tried to put a brave face on his departure, which was amicable. "I'm sorry I couldn't come through with the Pirates," he said. "I had my heart set on a winning team and a pennant.... I'm glad to step out in accord with their wishes." Before leaving, he spoke to Traynor and the players, wishing them all the best.[6] Gibson returned to his farm west of London, Ontario, and remained active in baseball. In 1958 he was the first baseball player elected to Canada's Sports Hall of Fame. He died in 1967 and in 1987 was inducted into the Canadian Baseball Hall of Fame.

June 30, 1934, marked the 25th anniversary of Forbes Field and club management wanted to make it a memorable day. A large monument to Barney and Sam Dreyfuss was unveiled in center field, a six-foot tall granite marker with a circular brass plaque honoring Dreyfuss father and son. Bandleader Danny Nirella led the same musicians who played for him at the official opening of the park in 1909, reprising tunes from that day including "Take Me Out to the Ballgame," and "In the Good Old Summertime." Baseball notables gathered at the monument, which was unveiled by Barney's young grandson, Billy Benswanger, Jr. National League president John Heydler placed a wreath at its base and in somber tones paid tribute to Barney, whom he described as "the senior member of the league and its major leader in thought, action and courage."[7] History repeated itself that day on the diamond. The Pirates faced the Chicago Cubs, their opponents on opening day June 30, 1909, when the Bucs lost 3–2. This time, 25 years later, against the same team, they lost 6–4. The Cubs were again party poopers. The balance of the 1934 season was a disappointment and the Pirates finished fifth, 19½ games back of pennant-winning St. Louis.

In early 1935, Boston Braves owner Emil Fuchs hired the aging Babe Ruth, promising he'd eventually become manager, a job the 40-year-old Ruth coveted. Ruth and the Braves appeared at Forbes Field late in May where Ruth made some baseball history. By the time of the three-game series, Ruth was already feuding with Fuchs and his batting

Two years after he died in 1932, this plaque honoring Barney Dreyfuss and his son Sammy was unveiled at Forbes Field. It was relocated to Three Rivers Stadium when the Pirates moved there and today can be found in the main concourse at PNC Park (Len Martin).

average that month hovered around .150, with only three homers. Ruth had become disillusioned with Boston, as well as with Fuchs and was playing poorly. He spoke about wanting to retire but agreed to remain until the end of the month at the insistence of Fuchs who knew both Cincinnati and Philadelphia had special (and lucrative) Babe Ruth Days planned for upcoming visits of the Braves. Ruth went hitless in the first game in Pittsburgh, but drove a ball to deep right field where Paul Waner made a leaping catch. In the second game, he hit another to deep right where Waner was forced to make a one-handed catch against the wall. Ruth's only hit was a single in the fourth inning. The final game was Saturday, May 25 and the Ruth of old suddenly came to life. He belted a two-run homer off starter Red Lucas in the first inning, then in the third connected for a two-run dinger off reliever Guy Bush. Two innings later he singled off Bush to drive in a run. Bush was still on the mound in the seventh when Ruth blasted his third home run, this one with bases empty. It was a massive clout that cleared the 86-foot-high double-decked stands along right field, the longest home run ever seen in Forbes Field. He went four-for-four and drove in six runs that day, but his heroics were wasted as the Pirates completed their three-game sweep with an 11–7 victory. It was Babe's 714th and last home run of his storied career. Pittsburgh and the players were left buzzing. "I never saw a ball hit so hard before or since," Bush admitted afterward. "I can't remember anything about the first home run he hit off me that day.... But I can't forget that last one. It's probably still going."[8] After obliging Fuchs by appearing in Cincinnati and Philadelphia—without any further hits—Ruth retired.

During the 1930s, Bill Benswanger and Florence Dreyfuss improved Forbes Field by installing loudspeakers and adding some padding to its concrete outfield walls. Permanent lights were installed at the end of the decade and the Pirates played their first night game at the park on June 4, 1940, when they embarrassed the Boston Braves 14–2. Pittsburgh was a bit late to night-time baseball, five years after the first night game was played at Crosley Field in Cincinnati. Beginning in 1929, Forbes Field was used by the Homestead Grays as their home park, although players were barred from using the clubhouse and showers. The successful Negro League team featured such outstanding players as Cool Papa Bell, Buck Leonard and Josh Gibson.[9] On July 18, 1930, the Grays played the Kansas City Monarchs in the first night-time baseball game ever played at Forbes Field, using portable floodlights. The game went 12 innings before the Grays prevailed, 5–4. Football games were also played at night with temporary lighting and the park was used for political rallies and boxing matches.

In 1936, Honus Wagner was among the first inductees into the National Baseball Hall of Fame in Cooperstown, along with Babe Ruth, Ty Cobb, Walter Johnson and Christy Mathewson. In 1938, regular radio broadcasts of Pirates games began.

The Pirates generally finished in the middle of the pack until 1944 when they again reached second, but were back in fourth the following year. In 1946, Ralph Kiner joined the club, playing left field, and making an immediate impact with his bat. He led the National League with 23 home runs in his rookie season and continued to be an offensive wonder for the Pirates until 1952, after which he was traded to Chicago. Kiner gave Pittsburgh fans something to lift their spirits as the Bucs remained a second-division team for all but one year. Kiner was the league's home run king from 1949 to 1952 with 54, 47, 42 and 37 round-trippers.

In early 1946, Barney Dreyfuss was among 39 baseball executives, managers, umpires and sportswriters appointed to the new "Honor Rolls of Baseball" at the National Baseball Hall of Fame in Cooperstown. Baseball writers elect members to the Hall of Fame but were having trouble agreeing in recent years. Meanwhile, the Hall trustees were faced with a recent expansion of the building with empty walls they wanted to fill. An affiliated group originally known as the "Old-Timers Committee," now operating as the "Permanent Committee," took it upon itself to recognize 11 players for formal induction. But the 39 non-playing members of the baseball community would not be inducted like the players. They were simply named to the "Honor Rolls." Dreyfuss was among 11 executives so honored in April, along with others including Ed Barrow of the Yankees, John T. Brush of the Giants, Charles Ebbets of Brooklyn, Ernest Barnard of the American League, and John T. Heydler and Nick Young of the National League. Also named was Dreyfuss's nemesis Garry Herrmann, chair of the old National Commission.

The Permanent Committee stressed that being named to the new Honor Rolls (often referred to in the singular) did not preclude anyone so honored from being formally inducted later into the Hall of Fame. This created some confusion and as baseball historian David L. Fleitz found, "reaction to the new designation was swift and almost universally negative."[10] *The Sporting News* decried creation of what it deemed an inferior honor. "There was no demand for a new list of sub-greats," it editorialized. "There will never be any cogent reason for that phony type of baseball beatification. If a man was a great umpire or an outstanding writer, he should be elected to the diamond Pantheon, and not placed in an annex to that office, so to speak."[11] The publication said the entire election process had been called into question and needed "a complete overhauling." Few sportswriters placed any value on the Honor Rolls and complained that two of the executives so honored, Barrow and Bob Quinn of the Boston Braves, were members of the committee that made the selections, undermining its legitimacy. No plaques or physical "honor roll" were created, no ceremony provided for the 39, and nothing about it was displayed at the Hall of Fame. No further appointments were ever made by Barrow and his committee and the rolls were quickly forgotten. The Dreyfuss family was pleased with the recognition, some of them apparently believing it amounted to full induction and well-deserved recognition. For its part, however, the Hall of Fame seemed anxious to forget the "Honor Rolls" as a well-intentioned mistake. The episode is little remembered today.

Shortly after the war, Florence Dreyfuss grew tired of owning a ball club. By 1946 there were rumblings that players were forming a union and Pittsburgh was one of the first cities targeted by organizers because of its strong union movement. A player strike was narrowly averted, but the situation had been stressful for ownership. Then the front office suffered a black eye and public criticism for fumbling a "free day" for 500 carriers of the *Pittsburgh Post-Gazette*. The game chosen for the special promotion was rained out and when the carriers appeared at Forbes Field the following day they were abruptly shooed away by club secretary Sam Watters. The newspaper carried a strong editorial critical of Pirates management, stinging the club owner who suggested to her son-in-law that the time had come to sell.[12] On August 8, Florence Dreyfuss announced the sale of the club for $2.5 million to a syndicate including banker Frank McKinney of Indianapolis, John W. Galbreath, a Columbus realtor, Tom Johnson, of the Standard Steel Spring Company and Bing Crosby, the popular singer and Hollywood movie star. McKinney became president and Crosby vice-president while Benswanger remained for a time as assistant to McKinney.[13]

In 1951, Forbes Field had a starring role in the Hollywood movie *Angels in the Outfield* which was filmed mainly in Pittsburgh. It was a story about a Pirates manager who received divine help to put his team on a winning track. (Ironically, by then, many of the long-suffering real Pirates faithful may have been hoping for similar intervention.) On April 30, 1955, a frail Honus Wagner was honored publicly when a bronze statue of him was unveiled just beyond the left outfield wall, while he sat in a nearby convertible, unable to join the dignitaries who included baseball commissioner Ford Frick, Mooney Gibson, Fred Clarke and Cy Young. The monument was 10 feet high, weighed 1,800 pounds and cost $40,000. "In honor of a baseball immortal, a champion among champions," the inscription read. The idea for the statue came from former Pittsburgh players and a public fundraising campaign was led by former Pirates president Bill Benswanger, who acted as master of ceremonies. About 1,000 guests were on hand to honor the modest old ballplayer who softly murmured "How about that!" when it was unveiled and a tear streamed down his cheek.[14] On December 6 that same year, Wagner died at the age of 81.

Honus Wagner passed away in 1955 and is buried in Jefferson Memorial Park south of Pittsburgh. His simple marker makes no mention of his hall-of-fame career. Visitors often leave baseballs and other items to salute the greatest of all Pirates (Kaitlyn Larsen).

18. After the Little Colonel

After a couple of decades of mostly second-division play, the Pirates captured the National League pennant in 1960, thrilling their long-suffering fans. Their last pennant was 33 years earlier when they fell to the Yankees in the World Series in four games straight. And for the 1960 fall classic it was the Yankees they would face again, a team which had become the most successful franchise in all of baseball while Pittsburgh had languished. New York had appeared in nine of the last 11 World Series, winning seven of them and they were heavily favored to repeat. Outfielders Mickey Mantle and Roger Maris collected 40 and 39 home runs respectively during the season, which began poorly for New York. But the Yankees regained their winning ways and took the final 15 games of the season to finish eight games up on Baltimore. The Pirates featured League all-stars Roberto Clemente in right field and Bill Mazeroski at second base, leading the pennant race most of the season with a powerful and balanced offense. They finished seven games ahead of Milwaukee. The 1960 World Series pitted a team that had spent 33 years in the wilderness against the high-flying Bronx Bombers for whom success had become routine. And was expected.

The showdown began at Forbes Field before 36,676 fans on October 5 with a 6–4 victory for the Pirates. The following day at Forbes, the Yankee bats exploded in a 16–3 romp before 37,308 witnesses, victimizing right-hander Bob Friend and five Pirate relievers. Mantle homered twice and batted in five runs in a game that featured 32 hits in all. Game Three was October 8 at Yankee Stadium before 70,000 fans. Left-hander Whitey Ford shut out the Pirates on four hits. Meanwhile, Bobby Richardson belted a grand-slam home run off reliever Clem Labine, while Mantle collected another homer and four hits as the Yankees won 10–0. The next day, with Vernon Law on the mound, the Pirates eked out a 3–2 win, disappointing the New York crowd of 67,812. Law and reliever Roy Face held the powerful Yankee offense to eight hits, a change of pace from the slugging displayed in the previous two games. With the Series tied two games apiece, Game Five was October 10 at Yankee Stadium before 62,753 fans. New York starter Art Ditmar was pulled in the second inning when the Bucs scored three runs. Maris homered in the bottom of the third, but reliever Face retired eight of the nine Yankees he faced to keep their offense largely in check. The powerful outfield arm of Roberto Clemente kept New York base runners honest as the Pirates won 5–2. The Series returned to Pittsburgh for Game Six where 38,580 fans crammed into Forbes Field and saw Ford shut out the Bucs 12–0.

With the Series tied three games apiece, the deciding game was October 13 at Forbes Field before a crowd of 36,683. Yankee manager Casey Stengel sent nine-game winner Bob Turley to the mound to face Law, winner of Games One and Four. Pittsburgh took an early 4–0 lead but after six complete innings, the Yankees led 5–4. Neither team scored in the seventh. In the top of the eighth, the Pirates went ahead 9–7, driving the crowd delirious with joy. Friend was called upon to hold the lead for the Pirates in the ninth but couldn't and the Yankees scored twice to tie the score 9–9.

Ralph Terry returned to the mound for New York in the bottom of the ninth and the Pirates faithful remained tense. The first batter he faced was Mazeroski, a player known more for his glove than his bat. In his career, the future hall of famer won eight gold gloves in his 17 seasons and had a lifetime batting average of .260. He let Terry's first offering sail by, high and outside. On the second pitch, a slider that failed to break low in the strike zone and stayed letter-high, Mazeroski connected for a drive over the left field wall near the 407-foot mark, a blast that drove the crowd wild and fans streamed onto the field to celebrate the dramatic victory. "It was, for the Pirates fans, a moment frozen in time," lifelong fan and author John McCollister wrote in his history of the Bucs. Pittsburgh partied all night, with fans dancing in the streets, singing, shouting and hugging each other. "There was no destruction of property that day," McCollister recalled, "only joy and true celebration."[15] Mazeroski's walk-off homer brought the Pirates their first World Series in 35 years. And he became the first player ever to hit a walk-off homer to win the fall classic. The only other player to do so was Toronto Blue Jay Joe Carter 33 years later, in game six of the 1993 World Series against Philadelphia. It, too, was a dramatic clout, but not quite like Mazeroski's game-seven blast. Barney Dreyfuss would have smiled his famous smile at getting sweet revenge for that humiliating four-games-straight loss to the Yankees back in 1927. And going the full seven games.

The heroics of the 1960 Pirates and "Maz" are still celebrated to this day. On October 13 every year, diehard fans gather at the remnants of the Forbes Field wall not far from the spot where Mazeroski's ball sailed into Pittsburgh sports history. They listen to a taped radio broadcast of the game in a tradition that began in 1985. The event has included some red, white and blue bunting that adorned Forbes Field that memorable day. A group calling itself the Game 7 Gang was organized in 2007 to keep the tradition alive and it includes regulars such as leader Herb Soltman and local baseball historian George Skornickel among the hundreds of regulars. They sing the national anthem, applaud and cheer when the Pirates score and lament and fret when the Yankees go ahead. Mazeroski's magic home run always draws the biggest cheers. Soltman attended the 1960 game with his parents and grandmother and he joined the throng that swarmed onto the field to greet Mazeroski at home plate. He said he loves listening to the replay at the wall with hundreds of others, which he has done every year since 1990 "and it is still exciting now, 50 years later, as it was in 1960," Soltman recalled in a brief memoir in 2010. The homer and the victory he said, "were, are now, and always will be my defining moment in sports."[16]

By the late 1960s Forbes Field was showing its age. The "House of Thrills" as it had become known, had chunks of concrete falling from its walls and it lacked many modern amenities, including unobstructed viewing and sufficient parking nearby. Meanwhile, its neighbor the University of Pittsburgh was looking to expand. The university purchased Forbes Field for $3 million in 1958 and allowed the Pirates to remain until they found a new home. The North Side, where Exposition Park once stood, was being revitalized and city officials decided a new multisport municipal stadium would provide a fine focal point for redevelopment of the former industrial area. It took more than two years to build the circular, five-tiered structure that would seat 48,000 for baseball and 59,000 for football. The $55 million park featured artificial turf and was inward-looking by design, unlike Forbes Field with its leafy vista beyond the outfield walls. The Pirates, whom it was feared might relocate to another city if they didn't get the new city-owned park, contributed nothing to the capital cost. The new park was named Three Rivers Stadium, marking its location near the confluence of the Allegheny, Monongahela and Ohio rivers.

The curtain call for Forbes Field came June 28, 1970, when nearly 41,000 fans crammed into the 35,000-capacity park for a doubleheader against the Cubs. The Pirates won both games to put them two percentage points behind the first-place New York Mets. After the final game, souvenirs of the venerable park were on sale but fans preferred to help themselves to mementoes ranging from bats to bases, scoreboard pieces and seats while, for the most part, police looked the other way. Two youths made off with the circular brass plaque from the centerfield monument to Barney and Sam Dreyfuss, but four

18. *After the Little Colonel* 195

Longtime Pirate fans Herb Soltman, left, and George Skornickel are regular visitors to a remaining section of the Forbes Field wall that sits on city-owned land. They are members of the Game 7 Gang who gather every October 13 at the wall over which Bill Mazeroski's homer sailed to win the 1960 World Series for the Bucs. The annual event features the playing of a tape of the radio broadcast of that game (author's photograph).

other youngsters wrested the booty from the pair and turned it over to the Pirates office.[17] It would be mounted in Three Rivers Stadium and later at the stadium's successor, PNC Park.

In 1971, the Pirates captured the National League pennant and defeated the Baltimore Orioles to take their fourth World Series. Roberto Clemente was outstanding and

A portion of the center field wall and the giant flagpole from Forbes Field have been retained by the city from which Barney Dreyfuss leased land to complete his outfield. It is often visited by Pittsburghers and tourists alike (Kaitlyn Larsen).

18. After the Little Colonel

had at least one hit in each of the seven games, with clutch home runs in Game Six and Seven. He batted .414 and was named most valuable player of the series. Tragically, he died in a plane crash the following year. Eight years later, the Pirates repeated as World Series winners, again downing the Orioles, to take their fifth world championship. Aging slugger Willie Stargell was the star for the Bucs, who rallied behind him and the "We Are Family" song they adopted for motivation. He pounded three home runs in the Series, batted .400 and was named most valuable player.

Bill Benswanger passed away in 1972 and two years later his widow Eleanor, Barney's daughter, donated some of her father's correspondence, agreements, rosters, programs and financial information to the Baseball Hall of Fame. At some point, the family also donated a trophy given Dreyfuss in 1901 to commemorate the Pirates winning the National League pennant and a silver cup presented to him in 1924, his 25th year as team owner.[18] The Hall also obtained a silver trophy baseball inscribed with the scores of two games played between Dreyfuss's Paducah ball club and its rivals in Cairo, Illinois, during the summer of 1885. Not all items are on display at the hall at any one time.[19]

In 1979, Barney Dreyfuss was elected to the International Jewish Sports Hall of Fame, honored as "an innovator during baseball's tumultuous formative years ... a visionary who rose above the petty disputes rampant in the sport at the turn of the century."[20]

After a successful decade in the seventies, the Pirates fell off the pace again and fans were left living off memories of past glories. After the 2000 season, Three Rivers Stadium was imploded, with $40 million still owing on it. It was replaced by 38,362-seat, baseball-only PNC Park which offers a fine view of the downtown Pittsburgh skyline and adjacent Roberto Clemente Bridge. It cost $262 million, with $143 coming from the city and $75 million from the state. PNC Park is considered one of the most beautiful parks

In 2005, a Pennsylvania state historical plaque honoring Barney Dreyfuss was unveiled near the remnants of the Forbes Field outfield wall. On hand were, from left, baseball historians Dennis DeValeria and Len Martin, Bill Benswanger, Jr., Aimee Benswanger, and baseball historian Dan Bonk (Len Martin and Dan Bonk).

in the game. Near its entrances are statues of Pirate immortals Honus Wagner, Roberto Clemente, Willie Stargell and Bill Mazeroski. The granite monument and plaque to Barney and Sam Dreyfuss, originally unveiled at Forbes Field, and briefly purloined upon its closing, can be found inside the concourse behind home plate. The opening game at PNC Park was April 9, 2001, against the Cincinnati Reds. And in what had become an unfortunate tradition on Pittsburgh ballpark opening days, the Reds spoiled the party by winning 8–2.

Large amounts of public money were required to build both Three Rivers Stadium and PNC Park, unlike Forbes Field. Back in 1909 Barney Dreyfuss built his state-of-the-art ballpark in a mere six months with $1 million of his own money. Pittsburghers grew to love his park and learned how much a baseball team could mean to the city. So it's not surprising crowds gather at the remains of the Forbes Field wall to recall a glorious moment in sports history when a ball sailed over it and brought glory to Pittsburgh.

Along what used to be the base of the left field wall of Forbes field lies a small plaque indicating where Mazeroski's homer cleared it in 1960. It was placed there in the mid–1970s. A few steps away can be found a more substantial historic marker unveiled by the Pennsylvania Historical and Museum Commission in 2005 honoring Barney Dreyfuss. It describes the builder of Forbes Field as a "legendary leader influential in initiating the first World Series, 1903" and notes his Pirates won six National League titles and two World Series. On hand for the official unveiling were his grandson, Bill Benswanger, Jr., and his wife Aimee, along with Forbes Field historians Len Martin and Dan Bonk, and Honus Wagner biographer Dennis DeValeria.

As time goes on, memories of Barney Dreyfuss and the fine baseball palace he gave Pittsburgh are fading. It's a shame, really, because Dreyfuss was so good for Pittsburgh and for all of baseball. His legacy will always be considered enormous.

Epilogue

As the on-field struggles of the Pirates continued into the latter years of the twentieth century and into the next, nostalgia for the team's glory days under Barney Dreyfuss only seemed to grow.

The unveiling of the plaque to him near the Forbes Field wall in 2005 was followed by an even greater honor. In 2008, he was inducted into the National Baseball Hall of Fame in Cooperstown, New York, in the executive category, along with former commissioner Bowie Kuhn and Dodger owner Walter O'Malley. The news came as a thrill to Barney's descendants, especially the widely scattered Dreyfuss clan. His great grandson Evan Dreyfuss, living in upstate New York about 100 miles from Cooperstown, was particularly pleased. "He was baseball's quiet giant," he told the *Pittsburgh Post-Gazette*. "He sort of got overlooked. His life and vision for baseball very much parallels the story of the American Dream—that success comes from hard work, taking risks, being of strong moral fiber and treating people well. The family is very, very proud of him."[21]

The induction ceremony attracted more than a dozen members of the Dreyfuss family but those in the Benswanger branch boycotted the event, believing the appointment of Dreyfuss to the ill-fated "Honor Rolls" of 1946 meant he was already ensconced in the Hall of Fame. His widow Florence apparently thought so, passing away four years later. The Benswangers felt the recognition granted 62 years earlier was more appropriate anyway and were unimpressed with how the Hall of Fame had handled things. They didn't want to be seen as endorsing the Hall which they felt had misled them years earlier. Their displeasure was reflected further when they sought the return of some Dreyfuss memorabilia they had earlier donated to the Hall. They were unsuccessful because the Hall understandably wants to dissuade those who might seek to cash in on the rising values of baseball memorabilia over the years by demanding the return of artifacts. Not that this was the Benswanger plan, but the family declined to discuss the matter publicly.

At the ceremony, Andrew Dreyfuss, Evan's twin brother, spoke for the family. Their older brother, Terry, whose given name was Barney Dreyfuss III, was among those on hand. Their father, Barney Dreyfuss II passed away suddenly in 1991 in his early 60s. In remarks recounting the career of his great grandfather, Andrew noted he "introduced or supported every piece of progressive legislation during the 30-year time span" he owned the Pirates. He helped end the war with the American League, helped establish the World Series and built a grand and permanent ballpark that demonstrated his faith in the game. He reminded the crowd that Branch Rickey once called Dreyfuss the best judge of players he'd seen and that 12 future Hall of Famers started their careers in Louisville or Pittsburgh when Barney was in charge. Andrew Dreyfuss pointed out that Barney's generosity and dedication to baseball were being saluted that same night in Columbia, South Carolina,

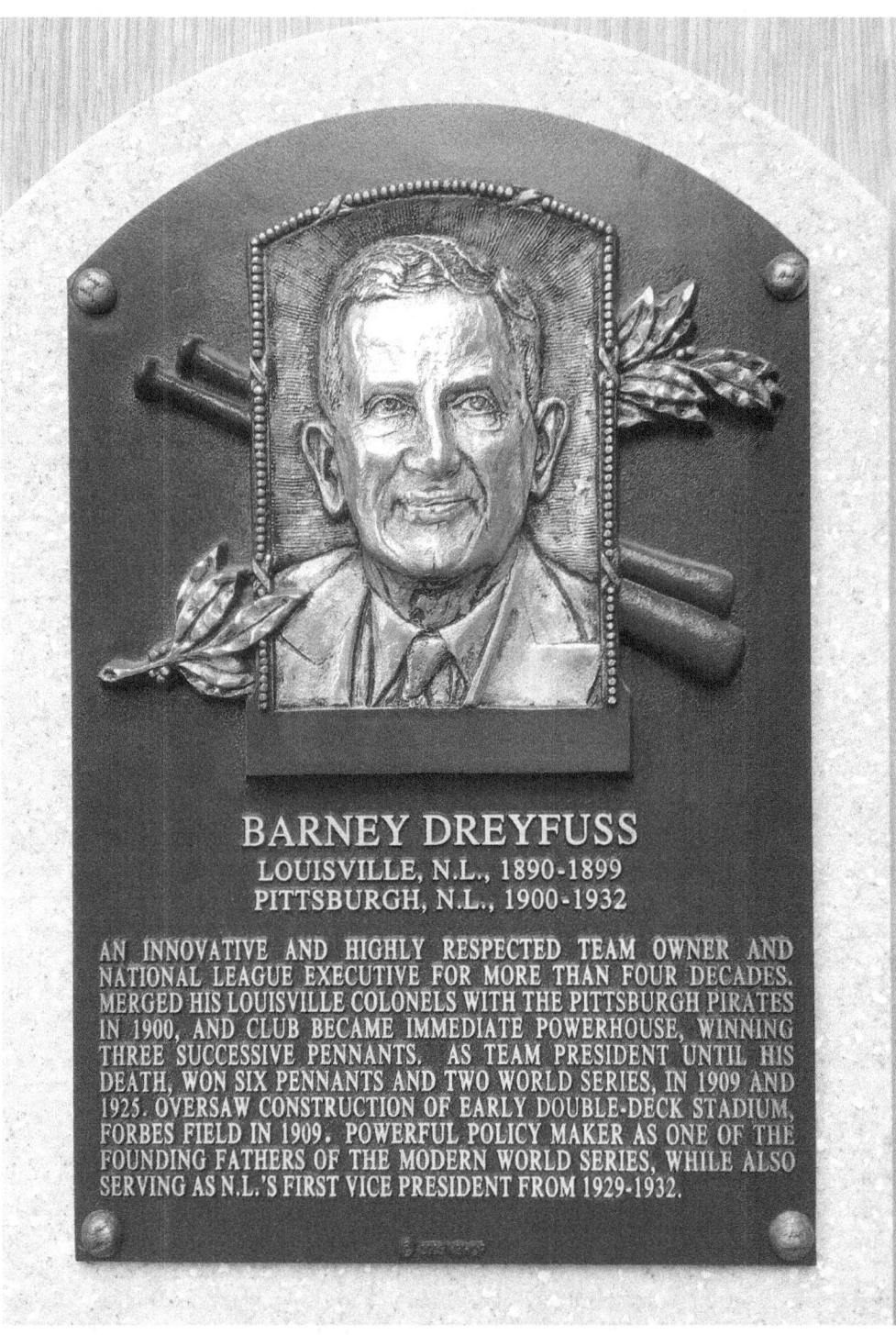

In 2008, Barney Dreyfuss was inducted into the National Baseball Hall of Fame in Cooperstown, New York. He is in the executive category, alongside baseball pioneers and notables Ed Barrow, Henry Chadwick, Charlie Comiskey, Ban Johnson, Kenesaw Mountain Landis, Al Spalding, Branch Rickey and Harry and George Wright (author's photograph).

where in 1927 he replaced their baseball stadium that had burned down the previous year. The Columbia Blowfish of the Coastal Plain League would be taking the field wearing 1927 replica jerseys of the Columbia Comers to recall the city's baseball benefactor.[22]

His plaque at the Hall of Fame calls Dreyfuss "an innovative and highly respected team owner and National League executive for more than four decades" and a "powerful policy maker as one of the founding fathers of the modern World Series." He is among executives such as Ed Barrow of the Yankees, Henry Chadwick, the Father of Baseball, Charles Comiskey of Chicago, Walter O'Malley of the Dodgers, Branch Rickey of the Cardinals and Dodgers, Jacob Ruppert of the Yankees and commissioners Ford Frick, Bowie Kuhn, and Kenesaw Mountain Landis. Also there is American League founder Ban Johnson. Others in the same category include baseball pioneers Albert Goodwill Spalding and brothers George and Harry Wright. Dreyfuss is in distinguished company.

Barney Dreyfuss really did live the American Dream. As a young man from a foreign land with a different language, he soon discovered that hard work had tangible rewards. But he wasn't all about work, early on discovering much pleasure from a game that he'd help develop into the national pastime—and a viable business. He treated people well but could not tolerate greed or dishonesty in anyone—players, managers or fellow executives. He always was guided by doing what he felt was best for the game, from efforts as small as banning the spitball and retiring the "rabbit ball," to grand ventures like investing $1 million in a permanent ballpark at a time in history when the future of professional baseball was anything but assured.

Dreyfuss realized the game was governed poorly and was instrumental in pushing for a Commissioner to clean it up once and for all. He loved the game for itself, not for the money it could generate, unlike magnates such as Andrew Freedman and John T. Brush. And Dreyfuss had a rare ability to find players able to play at its highest level. His "dope book" and the network of contacts and scouts he developed helped him field some of the finest teams in the game. "First Division Barney" hated losing and remained a fan his entire life. Other owners might sit back and leave managing to others. Not Dreyfuss, a real student of the game, who attended every Louisville Colonels and Pittsburgh Pirates home game he could, studying the play and making notes, keeping score and constantly pursuing a winning formula for his team. He was stubborn and became a force in the corridors of power of the National League. Dreyfuss survived several attempts to squeeze him out of baseball. He broke down barriers by playing peacemaker to recognize the American League and then arranged to have his Pirates play the best of that rival loop. He took chances on players that other owners had passed up and he risked most of his hard-earned wealth by opening Forbes Field, a move many critics dubbed his "folly." For some, the task of scheduling was onerous and fraught with pitfalls and accusations of favoritism. Not for the onetime distillery credit manager. He could come up with a fair schedule for all concerned with relative ease, juggling cities with Sunday games with those unable to play that day and by considering logical road trips to minimize travel costs and improve profitability for all teams. His scheduling was usually flawless and when he had to make occasional adjustments, Dreyfuss did so quickly, to the amazement of his fellow magnates. He could be generous, as in 1903 when he allocated his owner's share of that year's world championship to his players and later when he helped that ball club in South Carolina get back on its feet with a new stadium. Dreyfuss's ego seldom affected his decisions. Many friends urged him to put his name on his marvelous new stadium, but he instead chose that of a key figure in the history of Pittsburgh, British

General John Forbes who named the city after Prime Minister William Pitt. Dreyfuss was wealthy and could have become even more so had he agreed to extend the baseball season or sold advertising on the walls of Forbes Field. Such advertising was so much clutter, he felt, and detracted from the game and the fine setting the Pirates called home. Other owners derived good revenue from advertising at their parks, but he wanted none of it. Dreyfuss prized loyalty in his players and was loyal to them, especially Fred Clarke, Tommy Leach, Honus Wagner and George "Mooney" Gibson. Dreyfuss treated and paid his players well but if they held out for more money than he offered, he considered that disloyalty and would sever his connection with them.

Over the years much has been written about his sometimes titanic struggles and the contributions he made to the game in Paducah, Louisville and Pittsburgh.

In their fine history of Forbes Field, editors David Cicotello and Angelo J. Louisa conclude that Dreyfuss's legacy was "enormous" as a peacemaker and builder. But there was so much more:

> He was a facilitator, and when conflicts of interest arose that threatened to tear the structure of the game apart, Barney Dreyfuss was there to mediate the important issues by creating a path towards resolution. Between 1895 and 1932, Dreyfuss was in the middle of every important decision facing professional baseball including syndication, contraction, league conflicts, the Federal League, schedules, and of course, the scandal arising out of the 1919 World Series.[23]

Authors Mark L. Armour and Daniel R. Levitt cited Dreyfuss as a topflight owner and operator in their 2015 book *In Pursuit of Pennants,* which reviewed baseball's evolution from the deadball era to modern "moneyball." They noted that during his 32 years operating the Pirates, Barney's club finished in the first division an impressive 26 times while collecting six National League pennants and winning two World Series.

> Dreyfuss succeeded in this era because his unique attention to detail combined with his competitive fire, a knack for negotiating the charged politics of the league, and his ability to engender loyalty from his players created an organization one step ahead of most of the competition. At a time when the man in charge needed to be a jack-of-all-trades, Dreyfuss effectively understood both the detail and the general to assemble one of the great franchises of the early twentieth century.[24]

In their study of eight owners who shaped the game of baseball, Burton and Benita Boxerman noted that Dreyfuss was a stickler for integrity. He felt it should be against the law for anyone to sell tickets above their face value and he didn't want gambling in or near his ballpark. He urged police to take the scourge of gambling as seriously as he did. He retained a soft spot for his players and tried to do his best for them. Sometimes he helped them establish bank accounts for the benefit of their families and for some of his better-paid players he invested their pay for them and guaranteed the principal amount even if their investments turned sour.[25] His contributions to the game were his greatest contribution, however. The Boxermans cited one sportswriter who insisted no owner was more progressive in his approach to professional baseball than Dreyfuss:

> "If Charles Ebbets may be credited with the statement 'Baseball is in its infancy,' then Barney Dreyfuss must be given credit as the sportsman who [nourished] that infant into a lusty giant, a sportsman who wanted to know the score before he learned attendance figures ... and who was constantly striving for something new and progressive that would improve and advance the game."[26]

The view of Dreyfuss as a nurturer was not isolated. Other sportswriters who saw Dreyfuss operate were also moved to write about the contributions made to the game by the little Kentucky Colonel with the German accent. John Kieran covered baseball for the *New York Tribune* and the *New York Times* and witnessed his handiwork. In a *Times* column Kieran called the passing of Barney Dreyfuss "a great loss to baseball." He said the Pittsburgh owner "was looked upon by many as the shrewdest businessman in baseball" and "reaped a fortune" from it, but "was not looking to extract the last quarter or thin dime that baseball could produce for him." Kieran gave an example. He recalled that for the 1925 World Series, Dreyfuss erected an extra section for fans in Forbes Field at a cost of $25,000. The total income derived from the additional seating came to $8,000 of which the Pirates received a mere $1,200, a poor return on the investment. And after the Series, the stands were dismantled. "Mr. Dreyfuss always considered the money well spent," Kieran observed.[27]

PNC Park in Pittsburgh, the current home of the Pittsburgh Pirates, lies across the Allegheny River from downtown, in an area known as the North Side. It is near where Exposition Park and Three Rivers Stadium once stood. PNC is considered one of the most beautiful parks in baseball (author's photograph).

Frederick G. Lieb also followed the exploits of Dreyfuss and his Pirates for a variety of publications and wrote a book in 1948 about the team, one of six he penned about ball clubs for G.P. Putnam's Sons. Lieb noted Dreyfuss drank little and never touched tobacco. Lieb added he "could be severe, dominating and critical," and occasionally found himself at odds with fan sentiment, such as for his handling of their favorites Kiki Cuyler and Rabbit Maranville. Dreyfuss, however, was one of the larger-than-life characters in baseball for whom Lieb had great respect and he lamented Dreyfuss leaving the scene.

Yet when the former Paducah bookkeeper closed his earthly books, his contribution to baseball was large. He was one of the game's greatest and most far-seeing club owners. If, when in a moment of anger or peeve, he occasionally did a small thing, his vision was wide and his heart and keen mind were always on the side of better baseball. He said baseball was his business, so it was his business to keep the game and his club prosperous. Instinctively he recognized that clean baseball—a game above the slightest breath of suspicion—was the only baseball that paid.[28]

Writers Kieran and Lieb were both honored posthumously by the Baseball Writers' Association of America with the J.G. Taylor Spink Award, awarded annually since 1962 "for meritorious contributions to baseball writing."

Barney Dreyfuss lived a full and successful life. A man small in stature, he became a giant in baseball, a visionary, an innovator. He helped grow the game from a hit-and-miss proposition financially and overseen by clashing egos into a multimillion-dollar operation. Dreyfuss always put the game first, ahead of profit, ahead of ego. He gave his adopted home, the hard-working industrial city of Pittsburgh a great deal of pride, a winner, and the confidence it could compete against the best teams in baseball and the biggest cities in America. And yet, as the years pass and stadiums have come and gone, his name is no longer well-known in Pittsburgh. There is no statue to Dreyfuss like those for Pirate heroes Honus Wagner, Roberto Clemente, Bill Mazeroski, and Willie Stargell. Dreyfuss would be fine with that, no doubt, and possibly embarrassed at the historical marker bearing his name near the Forbes Field wall and the plaque now mounted at PNC Park. Baseball always came first for him, not personal gain nor public acclaim, so he'd be pleased to know that the game he loved eventually loved him back by recognizing his many contributions in Cooperstown.

In the end, the follies of Barney Dreyfuss were few. His successes were many.

Chapter Notes

Chapter 1

1. "Forbes Field, the World's Finest Baseball Grounds," *Pittsburgh Post*, June 27, 1909, 30.
2. Daniel L. Bonk, "Ballpark Figures: The Story of Forbes Field," *Pittsburgh History Magazine*, Summer 1993, 56.
3. "New Ballpark Will Surpass Expectations," *Pittsburgh Press*, March 7, 1909, 1.
4. Bonk, 57, 64.
5. "Two Shifts Will Work on New Baseball Park," *Pittsburgh Post*, March 28, 1909, 15.
6. Robert C. Trumpbour, "Forbes Field: Ahead of Its Time in 1909," accessed November 21, 2019, https://sabr.org/research/forbes-field-ahead-its-time-1909.
7. Dreyfuss's height is mis-stated in some accounts. This figure is taken from his 1925 day planner, written in his own hand, which is among the artifacts held at the Western Pennsylvania Sports Museum, Pittsburgh, and shared by assistant curator Craig Britcher. Dreyfuss also indicated that same height on a passport application.
8. Barney Dreyfuss, National Baseball Hall of Fame biography, accessed November 20, 2019, https://baseballhall.org/hall-of-famers/dreyfuss-barney.
9. Ralph S. Davis, "Barney Dreyfuss—The Man," *The Baseball Magazine*, Vol 1., No. 3., July 1908, 27.
10. "Dreyfuss, as Fan, Forgot Self as Owner of Club," *The Sporting News*, February 18, 1932, 7.
11. Wording on Dreyfuss's plaque at the National Baseball Hall of Fame and Museum, Cooperstown, New York.
12. Bonk, 55.
13. John McCollister, *The Bucs: The Story of the Pittsburgh Pirates* (Lanexa, KS: Addax Publishing Group, 1998), 63.
14. Bonk, 56.
15. "They Said Dreyfuss Was Crazy: 1909… When Forbes Was the Ball Park," *Pittsburgh Press*, June 29, 1969, 81.
16. Curt Smith, "Forbes Field (Pittsburgh)," Society for American Baseball Research, accessed April 5, 2019, https://sabr.org/bioproj/park/forbes-field-pittsburgh.
17. James Lincoln Ray, "Connie Mack Stadium (Philadelphia)," Society for American Baseball Research, accessed April 8, 2019, https://sabr.org/bioproj/parks/connie-mack-stadium.
18. Bob Bailey, "Eclipse Park," SABR BioProject, accessed January 2, 2020, https://sabr.org/bioproj/parks/cf040064
19. John Thorn, quoted in Vince Guerrieri, "How Concrete and Steel Built Baseball," Deadspin.com, accessed July 9, 2019, https://deadspin.com/how-concrete-and-steel-built-baseball-1835946538/amp?_twitter_impression=true.
20. Dennis DeValeria and Jeanne Burke DeValeria, *Honus Wagner: A Biography* (Pittsburgh: University of Pittsburgh Press, 1998), 210.
21. Harry Schoger, "Forbes Field, the House of Thrills, Celebrates Opening Day," in *Moments of Joy and Heartbreak: Significant Episodes in the History of the Pittsburgh Pirates* (Phoenix: Society for American Baseball Research, 2018), 22.
22. "Forbes Field, the World's Finest Baseball Grounds," *Pittsburgh Post*, June 27, 1909, 30, and "35,000 Fans Help Dedicate Ball Park: Largest Assemblage Ever Gathered in Any Ball Park Anywhere Enjoys Ideal Weather Conditions," *Pittsburgh Press*, June 30, 1909, 1.
23. "The National League's Showplace," *The Reach Official American League Baseball Guide for 1910* (Philadelphia: A.J. Reach Company, 1910). 126.
24. L.H. Constans, "Forbes Field: The Great Stadium of the Pittsburgh Pirates," *Baseball Magazine*, May 1913, 89.
25. "35,000 Fans Help to Dedicate Ball Park," *Pittsburgh Press*, June 30, 1909, 1.
26. *Pittsburgh Post*, June 18, 1860, 1.
27. "Base Ball," *Pittsburgh Gazette*, August 4, 1860, 3.
28. "Base Ball," *Pittsburgh Gazette*, August 28, 1865, 3.
29. "The Athletic Base Ball Contest," *Pittsburgh Gazette*, Sept. 14, 1865, 4.
30. "The Base Ball Tournament," *Pittsburgh Gazette*, September 15, 1865, 4.
31. Craig Britcher, "A Great Base Ball Tournament," *Making History*, the Heinz History Center Blog, accessed April 12, 2019, http://heinzhistorycenter.org/blog/western-pennsylvania-history/a-great-base-ball-tournament.
32. "Base Ball," *Pittsburgh Gazette*, August 18, 1865, 3.

33. "The Base Ball Tournament," *Detroit Free Press,* August 21, 1867, 1.
34. Peter Morris, "Allegheny Baseball Club," in *Base Ball Pioneers: 1850–1870,* edited by Peter Morris, William J. Ryczek, Jan Finkel, Leonard Levin and Richard Malatzky (Jefferson, NC: McFarland, 2012), 123.
35. James M. Egan, Jr., *Base Ball on the Western Reserve: The Early Game in Cleveland and Northeast Ohio by Year and Town, 1865–1900* (Jefferson, NC: McFarland, 2008), 33.
36. "Albert George Pratt," in *Baseball's First Stars,* editors Frederick Ivor-Campbell, Robert L. Tiemann and Mark Rucker (Cleveland: Society for American Baseball Research, 1996), 128.
37. Frederick G. Lieb, *The Pittsburgh Pirates* (Carbondale: Southern Illinois University Press, 2002, reprint of 1948 G.P. Putnam edition), 3–4.
38. Brian Martin, *Pud Galvin: Baseball's First 300-Game Winner* (Jefferson, NC: McFarland, 2016), 36.
39. Brian Martin, *The Tecumsehs of the International Association: Canada's First Major League Champions* (Jefferson, NC: McFarland, 2015), 142–144.
40. Martin, *Galvin,* 76.
41. Martin, *The Tecumsehs of the International Association,* 193–196.
42. Donald Dewey and Nicholas Acocella, "Al Pratt," *The Biographical History of Baseball* (Chicago: Triumph Books, 2002), 334.
43. David Nemec, *The Beer & Whiskey League: The Illustrated History of the American Association—Baseball's Renegade Major League* (New York: Lyons & Burford, 1994), 19–21.
44. "Denny McKnight," *Baseball's First Stars,* SABR., 109.
45. Martin, *Galvin,* 170–178.
46. Lieb, 21.
47. David Nemec, "William Warren Kerr," *Major League Baseball Profiles, 1871–1900, Volume 2: The Hall of Famers and Memorable Performers Who Shaped the Game* (Lincoln: University of Nebraska Press, 2011), 167.
48. Sam Bernstein, "Barney Dreyfuss and the Legacy of Forbes Field," in *Forbes Field: Essays and Memories of the Pirates' Historic Ballpark, 1909–1971,* edited by David Cicotello and Angelo J. Louisa (Jefferson, NC: McFarland, 2007), 16.
49. "Music-Maker Danny Nirella Dead at 83," *Pittsburgh Post-Gazette,* March 9, 1956, 1.
50. "June 30, 1909: Forbes Field, Pirates' House of Thrills, Celebrates Opening Day," SABR Games Project, accessed November 28, 2019, https://sabr.org/gamesproj/game/june-30-1909-forbes-field-pirates-house-thrills-celebrates-opening-day.
51. "35,000 Fans Help to Dedicate Ball Park," *Pittsburgh Press,* June 30, 1909, 1.
52. "How the Game Was Lost by Pirates' Ball Club," *Pittsburgh Post,* July 1, 1909, 10.
53. Lieb, 133.
54. Dan Bonk and Len Martin "Bourbon, Baseball and Barney: The Story of Barney Dreyfuss—'Last of the Baseball Squires,'" *A Celebration of Louisville Baseball in the Major and Minor Leagues* (Cleveland: Society For American Baseball Research, 1997), 63.

Chapter 2

1. Isaac Wolfe Bernheim, *The Story of the Bernheim Family* (Louisville, KY: John P. Morton & Co., 1910), 65, accessed December 1, 2019, https://babel.hathitrust.org/cgi/pt?id=wu.89060747300.
2. "Germany from 1871 to 1918: German Empire, 1871–1914," *Encyclopedia Britannica,* accessed December 5, 2019, https://www.Britannica.Com/Place/Germany/Germany-From-1871-To-1918.
3. "Germany: The Economy, 1870–90," *Encyclopedia Britannica,* accessed December 5, 2019, https://www.britannica.com/place/Germany/The-economy-1870-90.
4. "German Unification," Boundless World History by Lumen Learning, accessed December 4, 2019, https://courses.lumenlearning.com/boundless-worldhistory/chapter/german-unification/.
5. "Virtual Jewish World: Baden Germany," Virtual Jewish Library, accessed May 22, 2019, https://www.jewishvirtuallibrary.org/baden-germany-virtual-jewish-history-tour.
6. Barney Bernhard Dreyfuss baptism, February 26, 1865, Breisgau u. Freiburg, Baden, Deutschland, from Baden Germany Lutheran Baptisms, Marriages and Burials, 1783–1875, Dreyfuss Family tree, ancestry.com.
7. Bernheim, *The Story of the Bernheim Family,* 4–6.
8. Darrell E. Bigham, *Towns and Villages of the Lower Ohio* (Lexington: University Press of Kentucky, 1998), 63–64, 75.
9. *Ibid.,* 111.
10. "Weille Brothers Houses," *Paducah Sun,* September 2, 1982, 32.
11. Bernheim, *The Story of the Bernheim Family,* 7.
12. "Phantoms of Ellis Island: Livingston, Germany," *Paducah Sun,* July 4, 1996, 33.
13. Isaac W. Bernheim, "History of the Settlement of Jews in Paducah and the Lower Ohio Valley" (Paducah, KY: Temple Israel by reason of the generosity of Mr. Joseph L. Friedman, 1912), 21–23, https://catalog.hathitrust.org/Record/0095629 77.
14. Bigham, 150.
15. "Cincinnati: The Jewish Community of Cincinnati," accessed May 3, 2019, https://dbs.bh.org.il/place/cincinnati.
16. Bernheim, *The Story of the Bernheim Family,* 6.
17. *Ibid.,* 64.
18. Brien Bouyea, "Historic Horse Racing: Longfellow and Ten Broeck: The Pride of Old Kentucky," *The Saratogian,* August 15, 2017, accessed December 9, 2019, https://www.saratogian.com/news/historic-horse-racing-longfellow-

and-ten-broeck-the-pride-of/article_5a128652-1949-55a4-9203-c868aa164556.html

19. Reid Mitenbuler, "The Jewish Origins of Kentucky Bourbon," *The Atlantic*, May 12, 2015, accessed December 1, 2019, https://www.theatlantic.com/business/archive/2015/05/the-jewish-origins-of-kentucky-bourbon/392408/.

20. Gary Regan and Mardee Haidin Regan, *The Book of Bourbon and Other Fine American Whiskeys* (London: Mixellany Books, 2009), 139–140.

21. Marni Davis, *Jews and Booze: Becoming American in the Age of Prohibition* (New York: New York University Press, 2012), 18.

22. Mitenbuler, "The Jewish Origins of Kentucky Bourbon."

23. Davis, 7.

24. *Ibid.*, 29.

25. "Bourbon Barons: Isaac Wolfe Bernheim," Bourbonveach.com, Bourbon History, accessed December 5, 2019, https://bourbonveach.com/2019/10/07/bourbon-barons-isaac-wolfe-bernheim/

26. Davis, 16.

27. Bernheim, *The Story of the Bernheim Family*, 65.

Chapter 3

1. John Thorn, *Baseball in the Garden of Eden: The Secret History of the Early Game* (New York: Simon & Schuster, 2011), 57.

2. "Earliest Baseball Games," Baseball Memory Lab, accessed December 20, 2019, http://mlb.mlb.com/memorylab/spread_of_baseball/earliest_games.jsp.

3. Philip von Borries, *The Louisville Baseball Almanac* (Charleston, SC: The History Press, 2010), 19.

4. "Earliest Baseball Games," Baseball Memory Lab.

5. Randy Morgan, *Paducah's Native Baseball Team* (Paducah, KY: self-published, 2015), 1.

6. "Town Ball," *Evansville Journal*, July 17, 1865, 2.

7. "The Match Game of Base Ball," *Evansville Journal*, August 13, 1867, 8.

8. Thorn, 147.

9. "Base Ball," *Cairo Bulletin*, June 8, 1876, 3.

10. "Home Items," *Paducah News*, August 23, 1882, 3.

11. Dan Bonk and Len Martin, "Bourbon, Baseball and Barney: The Story of Barney Dreyfuss—'Last of the Baseball Squires,'" *A Celebration of Louisville Baseball in the Major and Minor Leagues* (Cleveland: Society for American Baseball Research, 1997), 63.

12. Jeff Youngblood (historian and Paducah native), "Paducah and the World Series: The Life and Times of Barney Dreyfuss," unpublished monograph, 2002, Kentucky Historical Society, accessed December 1, 2019, https://www.booksie.com/posting/per-jensen/paducah-and-the-world-series-the-life-and-times-of-barney-dreyfuss-71656. A copy is held by the National Baseball Hall of Fame Museum and Library, Cooperstown.

13. "Did You Know: That the Biggest Whisky House on Earth Is in Louisville?," *Louisville Courier-Journal*, July 4, 1897, 9.

14. "Base Ball," *Memphis Public Ledger*, August 21 and 22, 1882, 4.

15. "Personal and Otherwise," *Louisville Courier-Journal*, August 13, 1882, 3.

16. "General Local Items," *Cairo Bulletin*, August 10, 1882, 4.

17. "Will You Play?," *Paducah News*, August 11, 1882, 4.

18. "General Local Items," *Cairo Bulletin*, August 14, 1883, 4.

19. "General Local News," *Cairo Bulletin*, September 26, 1883, 4.

20. "General Local Items," *Cairo Bulletin*, September 27, 1883, 4.

21. "Enclosed Base Ball Grounds," *Paducah News*, September 1, 1882, 3.

22. Youngblood, "Early Life and Times of Barney Dreyfuss."

23. Mark L. Armour and Daniel R. Levitt, *In Pursuit of Pennants: Baseball Operations from Deadball to Moneyball* (Lincoln: University of Nebraska Press, 2015), 4.

24. Morgan, 1, and "Baseball Men Mourn Death of Dreyfuss," *Louisville Courier-Journal*, February 6, 1932, 13.

25. Upon the sudden death of old-time Paducah player George B. Dovey, who was president of the Boston Braves at the time of his passing, the *Pittsburgh Post* reported that Dovey joined the Paducah club "Where he met Barney Dreyfuss, who was then playing second base." The paper's account was likely derived from information from Dreyfuss himself, then the owner of the Pittsburgh Pirates and a close friend of Dovey who had met with the Boston owner shortly before his death. "George B. Dovey Dies Suddenly on a Train," *Pittsburgh Post*, June 20, 1909, 2.

26. "General Local News," *Cairo Bulletin*, August 10, 1882, 4.

27. "In the Ball Field," *Louisville Courier-Journal*, September 2, 1884, 3.

28. "Keep Your Eyes on Boston Team—George B. Dovey," *Evansville Press*, Jan. 11, 1907, 3.

29. For the former, see: "George Dovey, of Boston Team, Has Seen Last Game," *Paducah Sun*, June 19, 1909, 1 and for the latter see "Baseball President Dead," *New York Times*, June 20, 1909, 33, and Find-A-Grave, accessed December 28, 2019, https://www.findagrave.com/memorial/76493547/george-b_-dovey.

30. "General Local Items," *Cairo Bulletin*, August 29, 1884, 4.

31. "Local News," *Cairo Bulletin*, August 30, 1884, 3.

32. "Local News," *Cairo Bulletin*, August 28, 1884, 3.

33. "General Local News," *Cairo Bulletin*, September 7 and 9, 1884, 4, 3.

34. The stock certificate and accompanying letter sent to Dreyfuss many years later by a friend who found it and can be found here: https://collection.baseballhall.org/PASTIME/letter-and-attachment-adolph-weil-barney-dreyfuss-1913-april-19#page/1/mode/1up
35. "The Open Air," *Memphis Appeal,* June 9, 1885, 4.
36. "Hotel Arrivals," *Memphis Appeal,* June 9, 1885, 4.
37. "Local Paragraphs," *Memphis Appeal,* August 6, 1885, 4.
38. "Base Ball To-Day," *Owensboro Messenger,* August 8, 1885, 4.
39. "Cairo Defeats Paducah," *The Sporting News,* August 23, 1886, 1.
40. "Base Ball," *Owensboro Messenger,* February 4, 1887, 4.
41. "Cairo Defeats Paducah," *The Sporting News,* August 23, 1886, 1.
42. "Base-Ball, Records of Former Players of Paducah," *The Paducah Sun,* January 30, 1897, 2.
43. "Facts About George Dovey," *Louisville Courier-Journal,* February 17, 1907, 18.
44. "W.H. Dovey Dead," *Louisville Courier-Journal,* June 3, 1899, 4.
45. "Dovey Coal Company," *Louisville Courier-Journal,* November 28, 1911, 4.
46. Isaac Wolfe Bernheim, *The Story of the Bernheim Family* (Louisville, KY: John P. Morton & Company, 1910), 58.
47. Gary Regan and Mardee Haidin Regan, *The Book of Bourbon and Other Fine American Whiskeys* (London: Mixellany Books, 2009), 140.
48. Ibid.
49. "Bernheim Brothers & Uri," in "Distillers and Wholesale Liquor Dealers, *Louisville Courier-Journal,* January 1, 1891, 19.
50. "Did You Know: That the Biggest Whisky House on Earth Is in Louisville?," *Louisville Courier-Journal,* July 4, 1897, 9.
51. On May 13, 1887, from 1920 U.S. Census.
52. John Kieran, "The Passing of Barney Dreyfuss," *New York Times,* February 6, 1932, 22.

Chapter 4

1. Philip Von Borries, *The Louisville Baseball Almanac* (Charleston, SC: The History Press, 2010), 15.
2. Ibid., back cover.
3. Bob Bailey, "Eclipse Park (Louisville)," SABR Bioproject, accessed January 2, 2020, https://sabr.org/bioproj/park/cf040064.
4. Bill Mooney, "The Tattletale Grays," from the *Sports Illustrated* Vault, accessed January 7, 2020, https://www.si.com/vault/1974/06/10616133/the-tattletale-grays.
5. Von Borries, 204.
6. Harold Seymour and Dorothy Seymour Mills, *Baseball: The Early Years* (Oxford, New York: Oxford University Press, 1989 paperback edition), 79.
7. "Good Enough! The Finest Game of Base Ball Ever Witnessed in Louisville," *Louisville Courier-Journal,* April 26, 1876, 4.
8. Michael Haupert, "1876. In the Face of Crisis: The 1876 Winter Meetings," *Baseball's 19th Century "Winter" Meetings, 1857–1900* (Phoenix: The Society for American Baseball Research, 2018), 140, citing *Chicago Cubs Records,* NUCMC MS 71–888, Chicago Historical Society, cash books, 1875–76.
9. Ibid., 145.
10. David Nemec, *The Great Encyclopedia of 19th Century Major League Baseball* (New York: Donald I. Fine Books, 1997), 98.
11. Mooney, "The Tattletale Grays."
12. Daniel E. Ginsburg, "The Louisville Scandal," *A Celebration of Louisville Baseball in the Major and Minor Leagues* (Cleveland: Society for American Baseball Research, 1997), 59–60.
13. "The Tattletale Grays."
14. "August 20, 1877: Gray Outcomes for 'Louisville Four,'" Society for American Baseball Games Project, accessed January 4, 2020, https://sabr.org/gamesproj/game/august-20-1877-gray-outcomes-louisville-four.
15. "Ball Talk," *New York Clipper,* March 16, 1878, 402.
16. Dennis Pajot, "1877. Scandals, New Rules, and Franchise Changes: The 1877 National League Winter Meetings," *Baseball's 19th Century "Winter Meetings," 1857–1900,* 151.
17. Ibid., 150.
18. Brian Martin, *The Tecumsehs of the International Association: Canada's First Major League Champions* (Jefferson, NC: McFarland, 2015), 178–182.
19. Brian Martin, *Pud Galvin: Baseball's First 300-Game Winner* (Jefferson, NC: McFarland, 2016), 75–76.
20. Von Borries, 145.
21. Bob Bailey, 1999. "Back in the Major Leagues," unpublished paper, supplied its author, an expert in Louisville baseball and member of the Society for American Baseball Research.
22. Clyde F. Crews, "Slow Tragedy: The Saga of Pete Browning," *A Celebration of Louisville Baseball in the Major and Minor Leagues* (Cleveland: Society for American Baseball Research, 1997), 23–24.
23. Bob Bailey, "Hunting for the First Louisville Slugger: A Look at the Browning Myth," *Baseball Research Journal,* No. 30 (Cleveland: Society for American Baseball Research, 2001), 96–98.
24. "A Disabled Club: Cleveland, Short Their Best Player, Defeated by the Eclipse," *Louisville Courier-Journal,* August 22, 1881, 8.
25. Email explanation to author from Louisville baseball historian Bob Bailey, January 20, 2020.
26. John R. Husman, "June 21, 1879: The Cameo of William Edward White," SABR Games Project, accessed January 14, 2020, https://sabr.org/gamesproj/game/june-21-1879-cameo-william-edward-white.
27. Bailey, "Back in the Major Leagues."
28. David Nemec, *The Beer & Whiskey League: The Illustrated History of the American*

Association—Baseball's Renegade Major League (New York: Lyons & Burford, 1994), 39.

Chapter 5

1. Bob Bailey, "Back in the Major Leagues," unpublished paper shared with author, 1999.
2. "That 'Pankey' Note: The President of the Base Ball Club Sued on a Note He Claims He Did Not Give—The Trouble with the Eclipse Club," *Louisville Courier-Journal*, January 15, 1884, 8.
3. David Nemec, *The Beer & Whiskey League: The Illustrated History of the American Association—Baseball's Renegade Major League* (New York: Lyons & Burford, 1994), 67–68.
4. David Pietrusza, *Major Leagues: Professional Baseball Organizations, 1871 to Present* (Jefferson, NC: McFarland, 1991), 80.
5. "The Louisvilles Sold," *Louisville Courier-Journal*, June 7, 1888, 6.
6. Ibid.
7. "Fresh Ball News," *Louisville Courier-Journal*, November 26, 1888, 2.
8. Bob Bailey, "And the Last Shall Be First: Louisville Club Zooms from Cellar to Pennant in 1890," *A Celebration of Louisville Baseball in the Major and Minor Leagues* (Cleveland: Society for American Baseball Research, 1997), 11.
9. "Sports with the Ball," *Louisville Courier-Journal*, January 6, 1889, 11.
10. "Made Him an Offer," *Louisville Courier-Journal*, February 19, 1889, 6.
11. "A Scheme to Buy," *Louisville Courier-Journal*, June 12, 1889, 6.
12. James H. Bready, "First Strike in Baseball History: The More Things Change….," *Baltimore Sun*, October 16, 1994, 70.
13. "The Strike Off," *Louisville Courier-Journal*, June 16, 1889, 14.
14. "Davidson Explains," *Louisville Courier-Journal*, June 21, 1889, 6.
15. "In Debt to Davidson," *Louisville Courier-Journal*, June 22, 1889, 6.
16. "Quit the Business," *Louisville Courier-Journal*, July 3, 1889, 6.
17. "Bought by a Syndicate," *Louisville Courier-Journal*, July 4, 1889, 2.
18. "Adjusting the Fines," *Louisville Courier-Journal*, July 6, 1889, 6.
19. "And the Last Shall Be First," Bailey, 12.
20. David Nemec, *The Great Encyclopedia of 19th Century Major League Baseball* (New York: Donald I. Fine Books, 1997), 405.
21. Philip Von Borries, *The Louisville Baseball Almanac* (Charleston, SC: The History Press, 2010), 205.
22. Dan Bonk and Len Martin, "Bourbon, Baseball and Barney: The Story of Barney Dreyfuss—'Last of the Baseball Squires,'" *A Celebration of Louisville Baseball in the Major and Minor Leagues* (Cleveland: Society for American Baseball Research, 1997), 63.
23. John Bauer, "1890. Three Divides Into Two: The 1890 Winter Meetings," *Baseball's 19th Century 'Winter' Meetings. 1857–1900* (Phoenix: Society for American Baseball Research, 2018), 288.
24. John Bauer, "1891. The Making of the Big League: The 1891 Winter Meetings," *Baseball's 19th Century 'Winter' Meetings: 1857–1900* (Phoenix: Society for American Baseball Research, 2018), 307.
25. Nemec, *The Great Encyclopedia…*, 235.
26. "That League Meeting," *Louisville Courier-Journal*, June 13, 1892, 6.
27. "Dealers Vanquish Brokers," *Louisville Courier-Journal*, August 12, 1894, 16.
28. Harold Seymour and Dorothy Mills Seymour, *Baseball: The Early Years* (New York: Oxford University Press, 1960), 265.
29. "Your Uncle Nick Talks Shop," *Sporting News*, November 5, 1892, 3.
30. John Bauer, "1892. The Price of Monopoly and the Start of the Modern Game: The 1892 Winter Meetings," *Baseball's 'Winter' Meetings. 1857–1900* (Phoenix: Society for American Baseball Research, 2018), 315.
31. "In a Blaze," *Louisville Courier-Journal*, September 27, 1892, 2.
32. "Ball Park Bought," *Louisville Courier-Journal*, February 28, 1893, 5.
33. John Bauer, "1893. How I Learned to Stop Worrying and Love the Bunt: The 1893 Winter Meetings," *Baseball's 'Winter' Meetings. 1857–1900* (Phoenix: Society for American Baseball Research, 2018), 322.
34. "Last Game. Base-Ball Season of 1895 Closes To-Day," *Louisville Courier-Journal*, September 29, 1895, 4.
35. "Panic of 1893," accessed January 31, 2020, https://www.u-s-history.com/pages/h792.html.
36. "It Is Still President Drexler," *Louisville Courier-Journal*, December 5, 1893, 5.
37. "Deferred Electing Officers," *Louisville Courier-Journal*, December 15, 1894, 6.
38. "News and Comment," *Louisville Courier-Journal*, October 3, 1894, 1.
39. "Lost Several Thousands," *Louisville Courier-Journal*, October 3, 1894, 2.
40. Bill Lamberty, "Harry Pulliam," SABR BioProject, accessed January 9, 2020, https://sabr.org/bioproj/person/6e05b19c.
41. Mark Peavey, *Take Nothing for Granted in Baseball: The Harry Pulliam Story* (No place of publication given: Deadball Books, 2018), 5.

Chapter 6

1. *Sporting Life* of January 1895, quoted in "In Pfeffer's Favor," *Louisville Courier-Journal*, February 3, 1895, 2.
2. "Loaned by the League," *Louisville Courier-Journal*, March 5, 1895, 5.
3. Mark Peavey, *Take Nothing for Granted in Baseball: The Harry Pulliam Story* (no place of publication given: Deadball Books, 2018), 44.

4. Mark L. Armour and Daniel R. Levitt, *In Pursuit of Pennants: Baseball Operations from Deadball to Moneyball* (Lincoln: University of Nebraska Press, 2015), 7–8, quoting from Ronald T. Waldo, *Fred Clarke: A Biography of a Baseball Hall of Fame Player-Manager* (Jefferson, NC: McFarland, 2011), 23–24.
5. Armour and Levitt, 7.
6. "Last Game," *Louisville Courier-Journal*, September 29, 1895, 13.
7. "Even the Colonels Prospered," *Pittsburgh Press*, September 30, 1895, 5.
8. "Enthusiastic. Was the Annual Meeting of the Louisville Club," *Louisville Courier-Journal*, December 27, 1895, 8.
9. "A Great Game of Ball," *Louisville Courier-Journal*, April 17, 1896, 6.
10. "Riot on the Diamond," *Louisville Courier-Journal*, June 27, 1896, 3.
11. "Pulliam," *Louisville Courier-Journal*, October 15, 1896, 6.
12. "Meet To-Night," *Louisville Courier-Journal*, January 6, 1897, 6.
13. "Pulliam. In Supreme Control of the Base-Ball Club," *Louisville Courier-Journal*, January 7, 1897, 6.
14. David Nemec, *The Great Encyclopedia of 19th Century Major League Baseball* (New York: Donald I. Fine Books, 1997), 580.
15. "Awful Work," *Louisville Courier-Journal*, June 30, 1897, 6.
16. "Colts Make a Record," *Chicago Tribune*, June 30, 1897, 4.
17. Angelo Louisa, "Fred Clarke," SABR BioProject, accessed February 25, 2020, https://sabr.org/bioproj/person/6f6673ea.
18. Arthur D. Hittner, *Honus Wagner: The Life and Times of Baseball's 'Flying Dutchman'* (Jefferson, NC: McFarland, 1996), 44–45.
19. A.H. Tarvin, "Another Wagner Tale," *Baseball Magazine*, February 1948, 318, quoted in Hittner, 45.
20. Dennis DeValeria and Jeanne Burke DeValeria, *Honus Wagner: A Biography* (Pittsburgh: University of Pittsburgh Press, 1996), 42.
21. William Hageman, *Honus: The Life and Times of a Baseball Hero* (Champaign, IL: Sagamore Publishing, 1996), 12–13.
22. Ibid., 17.
23. Dan O'Brien, "Rube Waddell," SABR BioProject, accessed January 30, 2010, https:sabr.org/bioproj/person/a5b2c2b4.
24. Lawrence S. Ritter, *The Glory of Their Times: The Story of the Early Days of Baseball Told by the Men Who Played It* (New York: Perennial, 2002), 25.
25. Alan H. Levy, *Rube Waddell: The Zany, Brilliant Life of a Strikeout Artist* (Jefferson, NC: McFarland, 2000), 15. This story was also related in "Waddell Is Witty," *Louisville Courier-Journal*, September 16, 1897, 6.
26. Levy, 19.
27. Peavey, 48–50.
28. "Two Changes Among Officers," *Louisville Courier-Journal*, December 29, 1897, 6.
29. "Barney Would Gain Control," *Louisville Courier-Journal*, January 30, 1898, 8.
30. "Brush Makes Another Offer," *Louisville Courier-Journal*, February 2, 1898, 6.
31. "Preparations For Opening-Day Game," *Louisville Courier-Journal*, April 10, 1898, 10.
32. "Prodigal Sons Return Today," *Louisville Courier-Journal*, July 24, 1898, 13.
33. "Louisville Magnates Trying to Sell the Local Club," *Louisville Courier-Journal*, December 1, 1898, 6.
34. Jeff Samoray, "George A. Vanderbeck," SABR BioProject, accessed February 17, 2002, https://sabr.org/node/41074.
35. "Detroit Makes Another Offer," *Louisville Courier-Journal*, December 2, 1898, 3.
36. "Why the Club Owners Are Anxious to Sell," *Louisville Courier-Journal*, December 4, 1898, 15.
37. Jamie Talbot, "1898: The 1898–1899 National League Winter Meetings," *Baseball's 19th Century 'Winter' Meetings. 1857–1900* (Phoenix: Society for American Baseball Research, 2018), 356.

Chapter 7

1. "The Base-Ball Secret Out at Last," *Louisville Courier-Journal*, January 1, 1899, 8.
2. "Louisville Lines. Barney Dreyfuss to Take a Hand in the Game," *Sporting Life*, November 26, 1898, 9.
3. "Louisville Is Safe," *Sporting Life*, January 28, 1899, 4.
4. "The Passing of the Colonels," *Louisville Courier-Journal*, September 3, 1899, 6.
5. "News and Comment," *Sporting Life*, February 11, 1899, 3.
6. "Subscribed For Stock," *Louisville Courier-Journal*, January 10, 1899, 6.
7. "Stock Plan to Be Abandoned," *Louisville Courier-Journal*, February 1, 1899, 6.
8. "Change in Management," *Louisville Courier-Journal*, February 17, 1899, 6.
9. "Games For Ten Clubs," *Louisville Courier-Journal*, March 23, 1899, 6.
10. "Pittsburgh Points," *Sporting Life*, November 4, 1899, 5.
11. "Louisville's Lament," *Sporting Life*, November 11, 1899, 7.
12. "Change in Management," *Louisville Courier-Journal*, February 17, 1899, 6.
13. "Not For Sale at Any Price," *Louisville Courier-Journal*, February 28, 1899, 6.
14. "What's This? The Pennant," *Louisville Courier-Journal*, March 10, 1899, 6.
15. Robert Peyton Wiggins, *The Deacon and the Schoolmaster: Phillippe and Leever, Pittsburgh's Great Turn-Of-The-Century Pitchers* (Jefferson, NC: McFarland, 2011), 18–19.
16. Mark Armour, "Tommy Leach," SABR BioProject, accessed February 29, 2020, https://sabr.org/bioproj/person/ba1b7d5b.
17. "Schedule Is Adopted," *Louisville Courier-Journal*, March 26, 1899, 21.

18. "Serious Charges Are Made," *Louisville Courier-Journal,* March 27, 1899, 6.
19. "The Wind-Up," and "How Was It Done?," *Sporting News,* April 1, 1899, 3.
20. "To Destroy the League," *Louisville Courier-Journal,* March 28, 1899, 6.
21. "Louisville Club's Statement," *Louisville Courier-Journal,* March 29, 1899, 6.
22. "Soden Was Bulldozed," *Louisville Courier-Journal,* March 30, 1899, 6.
23. "Hart Declares Himself," *Louisville Courier-Journal,* March 31, 1899, 6.
24. Bill Lamb, "Andrew Freedman," SABR BioProject, accessed February 21, 2020, https://sabr.org/bioproj/person/51545e58.
25. *Sporting Life,* April 1, 1899, 5.
26. "Louisville Tears," *Sporting Life,* April 1, 1899, 6.
27. "May Enjoin the League," *Louisville Courier-Journal,* April 4, 1899, 8.
28. "Can Not Force Them," *Louisville Courier-Journal,* April 6, 1899, 6.
29. "We Get Back the Dates," *Louisville Courier-Journal,* April 12, 1899, 6.
30. "Attendance Figures," *Sporting Life,* June 3, 1899, 4.
31. "Phillipe's Fine Work," *Louisville Courier-Journal,* May 26, 1899, 6.
32. Steven V. Rice, "Chief Zimmer," SABR BioProject, accessed February 23, 2020, https://sabr.org/bioproj/person/8ade3747.
33. Steven V. Rice, "June 16, 1899: Honus Wagner and the Louisville Colonels Rally in 9th to Defeat Cy Young," SABR Games Project, accessed February 20, 2020, https://sabr.org/gamesproj/june-16-1899-honus-wagner-and-louisville-colonels-rally-9th-defeat-cy-young.
34. "Destroyed," *Louisville Courier-Journal,* August 13, 1899, 10.
35. "Made Six Home Runs," *Louisville Courier-Journal,* September 3, 1899, 6.
36. "The Passing of the Colonels," *Louisville Courier-Journal,* September 3, 1899, 6.
37. Editorial in *Sporting News,* quoting the *Louisville Courier-Journal,* September 9, 1899, 4.
38. "Strikes Out Thirteen," *Chicago Tribune,* October 3, 1899, 4.
39. "Made Some Profit," *Sporting Life,* October 7, 1899, 4.
40. "Louisville Lines," *Sporting Life,* November 4, 1889, 5.
41. "Louisville Lines," *Sporting Life,* October 7, 1889, 9.

Chapter 8

1. Frederick G. Lieb, *The Pittsburgh Pirates* (Carbondale: Southern Illinois University Press, 2002), 42–43.
2. "Heard in the Corridors [of the December 1899 National League Meeting]," *Pittsburgh Press,* December 14, 1899, 5.
3. John McCollister, *The Bucs! the Story of the Pittsburgh Pirates* (Lenexa, KS: Addax Publishing, 1998), 35.
4. "Pittsburgh Points," *Sporting Life,* December 2, 1899, 3.
5. "Baseball Gossip," *Pittsburgh Press,* October 24, 1899, 5.
6. "Baseball Deal Off," *Pittsburgh Press,* October 26, 1899, 1.
7. The Deal is Off," *Pittsburgh Commercial Gazette,* October 27, 1899, 6.
8. "Watkins Is Talking Now," *Pittsburgh Post,* October 28, 1899, 6.
9. "Baseball Gossip," *Pittsburgh Press,* October 27, 1899, 5.
10. "Pittsburgh Story Again," *Louisville Courier-Journal,* October 29, 1899, 9.
11. "Baseball Gossip," *Pittsburgh Press,* October 31, 1899, 5.
12. "Another Baseball Deal," *Pittsburgh Post,* October 31, 1899, 6.
13. "Baseball Gossip," *Pittsburgh Press,* November 1, 1899, 5.
14. Sam Bernstein, "Barney Dreyfuss," SABR BioProject, accessed December 31, 2019,. https://sabr.org/bioproj/person/29ceb9e0
15. "President Kerr Admits That the Louisville Man May Buy the Pittsburgh Club," *Pittsburgh Commercial Gazette,* November 1, 1899, 6.
16. "The Local Baseball Deal," *Pittsburgh Post,* November 2, 1899, 6.
17. "Pittsburgh Points," *Sporting Life,* November 4, 1899, 5.
18. "Baseball Deal Delayed," *Pittsburgh Press,* November 4, 1899, 1.
19. "Another Deal Declared Off," *Pittsburgh Press,* November 5, 1899, 15.
20. "Club Will Not Be Sold," *Pittsburgh Post,* November 5, 1899, 7.
21. "Pittsburgh Points" *Sporting Life,* November 18, 1889, 6.
22. "Casting an Anchor," *Sporting Life,* December 2, 1899, 7.
23. Mark Peavey, *Take Nothing for Granted in Baseball: The Harry Pulliam Story* (No place of publication given, Dead Ball Books, 2018), 91.
24. "Baseball Deal Closed Today," *Pittsburgh Press,* December 8, 1899, 1.
25. Francis C. Richter, "Dreyfuss Wins Out," *Sporting Life,* February 23, 1901, 8.
26. *Pittsburgh Post,* December 9, 1899, 4.
27. "Their Price Is $20,000," *Louisville Courier-Journal,* December 12, 1899, 6.
28. "Musical Romance That Bloomed in Louisville Founded a Baseball Dynasty at Pittsburgh," *Louisville Courier-Journal,* January 25, 1942, 47.
29. Jamie Talbot, "1899. The National League Winter Meetings of 1899–1900," *Baseball's 19th Century 'Winter' Meetings, 1857–1900* (Phoenix: Society for American Baseball Research, 2018), 361–362.
30. "Dreyfuss Has a New Scheme," *Pittsburgh Press,* December 13, 1899, 5.

31. Jamie Talbot, "1899. The National League Winter Meetings of 1899–1900," *Baseball's 19th Century 'Winter' Meetings, 1857–1900* (Phoenix: Society for American Baseball Research, 2018), 362.
32. David Pietrusza, *Major Leagues: Professional Baseball Organizations, 1871 to Present* (Jefferson, NC: McFarland, 1991), 140–144.
33. Joe Santry, "Ban Johnson," SABR BioProject, https://sabr.org/bioproj/person/dabf79f8.
34. "Hart Consented," *Sporting News*, March 24, 1900, 7.
35. "Pirates Made a Great Finish," *Pittsburgh Press*, April 5, 1900, 5.
36. "Drift of the Diamond," *Pittsburgh Press*, April 12, 1900, 5.
37. "Drift of the Diamond," *Pittsburgh Press*, April 7, 1900, 5.
38. "Drift of the Diamond," *Pittsburgh Press*, April 6, 1900, 5.
39. "Rain and Snow at Indianapolis," *Pittsburgh Post*, April 13, 1900, 6.
40. "Fans Went Wild in Last Inning," *Pittsburgh Post*, April 26, 1900, 1.
41. Arthur D. Hittner, *Honus Wagner: The Life of Baseball's 'Flying Dutchman'* (Jefferson, NC: McFarland, 1996), 76–77.
42. "Pirates Lost a Great Game," *Pittsburgh Press*, June 20, 1900, 5.
43. Mark L. Armour and Daniel R. Levitt, *In Pursuit of Pennants: Baseball Operations from Deadball to Moneyball* (Lincoln: University of Nebraska Press, 2015), 17.
44. "Baseball Chatter," *Pittsburgh Post*, July 8, 1900, 6.
45. Dan O'Brien, "Rube Waddell," SABR BioProject, accessed January 16, 2020, https://sabr.org/bioproj/person/a5b2c2b4.
46. "News and Comment," *Sporting Life*, September 1, 1900, 3.
47. "News and Comment," *Sporting Life*, September 1, 1900, 3.
48. "Pirates Look Like Winners," *Pittsburgh Post*, September 26, 1900, 6.
49. "Brooklyn on Top," *Sporting Life*, October 27, 1900, 7.
50. Francis C. Richter, "Dreyfuss Wins Out," *Sporting Life*, February 23, 1901, 8.

Chapter 9

1. Francis C. Richter, "Dreyfuss Wins Out," *Sporting Life*, February 23, 1901, 8.
2. "Place For Harry Pulliam," *Pittsburgh Post*, December 15, 1900, 6.
3. "Pulliam Generous," *Pittsburgh Press*, December 22, 1900, 5.
4. Editorial, *Sporting News*, December 29, 1900, 4.
5. "Dreyfuss Is Wanted in Two League Towns," *Pittsburgh Press*, December 31, 1900, 5.
6. "Pittsburgh Club Will Meet at Jersey City," *Pittsburgh Post*, January 12, 1901, 6.

7. "Meeting Blocked by Dreyfuss," *Pittsburgh Post*, January 13, 1901, 13.
8. "Action Postponed Until February," *Pittsburgh Post*, January 19, 1901, 6.
9. "Dreyfuss Comes to Pittsburgh," *Pittsburgh Post*, January 21, 1901, 6.
10. Francis C. Richter, "Dreyfuss Wins Out," *Sporting Life*, February 23, 1901, 8.
11. Mark L. Armour and Daniel R. Levitt, *In Pursuit of Pennants: Baseball Operations from Deadball to Moneyball* (Lincoln: University of Nebraska Press, 2015), 18.
12. Harold Seymour and Dorothy Mills Seymour, *Baseball: The Early Years* (New York: Oxford University Press, 1989), 316–317.
13. Mike Lynch, "1899–1900. The American League Winter Meetings of 1899–1901," *Baseball's 19th Century 'Winter' Meetings, 1857–1900* (Phoenix: Society for American Baseball Research, 2018), 378.
14. Joe Santry, "Ban Johnson," SABR BioProject, accessed March 12, 2020, https://sabr.or/bioproj/person/dabf79f8.
15. "Not Afraid of the Pirates," *Pittsburgh Post-Gazette*, March 5, 1901, 6.
16. Frederick G. Lieb, *The Pittsburgh Pirates* (Carbondale: Southern Illinois University Press, 2002), 78
17. Armour and Levitt, 18–19.
18. Arthur D. Hittner, *Honus Wagner: The Life of Baseball's 'Flying Dutchman'* (Jefferson, NC: McFarland, 1996), 94.
19. Ibid., 87.
20. Lieb, 46.
21. Hans Wagner, "Hans Wagner's Story, Chapter XXXII, Famous Fans in Baseball History," *Los Angeles Times*, January 14, 1924, B2 (or 38).
22. "Ball Men's Bad Start," *Pittsburgh Post*, April 28, 1901, 1.
23. Sam Bernstein, "Barney Dreyfuss," SABR BioProject, accessed December 31, 2019, https://sabr.org/bioproj/person/29ceb9eO.
24. Francis C. Richter, ed., "The Champion Pittsburgh Team," *Sporting Life*, October 19, 1901, 4.
25. "The Famous Pittsburgh Team," *Sporting Life*, October 26, 1901, 1.
26. "The League Season of 1901," *Spalding's Official Base Ball Guide* (New York: American Sports Publishing, 1902), 36.
27. "Champions' Cheer," *Sporting Life*, October 26, 1901, 3.
28. "Royally Treated," *Sporting News*, October 19, 1901, 3.
29. "The League Race," *Sporting Life*, October 12, 1901, 4.
30. Lieb, 85.
31. Jeremy Green, "1901. Firsts, Foibles and Failures," *Baseball's Business: The Winter Meetings, Volume 1, 1901–1957* (Phoenix: Society for American Baseball Research, 2016), 8–9.
32. "A.G. Spalding Is Made President," *Chicago Tribune*, December 14, 1901, 6.
33. Lieb, 86.
34. Ibid., 88.

35. Ronald T. Waldo, *The 1902 Pittsburgh Pirates* (Jefferson, NC: McFarland, 2015), 252–253.
36. "Sensation in Baseball," *Pittsburgh Post*, June 12, 1902, 8.
37. "Champions Will Stick," *Pittsburgh Press*, July 24, 1902, 12.
38. "Wagner Rejects Fortune," *Pittsburgh Press*, August 21, 1902, 10.
39. Hittner, 105.
40. Louis P. Masur, *Autumn Glory: Baseball's First World Series* (New York: Hill and Wang, 2003), 45.
41. *Pittsburgh Gazette*, September 11, 1902
42. Hittner, 105.
43. Lieb, 92.
44. "Pittsburgh Pained," *Sporting Life*, October 25, 1902, 4.
45. "The Financial Results," *Sporting Life*, October 11, 1902, 6.
46. Francis C. Richter, "Inter-League Clash," *Sporting Life*, October 18, 1902, 7.

Chapter 10

1. "Pittsburgh Team Has Advantage," *Pittsburgh Press*, November 19, 1902, 12.
2. "New York Selected; Pittsburgh Rejected," *Sporting Life*, November 15, 1902, 3.
3. "C.W. Somers Shifts Toward Pittsburgh," *Sporting Life*, December 6, 1902, 7.
4. "President Dreyfuss Due Today," *Pittsburgh Press*, November 2, 1902, 18.
5. "National League News," *Sporting Life*, November 22, 1902, 6.
6. "Baseball History Is Being Made," *Pittsburgh Press*, November 16, 1902, 21.
7. "Lining Up Votes," *Sporting News*, December 6, 1902, 1.
8. "Cincinnati Magnate Still on the Fence," *Pittsburgh Press*, December 10, 1902, 16.
9. "Wise Move Made by the National," *Pittsburgh Press*, December 13, 1902, 10.
10. Arthur D. Hittner, *Honus Wagner: The Life of Baseball's 'Flying Dutchman'* (Jefferson, NC: McFarland, 1996), 109.
11. Ronald T. Waldo, *The 1902 Pittsburgh Pirates: Treachery and Triumph* (Jefferson, NC: McFarland, 2015), 231.
12. Armour and Levitt, 24.
13. Frederick G. Lieb, *The Pittsburgh Pirates* (Carbondale: Southern Illinois University Press, 2002), 95.
14. Waldo, 243.
15. "Sensible Policy," *Sporting News*, November 8, 1902, 5.
16. Hittner, 110.
17. Honus Wagner, as told to Les Biederman, "Circling the Bases with the Flying Dutchman," *Sporting News*, November 22, 1950, 14.
18. Hittner, 111–112.
19. "Refuses to Talk," *Sporting News*, July 4, 1903, 1.
20. Seamus Kearney and Tom Simon, "Ed Doheny," SABR BioProject, accessed March 30, 2020, https://sabr.org/bioproj/person/023bfd7e.
21. Lieb, 98.
22. "Season's Success Pleases Pulliam," *Sporting Life*, October 24, 1903, 3.
23. Armour and Levitt, 25.
24. "Ban Johnson at the Game," *Boston Globe*, August 11, 1903, 5.
25. "Brush Refuses," *Boston Globe*, August 11, 1903, 5.
26. "Will Talk It Over," *Pittsburgh Press*, September 2, 1903, 10.
27. "As to the Post-Series," *Boston Globe*, September 14, 1903, 5.
28. One-page contract for 1903 post-season play between the Pittsburgh Pirates and Boston Americans, signed September 16, 1903 by Barney Dreyfuss and Henry Killilea. Source: Len Martin, Pittsburgh baseball historian.
29. Hittner, 119–120.
30. *Ibid.*, 126.
31. "President Dreyfuss Shocked," *Sporting Life*, October 17, 1903, 6.
32. "Dinneen's Curves Fooled Pirates," *Pittsburgh Gazette*, October 14, 1903, 9.
33. Francis C. Richter, "The World's Series a Splendid Event," *Sporting Life*, October 17, 1903, 4.
34. Lieb, 110.
35. Dennis DeValeria and Jeanne Burke DeValeria, *Honus Wagner: A Biography* (Pittsburgh: University of Pittsburgh Press, 1995), 136.

Chapter 11

1. "Longer Season on Ball Field," *Chicago Tribune*, December 10, 1903, 8.
2. "Longer Baseball Season," *New York Times*, December 10, 1903, 7.
3. "Longer Season on Ball Field," *Chicago Tribune*, December 10, 1903, 8.
4. "Long Schedule," *Boston Globe*, December 18, 1903, 5.
5. Dan Bonk and Len Martin, "Bourbon, Baseball and Barney," *A Celebration of Louisville Baseball in the Major and Minor Leagues* (Cleveland: Society for American Baseball Research, 1997), 64.
6. Don Jensen, "John McGraw," SABR BioProject, accessed April 5, 2020, https://sabr.org/bioproj/person/fef5035f.
7. William F.H. Koelsch, "New York Nuggets," *Sporting Life*, April 16, 2.
8. "Pittsburgh Gets McCormick," *Pittsburgh Post*, August 5, 1904, 6.
9. Arthur D. Hittner, *Honus Wagner: The Life of Baseball's 'Flying Dutchman'* (Jefferson, NC: McFarland, 1996), 133.
10. Ralph S. Davis, "Gameness of Dreyfuss Causing Much Comment," *Pittsburgh Press*, August 14, 1904, 19.
11. "World's Series Possible," *Sporting Life*, October 22, 1904, 4.
12. "Timely Topics," *Sporting Life*, October 22, 1904, 4.

13. Fred Lieb, *The Pittsburgh Pirates* (Carbondale: Southern Illinois University Press, 2002), 113–114.
14. Hittner, 139–140.
15. Lieb, 118–119.
16. "Refuses to Shake Hands with Brush," *Pittsburgh Gazette,* June 11, 1905, 34.
17. Richard C. Armstrong and Martin Healy, Jr., *George "Mooney" Gibson: Canadian Catcher for the Deadball Era Pirates* (Jefferson, NC: McFarland, 2020), 57–61.
18. "Pittsburgh Fans Have Gone Baseball Crazy," *Pittsburgh Press,* August 4, 1905, 16, and "Slugged Dreyfuss During the Climax," *Pittsburgh Post,* August 4, 1905, 3.
19. "Priest Said He Was Sorry," *Pittsburgh Press,* August 4, 1905, 7.
20. "Baseball Nuggets," *Pittsburgh Press,* December 14, 1904, 18.
21. "The League Business," *Sporting Life,* December 24, 1904, 6.
22. Dan Levitt, "Vic Willis," SABR BioProject, accessed April 13, 2020, https://sabr.org/bioproj/person/3c061442.
23. William A. Cook, *August "Garry" Herrmann: A Baseball Biography* (Jefferson, NC: McFarland, 2008), 77–78.
24. Bob LeMoine, "Boston Braves Team Ownership History," accessed February 5, 2019, https://sabr.org/research/boston-braves-team-ownership-history.
25. Lieb, 122.
26. Hittner, 164.
27. Lieb, 125.
28. "Progress—1908—Prosperity," *Sporting Life,* October 17, 1908, 3.
29. "Merkle Bonehead Play," accessed April 10, 2020, https://www.baseball-reference.com/bullpen/Merkle_Bonehead_Play.
30. National League Board of Directors Meeting Minutes, October 5, 1908, quoted in John Zinn, *Charles Ebbets: The Man Behind the Dodgers and Brooklyn's Beloved Ballpark* (Jefferson, NC: McFarland, 2019).
31. "Cubs Protest Yesterday's Ball Game Claiming Clarke's Run Should Not Go," *Pittsburgh Post,* September 5, 1908, 7.
32. Recollection of the play and O'Day comment by Tommy Leach of the Pirates, in Lieb, 127.
33. Ralph S. Davis, "Barney Dreyfuss—The Man," *Baseball Magazine, Volume 1, Number 3,* July 1908, 27–28.
34. Hittner, 168.
35. Cait Murphy, *Crazy '08: How a Cast of Cranks, Rogues, Boneheads and Magnates Created the Greatest Year in Baseball History* (New York: Smithsonian Books/HarperCollins, 2007), xiv.

Chapter 12

1. "New Ball Park in Oakland," *Pittsburgh Press,* October 18, 1908, 1.
2. Robert C. Trumpbour, "Forbes Field: Ahead of Its Time in 1909," *The National Pastime: Steel City Stories* (Phoenix: Society for American Baseball Research, 2018), 8.
3. ""One of Finest Baseball and Athletic Fields in the Country for Pittsburgh, *Pittsburgh Post,* October 18, 1908, 1.
4. "The Panic of 1907," Federal Reserve History, accessed April 23, 2020, https://www.federalreservehistory.org/essays/panic_of_1907.
5. "A Poor Financial Season," *Sporting Life,* October 17, 1908, 10.
6. Trumpbour, 9.
7. "Collusion Intimated in Ticket Scalping Case," *Chicago Tribune,* November 13, 1908, 10.
8. "The Ticket Scandal," *Sporting Life,* December 12, 1908, 1.
9. "Court Decrees," *Sporting Life,* November 21, 1908, 7.
10. Lenny Jacobsen, "Charles Murphy," SABR BioProfile, accessed April 15, 2020, https://sabr.org/bioproj/person/e707728f.
11. "Asks $7,000 for Dahlen," *Boston Globe,* December 9, 1908, 8.
12. "Splendid Results," *Sporting Life,* December 19, 1908, 6.
13. "Majors Meet," *Sporting Life,* December 19, 1908, 4.
14. Minutes of National League Owners Meeting, December 8, 1980, 349–350, 353–358, quoted in Zinn.
15. "Refuses to Comment on Decision," *Pittsburgh Press,* October 8, 1908, 16.
16. "Dreyfuss Will Protest," *New York Times,* October 7, 1908, 7.
17. Mark Peavey, *Take Nothing for Granted in Baseball: The Harry Pulliam Story* (No place of publication: Dead Ball Books, 2018), 208–212.
18. "No Contracts from Players," *Louisville Courier-Journal,* January 19, 1909, 31.
19. "No Developments," *Sporting News,* January 28, 1909, 1.
20. "President of the National League Declares His Position Is No Sinecure," *Pittsburgh Press,* January 11, 1909, 12.
21. John G. Zinn, *Charles Ebbets: The Man Behind the Dodgers and Brooklyn's Beloved Ballpark* (Jefferson, NC: McFarland, 2019), 105.
22. "Jones 'Kidding' Coast 'Bugs,'" *Chicago Tribune,* January 19, 1909, 8.
23. "Cap Anson Is Down But Far from Out," *Pittsburgh Press,* February 3, 1909, 8.
24. "Murphy-Pulliam Feud Is Growing Interesting," *Pittsburgh Press,* February 9, 1909, 15.
25. "War of Magnates Breaks Out Anew," *Chicago Tribune,* February 18, 1909, 10.
26. "League President May Not Be Re-Elected," *Pittsburgh Gazette Times,* February 18, 1909, 9.
27. "Pulliam Quits Until Owners Regain Senses," *St. Louis Post-Dispatch,* February 18, 1909, 14.
28. "Pulliam Gets Leave of Absence and Heydler Will Fill Vacancy," *Pittsburgh Post,* February 18, 1909, 9.

29. "Pulliam to Take Indefinite Rest," *Chicago Tribune,* February 19, 1909, 6.
30. "Pulliam Officially States His Position," *Chicago Tribune,* February 19, 1909, 6.
31. Peavey, 216.
32. "Alleged Briber Barred," *New York Times,* April 20, 1909, 7.
33. Harvey T. Woodruff, "Bar 'Dr. Creamer' from Ball Parks," *Chicago Tribune,* April 24, 1909, 8.
34. "East Hears of 'Dr. Creamer,'" *Chicago Tribune,* April 25, 1909, 31.
35. W.A. Phelon, "Chicago Chat," *Sporting Life,* December, 18, 1909, 2.
36. Cait Murphy, *Crazy '08: How a Cast of Cranks, Rogues, Boneheads and Magnates Created the Greatest Year in Baseball History* (New York: Smithsonian Books, 2007), 285, citing the minutes of the annual meeting of the National League, February 1909, 169, National Baseball Hall of Fame Library.
37. "Pulliam. Is Here on a Visit," *Cincinnati Enquirer,* July 17, 1909, 9.
38. Bill Lamberty, "Harry Pulliam," SABR BioProject, accessed January 9, 2020, https://sabr.org/bioproj/person/6e05b19c.
39. "Pulliam Puts Bullet in Head," *Louisville Courier-Journal,* July 29, 1909, 1.
40. Lamberty, "Harry Pulliam."
41. Peavey, 219–220.
42. "President of National League Succumbs to a Self-Inflicted Wound," *Pittsburgh Press,* July 29, 1909, 1.
43. Murphy, 295.
44. "Thirty Professional Teams Declare Games Off on Funeral Day," *Boston Globe,* August 3, 1909, 5.
45. Peavey, 220–221.
46. "Harry Clay Pulliam," *Louisville Courier-Journal,* August 2, 1909, 4.
47. "Commission Honors Memory of Baseball's Best Friend," *Pittsburgh Press,* October 8, 1909, 24.

Chapter 13

1. "Taft Roots for Pirate Success," *Pittsburgh Gazette Times,* May 30, 1909, 1.
2. "Taft Asks for Seat Back of First Base at Ball Ground," *Pittsburgh Post,* May 30, 1909, 1.
3. David Zax, "A Brief History of the Honus Wagner Baseball Card," *Smithsonian Magazine,* April 30, 2007, accessed May 8, 2020, https://www.smithsonianmag.com/history/a-brief-history-of-the-honus-wagner-baseball-card-153567429/.
4. Ralph S. Davis, "Davis' Dope," *Pittsburgh Press,* September 8, 1909, 12.
5. "Sleepy Game Won by the Pittsburghs," *Pittsburgh Gazette Times,* September 9, 1909, 7.
6. Frederick G. Lieb, *The Pittsburgh Pirates* (Carbondale: Southern Illinois University Press, 2002), 137–138.
7. Ibid., 134.
8. "Wild Baseball Yarns are Being Circulated," *Pittsburgh Post,* October 6, 1909, 8.

9. "Wagner's Hit as Fans Chirp Brings Him Supreme Moment" (from the syndicated Hans Wagner autobiographical series) *Pittsburgh Gazette Times,* February 8, 1924, 16.
10. "Clarke Is Jubilant; Jennings Praises Team," *Pittsburgh Post,* October 17, 1909, 1.
11. Ibid.
12. "Pittsburgh Is Winner of World Championship," *Pittsburgh Gazette Times,* October 17, 1909, 18.
13. Lieb, 139.
14. Ibid., 155.
15. Lawrence S. Ritter, *The Glory of Their Times: The Story of the Early Days of Baseball Told by the Men Who Played It* (New York: Perennial, 2002), 74–75.
16. "Baseball Magnates Coming to New York," *New York Times,* December 9, 1909, 12.
17. "Herrmann Is Here to Elect Heydler," *New York Times,* December 10, 1909, 12.
18. "Fogel on the Grill," *Washington Post,* December 12, 1909, S1.
19. "Dreyfuss Believes Heydler Will Win," *New York Times,* December 13, 1909, 7.
20. "Back Ban Johnson," *Washington Post,* December 12, 1909, S1.
21. "Garry Threatens to Jump," *Chicago Tribune,* December 13, 1909, 14.
22. "Big Leaguers' Horns Locked," *Los Angeles Times,* December 18, 1909, 7.
23. L.E. Sanborn, "National League Elects T.J. Lynch," *Chicago Tribune,* December 19, 1909, C1.
24. "Cap Anson," accessed April 30, 2020, https://www.baseball-reference.com/bullpen/Cap_Anson.
25. A.R. Cratty, "In Pittsburgh," *Sporting Life,* December 25, 1909, 10.
26. "Clarke Will Be in Charge of Pirates for Two More Years," *Pittsburgh Press,* December 14, 1909, 18.
27. John G. Zinn, *Charles Ebbets: The Man Behind the Dodgers and Brooklyn's Beloved Ballpark* (Jefferson, NC: McFarland, 2019), 113.
28. "Sports of Past Week Bring National Game Again Into Limelight," *Pittsburgh Post,* December 18, 1910, 17.

Chapter 14

1. Daniel R. Levitt, "Vic Willis," SABR BioProject, accessed April 2, 2020, https://sabr.org/bioproj/person/3c061442.
2. Jan Finkel, "Honus Wagner," SABR BioProject, accessed April 30, 2020, https://sabr.org/bioproj/person/30b27632.
3. Ralph S. Davis, "Something Wrong," *Sporting News,* July 14, 1910, 1.
4. Ralph S. Davis, "Hans Is Patriotic," *Sporting News,* February 16, 1911, 3.
5. "Other Managers Adopt Temperance Measure Originated by Fred Clarke," *Pittsburgh Press,* December 25, 1910, 15.
6. Frederick G. Lieb, *The Pittsburgh Pirates*

(Carbondale: Southern Illinois University Press, 2002), 161–162.

7. John McCollister, *The Bucs! the Story of the Pittsburgh Pirates* (Lanexa, KS: Addax Publishing, 1998), 69.

8. "Tommy Leach," BR Bullpen, accessed May 6, 2020, https://www.baseball-reference.com/bullpen/Tommy_Leach.

9. "The Welte Company," accessed May 4, 2020, http://120years.Net/The-Welte-Licht-Ton-Orgele-Weltegermany1936/ and *The Pianola Journal, Volume 17 and Volume 18,* accessed May 4, 2020, http://www.pianola.org/journal/journal.vol17–18.cfm.

10. McCollister, 71.

11. David Pietrusza, *Major Leagues: Professional Baseball Organizations, 1871 to Present* (Jefferson, NC: McFarland, 1991), 223.

12. Ibid., 227.

13. "Federal League," BR Bullpen, accessed May 7, 2020, https://Www.Baseball-Reference.Com/Bullpen/Federal_League and David Quentin Voigt, *American Baseball: from the Commissioners to Continental Expansion* (University Park: Pennsylvania State University Press, 1983), 118.

14. Lenny Jacobsen, "Charles Murphy," SABR BioProject, accessed May 7, 2020, https://sabr.org/bioproj/person/e707728f.

15. Lieb, 173.

16. William A. Cook, *August "Garry" Herrmann: A Baseball Biography* (Jefferson, NC: McFarland, 2008), 190.

17. "Gaffney May Buy Pirates," *New York Times,* December 15, 1916, 14.

18. Cook, 190.

19. "George Gibson, Veteran Catcher, Is Released," *Pittsburgh Press,* August 15, 1916, 24.

20. Lawrence S. Ritter, *The Glory of Their Times: The Story of the Early Days of Baseball Told by the Men Who Played It* (New York: Perennial, 2002), 75–76.

21. Cook, 213.

22. McCollister, 74–75.

23. Daniel Ginsburg, "John Tener," SABR BioProject, accessed May 9, 2020, https://sabr.org/bioproj/person/c90d4ea.

24. "Baseball Magnates Must Clean House," *New York Herald,* November 24, 1918, 21.

25. "Dreyfuss Original Advocate of Taft," *New York Herald,* November 28, 1918, 13.

26. "Dreyfuss Peeved Because of Leak in New York," *Pittsburgh Gazette Times,* November 25, 1918, 8.

27. "Taft Refuses to Serve as Baseball Commissioner," *Pittsburgh Press,* December 1, 1918, 26.

28. "National League to Bar Mitchell," *New York Herald,* December 10, 1918, 13.

29. Jacob Pomrenke, "1981: Baseball Returns from the Great War," *Baseball's Business, the Winter Meetings, Volume 1, 1901–1975* (Phoenix: Society for American Baseball Research, 2016), 121.

30. Mark L. Armour and Daniel R. Levitt, *In Pursuit of Pennants: Baseball Operations from Deadball to Moneyball"* (Lincoln: University of Nebraska Press, 2015), 28.

31. Richard C. Armstrong and Martin Healy, Jr., *George "Mooney" Gibson: Canadian Catcher in the Deadball Era Pirates* (Jefferson, NC: McFarland, 2020), 166.

32. From the recording of interviews conducted by Lawrence S. Ritter in 1963 and 1965 with Gibson, cited in Armstrong and Healy, Jr., 166.

33. Ritter, 77.

34. Ritter interview, cited in Armstrong and Healy, 169.

35. Edward F. Balinger, "Baseball Progress Slightly Held Up by Petty Quarrel," *Pittsburgh Post,* December 14, 1919, 19.

36. Ralph S. Davis, "Choice of Gibson Is Popular," *Pittsburgh Press,* December 14, 1918, 24.

Chapter 15

1. Harold and Dorothy Seymour, *Baseball: The Golden Age* (New York: Oxford University Press, 1971), 264–266, cited in Jacob Pomrenke, "1919. The End of the Deadball Era," *Baseball's Business. the Winter Meetings, Volume 1, 1901–1957* (Phoenix: Society for American Baseball Research, 2016), 123–125.

2. "Nothing Doing for Pirates in Trades," *Sporting News,* February 19, 1920, 2.

3. "Herrmann Offers to Quit National Commission Chair if Moguls Insist," *Pittsburgh Post,* December 11, 1919, 6.

4. "The Spitball, End of a Baseball Era," *Sports History Weekly,* accessed May 19, 2020, http:sportshistoryweekly.com/stories/spitball-baseball-mlb-burleigh-grimes-deadball-era-babe-ruth,778.

5. "Refuse to Let Garry Off," *Cincinnati Enquirer,* January 9, 1920, 6.

6. "Reformers Object to Fun Being Made," *Sporting News,* October 28, 1920, 3.

7. "To War on Gambling," *New York Times,* December 19, 1919, 18.

8. William Lamb, "The Black Sox Scandal," accessed May 10, 2020, https://sabr.org/research/black-sox-scandal-bill-lamb.

9. Jacob Pomrenke, "Gambling in the Deadball Era," accessed May 12, 2020, https://jacobpomrenke.com/black-sox/gambling-in-the-deadball-era/.

10. Philip Dixon, "September 28, 1865: The First Fixed Baseball Game," accessed May 14, 2020, https://sabr.org/gamesproj/game/september-28-1865-first-fixed-baseball-game

11. Steve Krah, "Lou Criger," SABR BioProject, accessed May 14, 2020, https://sabr.org/bioproj/person/95e23fdd.

12. Marshall Adesman, "1920: The Year That Rocked Baseball and Changed It Forever," *Baseball's Business: The Winter Meetings, Volume 1, 1901–1957* (Phoenix: Society for American Baseball Research, 2016), 128.

13. "A Timely Reform: Allegheny's New Mayor Announces That He Will Stamp Out Gambling on Base Ball Games," *Sporting Life,* April 21, 1906, 5.

14. "Pirates Place Anti-Gambling Squad at Park," *Chicago Tribune,* June 9, 1921, 12.

15. Frederick G. Lieb, *The Pittsburgh Pirates* (Carbondale: Southern Illinois University Press, 2002), 185–186.
16. "Jurors Cheer as Judge Orders Baseball Quiz," *Chicago Tribune*, September 8, 1920, 9.
17. Lamb, "The Black Sox Scandal."
18. "Baseball Quiz on Today Before Grand Jurymen," *Chicago Tribune*, September 21, 1920, 17.
19. Lamb, "The Black Sox Scandal."
20. "Crooks Scared Out of Baseball, Says McDonald," *Chicago Tribune*, August 4, 1921, 21.
21. Lamb, "The Black Sox Scandal."
22. "Dreyfuss Admits Baseball Men Not Likely to Yield Control," *Sporting News*, October 7, 1920, 1.
23. "1920," Adesman, 129.
24. Dan Busby "Kenesaw Mountain Landis,", accessed May 14, 2020, https://sabr.org/node/33871.
25. "Outlaw Anti-Trust Suit Is Dismissed by Judge Landis," George S. Robbins, *Sporting News*, February 10, 1916, 1.
26. "12-Club Major League Built Upon Ruins of Old; Landis Offered Presidency of Tribunal at $50,000," *Pittsburgh Gazette Times*, November 9, 1920, 1.
27. "Landis Terms Offer of Ball Post an Honor," *Chicago Tribune*, November 9, 1920, 1.
28. "Some High Points from Kansas City," *Sporting News*, November 18, 1920, 3.
29. "Landis Confers with Herrmann," *Boston Globe*, November 21, 1920, 21.
30. "1920," Adesman, 137.
31. Lieb, 188.
32. M'Graw, "Giants Must Beat Pirates to Win Flag—Gibson Has Club Hustling" *Pittsburgh Post*, May 25, 1921, 10.
33. "World Series Game and New York Presentations Feature WCAE Program," *Pittsburgh Press*, October 7, 1925, 10.
34. Peter Morris, *A Game of Inches: The Story Behind the Innovations That Shaped Baseball* (Chicago: Ivan R. Dee, 2010), 442–443.
35. W.J. McGoogan "Ball to Oppose, Breadon to Back up Broadcasts of Ball Games,", *St. Louis Post-Dispatch*, December 8, 1929, 20.
36. "Barnard Favors $50,000 Broadcasting Charge," *Sporting News*, December 5, 1929, 1.
37. Richard C. Armstrong and Martin Healy, Jr., *George "Mooney" Gibson: Canadian Catcher for the Deadball Era Pirates* (Jefferson, NC: McFarland, 2020), 186, citing an interview Gibson conducted with Lawrence S. Ritter late in Gibson's life.

Chapter 16

1. Frederick G. Lieb, *The Pittsburgh Pirates* (Carbondale: Southern Illinois University Press, 2002), 199.
2. "Ghosts of Bribe Scandal Fail to Effect Playing of Games," *Sporting News*, October 9, 1924, 1.
3. "Ban Johnson Demands Federal Inquiry," *Sporting News*, October 9, 1924, 2.
4. "Landis Refuses to Talk to Dreyfuss," *Sporting News*, October 16, 1924.
5. Ralph S. Davis, "Dreyfuss Credit to Baseball," *Pittsburgh Press*, October 26, 1924, 19.
6. "Barney Dreyfuss Lauded at Silver Anniversary Banquet," Ralph S. Davis, *Pittsburgh Press*, October 26, 1924, 21.
7. "1,000 Fans, Baseball 'Greats' and Officials Pay Dreyfuss Tribute," *Pittsburgh Post-Gazette*, October 26, 1924, 18.
8. Lieb, 202.
9. "Dreyfuss Will Enlarge Forbes Field to Seat 40,000 Fans," *Pittsburgh Post*, January 25, 1925, 27.
10. John McCollister, *The Bucs! the Story of the Pittsburgh Pirate* (Lanexa, KS: Addax Publishing, 1998), 84.
11. Lieb, 206.
12. *Ibid.*, 211.
13. "Uphill Struggle Brings Success," *Pittsburgh Press*, October 16, 1925, 38.
14. "Pirates Gamest Club I Ever Saw—Heydler," *Pittsburgh Gazette Times*, October 16, 1925, 11.
15. "Keeping Johnson in Lost Series, League Head Says as He Criticizes Harris," *Pittsburgh Gazette Times*, October 16, 1925, 1.
16. Chilly Doyle, "Chillysauce," *Pittsburgh Gazette Times*, October 18, 1925, 28.
17. "The Crowd and the Money," *Pittsburgh Gazette Times*, October 16, 1925, 1.
18. Lieb, 219–220.
19. McCollister, 86.
20. Lieb, 223.
21. Dan Busby, "Kenesaw Mountain Landis," SABR BioProject, accessed May 18, 2020, https://sabr.org/node/33871.
22. "Old Clubs Reject Speaker and Cobb," *Chicago Tribune*, January 26, 1927, 17.
23. Joe Santry, "Ban Johnson," SABR BioProject, accessed May 18, 2020, https://sabr.org/bioproj/person/dabf79f8.
24. Branch Rickey with Robert Riger, *The American Diamond: A Documentary of the Game of Baseball* (New York: Simon & Schuster, 1965), 23, cited in Joe Santry, "Ban Johnson," SABR BioProject.

Chapter 17

1. Matt Rothenberg, "A Hidden Legacy in Plain Sight," National Baseball Hall of Fame, accessed May 8, 2019, https://baseballhall.org/discover-more/stories/short-stops/hidden-legacy-in-plain-sight.
2. Joseph Wancho, "Lloyd Waner," SABR BioProject, accessed May 23, 2020, https://sabr.org/bioproj/person/ca302f54.
3. Gregory H. Wolf, "Kiki Cuyler," SABR BioProject, accessed May 23, 2020, https://sabr.org/bioproj/person/7107706b.
4. Frederick G. Lieb, *The Pittsburgh Pirates* (Carbondale: Southern Illinois University Press, 2002), 228.
5. "Yankees Overjoyed Over Clean Sweep," *New York Times*, October 9, 1927, S5.

6. "Dreyfuss Crushed by Four Losses in Row to Yankees," *Sporting News,* October 5, 1960, 12.
7. "Casual Comment," *Sporting News,* October 20, 1927, 4.
8. "Landis Slices Juicy Melon Among Series Combatants," *Sporting News,* October 20, 1927, 6.
9. "Miljus Signs Buc Contract," *Pittsburgh Press,* October 11, 1927, 1.
10. "Sale of Pirate Team Is Denied," *Pittsburgh Press,* October 9, 1927.
11. John McCollister, *The Bucs! the Story of the Pittsburgh Pirates* (Lanexa, KS: Addax Publishing, 1998), 95.
12. Havey J. Boyle, "Mirrors of Sport," *Pittsburgh Post-Gazette,* February 23, 1931, 17.
13. "Death of Samuel Dreyfuss," *Pittsburgh Press,* February 24, 1931, 10.
14. "Sam W. Dreyfuss," *Sporting News,* February 26, 1931, 4.
15. Ralph S. Davis, "Death of Junior Dreyfuss May Bring New Pirate Regime Here," *Pittsburgh Press,* February 23, 1931, 13.
16. "Jewel Ens Calls Off Workout," *Pittsburgh Press,* February 23, 13.
17. Lieb, 243.
18. McCollister, 100.
19. Lieb, 248.
20. Richard C. Armstrong and Martin Healy, Jr., *George "Mooney" Gibson: Canadian Catcher for the Deadball Era Pirates* (Jefferson, NC: McFarland, 2020), 196.
21. *Ibid.,* 195.
22. Peter Morris, *A Game of Inches: The Story Behind the Innovations That Shaped Baseball* (Chicago: Ivan R. Dee, 2010), 279.
23. David Schoenfeld, "The History of Juiced Balls and How Today's Home Run Binge Fits In," ESPN.com, accessed May 31, 2020, https://www.espn.com/mlb/story/_/id/26960922/the-history-juiced-balls-how-today-home-run-binge-fits-in.
24. "Lively Ball All Washed Up, Barney Dreyfuss Declares," *Pittsburgh Press,* July 12, 1931, 46.
25. "Major Leagues Hear Minors' Appeal," *Pittsburgh Post-Gazette,* December 9, 1931, 18.
26. Havey J. Boyle, "Mirrors of Sport," *Pittsburgh Post-Gazette,* December 1, 1931, 19.
27. "Gibson Made 'Buc' Pilot for 1932," *Pittsburgh Press,* November 30, 1931, 28.
28. Edward F. Balinger, "Baseball Gossip," *Pittsburgh Post-Gazette,* December 3, 1931, 16.
29. "Major Leagues Hear Minors' Appeal," *Pittsburgh Post-Gazette,* December 9, 1931, 18.
30. "Distribute Personal Estate of Dreyfuss," *Pittsburgh Post-Gazette,* December 11, 1931, 22.
31. Last Will and Testament of Barney Dreyfuss, dated December 14, 1931, courtesy of Pittsburgh baseball historian Len Martin.
32. "Dreyfuss Goes to New York," *Pittsburgh Post-Gazette,* December 16, 1931, 18.
33. "Grim Reaper Takes Heavy Baseball Toll," *Pittsburgh Post-Gazette,* February 6, 1932, 14.
34. Dan Bonk and Len Martin, "Bourbon, Baseball and Barney: The Story of Barney Dreyfuss—'Last of the Baseball Squires,'" in *A Celebration of Louisville Baseball in the Major and Minor Leagues* (Cleveland: Society for American Baseball Research, 1997), 64.
35. "Dreyfuss, 66, Dead; Owner of Pirates," *New York Times,* February 6, 1932, 21.
36. "Baseball Leaders, Friends Pay Tribute to Dreyfuss," *Pittsburgh Post-Gazette,* February 6, 1932, 14.
37. "Harridge Pays Tribute," *New York Times,* February 6, 1932, 21.
38. "Impressive Ceremony for Pirate Prexy," *Pittsburgh Press,* February 8, 1932, 24.
39. "Widow Named Pirate Owner," *Pittsburgh Post-Gazette,* February 11, 1932, 2.
40. Joan M. Thomas, "Helene Britton," SABR BioProject, accessed June 10, 2020, https://sabr.org/bioproj/person/ecd910f9.

Chapter 18

1. Dennis DeValeria and Jeanne Burke DeValeria, *Honus Wagner: A Biography* (Pittsburgh: University of Pittsburgh Press, 1998), 284–288.
2. Richard C. Armstrong and Martin Healy, Jr., *George "Mooney" Gibson: Canadian Catcher for the Deadball Era Pirates* (Jefferson, NC: McFarland, 2020), 201.
3. DeValeria and DeValeria, 289.
4. "Is Gibby to Get the Axe? No, Says Buc Head," *Pittsburgh Press,* July 25, 1933, 21.
5. "Gibson 'On Spot,' But He Laughs at Fans' Boos," *Pittsburgh Press,* June 18, 1934, 27.
6. "Gibson Fired, Traynor Named Manager," *Pittsburgh Press,* June 19, 1934, 1.
7. "Notables Help Unveil Tablet to Dreyfusses," *Pittsburgh Sun-Telegraph,* July 1, 1934, 17.
8. Robert W. Creamer, *Babe: The Legend Comes to Life* (New York: Simon & Schuster, 2005), 397.
9. "Forbes Field," at This Great Game, accessed June 15, 2020, http://www.thisgreatgame.com/ballparks-forbes-field.html.
10. David L. Fleitz, "The Honor Rolls of Baseball," *Baseball Research Journal,* No. 34 (Cleveland: Society for American Baseball Research, 2005), 53.
11. "Hall of Fame Committee Invites Criticism," *Sporting News,* May 2, 1946, 12.
12. John McCollister, *The Bucs! The Story of the Pittsburgh Pirates* (Lanexa, KS: Addax Publishing, 1998), 129.
13. Fredrick G. Lieb, *The Pittsburgh Pirates* (Carbondale: Southern Illinois University Press, 2002), 285.
14. DeValeria and DeValeria, 298–300, and Arthur D. Hittner, *Honus Wagner: The Life of Baseball's 'Flying Dutchman'* (Jefferson, NC: McFarland, 1996).
15. McCollister, 162, 163.
16. Herbert S. Soltman, "October 13, 1960, 3:36 p.m.—My Defining Moment in Sports," a memoir penned in 2010 and shared with the author after Soltman provided a guided tour of the remains of Forbes Field in September of 2017.

Notes—Chapter 18

17. "Pirates Close Forbes Field with Two Wins," *Pittsburgh Post-Gazette,* June 29, 1970, 1.

18. "Old Pirate Finds Fame 76 Years After His Death," *Pittsburgh Post-Gazette,* July 28, 2008, 1.

19. Emails to author from Hall of Fame reference librarian Cassidy Lent and the hall's manuscript archivist Claudette Scrafford, October 19, 2020.

20. "Barney Dreyfuss," International Jewish Hall of Fame, accessed June 22, 2020, http://www.jewishsports.net/BioPages/BarneyDreyfuss.htm.

21. Robert Dvorchak, "Fame Finally Comes to Barney Dreyfuss," *Pittsburgh Gazette,* July 20, 2008, 1.

22. Andrew Dreyfuss address at the induction of Barney Dreyfuss into the National Baseball Hall of Fame, Cooperstown, New York, July 27, 2008, courtesy HOF reference librarian Cassidy Lent.

23. David Cicotello and Angelo J. Louisa, *Forbes Field: Essays and Memories of the Pirates' Historic Ballpark, 1909–1971* (Jefferson, NC: McFarland, 2007), 23.

24. Mark L. Armour and Daniel R. Levitt, *In Pursuit of Pennants: Baseball Operations from Deadball to Moneyball* (Lincoln: University of Nebraska Press, 2015), 28.

25. Burton A. Boxerman and Benita W. Boxerman, *Ebbets to Veeck to Busch: Eight Owners Who Shaped Baseball* (Jefferson, NC: McFarland, 2003), 39–40.

26. *Ibid.,* 53–54.

27. John Kieran, "Sports of the Times," *New York Times,* February 6, 1932, 22.

28. Frederick G. Lieb, *The Pittsburgh Pirates* (Carbondale: Southern Illinois University Press, 2002), 46–47.

Bibliography

Books

Armour, Mark L., and Daniel R. Levitt. *In Pursuit of Pennants: Baseball Operations from Deadball to Moneyball*. Lincoln: University of Nebraska Press, 2015.
Armstrong, Richard C., and Martin Healy, Jr. *George "Mooney" Gibson: Canadian Catcher for the Deadball Era Pirates*. Jefferson, NC: McFarland, 2020.
Bernheim, Isaac W. *History of the Settlement of Jews in Paducah and the Lower Ohio Valley*. Paducah, KY: Temple Israel, 1912, https://catalog.hathitrust.org/Record/009562977.
Bernheim, Isaac Wolfe. *The Story of the Bernheim Family*. Louisville, KY: John P. Morton & Co., 1910, https://babel.hathitrust.org/cgi/pt?id=wu.89060747300.
Bigham, Darrell E. *Towns and Villages of the Lower Ohio*. Lexington: University Press of Kentucky, 1998.
Boxerman, Burton A., and Benita W. Boxerman. *Ebbets to Veeck to Busch: Eight Owners Who Shaped Baseball*. Jefferson, NC: McFarland, 2003.
Cook, William A. *August "Garry" Herrmann: A Baseball Biography*. Jefferson, NC: McFarland, 2008.
Creamer, Robert W. *Babe: The Legend Comes to Life*. New York: Simon & Schuster, 1974.
Davis, Marni. *Jews and Booze: Becoming American in the Age of Prohibition*. New York: New York University Press, 2012.
DeValeria, Dennis, and Jeanne Burke DeValeria. *Honus Wagner: A Biography*. Pittsburgh: University of Pittsburgh Press, 1998.
Dewey, Donald, and Nicholas Acocella. *The Biographical History of Baseball*. Chicago: Triumph Books, 2002.
Dicotello, David, and Angelo J. Louisa, eds. *Forbes Field: Essays and Memories of the Pirates' Historic Ballpark, 1909–1971*. Jefferson, NC: McFarland, 2007.
Egan, James M., Jr. *Base Ball on the Western Reserve: The Early Game in Cleveland and Northeast Ohio by Year and Town, 1865–1900*. Jefferson, NC: McFarland, 2008.
Hageman, William. *Honus: The Life and Times of a Baseball Hero*. Champaign, IL: Sagamore Publishing, 1996.
Hittner, Arthur D. *Honus Wagner: The Life of Baseball's "Flying Dutchman."* Jefferson, NC: McFarland, 1996.
Hodges, Jeremy K., and Bill Nowlin, eds. *Baseball's 19th Century Winter Meetings, 1857–1900*. Phoenix: Society for American Baseball Research, 2018.
Ivor-Campbell, Frederick, Robert L. Tiemann and Mark Rucker, eds. *Baseball's First Stars*. Cleveland: Society for American Baseball Research, 1996.
Levy, Alan H. *Rube Waddell: The Zany, Brilliant Life of a Strikeout Artist*. Jefferson, NC: McFarland, 2000.
Lieb, Frederick G. *The Pittsburgh Pirates*. Carbondale and Edwardsville: Southern Illinois University Press, 2002.
Martin, Brian. *Pud Galvin: Baseball's First 300-Game Winner*. Jefferson, NC: McFarland, 2016.
Masur, Louis P. *Autumn Glory: Baseball's First World Series*. New York: Hill and Wang, 2003.
McCollister, John. *The Bucs! The Story of the Pittsburgh Pirates*. Lanexa KS, 1998.
Morgan, Randy. *Paducah's Native Baseball Team*. Paducah, KY: Self-published, 2015.
Morris, Peter. *A Game of Inches: The Story Behind the Innovations That Shaped Baseball*. Chicago: Ivan R. Dee, 2010.
Morris, Peter, William J. Ryczek, Jan Finkel, Leonard Levin and Richard Malatzky, eds. *Baseball Pioneers: 1859–1870*. Jefferson, NC: McFarland, 2012.
Murphy, Cait. *Crazy '08: How a Cast of Cranks, Rogues, Boneheads and Magnates Created the Greatest Year in Baseball History*. New York: Smithsonian Books/HarperCollins, 2007.
Neft, David S., and Richard M. Cohen. *The Sports Encyclopedia: Baseball*. New York: St. Martin's Press, 1993
Nemec, David. *The Beer & Whiskey League*. New York: Lyons & Burford, 1994.
Nemec, David. *The Great Encyclopedia of 19th Century Major League Baseball*. New York: Donald I. Fine Books, 1997.
Nemec, David. *Major League Baseball Profiles, 1871–1900, Volume 2: The Hall of Famers and Memorable Performers Who Shaped the Game*. Lincoln, NB: University of Nebraska Press, 2011.

Peavey, Mark. *Take Nothing for Granted in Baseball: The Harry Pulliam Story*. No place of publication: Deadball Books, 2018.
Pietrusza, David. *Major Leagues: Professional Baseball Organizations, 1871 to Present*. Jefferson, NC: McFarland, 1991.
Reach Official American League Baseball Guide for 1910. Philadelphia: A. J. Reach Company, 1910.
Regan, Gary, and Mardee Haidin Regan. *The Book of Bourbon and Other Fine American Whiskeys*. London: Mixellany Books, 2009.
Ritter, Lawrence S. *The Glory of Their Times*. New York: Perennial, 2002.
Sarnoff, Gary A. *The First Yankees Dynasty: Babe Ruth, Miller Huggins and the Bronx Bombers of the 1920s*. Jefferson, NC: McFarland, 2014.
Seymour, Harold, and Dorothy Mills Seymour. *Baseball: The Early Years*. New York: Oxford University Press, 1989.
Spalding's Official Base Ball Guide, 1901. New York: American Sports Publishing, 1902.
Thorn, John. *Baseball in the Garden of Eden*. New York: Simon & Schuster, 2011.
Tiemann, Robert L., and Mark Rucker, eds. *Nineteenth Century Stars*. Phoenix: Society for American Baseball Research, 2012.
Voigt, David Quentin. *American Baseball: From the Commissioners to Continental Expansion, Volume Two*. University Park: The Pennsylvania State University Press, 1983.
von Borries, Philip. *The Louisville Baseball Almanac*. Charleston, SC: The History Press, 2010.
Waldo, Ronald T. *The 1902 Pittsburgh Pirates*. Jefferson, NC: McFarland, 2015.
Weingarden, Steven, and Bill Nowlin, eds. *Baseball's Business: The Winter Meetings, Volume 1, 1901–1957*. Phoenix: Society for American Baseball Research, 2016.
White, G. Edward. *Creating the National Pastime: Baseball Transforms Itself, 1903–1953*. Princeton, NJ: Princeton University Press, 1996.
Wiggins, Robert Peyton. *The Deacon and the Schoolmaster: Phillippe and Leever, Pittsburgh's Great Turn-of-the-Century Pitchers*. Jefferson, NC: McFarland, 2011.
Zinn, John G. *Charles Ebbets: The Man Behind the Dodgers and Brooklyn's Beloved Ballpark*. Jefferson, NC: McFarland, 2019.

Articles

Armour, Mark. "Deacon Phillippe." SABR BioProject, https://sabr.org/bioproj/person/939999be.
Armour, Mark. "Tommy Leach." SABR BioProject, https://sabr.org/bioproj/person/ba1b7d5b.
"August 20, 1877: Gray Outcomes for 'Louisville Four,'" SABR Games Project, https://sabr.org//gamesproj/game/august-20-1877-gray-outcomes-louisville-four.
Backer, Ron. "The Pittsburgh Pirates Go to the Movies." *The National Pastime: Steel City Stories*. Phoenix: Society for American Baseball Research, 2018.
Bailey, Bob. "And the Last Shall Be First: Louisville Club Zooms from Cellar to Pennant in 1890,", *A Celebration of Louisville Baseball in the Major and Minor Leagues*. Cleveland: Society for American Baseball Research, 1997.
Bailey, Bob. "Back in the Major Leagues." unpublished paper by the Louisville baseball historian and member of the Society for American Baseball Research.
Bailey, Bob. "Eclipse Park (Louisville)." SABR BioProject, https://sabr.org/bioproj/parks/cf040064.
Bailey, Bob. "Hunting for the First Louisville Slugger." *Baseball Research Journal, No. 30*. Cleveland: Society for American Baseball Research, 2001.
"Barney Dreyfuss." National Baseball Hall of Fame Biography, https://baseballhall.org/hall-of-famers/dreyfuss-barney.
Bernstein, Sam. "Barney Dreyfuss." SABR BioProject, https://sabr.org/bioproj/person/29ceb9e0.
Bernstein, Sam. "Barney Dreyfuss and the Legacy of Forbes Field." *Forbes Field: Essays and Memories of the Pirates' Historic Ballpark, 1909–1971*. Jefferson, NC: McFarland, 2007.
Bonk, Dan, and Len Martin. "Bourbon, Baseball and Barney: The Story of Barney Dreyfuss—'Last of the Baseball Squires.'" *A Celebration of Louisville Baseball in the Major and Minor Leagues*. Cleveland: Society for American Baseball Research, 1997.
Bonk, Daniel L. "Ballpark Figures: The Story of Forbes Field." *Pittsburgh History Magazine*, Summer 1993.
"Bourbon Barons: Isaac Wolfe Bernheim." Bourbonveach.com, Bourbon History, https://bourbonveach.com/2019/10/07/bourbon-barons-isaac-wolfe-bernheim/.
Bouyea, Brien. "Historic Horse Racing: Longfellow and Ten Broeck: The Pride of Old Kentucky." *The Saratogan*, August 15, 2017.
Britcher, Craig. "A Great Base Ball Tournament." *Making History, the Heinz Center Blog*, http://heinzhistorycenter.org//blog/western-pennsylvania—history/a-great-base-ball-tournament.
"Cap Anson." https://www.baseball-reference.com/bullpen/Cap_Anson.
"Cincinnati: The Jewish Community of Cincinnati." https://dbs.bh.org.il/place/cincinnati.
Constans, L.H. "Forbes Field: The Great Stadium of the Pittsburgh Pirates." *Baseball Magazine*, May 1913.
Crews, Clyde F. "Slow Tragedy: The Saga of Pete Browning." *A Celebration of Louisville Baseball in the Major and Minor Leagues*. Cleveland: Society for American Baseball Research, 1997.

Bibliography

Davis, Ralph S. "Barney Dreyfuss—The Man." *Baseball Magazine, Volume 1, No. 3,* July 1908.
Dixon, Philip. "September 28, 1865: The First Fixed Baseball Game." SABR Games Project, https://sabr.org/gamesproj/game/september-28–1865-first-fixed-baseball-game.
"Earliest Baseball Games." Baseball Memory Lab, http://mlb.mlb.com/memorylab/spread_of_baseball/earliest_games.jsp.
"Federal League." https://www.baseball-reference.com/bullpen/Federal_League.
Finkel, Jan. "Honus Wagner." SABR BioProject, https://sabr.org/bioproj/person/30b27632.
"Forbes Field." This Great Game, http://www.thisgreatgame.com/ballparks-forbes-field.html.
"German Unification." *Boundless World History by Lumen Learning,* https://courses.lumenlearningl.com/boundless-worldhistory/chapter/german-unification/.
"Germany from 1871 to 1918: German Empire, 1871–1914." *Encyclopedia Britannica,* https://www.britannica.com/place/Germany/Germany-from-1871-to-1918.
"Germany: The Economy, 1870–1890." *Encyclopedia Britannica,* https://www.britannica.com/place/Germany/The-economy-1870-90.
Ginsburg, Daniel. "John Tener." SABR BioProject, https://sabr.org/bioproj/person/c90d4ea.
Ginsburg, Daniel E. "The Louisville Scandal." *A Celebration of Louisville Baseball in the Major and Minor Leagues.* Cleveland: Society for American Baseball Research, 1997.
Greene, Nelson "Chip." "Three Rivers Stadium." SABR BioProject, https://sabr.org/bioproj/park/three-river-stadium.
Guerrieri, Vince. "How Concrete and Steel Built Baseball." Deadspin.com, https://deadspin.com/how-concrete-and-steel-built-baseball-1835946538/amp_twitter_impression=true.
Husman, John R. "June 21, 1879: The Cameo of William Edward White." SABR Games Project, https://sabr.org/gamesproj/game/june-21–1879-the-cameo-of-william-edward-white/.
Jacobsen, Lenny. "Charles Murphy." SABR BioProject, https://sabr.org/bioproj/person/e707728f.
Jensen, Don. "John McGraw." SABR BioProject, htttps://sabr.org/bioproj/person/fef5035f.
"Kenesaw Mountain Landis." https://sabr.org/node/33871.
Kennedy, Seamus, and Tom Simon. "Ed Doheny." SABR BioProject, https://sabr.org/bioproj/person/0233bfd7e.
Krah, Steve. "Lou Criger." SABR BioProject, https://sabr.org/bioproj/person/95e23fdd.
Lamb, Bill. "Andrew Freedman." SABR BioProject, https://sabr.org/bioproj/person/51545e58.
Lamb, Bill. "The Black Sox Scandal." https://sabr.org/research/black-sox-scandal-bill-lamb.
Lamberty, Bill. "Harry Pulliam." SABR BioProject, https://sabr.org/bioproj/person/6e05b19c.
LeMoine, Bob. "Boston Braves Team Ownership History." https://sabr.org/research/boston-braves-team-ownership-history.
Levitt, Dan. "Vic Willis." SABR BioProject, https://sabr.org/bioproj/person/3c061442.
Louisa, Angelo. "Fred Clarke." SABR BioProject, https://sabr.org/bioproj/person/6f6673ea.
"Merkle Bonehead Play." https://www.baseball-reference.com/bullpen/Merkle_Bonehead_Play.
Mitenbuler, Reid. "The Jewish Origins of Kentucky Bourbon." *The Atlantic,* May 12, 2015.
Mooney, Bill. "The Tattletale Grays." *Sports Illustrated* Vault, https://www.si.com/fault/1974/06//10616133/the-tattletale-grays.
Morris, Peter. "Allegheny Baseball Club." *Base Ball Pioneers: 1850–1870.* Jefferson, NC: McFarland, 2012.
O'Brien, Dan. "Rube Waddell." SABR BioProject, https://sabr.org/bioproj/person/a5b2c2b4.
"Panic of 1893." U.S. History, https://www.u-s-history.com/pages/h792.htm.
"The Panic of 1907." Federal Reserve History, https://www.federalreservehistory.org/essays/panic_of_1907.
Pomrenke, Jacob. "Gambling in the Deadball Era." https://jacobpomrenke.com/black-sox/gambling-in-the-deadball-era/.
Puerzer, Richard J. "The Annual Forbes Field Celebration." *The National Pastime: Steel City Stories.* Phoenix: Society for American Baseball Research, 2018.
Ray, James Lincoln. "Connie Mack Stadium (Philadelphia)." SABR BioProject, https://sabr.org/bioproj/parks/connie-mack-stadium.
Rice, Steven V. "Chief Zimmer." SABR BioProject, https://sabr.org/bioproj/person/8ade3747.
Rice, Steven V. "June 16, 1899: Honus Wagner and the Louisville Colonels Rally in 9th to Defeat Cy Young." SABR Games Project, https://sabr.org/gamesproj/june-16–1899-honus-wagner-and-louisville-colonels-rally-9th-defeat-cy-young.
Rothenberg, Matt. "A Hidden Legacy in Plain Sight." National Baseball Hall of Fame, https://baseballhall.org/discover-more/stories-short-stops/hidden-legacy-in-plain-sight.
Samoray, Jeff. "George A. Vanderbeck." SABR BioProject, https://sabr.org/node/41074.
Santry, Joe. "Ban Johnson." SABR BioProject, https://sabr.org/bioproj/person/dabf79f8.
Schoenfeld, David. "The History of Juiced Balls and How Today's Home Run Binge Fits In." ESPN.com, https://www.espn.com/mlb/story//../id/26960922/the-history-juiced-balls-how-today-home-run-binge-fits-in.
Schoger, Harry. "Forbes Field, the House of Thrills, Celebrates Opening Day." *Moments of Joy and Heartbreak; 66 Significant Episodes in the History of the Pittsburgh Pirates.* Phoenix: Society for American Baseball Research, 2018.

Smith, Curt. "Forbes Field (Pittsburgh)." SABR BioProject, https://sabr.org/bioproj/park/forbes-field-pittsburgh.
"The Spitball, End of a Baseball Era." *Sports History Weekly*, http:sportshistoryweekly.com/stories/spitball-baseball-mlb-burleigh-grimes-deadball-era-babe-ruth.
Tarvin, A.H. "Another Wagner Tale." *Baseball Magazine*, February 1948.
Thomas, Joan M. "Helene Britton." SABR BioProject, https://sabr.org/bioproj/person/ecd910f9.
Trumpbour, Robert C. "Forbes Field: Ahead of Its Time in 1909." *The National Pastime: Steel City Stories*. Phoenix: Society for American Baseball Research, 2018.
"Virtual Jewish World: Baden Germany." Virtual Jewish Library, https://www.jewishvirtuallibrary.org/baden-germany-virtual-jewish-history-tour.
Wancho, Joseph. "Lloyd Waner." SABR BioProject, https://sabr.org/bioproj/person/ca302f54.
"The Welte Company." *The Pianola Journal, Volume 18 and 18,* http://120years.net/the-welte-lichte-ton-orgele-weltegermany1936/ and http://www.pianola.org/journal/journal.vol17–18.cfm.
Wolf, Gregory H. "KiKi Cuyler." SABR BioProject, https://sabr.org/bioproj/person/7107706b.
Youngblood, Jeff. "Paducah and the World Series: The Life and Times of Barney Dreyfuss." https://www.booksie.com/posting/per-jensen/paducah-and-the-world-series-the-life-and-times-of-barney-dreyfuss-71656 also available at National Baseball Hall of Fame and Library, Cooperstown, New York.
Zax, David. "A Brief History of the Honus Wagner Baseball Card." *Smithsonian Magazine,* April 20, 2007, https://www.smithsonianmag.com/history/a-brief-history-of-the-honus-wagner-baseball-card-153567429/.

Magazines

The Atlantic
Baseball Magazine
Baseball Research Journal
The National Pastime: Steel City Stories
New York Clipper
Pittsburgh History Magazine
Smithsonian Magazine
Sporting Life
Sporting News
Sports History Weekly

Newspapers

Baltimore Sun
Boston Globe
Cairo (Illinois) Bulletin
Chicago Tribune
Cincinnati Enquirer
Detroit Free Press
Evansville (Indiana) Journal
Evansville (Indiana) Press
Los Angeles Times
Louisville Courier-Journal
Memphis Appeal
Memphis Public Ledger
New York Herald
New York Times
Owensboro (Kentucky) Messenger
Paducah News
Paducah Sun
Pittsburgh Commercial Gazette
Pittsburgh Gazette
Pittsburgh Gazette Times
Pittsburgh Post
Pittsburgh Post-Gazette
Pittsburgh Press
St. Louis Dispatch
St. Louis Post-Dispatch
Washington Post

Blogs

Making History, the Heinz Center Blog
Our Game, by John Thorn

Online Resources

Ancestry.com
Baseball-reference.com
Bourbonveach.com
Encyclopedia Britannica
Federalreservehistory.org
Find-a-Grave
History.com
Jewishsports.net
Major League Baseball Memory Lab
Newspapers.com
Retrosheet.org
Smithsonianmag.com
Society for American Baseball Research BioProject Files
Society for American Baseball Research Games Project Files
Society for American Baseball Research Parks Project Files
Sportshistoryweekly.com
Thisgreatgame.com

Other

A Celebration of Louisville Baseball in the Major and Minor Leagues. Cleveland: Society for American Baseball Research, 1997.

Index

Numbers in ***bold italics*** indicate pages with illustrations

Abbaticchio, Ed 115, 116, 118, 138
Abell, Ferdinand 70
Abstein, Bill 13, 14, 129, 138, 140
Adams, Babe 129, 133, 135–138, 140, 144, 146, 150, 158, 163, 170, 173
Adams, Earl "Sparky" 179
Adesman, Marshall 161, 216–217
Aldridge, Vic 167–171, 177, 179
Alexander, Pete 158
Aliquippa Base Ball Club 8
Allegheny City 2, 6, 8–9, 81, 120, 157
Alleghenys (Pittsburgh ball club) 8, 10, 12, 38, 223
American Association 10–11, 30, 33–34, 38–39, 41–51, 58, 146, 206, 209
American League 87, 98, 102, 175
American Tobacco Company 134
Angels in the Outfield (movie) 191
Anson, Constantine "Cap" 35, 53, 55, 125, 128, 141–142, 214–215, 222
Arbuckle, John 11
Arbuckle Coffee Company 76
Armour, Mark L. 202, 207, 210, 212–213, 216, 219, 221–222
Atlantic Base Ball Club 8, 9
Auten, Phil 11, 76–77, 79, 86–88, 96

Bagby, Jim 165
Bailey, Bob 37, 39, 41, 45, 205, 208–209, 222
Baker, William 156
Balinger, Edward F. 153, 183, 216, 218
Ball, Phil 147, 163
Balliet, Frank 86
Ballou, Win 170
Baltimore Orioles 46, 52, 54–55, 57, 70, 88, 96, 100, 195, 197
Barbare, Walter 162
Barbeau, Jap 13–14, 129
Barnard, Ernest 163, 190, 217
Barnes, Ross 34–36
Barnhart, Clyde 168, 170
Barrow, Ed 59, 110–111, 181, 190–191, 200–201
Bartell, Dick 179
Baseball Magazine 4, 7, 118, 205, 210, 214–215, 222–224
Baseball Research Journal 39, 208, 218, 222, 224
Batman, Thomas 50–51
Beaumont, Clarence "Ginger" 77, 83, 93–94, 99, 102–103
Bechtel, George 35
"Beer and Whiskey League" 10, 42–43, 206, 208–209, 221

Bell, Cool Papa 190
Belmont Park Raceway 120
Bennett Park (Detroit) 137–138
Benswanger, Aimee ***197***
Benswanger, Billy, Jr. 188, ***197***
Benswanger, William 6, 181, 183–185, 187–188, 190–191
Bernheim, Bernhard 21, 31
Bernheim, Henry 16
Bernheim, Isaac Wolfe 19, 23, 64, 206–208, 221–222
Bernheim, Leon Solomon 16
Bernheim, Leopold 16, 19
Bernheim Brothers 19, 22–23, 25–28, 31–32, ***41***, 49–50, 64, 66–67, 208
Bezdek, Hugo Francis 151–153
Bierbauer, Louis 11
Bigbee, Carson 164, 171, 173
"Black Sox Scandal" 33, 158–162, 216–217, 223
Blake, Harry 73
Bloom, Moses 21–23
Blue Grass League 30
Bond, Tommy 36
Bonk, Dan ***197***, 198, 205–207, 209, 213, 218, 222
Boston Americans 88, 101, 103–104, 106
Boston Beaneaters 28, 51, 57, 63, 68, 115
Boston Braves 146, 148–149, 151, 154, 162, 169, 173, 178, 180, 188–191, 207, 214, 223
Boston Doves 15, 134
Boston Globe 92, 213–215, 217, 224
Boston Pilgrims 101
Boston Post 131
Boston Red Caps 36–37
Boston Red Sox 129, 151–152, 154
Bowerman, Frank 100
Boxerman, Benita 202, 219, 221
Boxerman, Burton 202, 219, 221
Boyle, Havey J. 180, 183, 218
Bradley, George 36
Brain, Dave 111, 114
Brame, Erv 180
Bransfield, Kitty 94, 99, 110, 117
Breadon, Sam 163, 186, 217
Bresnahan, Roger 100, 129
Bridwell, Al 117
Britcher, Craig 205, 222
Britton, Helene 184
Brooklyn Bridegrooms 49, 84, 102
Brooklyn Dodgers 42, 94, 179, 201, 214–215, 222
Brooklyn Eckfords 157
Brooklyn Robins 158

225

Brooklyn Superbas 84–85
Brown, Mordecai "Three Finger" 115
Browning, Pete 33, 38–41, **40**, 46–48, 208, 222
Brush, John T. 64, 68, 70–71, 76–77, 91–92, 96–98, 100–102, 106–107, 109–111, 113, 116, 122–124, 127–129, 140–142, 166, 190, 201, 210, 213–214
Brush-Freedman Trust plan 91–92, 122
Bryant, William Jennings 117
Buckeyes Base Ball Club (Columbus, Ohio) 9
Bush, Guy 189–190
Bush, Owen "Donie" 174, 176, 178–179, 187
Butler, Art 147

Cairo, Illinois 24–25, 27–39, 197
Cairo Bulletin 27–29, 207
California State League 124
Callahan, James "Nixey" 150–151
Camnitz, Howie 133–134, 136–137, 144, 146–147
Campbell, Vin 144, 146
Canadian Baseball Hall of Fame 188
Carey, Max (Maximilian Carnarius) 144, 150–152, 158, 163–165, 168, 171, 173
Carnegie, Andrew 5, 120
Carnegie, Pennsylvania 59–60, 77, 94, 99, 187
Carnegie Library 120
Carnegie Technical Schools 12, 120–120
Carroll, Frank 38
Carter, Joe 194
Case, Charlie 107
Caylor, O.P. 10
Central City, Kentucky 28, 30–31, 115
Chadwick, Henry 91, **200**, 201
Chance, Frank 12, 114–115, 117, 127
Chapman, Jack 35–36, 48
Charleston, Missouri 30
Chase, Charles E. 34–35
Chesbro, Jack 76, 79, 83, 88, 91, 93–95, 98
Chicago Cubs 4, 12–14, 107, 113–118, 122, 125, 127–129, 133, 135, 144–148, 151, 154, 158–160, 163, 167, 178–180, 184, 186, 188, 194, 208, 214
Chicago Orphans 71–72, 82–83
Chicago Tribune 58, 70, 75, 106, 128, 141, 159–160, 210–212, 214–217
Chicago Whales 160
Chicago White Sox 107, 113–115, 125, 150–152, 156, 158–161
Chicago White Stockings 10, 34–35, 53, 82
Childs, Cupid 73
Cicotello, David 202, 206, 219
Cicotte, Eddie 159
Cincinnati Enquirer 129, 156, 215–216
Cincinnati Reds 9–10, 12, 45, 76, 83, 97, 99, 114, 128, 142, 152, 156, 162–163, 187, 198
Civil War 8–9, 21, 24–25, 33, 41, 157
Clancy, Bill 110
Clarke, Fred 12, 33, 53–54, 58–59, 62–63, 65, 72–73, 79, **80**, 83, 88, 90, 93, 98–100, 102–104, 107, 110, 116–119, 121, 133, 135, 138, 140, 142, 144, 146–147, 149–150, 167–168, 171, 173–174, 191, 202, 210, 215, 223
Clemente, Roberto 193, 195, 197–198, 204
Cleveland Forest Citys 9
Cleveland Indians 156, 158, 165, 175
Cleveland Naps 109–110
Cleveland Spiders 54–57, 65, 72, 186
Clingman, Billy 65, 72, 83
Coastal Plain League 201
Cobb, Ty 116–117, 135–137, 140, 175, 179, 190, 217
Cole, Leonard "King" 144–146

Collins, Jimmy 33, 54, 88, 101
Columbia (South Carolina) Blowfish 201
Columbia (South Carolina) Comers 176, 201
Combs, Earle 178
Comiskey, Charles 31, 107, 125, 154, 156, 158–159, 200–201
Comorosky, Adam 179–180
Conroy, Wid 92, 94
Coolidge, Pres. Calvin 169
Cooper, Wilbur 151, 167
Cooperstown, New York 24, 26, 29–30, 39, 54, 190, 199, 204–205, 207, 219, 224
Coveleski, Stan 168–170
Craver, Bill 36–37
Crawford, Sam 116, 137–138
Creamer, Dr. Joseph 128–129, 166, 215
Criger, Lou 157, 216, 223
Cronin, Joe 174
Crosby, Bing 191
Cross, Lave 73
Cunningham, Bert 65, 72–74
Cutshaw, George 163
Cuyler, Hazen Shirley "Kiki" 165, 168–169, 171, 173, 176, 178–179, 203, 217, 224
Cvengros, Mike 177

Davidson, Mordecai 44–47, 209
Davis, Lefty 95
Davis, Marni 23, 207, 221
Davis, Ralph S. 109, 118, 134, 144, 153, 159, 166, 181, 205, 213–218, 223
Day, John 10
Deadball era 107, 155, 157, 182, 202, 221
Dehler, Charles 62–64, 66, 73–74
Delahanty, Jim 136
Detroit Tigers 14, 116, 135–139, 175
Detroit Wolverines 11, 63, 76
DeValeria, Dennis **197**, 198, 205, 210, 213, 218, 221
Devlin, Jim 35–37
Dexter, Charlie 65, 72–74
Dinneen, Bill 74, 101–104, 213
Ditmar, Art 193
Doheny, Ed 93, 100, 102–104, 213, 223
Dolan, Albert "Cozy" 147, 166
Donovan, Patsy 59–60, 76
Donovan, "Wild Bill" 137–138
Dooin, Red 145
Doubleday, Abner 39
Dougherty, Patsy 101–102
Dovey, George 28–31, 115–116, 128, 132, 207–208
Dovey, John 28, 115, 131
Dovey, Will 28, 30–31, 115
Dowling, Pete 74
Doyle, "Chilly" 172, 217
Drexler, Fred, Jr. 49, 52, 66, 209
Dreyfuss, Andrew 199
Dreyfuss, Babette 17–20
Dreyfuss, Barney 26, **126**, **142**, **155**, **180**; arranges first post-season championship series 101–102; arrives in Paducah 23; assaulted by inebriated gambler 111–113; bans advertising on walls of Forbes Field 143; birth and childhood 15–17; buys into Louisville Colonels; buys into Pittsburgh Pirates 49; death 183; donates owner share of 1903 "world's championship" proceeds to his players 104; fails to sign prospect Walter Johnson 11; final resting place in West View Cemetery **185**; funeral 184; hires Fred Clarke 54; hires Harry Pulliam 52; hires Honus Wagner; hires

Mooney Gibson to manage 153, 183; inducted into Baseball Hall of Fame 199, **200**, 201; joins Bernheim Brothers 23; manages baseball in Paducah 28; moves to Louisville 31; moves to Pittsburgh 81; named vice-president of the National League 180; opens Forbes Field 1–7, 11–14; opposition to radio broadcast of games 163–164; opposition to spitball 155; plaque unveiled at Forbes Field 188, **189**; supports Harry Pulliam for National League president 97; transfers best Louisville players to Pittsburgh 78–79; troubles with Exposition Park 89–90, 121; views on gambling 157; wins his first World Series title in 1909 135–139; wins the 1925 World Series 168–172
Dreyfuss, Barney II 199
Dreyfuss, Barney III (Terry) 199
Dreyfuss, Eleanor 81, 181, 183, 197
Dreyfuss, Elizabeth 19
Dreyfuss, Evan 199
Dreyfuss, Fanny 16, 19–20
Dreyfuss, Florence 81, 139, 183–84, 190–191, 199
Dreyfuss, Jeanette 17–19, 21
Dreyfuss, Rosa 19
Dreyfuss, Sammy 81, 152, 172, 179–181, 183–184, 189, 218
Dreyfuss, Samson 18, 20
Dreyfuss, Samuel 16–20
Dreyfuss Field (Columbia, S.C.) 17
Duffy, Hugh 88
Duquesne Base Ball Club (Pittsburgh) 8
Durbin, Blaine 14

Eastern League 111
Ebbets, Charlie 89, 118, 124–125, 127, 140–141, 143, 152, 156, 190, 202, 214–215, 219, 222
Eclipse Base Ball Club (Louisville) 34, 38, 41–42, 44, 209
Eclipse Park (Louisville) 34, 39, 41, 45, 49–51, 55, 67, 71–73, 205, 208, 222
Ehret, Red 46, 49
Ely, Bones 83, 88, 90
Emslie, Bob 14, 117
Ens, Jewel 179–180, 218
Enterprise Base Ball Club (Pittsburgh) 8–9, 22
Esterbrook, Dude 46
Evans, Billy 138
Evansville, Indiana 24, 27–30
Evansville Ball Club 25, 27–28
Evansville Journal 25
Evansville Press 28
Evansville Resolute Base Ball Club 25
Evansville Workingmen's Base Ball Club 26
Evers, Johnny 12, 115, 117–118, 148
Exposition Park (Pittsburgh) 2, 4–7, 11, 81, 83, 85, **90**, 91, 94–95, 99–100, **101**, 103, 109, 111, 115, 118, 121, 133–134, 145, 157, 194

Face, Elroy "Roy" 193
Falkenberg, Cy 98–99
Falls City Sluggers (bat) 41
Famous Slugger Yearbook, 1939 39
"Father Welsh" 112–113, 157
Federal League 147, 149–151, 160, 202, 216
Felsch, Happy 159
Ferguson, Alex 169–170
Flaherty, Pat 109
Flaherty, Patsy 107, 109
Fleischmann, Julius 97
Fogel, Horace 140

Forbes, British General John 6, 201–202
Forbes Field 1, 3–4, **5**, 7, 11–12, **13**, 14, 121, 128–129, **131**, 134, **136**, 137, 139–140, 143, 153, 156–157, 163, 167–168, 170, 172, **174**, 178, 182–184, 186, 188–191, 193–199, 201–206, 214, 218
Forbes Field Wall **195–196**, 198–199, 204
Ford, Whitey 193
Ford Pitt Base Ball Club (Pittsburgh) 8
Fort Duquesne 6
Fowle, Charles A. 34–35
Fowler, Bud 41–42
Franco-German War 21
Frazee, Harry 152, 154, 157
Freedman, Andrew **61**, 65, 68, 70–71, 81, 86, 91–92, 96, 98, 116, 122, 201, 211, 223
Freeman, Buck 74, 101
Freiburg, Duchy of Baden 15–16, 19–21, 23, 91, 146, 184
French, Larry 179–180
French Lick Springs, Indiana 76–77
Frick, Ford 191, 201
Friedburg, Amalie 20
Friend, Bob 193
Fuchs, Emil 188–190
Fulmer, Chick 35

Gaffney, James 149
Galbreath, John W. 191
Galvin, J.F. "Pud" 11, 206, 208, 221
Game 7 Gang 194, **195**
Gandil, Chick 159
Gatto, Larry 49
Gehrig, Lou 177–179, 182
Gibson, George (Mooney) 13–14, 111, **112**, 115–117, 134–138, 140, 145, 148, 150, 153, 158, 162, 164, 182–184, 186–188, 202, 214, 216–218, 221
Gibson, Josh 190
Gill, Warren 118
Glazer, Rabbi B.B. 184
Glazner, Whitey 162–163, 165
Goldenson, Rabbi Samuel H. 184
Goldsmith, Fred 10
Gooch, Johnny 178
Goslin, Goose 172
Grantham, George 167–168, 173, 179–180
Griffith, Clark 72, 83, 88, 98, 154
Griggs, Art 181
Grimes, Burleigh 151, 155, 179–180
Grimm, Charlie 152, 163, 165, 167
Groh, Heinie 162
Guelph (Ontario) Maple Leafs 10

Hague, Bill 36
Hahn, Noodles 83
Haldeman, John A. 34, 36
Haldeman, Walter N. 36
Hall, George 36
Hanlon, Ned 6, 11, 85
Harmon, Bob 147
Harper, John 22
Harridge, William 184, 218
Harris, Bucky 28, 169–170, 172
Harris, Joe 168, 171
Hart, James 68
Hartford Dark Blues 36
Hecker, Guy 33, 46–48
Hempstead, Harry 152
Hendrix, Claude 146–147
Herrmann, August "Garry" 12, 96–98, 106, 114, 122–

Index

132, 140–141, *142*, 147–149, 151–152, 154–157, 159, 162, 190, 214–217, 221
Hershman, Oliver 87
Hess, Otto 110
Heydler, John 12, 123, 127, 129–131, 140–141, 148, 152, 156, 159–160, 169, 171, 180–181, 184, 188, 190
Heyman, D.I. 86
Hill, Carmen 176–177
Hillerich, John A. "Bud" 33, 39
Hittner, Arthur D. 89, 94
Hofman, Solly 12–14, 117, 146
Holmes, Ducky 70–71, 81
Homestead Grays 190
Honor Rolls of Baseball (1946) 190–191, 199
Hornsby, Rogers 164
Hot Springs, Arkansas 88, 107, 116
Howard, Del 110, 114
Howell, Harry 84
Hoy, Dummy 62–63
Hoyne, Maclay 158
Hoyt, Waite 177, 187–188
Huggins, Miller 177
Hulbert, William 34–37
Huntington Avenue Grounds (Boston) 104
Hyatt, Ham 14, 133

Indiana-Kentucky League 30
International Association 10, 38, 41
International Jewish Sports Hall of Fame 197
I.W. Harper Bourbon 22–23, 31

Jackson, Shoeless Joe 159
Jackson, Will, Jr. 44
J.G. Taylor Spink Award 204
Johnson, Ban 12, 82, 87, 92–94, 96–97, 101, 107, 113, 122, 125, 127, 129, 131, 141, 147, 149, 151–152, 154, 158–161, 166, 170, 172, 175, *200*, 201
Johnson, Hiram 160
Johnson, Tom 191
Johnson, Walter 116, 168, 170, 190
Johnstone, James 124
Jones, Davy 137–138
Jones, Fielder 115
Judge, Joe 169

Kahn, Moses 20
Kansas City Cowboys 46
Kansas City Monarchs 190
Karlsruhe, Duchy of Baden 15, 19, 26
KDKA Radio (Pittsburgh) 163
Kelly, Billy 146
Kelly, John "Kick" 45
Kennedy, Bill "Brickyard" 98, 100, 103
Kerins, John 45
Kerr, W.W. 11, 70, 76–79, 86–88, 96, 206
Keystone Base Ball Club (Pittsburgh) 8
Kieran, John 203–204
Killian, Ed 116
Killilea, Henry 102, 104
Kiner, Ralph 190
Kitson, Frank 84–85
Kittridge, Malachi 65, 72–73
Klem, Bill 124, 128
Knowles, Fred 100
Koenig, Mark 178
Konetchy, Ed 147–149
Kremer, Ray 165, 168–171, 173, 177, 179–180
Kuhn, Bowie 199, 201

Labine, Clem 193
Laevison, A.E. 29
Lajoie, Nap 88, 95, 109
Lamb, Bill 158
Landis, Judge Kenesaw Mountain 158–160, *161*, 162, 166–171, 174–175, 184, 200–201, 217
Lasker, Albert 154
Lasker Plan 154, 159–162
Latimer, Tacks 75
Law, Vernon 193
Leach, Tommy 14, 33, 60, 62, 68, 79, 83, 88, 93–94, 99–100, 102, 109, 118, 133, 138, 140, 146, 202, 210, 216
Leavitt, Charles W. 12, 120
Leever, Sam 83, 85, 95, 98, 100, 102–104, 109, 116, 133, 145
Leifield, Lefty 115–116, 137, 144, 146
Leonard, Buck 190
Leonard, Dutch 175
Levitt, Daniel R. 202
Lieb, Frederick 11, 76, 89, 103, 110, 135, 144, 149, 151–152, 162, 167, 176, 181, 203–204
Lincoln Base Ball Club (Pittsburgh) 8
Lindaman, Vive 114
Lindstrom, Freddie 187–188
Livingston, Mangold 17–18, 20–21
Locke, Will 113, 126
Loeb, Reuben 21–23
London, Ontario 150, 153, 164, 188
London (Ontario) Tecumsehs 10, 38, 206, 208
Longfellow (racehorse) 22
Louisa, Angelo J. 202
Louisville Base-Ball Club 24, 33, 46, 52, 62, 65–66, 70–71, 78–79, 81
Louisville Colonels 6, *58*
Louisville Courier-Journal 32, 34–36, 41–42, 45–47, 50, 52–58, 62–63, 65, 71–74, 77, 79, 130–131
Louisville Cyclones 48–49
Louisville Eagles 33–34
Louisville Eclipse 30, 33–34, 38–39, 41–42, 44, 48
Louisville Grays 34–38, 42, 48
Louisville Olympics 34, 38
Louisville Scandal 33, 37
Louisville Slugger (bat) 33, 39, 41
Louisville Vogels 27
Lucas, Red 189
Lundgren, Carl 115
Lynch, Ambrose 9
Lynch, Thomas 129, 141, 148
Lynn (Massachusetts) Base Ball Team 10, 41
Lyons, W.L. 44–45

Mack, Connie 6, 60, 76, 84, 101, 113, 116, 145, 148, 179
Maddox, Nick 117, 137
Magee, Bill 65
Magee, Sherry 145
Magee, Pittsburgh Mayor William 12, 138, 167
Mamaux, Al 150, 151
Mantle, Mickey 193
Maranville, Walter "Rabbit" 162–163, 167, 203
Marberry, Firpo 169–170
Maris, Roger 193
Marquard, Rube 148
Martin, Len 198
Mathewson, Christy 90, 100, 107, 113, 129, 133–134, 144, 146, 169, 190
Mattern, Al 134
Mays, Carl 154
Mazeroski, Bill 193–195, 198, 204

McCarthy, Tom 134
McCollister, John 194
McCormick, Moose 109, 117
McDonald, Judge Charles A. 158, 160
McDonald, Jim 73
McFarlan, Alex 50
McFarlan, Claude 59–60
McGann, Dan 111
McGinnity, Joe 84–85, 90, 100, 107, 117
McGraw, John *80*, 88, 96, 100, 106–107, **108**, 109–111, 113, 116, 117, 123, 128–129, 131, 142, 145–147, 150, 153, 157, 159–160, 162–163, 165–166, 179, 182
McKechnie, Bill 164–171, 173–174, 179, 184
McKinney, Frank 191
McKnight, Harmar Denny 8–10, 42
McKnight, Robert 9
McMullin, Fred 159
McRoy, Robert 125
McVey, Cal 34
Meadows, Lee 165, 168, 173, 177
Memphis Appeal 29
Memphis Cotton Nine 29
Memphis Eckfords 29
Memphis Reds 27
Merkle, Fred 117–118
"Merkle's Boner" 117, 123
Meusel, Emil "Irish" 162, 163
Miljus, Johnny 178
Miller, Dots 13, 129, 133, 138, 147
Milwaukee Brewers 84, 102
Montreal Royals 111
Moore, Eddie 169–171
Moore, Wilcy 177
Morgan, Randy 24
Moriarity, George 138
Morin, John 12
Morris, Ed 11
Morris, Peter 42
Morrison, Johnny 165, 168, 171
Morrissey, Jack 99
Mowrey, Mike 147
Mueller, Ray 135
Mullin, George 136–138
Murpheysboro, Illinois 29
Murphy, Cait 119, 129
Murphy, Charles W. 12, 113–114, 118, 122, 124–125, 127, 129, 141, 148, 214
Mutual Base Ball Club of New York 34, 157

Nashville Cumberlands Base Ball Team 33
National Agreement 50, 64, 82, 88, 98, 122, 161
National Association of Professional Base Ball Players 9, 34–36
National Base-Ball Association (formerly International Association) 10
National Baseball Hall of Fame 1, 4, 29, 114–116, 129, 151, 162, 175, 190–192, 197, 199–201
National Commission 12, 98, 114, 122, **123**, 127–129, 132, 147, 149–152, 154, 156–162, 166
National League owners meeting, 1913 **148**
Navin, Frank 136
Nealon, Joe 114
Nemec, David 11
New York Athletic Club 130
New York Clipper 37
New York Giants *61*, 65, 70–72, 96, 101–102, 109–110, 112–113, 123–124, 128, 146–147, 166
New York Herald 151

New York Highlanders 98, 100, 109
New York Metropolitans (Mets) 10, 194
New York Mutuals 157
New York Times 130, 140, 149, 156, 184, 203
New York Tribune 203
New York Yankees 96, 154, 157, 163–164, 173, 177–179, 184, 187, 193–194
Nichols, Al 36–37
Nicholson, Fred 158
Nicola Building Company 121
Niehaus, Al 167
Nimick, William A. 10
Nirella, Danny 12, 186, 188

O'Connell, Jimmy 166
O'Connor, Jack 73, 93–94
O'Day, Hank 14, 102, 117
Old Continental Bourbon 31
Oldham, Red 171
O'Loughlin, Silk 137
Olympic Base Ball Club (Louisville) 34, 38
Olympic Base Ball Club (Pittsburgh) 8–9
O'Malley, Walter 199, 201
O'Neal, Bill 33
O'Neill, J. Palmer 11
O'Toole, Marty 146–147
Overall, Orvie 115, 117
Overton, Pennsylvania 21
Owensboro, Kentucky 25, 28, 30
Owensboro Messenger 30

Pacific Coast League 124
Paducah, Kentucky 16–32, 43, 50, 66, 115, 202, 204
Paducah Base Ball Association 29
Paducah Eckfords 26–27, 29
Paducah Idlewilds 25
Paducah News 24, 26–27, 29
Palmer, Elbridge 22
Panic of 1907 121–122
Pank, J.W. 38, 42, 44
Parsons, Lawrence 47, 49
Paso Robles, California 181
Peavey, Mark 131
Peckinpaugh, Roger 168–169, 171
Pedder, Charles J. 96
Peitz, Heinie 110
Pennock, Herb 177
Pennsylvania Historical and Museum Commission 198
Perry, Scott 151, 154
Perry, the Rev. Wallace C. 167
Pershing, Gen. John 160
Pesch, Joe 156
Petty, Jesse 179
Pfeffer, Fred "Dandelion" 38, 41, 53
Pfiester, Jack 117
Phelon, W.A. 128–129
Phelps, Eddie 99, 107, 110, 114
Phelps, Zach 44
Philadelphia Athletics 8, 11, 48, 90, 113, 116, 120, 136, 146, 149, 151, 154, 179–180
Philadelphia Phillies 65, 145, 158, 165
Phillippe, Deacon 33, 67–68, 72, 79, 83, 85, 88, 91, 93, 95, 98–99, 102–104, 107, 113, 116, 133, 138, 144–145, 167
Pipgras, George 177
Pittsburgh Athletic Association 11, 86
Pittsburgh Burghers 11, 76

Index

Pittsburgh Chronicle-Herald 85
Pittsburgh Filipinos 145
Pittsburgh Gazette Times 135
Pittsburgh Penguins 1
Pittsburgh Pirates, renamed from Alleghenys 2, 11
Pittsburgh Post 4, 7, 14, 78–79, 120, 153
Pittsburgh Post Gazette 180, 183, 191, 199
Pittsburgh Press 7–8, 55, 77, 87, 96, 109, 113, 118, 134, 153, 159, 163, 166, 181, 183, 188
Pittsburgh Rebels 149
Pittsburgh Steelers 1
Players' League 11, 48, 50
Pleasure Ridge Distillery 31
PNC Park (Pittsburgh) 2, 189, 195, 197–198, **203**–204
Polo Grounds (New York) **63**, 109–110, 115, 117–118, 124, 128, 134, 141, 146, 154, 162, 165–166
Pomrenke, Jacob 157
Pratt, Al 9–10, 12
Propst, L.L. 176
Providence Grays 42
Pulliam, Grace 131
Pulliam, Harry 12, 52–55, 57–64, 66–67, 74, 76–79, 82, 84–87, 91, 93–101, 106, 109–110, 113, 118, 122–132, 139–141, 148, 170

"rabbit ball" 182, 201
Rawlings, Johnny 165
Raymond, Harry 46
Reach Official American League Baseball Guide 7
Reccius, Billy 38, 42
Reccius, John 38, 41
Reccius, Phil 38
Reccius, William 38
Recreation Park (Allegheny City) 2, 10, 88
Redmon, Harry 156
Resolute Base Ball Club, Evansville 25
Resolute Base Ball Club, Pittsburgh 8
Reulbach, Ed 12
Revolution of 1848 16
Rice, Sam 169
Richardson, Bobby 193
Richter, Francis C. 79, 95, 104, 123
Rickey, Branch 149, 156, 175, 199–201
Riconda, Harry 179
Rigler, Cy 169
Risberg, Swede 159
Ritchey, Claude 73, 79, 83, 99, 115
Ritter, Lawrence S. 153
Robinson, Hank 147
Robinson, Jackie 42
Robison, Frank 65, 67–68, 92, 97, 186
Robison, Stanley 140, 186
Rodef Shalom Temple (Pittsburgh) 184
Rogers, Col. John I. 68
Roosevelt, Pres. Theodore 94
Rowe, Norman L. 87
Ruckstuhl, J. George 51
Ruppert, Jacob 154, 157, 178, 184, 201
Ruth, Babe 12, 155, 157, 159, 163–164, 177, 179–180, 182, 188–190

St. James Court (Louisville) 35
St. Louis Browns 9, 31, 46–47, 57, 65–66, 93, 147, 149, 163–164
St. Louis Cardinals 89, 99, 144, 147, 164, 173–174, 177, 179–180, 186, 201
St. Louis Perfectos 72–73
St. Louis Terriers 147

Sanborn, I.E. 141
Sand, Heinie 166
Saunders, John J. 81
Schenley Apartments **136**, 172, 174
Schenley Hotel 4, 91, 120, 136, 174
Schenley Park 6, 11, 94, 120
Schmidt, Charles "Boss" 137–138
Schoepf, W.K. 87
Scott, Floyd "Pete" 179
Sebring, Jimmy 99, 107, 109
Selee, Frank 114
Seven Weeks' War 20
Seymour, Cy 113–114
Seymour, Dorothy Mills 51
Seymour, Harold 35, 51
Shannon, Dan 46, 48
Sheckard, Jimmy 12–14
Sherman Anti-Trust Act 147
Shibe, Ben 6
Shibe Park (Philadelphia) 6, 120–121, 129
Shocker, Urban 177
Simon, Mike 147
Sisler, George 149–150, 152
Skornickel, George 194, **195**
Slagle, Jimmy 118
Smith, Bob 173
Smith, Earl 168–169, 171
Smith, Harry 92
Smithland, Kentucky 16–18
Society for American Baseball Research 1
Soden, Arthur 68, 70, 92, 115–116
Soltman, Herb 194, **195**
Somers, Charles W. 93–94, 96, 102
South End Grounds (Boston) 115
Southern League 27
Southworth, Billy 151, 162
Spalding, Albert Goodwill 34–35, 38, 92, 97
Speaker, Tris 175, 179
spitball 155, 157, 182, 201
Sporting Life 4, 53–54, 62, 65, 67, 70–72, 75, 78–79, 81, 84, 86, 91, 95, 98, 104, 107, 109, 117, 123–124, 128
Sporting News 4, 51, 60, 67–68, 74, 98, 124, 145, 155, 159–160, 166, 181, 191
Staley, Harry 11
Stargell, Willie 197–198, 204
Start, Joe 42
Steinfeldt, Harry 13–14, 115
Stengel, Casey 193
Storke, Alan 14
Stratton, Scott 49
Stucky, T. Hunt 49, 52–53, 55, 57, 62, 63, 79
Summers, Ed "Kickapoo" 137
Swetonic, Steve 186
syndication 79, 202

Taft, Charles P. 133, 141, 147–148
Taft, William Howard 117, 133, 160
Tannehill, Jesse 83, 85, 89, 93–95, 98
Taylor, Dummy 111
Tebeau, Patsy 55–57, 73
Temple, William C. 11, 91, 97
Ten Broeck (racehorse) 22
Tener, John **148**, 149, 151–152, 167, 184
Tenney, Fred 117
Terry, Bill 182
Terry, Ralph 193
Thompson, Gus 103
Thorn, John 6

Index

Thorner, Justus 10
Three Rivers Stadium (Pittsburgh) 194, 197–198
Tierney, Cotton 163–165
Tinker, Joe 13, 115, 118, 147
Titanic 146
Toledo Blade 42
Toledo Blue Stockings 42
Toronto Maple Leafs Baseball Club 153
Traynor, Harold Joseph "Pie" 162, 165–166, 168–170, 179–181, 187–188
Trimble baseball grounds (Paducah, KY) 27
Trumpbour, Robert C. 122
Turley, Bob 193

Union Base Ball Club (Pittsburgh) 8
Union Park (Pittsburgh) 2, 9–10
United States Baseball League 145
University of Pittsburgh 12, 120–121, 194
Uri, Amanda 22
Uri, Nathan M. 31

Vanderbilt, Cornelius 51
Vaughan, Floyd "Arky" 181, 186–188
Veach, Bobby 169
Veeck, William 156, 158–160
Veil, Bucky 98, 103
Vila, Joe 124
von Bismarck, Chancellor Otto 15–16
Von Borries, Philip 33
Von der Ahe, Chris 10, 31, 66

Waddell, Rube 33, 58, 60–61, 74–75, 79, 83–85, 90
Wagner, Bessie 187
Wagner, Honus 13, 33, 58, 60–61, 63, 68, **69**, 72–73, 77, 79, 83, 88–89, 93, 98–99, 107, 109, 111, 114, 116, 127, 129–130, 133–135, 144, 146, 151, 158, 162, 162, 165, 167, 173, 181, 184, 187, 190–192, 198, 202, 204; final resting place Jefferson Memorial Park **192**
Wagner, J. Earl 78
Waldo, Ronald T. 93, 98
Walker, Moses Fleetwood 33, 41
Wallace, Bobby 73
Waner, Lloyd 176, 178–180
Waner, Paul 173–174, 176, 178–180, 189
Ward, John Montgomery 97, 129, 140
Washington Park (Brooklyn) 49
Washington Senators 74, 78, 116, 154, 168–172, 175
Waterson, Henry 41
Watkins, William "Watty" 11, 76–78

Watters, Sam 181, 191
WCAE Radio (Pittsburgh) 163, 168, 172
Weaver, Buck 159
Weeghman, Charles 147–148
Weil, Meyer 18, 23
Weill, Louis 20
Weille, Benjamin 17, 21
Welte, Edwin 148
West View Cemetery (Pittsburgh) 184, ***185***
Western League 61, 63–64, 67–68, 79, 82, 150, 181
White, Deacon 34
White, William Edward 42
White Sewing Machine Company of Cleveland 41
Whitted, George "Possum" 163
Wikoff, Wheeler C. 46
Wilhelm, Irvin "Kaiser" 98
Wilkes-Barre, Pennsylvania 21
Willard Hotel (Washington) 166
William Pitt Hotel (Pittsburgh) 167
Williams, Jimmy 83, 88
Williams, Ken 164
Williams, Lefty 159
Willis, Vic 12, 114, 116–118, 133–134, 138, 144
Wills, Dave 73
Wilson, Owen "Chief" 147
Wolf, Florence (Mrs. Barney Dreyfuss) 81, 139, 183–184, 190, 191, 199
Wood, Smoky Joe 175
Woodruff, Harvey 128
Woods, Walt 73
World Series 1, 14, 49, 106, 109, 113–117, 119, 121–123, 125–126, 132, 140, 145–147, 149–152, 156–158, 163–164, 166, 174–175, 179–180, 183, 186, 195, 197–199, 201–203; (1903) 102–105; (1909) 135–139; (1925) 168–173; (1927) 177–178; (1960) 193–194
"World's Championship" of 1880s 76
Wright, George 201
Wright, Harry 201
Wrigley, William 163, 184

Yankee Stadium 177–179, 193–194
Yde, Emil 165, 168, 170
Young, Cy 72–73, 88, 95, 101–103, 116, 191
Young, Nick 51, 57, 64, 70, 75, 82, 91–92, 190
Youngblood, Jeff 28

Zachary, Tom 170
Zimmer, Chief 72, 79, 83, 87, 90, 135

www.ingramcontent.com/pod-product-compliance
Lightning Source LLC
Chambersburg PA
CBHW060341010526
44117CB00017B/2914